The Old Testament Is Dying

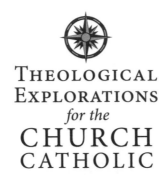

THEOLOGICAL
EXPLORATIONS
for the
CHURCH
CATHOLIC

"With passion, insight, and sober analysis, Strawn argues that the sharp drop in fluency in the use of the Old Testament in many North American congregations threatens the future of the church at its core. Strawn brilliantly develops the dual metaphors of a dying medical patient and a language hurtling toward linguistic extinction to illuminate the complex dynamics of how and why the Old Testament is increasingly neglected or misused in preaching, singing, and teaching. Using the book of Deuteronomy, Strawn offers helpful, practical but demanding recommendations for the recovery and resuscitation of the Old Testament in congregational life."

—**Dennis Olson**, Princeton Theological Seminary

"Beautifully and compellingly written! The linguistic analogy that the Old Testament is like a dying language is enthralling in the hands of Professor Strawn. Here we come face to face with the consequences of our pernicious neglect of the Old Testament. Strawn also makes good use of a medical metaphor: the doctor's diagnosis is in, and the patient is dying. For some, the patient has already been laid to rest without proper burial. But resurrection is possible. The good Dr. Strawn has prescribed here an important dose of medicine if the church will merely accept this healing tonic."

—**Bill T. Arnold**, Asbury Theological Seminary

"Drawing on the analogy of a dying language, Strawn brings his encyclopedic mind and seemingly limitless creativity to bear on the problem of the silence of the Old Testament in the church today. The diagnosis is daunting, but the prognosis, if followed, is hopeful. This important book promises to breathe life into the church's attempts to speak God's truth today, especially for those who still find the *viva vox* of the gospel in the Old Testament."

—**Rolf Jacobson**, Luther Seminary

"Strawn faces the fact that we are losing literacy in the Old Testament, if not the Bible as a whole. Many believers and church goers are unfamiliar with it and often puzzled about it, and people of influence—from atheistic scientists to health-and-wealth preachers—frequently misuse it for their own purposes. Strawn shows how serious the problem is for the Christian faith, threatening it to its very roots. The treatment for this deadly disease will not be easy, but there is a way forward that holds promise for the life and vitality of the believer and the church and the betterment of the world in which we live as salt and light."

—**Richard E. Averbeck**, Trinity Evangelical Divinity School

The Old Testament Is Dying

A Diagnosis and Recommended Treatment

Brent A. Strawn

Baker Academic

a division of Baker Publishing Group
Grand Rapids, Michigan

Published by Baker Academic
a division of Baker Publishing Group
P.O. Box 6287, Grand Rapids, MI 49516-6287
www.bakeracademic.com

Printed in the United States of America

Library of Congress Cataloging-in-Publication Data
Names: Strawn, Brent A., author.
Title: The Old Testament is dying : a diagnosis and recommended treatment / Brent A. Strawn.
Description: Grand Rapids : Baker Academic, 2017. | Includes bibliographical references and index.
Identifiers: LCCN 2016038828 | ISBN 9780801048883 (pbk.)
Subjects: LCSH: Bible. Old Testament—Criticism, interpretation, etc.
Classification: LCC BS1171.3 .S77 2017 | DDC 221.6—dc23
LC record available at https://lccn.loc.gov/2016038828

17 18 19 20 21 22 23   7 6 5 4 3 2 1

For my parents,
my first Bible teachers
שמע בני מוסר אביך
ואל תטש תורת אמך
(Prov. 1:8)

Contents

Contents

Series Preface

Long before it became popular to speak about a "generous orthodoxy," John Wesley attempted to carry out his ministry and engage in theological conversations with what he called a "catholic spirit." Although he tried to remain "united by the tenderest and closest ties to one particular congregation"[1] (i.e., Anglicanism) all his life, he also made it clear that he was committed to the orthodox Christianity of the ancient creeds, and his library included books from a variety of theological traditions within the church catholic. We at Nazarene Theological Seminary (NTS) remain committed to the theological tradition associated with Wesley but, like Wesley himself, are very conscious of the generous gifts we have received from a variety of theological traditions. One specific place this happens in the ongoing life of our community is in the public lectures funded by the generosity of various donors. It is from those lectures that the contributions to this series arise.

The books in this series are expanded forms of public lectures presented at NTS as installments in two ongoing, endowed lectureships: the Earle Lectures on Biblical Literature and the Grider-Winget Lectures in Theology. The Earle Lecture series is named in honor of the first professor of New Testament at NTS, Ralph Earle. Initiated in 1949 with W. F. Albright for the purpose of "stimulating further research in biblical literature," this series has brought outstanding biblical scholars to NTS, including F. F. Bruce, I. Howard Marshall, Walter Brueggemann, Richard Hays, Terence Fretheim, and Joel Green. The Grider-Winget Lecture series is named in honor of J. Kenneth Grider, longtime

---

1. John Wesley, *Sermon 39*, "Catholic Spirit," §III.4, in *Bicentennial Edition of the Works of John Wesley* (Nashville: Abingdon, 1985), 2:79–95. We know, however, that his public ties with Anglicanism were at some points in his life anything but tender and close.

professor of theology at NTS, and in memory of Dr. Wilfred L. Winget, a student of Dr. Grider and the son of Mabel Fransen Winget, who founded the series. The lectureship was initiated in 1991 with Thomas Langford for the purpose of "bringing outstanding guest theologians to NTS." Presenters for this lectureship have included Theodore Runyon, Donald Bloesch, Jürgen Moltmann, Robert Jenson, and Amy Plantinga Pauw.

The title of this monograph series indicates how we understand its character and purpose. First, even though the lectureships are geared toward biblical literature *and* systematic theology, we believe that the language of "theological explorations" is as appropriate to an engagement with Scripture as it is to an engagement with contemporary systematic theology. Though it is legitimate to approach at least some biblical texts with nontheological questions, we do not believe that doing so is to approach them *as Scripture*. Old and New Testament texts are not inert containers from which to draw theological insights; they are already witnesses to a serious theological engagement with particular historical, social, and political situations. Hence, biblical texts should be approached *on their own terms* through asking theological questions. Our intent, then, is that this series will be characterized by theological explorations from the fields of biblical studies and systematic theology.

Second, the word "explorations" is appropriate since we ask the lecturers to explore the cutting edge of their current interests and thinking. With the obvious time limitations of three public lectures, even their expanded versions will generally result not in long, detailed monographs but rather in shorter, suggestive treatments of a given topic—that is, explorations.

Finally, with the language of "the church catholic," we intend to convey our hope that these volumes should be *pro ecclesia* in the broadest sense—given by lecturers representing a variety of theological traditions for the benefit of the whole church of Jesus Christ. We at NTS have been generously gifted by those who fund these two lectureships. Our hope and prayer is that this series will become a generous gift to the church catholic, one means of equipping the people of God for participation in the *missio Dei*.

Andy Johnson
Lectures Coordinator
Nazarene Theological Seminary
Kansas City, Missouri

Author Preface

The chapters that follow were originally presented as the Earle Lectures on Biblical Literature at the Nazarene Theological Seminary (NTS) in Kansas City, Missouri, on April 16–17, 2012. I am thankful for the honor bestowed on me to give these lectures, which are named after a prominent biblical scholar in the Church of the Nazarene whose family is well known by my own. I am also grateful for the warm and gracious hospitality showed to me by the faculty, staff, and students of NTS, including the then-president Dr. David Busic, Academic Dean Roger Hahn, and especially Dr. Andy Johnson, the coordinator of the lectures, who first invited me to come to NTS and who edits the series within which the book is now housed. Although the material that follows has been significantly expanded beyond the original lectures, I have tried to retain something of the oral style of the lectures if for no other reason than to increase the readability of the book. Perhaps this will also help those parts intended as humorous to come across in the right way.

Even before the lectures at NTS, students in several years of introductory courses at the Candler School of Theology at Emory University listened to me discuss the problem of the Old Testament's linguistic death, even if only sporadically and inchoately. The same is true for an early presentation I made on the subject to Candler's Committee of 100 and to Grace Episcopal Church in Gainesville, Georgia. A more developed, but still incomplete form of the larger idea was given as the Marcy Preaching Lectures (March 2012) in Orlando, Florida, as a run-up to the NTS lectures. Since the NTS lectures, I've had the opportunity to speak on the topic at a number of different types of ecclesial gatherings in Atlanta and elsewhere in Georgia, Mississippi, Texas, and Florida, including the inaugural Thompson Lectureship at First United Methodist Church in Gainesville, Georgia, and in various academic settings, including the Thirteenth Annual Joe R. Engle Institute of Preaching at Princeton Theological Seminary (2015), and at Point Loma Nazarene University in San Diego (2015). I think I learned more each time I spoke about the topic, including more about all that I do not yet know about the subject matter! I remain thankful for each of these opportunities and for the people who helped to make them happen.

It is appropriate to acknowledge up front my intellectual debt to John McWhorter, whose wonderfully engaging lectures for the Teaching Company on linguistics, especially those devoted to language death, pidginization, and creolization, not only relieved the pain of my daily commute, but also served as my first formal introduction to these subjects. The combination of listening to McWhorter's lectures while driving to school to teach Old Testament to students training for Christian ministry is what first prompted me to consider the Old Testament in an analogical, linguistic fashion. Despite this debt to McWhorter, anyone familiar with his work will know (as do I) that he would no doubt quarrel with a number of the quite prescriptive ways to which I have put his (and others') largely descriptive linguistic research, especially on dialects and creole continua. Then again, McWhorter himself rarely shies away from the political ramifications of his scholarly work. In any event, I have taken great inspiration from McWhorter's teaching and writing—indeed, from the very inception of the idea. My further indebtedness to him and to other linguists can be traced in the footnotes and bibliography.

I must also mention my great debt to Jim Kinney. After many years of talking, it has been a pleasure to finally be able to work with Jim and all the wonderful people at Baker Academic. Jim has been exceedingly patient and gracious during the several delays the project encountered, which makes me even more appreciative of him and the press.

I'm also thankful to several individuals who read pieces of the manuscript, discussed its ideas with me, or provided help in one crucial way or another, especially (and alphabetically) the following: Bill T. Arnold, Lewis Ayres, Anthony A. Briggman, William P. Brown, Walter Brueggemann, Greg Carey, Stephen B. Chapman, Tracey A. Cook, Kenda Creasy Dean, Julie A. Duncan, Christy Lang Hearlson, E. Brooks Holifield, Luke Timothy Johnson, Steven J. Kraftchick, Joel M. LeMon, Thomas G. Long, Ian A. McFarland, R. W. L. Moberly, Ted A. Smith, Tim Suttle, and Reese A. Verner. Thanks, too, to my Emory colleagues Steven M. Tipton, for assistance with the U.S. Religious Knowledge Survey and its cultured despisers; to †John H. Hayes, Jonathan Strom, and Phillip Reynolds for thoughts on the Apocrypha, for which I also thank my more distant colleagues John Endres and David deSilva; and to Andrea White and Don E. Saliers on George Lindbeck and "post-post-liberal theology." Andrew Thomas gave me permission to cite lyrics from his song "You Are" featuring Kawan Moore. I am grateful to Timothy K. Beal for bibliography on Bible publishing and for his profound reflections on such in his wonderful book *The Rise and Fall of the Bible*. I also gladly acknowledge the help I received from several doctoral students who gathered needed items, listened to ideas, and occasionally brainstormed how to address certain problems: Harry Huberty, K. Parker Diggory, and Josey Bridges Snyder. A fourth, T. Collin Cornell, was especially helpful at the eleventh hour, offering me key encouragement and support. Collin also performed a final read-through and compiled the bibliography. I am also grateful to my Dean, Dr. Jan Love, for the sabbatical that afforded me the time to finish this and several other projects. Finally, I single out for special mention Ryan P. Bonfiglio, who read the entire manuscript (portions of it more than once) and, as is his custom, offered numerous suggestions that bettered it in virtually every possible way. It seems obligatory, but is nevertheless quite important given the number of people listed here and the arguments I make in what follows, to state that none of these individuals should be held responsible for my arguments even as I am more than happy to share with them the credit for any good ideas that might be found herein.

I also wish to thank my wife, Holly, sine qua non, who listens to me and to my thoughts about the Old Testament (and everything else) far more than anyone should ever have to, and my three children—Caleb (כלב), Hannah (חנה), and Micah (מיכה)—whose names bear evidence of their father's primary linguistic love, but equally also my love for them. I can't imagine more beautiful names (or kids).

Given the particular focus of this book, it is imperative that I recognize my first Bible professors: Dr. Reuben Welch, Dr. Robert W. Smith (my first Greek teacher), and Dr. Frank G. Carver (my first Hebrew teacher) of Point Loma Nazarene University. These three somehow put me on the path of lifelong study of Scripture in ways that continue to amaze me—ways I hope to emulate in my own teaching and somehow pass on to my own students.

Last, since this book is so much about language and, ultimately, about parents and their children, it seems only right to dedicate it to my parents, David and Sharon (two more Hebrew names—surely a sign of providence!). They were the first to teach me not only the English language but also the language of faith and Scripture, even, I'm quite sure, at *preverbal* stages and in embodied sorts of ways. I dedicate the book to them with profound love and gratitude—far beyond what words in any human language could express.

Abbreviations

General and Bibliographic

*	hypothetical/unattested form
√	verbal root
A	answer
AB	Anchor Bible
ABD	*Anchor Bible Dictionary*, ed. D. N. Freedman, 6 vols. (New York: Doubleday, 1992)
ABRL	Anchor Bible Reference Library
alt.	altered translation
AnBib	Analecta Biblica
ANF	*The Ante-Nicene Fathers*, ed. A. Roberts and J. Donaldson, 10 vols. (New York: Christian Literature, 1885–96; repr., Grand Rapids: Eerdmans, 1950–51)
AOS	American Oriental Series
app(s).	appendix(es)
ASR	*American Sociological Review*
ATJ	*Asbury Theological Journal*
AYBRL	Anchor Yale Bible Reference Library
BASOR	*Bulletin of the American Schools of Oriental Research*
BCP	Book of Common Prayer, used by the Episcopal Church
BCW	Book of Common Worship
BH	Biblical Hebrew
BR	*Biblical Research*
BT	*The Bible Translator*
BZAW	Beihefte zur Zeitschrift für die alttestamentliche Wissenschaft
CAL	Cambridge Approaches to Linguistics
CBQ	*Catholic Biblical Quarterly*
CBQMS	Catholic Biblical Quarterly Monograph Series
CBR	*Currents in Biblical Research*
CEB	Common English Bible
CEL	*Cambridge Encyclopedia of Language*, by David Crystal, 2nd ed. (Cambridge: Cambridge University Press, 1997)
cf.	*confer*, compare
chap(s).	chapter(s)
CSCD	Cambridge Studies in Christian Doctrine
CTL	Cambridge Textbooks in Linguistics
DBI	*Dictionary of Biblical Interpretation*, ed. J. Hayes, 2 vols. (Nashville: Abingdon, 1999)
ed(s).	editor(s), edited by, edition

EDSS	*Encyclopedia of the Dead Sea Scrolls*, ed. L. H. Schiffman and J. C. VanderKam, 2 vols. (New York: Oxford University Press, 2000)	LHBOTS	Library of Hebrew Bible / Old Testament Studies
		LSAWS	Linguistic Studies in Ancient West Semitic
		LXX	Septuagint
e.g.	*exempli gratia*, for example	MH	Mishnaic Hebrew
esp.	especially	*MoTh*	*Modern Theology*
et al.	*et alia*, and others	MT	Masoretic Text
etc.	et cetera, and the rest, and so forth	NAB	New American Bible
		NASB	New American Standard Bible
FAT	Forschungen zum Alten Testament	NCB	New Century Bible
GBS	Guides to Biblical Scholarship	NCBC	New Cambridge Bible Commentary
GNT	Greek New Testament	NICNT	New International Commentary on the New Testament
HB	Hebrew Bible		
HBM	Hebrew Bible Monographs	NICOT	New International Commentary on the Old Testament
HCOT	Historical Commentary on the Old Testament		
HSS	Harvard Semitic Studies	*NIDOTTE*	*New International Dictionary of Old Testament Theology and Exegesis*, ed. W. A. VanGemeren, 5 vols. (Grand Rapids: Zondervan, 1997)
HTS	Harvard Theological Studies		
ICC	International Critical Commentary		
i.e.	*id est*, that is		
IH	Israeli Hebrew		
Int	*Interpretation*	NIGTC	New International Greek Testament Commentary
JBL	*Journal of Biblical Literature*		
JCTCRS	Jewish and Christian Texts in Context and Related Studies	NIV	New International Version
		NJPS	*Tanakh: The Holy Scriptures* (New Jewish Publication Society Translation)
JSOT	*Journal for the Study of the Old Testament*		
JSOTSup	Journal for the Study of the Old Testament Supplement Series	NLT	New Living Translation
		NovTSup	Supplements to Novum Testamentum
JTI	*Journal for Theological Interpretation*	NRSV	New Revised Standard Version
JTISup	Journal for Theological Interpretation, Supplements	NT	New Testament
		NTA	New Testament Apocrypha
KJV	King James Version	NTM	New Testament Monographs
L1	First (native) language	OBT	Overtures to Biblical Theology
L2	Second (acquired) language		
LAI	Library of Ancient Israel	ODCC	*Oxford Dictionary of the Christian Church*, ed. F. L. Cross and E. A. Livingstone, 3rd ed. (Oxford: Oxford University Press, 1997)
LALD	Language Acquisition and Language Disorders		
LCC	Library of Christian Classics		
LDS	Latter-day Saints		

OED	Oxford English Dictionary, 2nd ed. (Oxford: Oxford University Press, 1989)	s.v.	sub verbo, under the word
		SymS	Symposium Series
		TDOT	Theological Dictionary of the Old Testament, ed. G. J. Botterweck and H. Ringgren, trans. J. T. Willis et al., 15 vols. (Grand Rapids: Eerdmans, 1974–2006)
OHLT	Oxford Handbooks for Language Teachers		
orig.	original		
OT	Old Testament		
OTA	Old Testament Apocrypha		
OTL	Old Testament Library	ThTo	Theology Today
OTM	Oxford Theological Monographs	TLOT	Theological Lexicon of the Old Testament, ed. E. Jenni, with assistance from C. Westermann, trans. M. E. Biddle, 3 vols. (Peabody, MA: Hendrickson, 1997)
OTP	Old Testament Pseudepigrapha		
OTT	Old Testament Theology		
PNG	Papua New Guinea		
PRSt	Perspectives in Religious Studies		
PSB	Princeton Seminary Bulletin	TLZ	Theologische Literaturzeitung
Q	question	trans.	translated by
RBS	Resources for Biblical Study	TU	Texte und Untersuchungen
RCL	Revised Common Lectionary	UBL	Ugaritisch-biblische Literatur
repr.	reprint	UBS	United Bible Societies
SB	Sources bibliques	vs.	versus
SBLDS	Society of Biblical Literature Dissertation Series	VT	Vetus Testamentum
		VTSup	Supplements to Vetus Testamentum
SBTS	Sources for Biblical and Theological Study	v(v).	verse(s)
SLA	Second-Language Acquisition	WBC	Word Biblical Commentary
STDJ	Studies on the Texts of the Desert of Judah	WTT	Westminster Morphologically Tagged Hebrew Text
STI	Studies in Theological Interpretation	WUNT	Wissenschaftliche Untersuchungen zum Neuen Testament
STR	Studies in Theology and Religion	ZAH	Zeitschrift für Althebräistik

Old Testament

Gen.	Genesis	Ezra	Ezra
Exod.	Exodus	Neh.	Nehemiah
Lev.	Leviticus	Esther	Esther
Num.	Numbers	Job	Job
Deut.	Deuteronomy	Ps(s).	Psalm(s)
Josh.	Joshua	Prov.	Proverbs
Judg.	Judges	Eccles.	Ecclesiastes
Ruth	Ruth	Song	Song of Songs
1–2 Sam.	1–2 Samuel	Isa.	Isaiah
1–2 Kings	1–2 Kings	Jer.	Jeremiah
1–2 Chron.	1–2 Chronicles	Lam.	Lamentations

Ezek.	Ezekiel		Mic.	Micah
Dan.	Daniel		Nah.	Nahum
Hosea	Hosea		Hab.	Habakkuk
Joel	Joel		Zeph.	Zephaniah
Amos	Amos		Hag.	Haggai
Obad.	Obadiah		Zech.	Zechariah
Jon.	Jonah		Mal.	Malachi

New Testament

Matt.	Matthew		1–2 Thess.	1–2 Thessalonians
Mark	Mark		1–2 Tim.	1–2 Timothy
Luke	Luke		Titus	Titus
John	John		Philem.	Philemon
Acts	Acts		Heb.	Hebrews
Rom.	Romans		James	James
1–2 Cor.	1–2 Corinthians		1–2 Pet.	1–2 Peter
Gal.	Galatians		1–3 John	1–3 John
Eph.	Ephesians		Jude	Jude
Phil.	Philippians		Rev.	Revelation
Col.	Colossians			

Old Testament Apocrypha

2 Esd.	2 Esdras		Tob.	Tobit
1–4 Macc.	1–4 Maccabees		Wis.	Wisdom of Solomon
Sir.	Sirach			

Other Ancient Sources

b.	Babylonian Talmud		*m.*	Mishnah
Ber.	tractate *Berakot*		*Sanh.*	tractate *Sanhedrin*

Testimonia

Tell me what you would strike from the Old Testament and I'll tell you what defect there is in your Christian knowledge.

—Wilhelm Vischer

Indeed, it would be no exaggeration to understand the hermeneutical problem of the Old Testament as *the* problem of Christian theology, and not just as one problem among others, seeing that all the other questions of theology are affected in one way or another by its resolution. . . . This question [of whether and why the Old Testament is part of the canon of Scripture and what its relevance is] affects the extent and also qualitatively the substance of what may be regarded as Christian. No more fundamental question can be posed in all theology; providing an answer for it defines the realm in which theology has to be done.

—A. H. J. Gunneweg

The passing of the debate over the higher criticism still leaves us with the real problem of the Old Testament: *should it have any authority in the Christian Church and if so how is that authority to be defined?* Once one has awakened to [the] commanding importance of this question one will be able to see that it runs through the whole of Christian history with a scarlet thread. Yea, more: one can see that much of the difference in theologies springs from the extent to which they build Old Testament ideas or impulses into the primitive Christian patterns. And the latter, one may discover, differ in themselves already because of the degree of Old Testament influence received. The Old Testament problem, therefore, is not just one of many. It is the master problem of theology. And even for those who regard the first half of the question, as formulated above, beyond debate, the second half still remains in force. All theology that operates in any way with [the] biblical heritage hangs in the air until it is settled.

—Emil G. Kraeling

The current fashion of thought has regarded the Old Testament as a monument of antiquity, interesting to the historian, the literary critic, and the archaeologist, but of little serious value for the life and thought of the modern Christian. Our approach to it has been by means of an overconfident "historicism," wherein it is assumed that, once we are able to trace the accurate, detailed history of the linguistics and institutions of the Hebrew people in their proper life-situation, our task is finished. In reality, however, it has scarcely begun. Those of us who are Christian theists are still faced with the fundamental question: What is the relevance of the prophetic "Thus said the Lord" for our day? . . . One reason for such confusion . . . may be the lack of familiarity with a positive treatment of Old Testament theology. Not merely is this subject neglected in modern biblical teaching; it is almost entirely forgotten.

—G. Ernest Wright

"I shall go to my grave," a friend of mine once wrote me, "feeling that Christian thought is a dead language—one that feeds many living ones to be sure, one that still sets these vibrating with echoes and undertones, but which I would no more use overtly than I would speak Latin." I suppose he is right, more right than wrong anyway. If the language that clothes Christianity is not dead, it is at least, for many, dying; and what is really surprising, I suppose, is that it has lasted as long as it has.

—Frederick Buechner

The language of faith, the language of public responsibility in which as Christians we are bound to speak, will inevitably be the language of the Bible, the Hebrew and the Greek Bible and the translations of them, and the language of Christian tradition, the language in the forms of the thoughts, concepts and ideas, in which in the course of centuries the Christian Church has gained and upheld and declared its knowledge. There is a specifically Church language. That is in order. Let us call it by the familiar name by saying that there is a "language of Canaan." And when the Christian confesses his faith, when we have to let the light that is kindled in us shine, no one can avoid speaking in this language. For this is how it is: if the things of Christian faith, if our trust in God and His Word is to be expressed precisely, so to speak in its essence— and time and again it is bitterly necessary for this to be done, so that things may be made clear—then it is inevitable that all undaunted the language of

Canaan should sound forth. For certain lights and indications and heartening warnings can be uttered directly in this language alone. . . . One thing is certain, that where the Christian Church does not venture to confess in its own language, it usually does not confess at all. Then it becomes the fellowship of the quiet, whereby it is much to be hoped that it does not become a community of dumb dogs.

—Karl Barth

Gather everyone—men, women, children, and the immigrants who live in your cities—in order that they hear it, learn it, and revere the LORD your God, carefully doing all the words of this Instruction, and so that their children, who don't yet know the Instruction, may hear it and learn to revere the LORD your God. . . . So in light of all that, you must write down this poem and teach it to the Israelites. Put it in their mouths so that the poem becomes a witness for me against them . . . this poem will witness against them, giving its testimony, because it won't be lost from the mouths of their descendants.

—Deuteronomy 31:12–13a, 19, 21 CEB

You've taught me since my youth, God,
   and I'm still proclaiming your wondrous deeds!
So, even in my old age with gray hair, don't abandon me, God!
   Not until I tell generations about your mighty arm,
tell all who are yet to come about your strength,
   and about your ultimate righteousness, God,
because you've done awesome things!
   Who can compare to you, God?

—Psalm 71:17–19 CEB

When I was a child, I used to speak like a child, reason like a child, think like a child. But now that I have become a man, I've put an end to childish things.

—1 Corinthians 13:11 CEB

God's goal is for us to become mature adults—to be fully grown, measured by the standard of the fullness of Christ. As a result, we aren't supposed to be infants any longer who can be tossed and blown around by every wind that comes from teaching with deceitful scheming and the tricks people play to deliberately mislead others.

—Ephesians 4:13a–14 CEB

The days are surely coming, says the LORD God,
>when I will send hunger and thirst on the land;
>neither a hunger for bread, nor a thirst for water,
>but of hearing the LORD's words.

They will wander from sea to sea,
>and from north to east;

they will roam all around,
>seeking the LORD's word,
>but they won't find it.

—Amos 8:11–12 CEB

PART 1

The Old Testament as a Dying Language

1

The Old Testament Is Dying

A (Non)Telling Vignette

Like many others who make their living as theological educators, I do a fair amount of teaching in local church settings. It is often and increasingly the case that the majority, if not the entirety, of the audiences at these events are senior citizens, with most more than a bit beyond the fifty-five-year age minimum to get cheaper coffee at McDonald's. Since I myself have school-age children at home, I understand and can sympathize with the fact that parents with children are stretched very thin, and if they aren't altogether absent from church that day due to soccer practice, cheerleading, or a debate team competition, they are perhaps assisting in children's worship, Sunday school, teen activities, or the like. While I have no doubt that this may very well be the case, the fact that so many of the regulars at the church events where I speak are septuagenarians, if not octogenarians or nonagenarians, is of great significance for the diagnosis that I offer here because one of the primary signs of language death is when only the elderly speak it.

Now let me be clear: I'm very thankful for the opportunities I get to teach, and I'm very thankful for any who will listen, whatever their age. Moreover, the elderly who so frequently predominate at my talks are, to borrow a churchy term, "the saints"—and that means that even if they aren't particularly holy, they've at least been around the church barn a few times. The odds are that they are fairly faithful people, on various fronts, that they know their Bibles decently well, and, although they may not like what's happening in the contemporary service, they'll almost certainly be back next Sunday along with their tithe envelopes. Then too there is the additional fact that the saints, especially the quite elderly ones, always seem happy to have someone—especially someone (relatively) younger—come and spend some time talking to them.

But as I was teaching in a church in metropolitan Atlanta a summer or two ago, something shocking took place that I had never experienced before. I admit to being momentarily dumbfounded when it happened, but the full significance of what transpired didn't hit me until later. I was teaching a two-week series on biblical poetry and was introducing the topic by pointing out the use of poetry at certain key junctures in the Bible. I had mentioned several examples from the Old Testament and had just turned to the New Testament. I began with the role of prophetic poetry at the start of Jesus's ministry (the citation from Isa. 40:3; Mal. 3:1; and Exod. 23:20 in Mark 1:2) and then moved to the Passion Narratives, at which point I quoted Jesus's well-known "cry of dereliction" from the cross: "My God, my God, why hast thou forsaken me?"—in the King James Version, no less (to tap the recall of the elderly audience). Given what I had just said, I figured the class was following me and that it was relatively clear that this saying from the cross was (a) poetic and (b) a citation from the Old Testament. So I asked the class of hoary heads what Jesus was quoting. Where, I questioned, did his words come from?

Total silence.

No one knew. Or if they did know, they certainly weren't telling. But the pause was long enough and the silence deafening enough to make it clear to me that this wasn't a case of being tight-lipped. It was a case of *not knowing.* One sweet-faced, white-haired woman finally shook her head, confirming my suspicion. No, they did not know the answer to my question. Not even this elderly group of "saints" knew that Jesus's cry was a direct quotation of Psalm 22.

That's when I realized, in a way that I had never realized before, that the Old Testament was dying.

The Diagnosis, in Brief, with a Caveat

That, in brief, is my claim—or to employ a medical metaphor, my diagnosis: the Old Testament is dying. Much needs to be said about this claim to explain it, let alone establish it, but for now let me gloss it further by stating my firm belief that for many contemporary Christians, at least in North America,[1] the

---

1. I make no claims about Christianity elsewhere; perhaps other places on the planet are doing better. For the similarities and differences between Judaism and Christianity with reference to my diagnosis, see note 43 below.

Old Testament has ceased to function in healthy ways in their lives as sacred, authoritative, canonical literature. These individuals—or in some cases, groups of individuals (even entire churches)[2]—do not regard the Old Testament in the same way (or as highly) as the New Testament, do not understand the Old Testament, would prefer to do without the Old Testament, and for all practical purposes do exactly that by means of their neglect and ignorance of it, whether in private devotion or public worship or both. All of that is what I mean by the shorthand claim "The Old Testament is dying." Indeed, in many circles, the claim "The Old Testament is dying," as stark as it is, is not nearly stark enough. "The Old Testament is dead" is far more accurate.

Before going further, I want to clarify what I do and do not mean by this claim that the Old Testament is dying if not already dead. First and foremost, I do not intend any connections with the earlier (in)famous "God Is Dead" controversy of the 1960s.[3] Given the not-so-serendipitous convergence of the language, I admit to having entertained a different title for the present book by rephrasing it altogether as a question, "Is the Old Testament Dying?" While I have opted for the indicative formulation, it is nevertheless true that what follows is an *essay*, not a final or definitive statement, and it is the nature of all such claims to be contestable.[4] Some will no doubt challenge what I present here, and that is well and good. I would be *beyond* delighted

2. As one example, I mention a church near my home whose sign reads "The Praise Center: A New Testament Church for the 21st Century." So-called New Testament churches of various sorts (typically of the low-church or free-church variety) are not uncommon in the United States; by contrast, I have never once seen an "Old Testament Church." Regardless, the root problem is not restricted to more conservative-evangelical wings of Christianity and may be even more pronounced outside such circles. Ellen F. Davis tracks the same trend in mainline Christianity: "The Old Testament is ceasing to function as Scripture in the European-American mainstream church" ("Losing a Friend," 83).

3. For the "God is dead" controversy, see Elson, "Theology: Toward a Hidden God," beginning on 82. The stark black-and-white cover of that issue of *Time* has "Is God Dead?" in red (http://content.time.com/time/covers/0,16641,19660408,00.html). Note also the slightly earlier treatment in Elson, "God Is Dead Movement"; the letters responding to "Theology: Toward a Hidden God" in *Time*, April 15, 1966, 13; April 22, 1966, 9; April 29, 1966, 19; and May 6, 1966, 9; and the publisher's letter on May 20, 1966, 23. The God-is-dead idea and Thomas J. J. Altizer, one of the theologians with whom it is inextricably linked, are also mentioned in the unsigned article by Elson, "Changing Theologies for a Changing World," 42–43; cf. the cover story in that issue, "Is God Coming Back to Life?," beginning on 40. More recently, see the autumn 2006 issue of *Emory Magazine*. In 1966, Anthony Towne wrote an entertaining obituary for God for the *New York Times* ("'Obituary' for God"): "God, creator of the universe, principal deity of the world's Jews, ultimate reality of Christians, and most eminent of all divinities, died late yesterday during major surgery undertaken to correct a massive diminishing influence." Long before Altizer et al., there was Nietzsche, *Gay Science*, esp. 181. Cf. R. Morgan with J. Barton, *Biblical Interpretation*, 60.

4. See, e.g., Booth, Colomb, and J. Williams, *Craft of Research*, 120–29.

to be proven wrong—indeed, to borrow words from Bill McKibben,[5] it is my prayer to be proven wrong, but thus far my prayers have gone unanswered, and so I remain convinced that my diagnosis is correct. I have based my assessment on the available data at hand and my interpretation of those data, but I admit that "the parties" involved in my study—the Old Testament and its life within contemporary Christianity—are very large subjects, and so any one person's assessment cannot help but be limited, perspectival, and to some degree anecdotal.[6]

Let me be clear: I have no doubt that the Old Testament is read, at least occasionally, by many Christians and in many churches, but part of my larger point—not to mention the larger problem—is not simply *if* the Old Testament is present (somehow), read (intermittently), or preached from (sporadically), but *how* it is present, read, preached from, and so on and so forth. The Old Testament was also present in Nazi Germany, at least for a while, but *how?*—which is to ask, *To what end?*[7]

Further, even at the points where I do make firm claims, where I do mean to describe the terminal state of the Old Testament among certain people or groups, my argument should not be confused with an affirmative or prescriptive statement on my part. As will be obvious in what follows, the death of the Old Testament is not something I endorse. Far from it! Instead, it constitutes my greatest sadness.

The Old Testament Is (Like) a Language

My diagnosis that the Old Testament is dying, if not already dead, depends on a linguistic analogy. The analogy is that the Old Testament is a language or very much like a language; hence, like other languages, it can die out relatively quickly, even definitively, never to return in living form. But what does it mean to say that the Old Testament is a language or very much like one? I begin with what I do *not* mean by this statement.

First, I do not mean to discuss the language of the Old Testament itself, which, in truth, is not one language but several. When studying the Old Testament "in the original," one must actually reckon with many ancient languages: Classical (or Biblical) Hebrew primarily, of course, but also Biblical

5. Cf. McKibben, *End of Nature*, xxiv (on environmental issues).
6. To be sure, anecdotes aren't all bad and comprise part of the arsenal in the New Historicism (see Hens-Piazza, *New Historicism*). Note also Prothero's instructive use of both hard data and anecdotes in his *Religious Literacy*. See chap. 2 below for some (semi)empirical data to support the diagnosis offered here.
7. See Bergen, *Twisted Cross*, 143–54; and chap. 5 below.

Aramaic for those bits of Genesis, Jeremiah, and especially Daniel and Ezra that exist in that language. Next in importance, though very important in and of itself, is the Greek of the Septuagint (LXX), which in turn is a complex entity comprising "one" (yet again, one out of many) of the most important textual witnesses to the Old Testament, together with those apocryphal or deuterocanonical books that survive exclusively or primarily in that language.[8] This listing doesn't yet include the many other languages that have preserved important versions of the Old Testament—the Latin Vulgate, for instance, or the Syriac Peshitta, both of which contain additional deuterocanonical material—nor does it include certain languages that have proved to be particularly useful for the study of the Old Testament in terms of understanding low-frequency words, analyzing poetry, or providing crucial historical and cultural contexts for the biblical texts. One thinks here of the ancient Near Eastern languages, especially of Hebrew's close Northwest Semitic cousin, Ugaritic, but also and especially the massive gold mine that is Akkadian in its various dialects and periods.

All of these languages are important, and the most competent biblical scholars work with several at a time, but it should be quickly admitted that a thorough knowledge of even just one, even Biblical Hebrew itself, while of great help, does not (re)solve every problem one encounters in the Old Testament. Part of why that is the case is precisely due to the nature of these languages and how they differ from our own.[9] Walter Brueggemann has this to say about Biblical Hebrew specifically:

> Of all that could be said of this script [the Bible], my initial point is a simple but crucial one. It is in Hebrew, not Latin. I do not say that to suggest that one cannot read it without knowledge of Hebrew grammar, though such knowledge is a good idea and a real advantage. I say it rather to make the point that this text, in its very utterance, in its ways of putting things, is completely unfamiliar to us. . . . Hebrew, even for those who know it much better than do I, is endlessly imprecise and unclear. It lacks the connecting words; it denotes rather than connotes; it points and opens and suggests, but it does not conclude or define.[10]

8. Hebrew fragments of some apocryphal books were found at Qumran—notably Sirach, Tobit, Psalm 151, and the Letter of Jeremiah. See Collins, "Apocrypha and Pseudepigrapha"; and chap. 7 below.

9. Similarly, neither does simply reading the Bible guarantee some sort of "faithful" engagement or response. See, anecdotally, Plotz, *Good Book*; and chaps. 2, 4–6 below. Some studies on correlations between Scripture reading and various ethical activities show this as an area that is at least theoretically open to social-scientific analysis. See, e.g., Fawcett and Linkletter, "Bible Reading and Adolescents' Attitudes."

10. Brueggemann, "Preaching a Sub-Version," 197.

Or, as another Old Testament scholar, Peter Enns, has written: "Knowing the original Hebrew does not always make the text 'come alive'! It often introduces obscurities that English readers are not aware of."[11]

The point here, however, is not the number of languages necessary for a minimally adequate interpretation of the Bible; neither is the point how difficult these various languages can be. Despite the truism about how much is "lost in translation,"[12] one hopes that one's native vernacular will suffice for much biblical interpretation (particularly if we are speaking of *minimum* competency), especially given the large number and range of excellent translations of the Bible into English, not to mention the countless resources for the study of the Bible that are based on its original languages, even for those who know none of them.[13] Instead, my point is that the Old Testament itself *is* a language, or, to back off ever so slightly, very much like a language.

What I mean by this linguistic analogy, then, is that the Old Testament, like any other piece of literature or art—like any other way of figuring the world—is, or at least can be, a way of constructing reality, a way of understanding the world, a way of perceiving all that is, including ourselves.[14] Just as language—preverbal, nonverbal, and verbal—allows us to make sense of the world and ourselves, the Old Testament provides (or can provide) a kind of grammar for constructing, perceiving, and understanding the same.[15]

There are several ways to unpack this notion of the language that is the Old Testament.

First, we might observe that the languages used in the Old Testament—Hebrew primarily, but also Aramaic, Greek, and all the others—reflect a certain way of perceiving reality (see further below). This is a basic insight regarding the social construction of reality familiar from the work of, among

11. Enns, *Inspiration and Incarnation*, 71–72.

12. Bly puts it memorably in *Eight Stages of Translation*, 15–16: "As we read the literal [translation of the poem], our first reaction is: What happened to the poem? Where did it go? So we read the original again and it's still marvelous; so evidently something has been left out [of the translation]—probably the meaning."

13. These, too, don't guarantee much of anything. See at note 9 above and chaps. 8–9 below.

14. For literature more generally, see Booth, *Company We Keep*, esp. his chapters on figurative language (293–373). For the "livability" of metaphor, see also Lakoff and M. Johnson, *Metaphors We Live By*.

15. John Calvin puts things similarly, though using a visual metaphor: "Just as old or bleary-eyed men and those with weak vision, if you thrust before them a most beautiful volume, even if they recognize it to be some sort of writing, yet can scarcely construe two words, but with the aid of spectacles will begin to read distinctly; so Scripture, gathering up the otherwise confused knowledge of God in our minds, having dispersed our dullness, clearly shows us the true God" (*Institutes of the Christian Religion*, 1:70 [1.6.1]).

others, Peter Berger and Thomas Luckman.[16] Biblical Hebrew (or Aramaic or Greek, etc.) is thus hardly unique at this point. Every society constructs reality in a certain way, with language serving as a primary vehicle of the construction.[17] The same holds true for *religious* societies and/or for *religious aspects* of a society.[18]

A second, closely related way to understand the notion would be to observe how the Old Testament itself—as a complex whole, not simply by means of its specific linguistic form(s)—is a way of constructing and understanding the world. In this view, the issue is not, for example, to notice how interesting (if not odd) it is that deep emotions are often associated with the bowels in Hebrew anthropology, or how rage is located in the nose.[19] Neither is the issue to wonder how Hebrew conceptions of time seem oriented, to some degree at least, toward the cardinal points of the compass, with the speaker evidently facing the past, since "the past" is קדם/*qdm*, a word related to what lies "before" or "in front of," which means the speaker rows backward into "the future," which in Hebrew is related to אחר/*ʾḥr*, "behind."[20]

The way Hebrew terms reflect anthropology and time are both interesting points and not without significance, yet to speak of the Old Testament writ large as a language says that it is more than the sum of its (specific Hebrew) parts in the same way that the book of Job is more than a list of its vocabulary items. Thus the language that is the Old Testament is more than just one book, such as Job. The book of Job may be one piece of the language—perhaps a lexical item or a syntactical unit, maybe even a sentence, paragraph, or larger unit of discourse—having to do with suffering, for example; yet certain other pieces of the language of the Old Testament also have something to contribute to that subject: Proverbs, say, or Deuteronomy. Calling the latter two "lexemes" that are antonyms to Job's "word," or calling them "sentences" that are antithetical to Job's, isn't entirely wrong, but it also isn't very helpful, mostly because the word/antonym structure is too simplistic for complex compositions like these ones.[21] Even so, an important point in this second way of understanding the linguistic analogy of the Old Testament as (like) a language is that, in this construal, in order to "speak

---

16. Berger and Luckman, *Social Construction of Reality*.

17. Cf. the following works, some of which are in debate: Deutscher, *Through the Language Glass*; McWhorter, *Language Hoax*; and Pinker, *Stuff of Thought*.

18. Cf., e.g., D. Morgan, *Visual Piety*, esp. 1–20.

19. See Wolff, *Anthropology of the Old Testament*, 63–66; M. Smith, "The Heart and Innards."

20. See Wolff, *Anthropology of the Old Testament*, 88; and Wyatt, "Vocabulary and Neurology of Orientation"; reprinted in Wyatt, *Mythic Mind*, 125–50.

21. For the dialogical complexity within Job, see, e.g., Newsom, *Book of Job*.

the language," especially with any sort of fluency, one would need to know *both* Job *and* Proverbs, Job *and* Deuteronomy, Deuteronomy *and* Proverbs, and so on and so forth. Otherwise one isn't speaking the full language but something significantly less than that: an incomplete or severely abbreviated version of the language—baby talk, as it were.[22]

A third way to understand the notion of the Old Testament as being (like) a language is to consider the possibility that someone could conceivably adopt one or both of the former approaches and so construct one's own world similarly. This would be an exercise in forming what is sometimes called a "biblical worldview." Such worldviews are rarely constructed in terms of the first understanding offered above. Few indeed would advocate reconceptualizing modern understandings of cognition so as to locate it where ancient Israelites believed cognition was housed, not in the brain at all, but in the "heart" (לב/ *lēb*). Only a very few and rather unique individuals, that is, have the wherewithal and zaniness to spend a year "living biblically"—in an extreme sort of way, at any rate—though evidently doing so can occasionally lead them to write best-selling books.[23] (But even these people can only stand a year of it!) Instead, the idea of a "biblical worldview" is almost always predicated on something similar to the second understanding: perceiving reality in terms commensurate with the Bible. In this perspective, Christianity is a way of "imagining the world Scripture imagines."[24] Of course, so too is Judaism, especially with the yearly remembrance of the exodus in the Passover Haggadah: "We were slaves in Egypt. . . ."[25]

For some people the idea of constructing a biblical worldview makes good sense (probably because they are thinking in terms of the more sober option above); to others the exact opposite is the case (especially if they are thinking in terms of the more zany option above). Either way, it is safe to say that, whether consciously or not, intentionally or otherwise, worldviews are being formed all the time—to one degree or another—and literature and other works of art are a part of that formation, if not the primary way they are formed.[26]

---

22. See further chaps. 3–7 below.

23. See Jacobs, *Year of Living Biblically*. Note also R. Evans, *Year of Biblical Womanhood*; B. Cohen, *My Jesus Year*; within the same orbit, Plotz, *Good Book*.

24. See L. Johnson, "Imagining the World Scripture Imagines." See also, inter alia, Brueggemann, *Book That Breathes New Life*, xv–xvi; Brueggemann, *Inscribing the Text*, 13–14; and more generally, Kort, *"Take, Read."*

25. Cf. Fishbane, *Exegetical Imagination*, 4; also chaps. 4–5 below on figural reading.

26. Booth, *Company We Keep*, is helpful on this point: such formation is neither automatic nor invariably "positive." Rather, readers are always making judgments about what they read, which, for Booth, ultimately comes down to a decision regarding whether or not the reader will choose to keep company with this or that piece of literature, deeming it a close friend, a distant

It thus should come as no surprise, and there is no obvious rebuttal to it (at least in theory), that the Old Testament could be used in similar ways. To put the matter more directly: it seems clear that the Old Testament works (or *can* work) on readers in these world-constructing ways quite apart from intentional use or conscious awareness. One example of this kind of "work" is found in the Revised Common Lectionary (RCL) and how it (re)presents the Bible as a lens through which one can and does—perhaps even must—reflect on a season in the Christian year or the themes of that particular liturgical season, assuming one uses it.[27] This example granted, there still remain significant problems with the notion of a biblical worldview and with constructing one—not the least of which is that there is no one, simple, unified "biblical worldview" (recall above on speaking "only Job"), and even if there were just "one," getting it from back there—from "Bible Land" where it was written in "Bible-ese"—to here and now is no small task or mean feat.

Despite the problems besetting this third approach—or at least simplistic versions of it—it remains reasonable to think that the Old Testament is (like) a language in the sense that the Old Testament could be used in the creation of a biblical worldview (the third approach), or in the sense that it could be used to perceive the world (the second approach), whether that perception is modern in orientation or outcome (the second and third approaches) or ancient—meaning, in the last case, Israel's articulation of its own reality (the first approach). Whether the Old Testament *would* be so used (and in the best-case scenarios) is precisely the question at hand.

One could appeal to yet other disciplines beyond those of the Bible or linguistics in support of the notion that the Old Testament is (like) a language, useful for understanding the world. In systematic theology, for example, George A. Lindbeck famously advocated a "cultural-linguistic" understanding of Christian doctrine.[28] More broadly and in truth more fundamentally (since

---

acquaintance, or a downright enemy. Other useful works include Ricoeur, *Rule of Metaphor*; and Goodman, *Ways of Worldmaking*.

27. See, e.g., Kaltner and McKenzie, *Back Door Introduction to the Bible*, 127–28. On the RCL, see chap. 2 below.

28. Lindbeck, *Nature of Doctrine*, esp. 18–27; also 152–65, with an extensive listing of reviews and secondary treatments of Lindbeck's work. Among others, note Tracy, "Lindbeck's New Program for Theology"; Michalson, "Response to Lindbeck"; and reviews by Corner; Raynal; G. Kaufman. See also Marshall, "Introduction: *The Nature of Doctrine* after 25 Years," which details many critiques of Lindbeck but also offers Marshall's own refutation of several of them. An OT scholar's perspective may be found in Childs, *New Testament as Canon*, 541–46; and Childs, *Biblical Theology of the Old and New Testaments*, 21–22. Lindbeck, in turn, contributed to one of Childs's *Festschriften*: "Postcritical Canonical Interpretation." Two other works that deal with linguistics and cultural factors are Blount, *Cultural Interpretation*; and Vanhoozer, *Drama of Doctrine*, esp. 3–25.

Lindbeck depended on anthropological theory), one could note the use of linguistic analogies, structures, and concepts in cultural anthropology in order to understand social systems along the lines of linguistic ones.[29] To quote Claire Jacobson, the translator of Claude Lévi-Strauss's classic work on the subject, *Structural Anthropology*: "Language can . . . be treated as a conceptual model for other aspects of culture; these aspects can also be regarded as systems of communication."[30] So it is that many fields have taken "the linguistic turn."[31] Close to the Old Testament proper, we might cite the iconographic work of Othmar Keel and Christoph Uehlinger, who have used similar insights to depict ancient Israelite religion as a massive "symbol system" replete with an artistic grammar and correlate syntax.[32]

Indeed, the linguistic analogy of Christian belief, along with its foundational texts, as being (like) a language has informed two recent books by two very different theologians, both of whom, despite their deep disagreements, write about "speaking Christian."[33] Marcus J. Borg argues that *to be* Christian is *to speak* Christian:

> Why do I express this crisis [in the ability to "speak Christian"] as a problem of language? Because language is the medium through which people participate in their religion. To be part of a religion means being able to speak and understand its language. Every religion has a basic vocabulary: its "big" words and collections of words, spoken and heard in worship, embodied in rituals and practices.
>
> Thus to be Jewish means "speaking Jewish"; to be Muslim means "speaking Muslim"; to be Buddhist means "speaking Buddhist"; and so forth. By "speaking" I do not mean merely knowing either the ancient languages of these religions or their modern descendants. I mean something more basic: the way practitioners use the concepts and ideas from their religion as a lens through which to see the world, the way they use them to connect their religion to their life in the world. . . .

29. Lindbeck is explicitly dependent on Clifford Geertz (esp. his essays "Thick Description: Toward an Interpretive Theory of Culture," "The Impact of the Concept of Culture on the Concept of Man," "The Growth of Culture and the Evolution of Mind," and "Religion as a Cultural System"—all in Geertz's *Interpretation of Cultures*, 1–30, 33–54, 55–86, 87–125, respectively) among others. Lindbeck's debt to Ludwig Wittgenstein is also notable (seen in the index to *Nature of Doctrine*, 170). See also the classic study by Lévi-Strauss, *Structural Anthropology*, esp. 31–97. Of course structuralism, which depends heavily on linguistic research and analogues (note Lévi-Strauss's dependence on Saussure), has also been vigorously debated and critiqued, esp. by thinkers writing from poststructuralist perspectives (including that of deconstruction).

30. Jacobson, "Translator's Preface," xii.

31. See, e.g., Rorty, *Linguistic Turn*.

32. Keel and Uehlinger, *Gods, Goddesses, and Images of God*.

33. Borg, *Speaking Christian*; and Hauerwas, *Working with Words*.

In this respect, being Christian (or Jewish or Muslim) is like being French (or Turkish or Korean). One of the criteria for being French is the ability to speak French. Another is being able to understand French. We would not think someone fluent in French if that person could speak it but not understand it. In the same way, literacy means more than simply being able to make sounds out of written words. It also involves having some understanding of what the words mean. Christian literacy means not simply the ability to recognize biblical and Christian words, but also to understand them.[34]

Stanley Hauerwas asserts that theology is "work with words," and therefore "the work of the theologian is word work."[35] Like Borg, he believes that the problem facing Christianity is mostly a linguistic one:

> I think the characterizations of the challenges facing those going into the ministry are the result of the loss of the ability of Christians to speak the language of our faith. The accommodated character of the church is at least partly due to the failure of the clergy to help those they serve know how to speak Christian. To learn to be a Christian, to learn the discipline of the faith, is not just similar to learning another language. It *is* learning another language.[36]

Not all of the disciplines of study mentioned above (systematic theology, cultural anthropology, ancient Israelite religion) use language in exactly the same way—no more than do Borg and Hauerwas agree on every detail—but they do represent a confluence around the usefulness of the linguistic analogy, which also commends its use and utility with reference to the Old Testament.

Plan of the Book and Two Additional Caveats

Now if the linguistic analogy is apt and instructive for the Old Testament, this would mean that, just like any other language, the Old Testament could be taught, learned, and spoken, whether well or poorly, fluently or haltingly. It would also mean that, like any other language, the Old Testament is subject to the same kinds of processes that affect all other languages. These processes include linguistic growth and change, but also, depending on the language and

---

34. Borg, *Speaking Christian*, 5–6; in this same context he explicitly cites Lindbeck. Cf. also ibid., 18: "It is the premise of this book that religions are like languages. If we take this seriously, it means that being Christian means speaking Christian. To cease to speak Christian would mean no longer being Christian—just as ceasing to speak French would mean no longer being French. Speaking Christian is essential to being Christian."
35. Hauerwas, *Working with Words*, x.
36. Ibid., 86–87, emphasis original.

the circumstances, linguistic decline, demise, and ultimately death—the full extent, in other words, of the language life cycle. The death of any human language is a tragedy, given the amazing repositories of knowledge that each encodes in its own unique way.[37] The death of religious language is similarly tragic, and often accompanied by serious sociohistorical, even geopolitical ramifications.[38] In the case of the (seemingly imminent) death of the Old Testament, the problem is acute for the reasons already expressed, as well as other reasons presented in chapters 2 and 4–6. But the gravity of the situation is already signaled in several of the *testimonia* used as the epigraphs to the present book. Deficient knowledge of the Old Testament leads to defects in Christian knowledge, according to Wilhelm Vischer; *all* theological questions are related in one way or another to the hermeneutical problem of the Old Testament, according to A. H. J. Gunneweg; indeed, understanding the Old Testament is the master problem of theology, according to Emil G. Kraeling. All of these points are made even more poignant by G. Ernest Wright's remark that, for many, the Old Testament is nothing but an ancient monument, which means that a "positive treatment" of its theology is a subject that is not only neglected but almost entirely forgotten; and by Frederick Buechner's comment: it is no small miracle that the language clothing Christianity "has lasted as long as it has." Finally, the passage from Karl Barth underscores once more what is at stake: the "language of Canaan" is absolutely necessary if one wishes to speak precisely about—or better, to *confess*—the essence of Christian faith.[39]

Given my diagnosis that the Old Testament is dying, the problem of language death is of special concern here. But before addressing that issue directly, it is helpful to step back and offer some (semi)empirical evidence as proof that the Old Testament qua language is truly in dire straits. This "initial testing" of the patient is carried out in chapter 2 with reference to four distinct data sets, the first of which concerns the health of the Old Testament (not to mention some other religious subjects) among the general populace, while the other three speak to the life (or rather, death) of the Old Testament in Christian liturgical practice(s).

With these preliminary tests confirming the initial diagnosis, chapter 3 addresses language death proper, including how languages die, why they die,

---

37. See, e.g., Harrison, *Last Speakers*; and D. Wheeler, "Death of Languages." See further chap. 3 below.

38. See Prothero, *Religious Literacy*.

39. Respectively: Vischer, "Das alte Testament als Gottes Wort," 386; Gunneweg, *Understanding the Old Testament*, 2; Kraeling, *Old Testament since the Reformation*, 7–8; G. E. Wright, *Challenge of Israel's Faith*, v–vi; Buechner, *Magnificent Defeat*, 110; Barth, *Dogmatics in Outline*, 31.

and what is lost when they die. Treating these matters requires some background on how languages grow and change, as well as some discussion of the linguistic processes known as pidginization and creolization, because these bear directly on how languages change and survive and how they disappear and die. Indeed, pidginization and creolization are on further display in the signs of morbidity that are the focus of chapters 4–6. On the one hand, the signs of the patient's demise discussed in those chapters offer nothing new: they simply confirm the diagnosis and the results of the initial testing. On the other hand, they are especially important and troubling because they showcase the death of the Old Testament in three discourses or areas that are in many ways larger and more public—and thus more problematic—than those treated in chapter 2. The three discourses are the so-called New Atheism, Marcionites Old and New, and what I am calling, for lack of a better term, the New Plastic Gospels of the "happiologists."[40] In each of these three areas, the Old Testament seems to be on its last breath. In truth, in the case of the first two, the patient has already been laid to rest, without even the dignity of a proper funeral. Regardless, chapters 4–6 demonstrate that it is precisely the death of the Old Testament as a language that permits these three discourses to flourish after their own fashion and in their own way—fashions and ways that, in my judgment, are deeply flawed both theologically and ethically.

Thus far, then, my primary claim is that the Old Testament is dying, if not already dead. I have referred to this claim, both here and in the book's subtitle, as a "diagnosis," a word typically defined as "determination of the nature of a diseased condition; identification of a disease by careful investigation of its symptoms and history."[41] The problem of language death and the signs and symptoms of this pathology in the life of the Old Testament are presented in chapters 2–6. But, lest I seem completely pessimistic about the patient's future—that the Old Testament is completely incurable, altogether terminal—let me also draw attention to the other part of the book's subtitle, the part that mentions "recommended treatment." Part of my diagnosis—a word that also means "the opinion (formally stated) resulting from . . . investigation" of an illness[42]—is that the disease need *not* be terminal and so, in chapters 7–9, I move from diagnosis to prognosis, asking what can be done

40. I take the term "happiologists" from Peterson, *Primer in Positive Psychology*, 7–8, who is careful to say that "happiology" is not the same as authentic happiness, one of the primary foci of Positive Psychology. Peterson does not use the term with reference to prosperity preachers, which is how I am employing it.

41. See *OED*, s.v. "diagnosis, n."

42. Ibid.

to prevent the death of this particular and precious language known in Christian circles as "the Old Testament."[43] Here too I draw from linguistics—not only with regard to the preservation, revival, and even resurrection of dead and dying languages, but also via insights from children's language learning and second-language acquisition. These theories will, in the end, highlight the importance of two crucial factors in the future life of the Old Testament as a vibrant living language of faith that is "spoken here": the significance of children and the important role of poetry and music. As we will see, these are profoundly interrelated.

Finally, two caveats are in order. First, I am aware that my linguistic analogy—that the Old Testament is (like) a language—like any other analogy, is imperfect. There are several reasons for this. One is the nature of analogy itself: there is no one-to-one correspondence in analogy. But further, on the linguistic side of the analogy, we might recognize that the study of languages is an inexact science, and it is inexact precisely on matters relating to several crucial differentiations—when, for instance, a dialect is no longer a dialect but a truly distinct "language," or how "languages" themselves are something of a construct because languages are, in truth, complex conglomerations of many smaller though similar idiolects spoken by individual speakers.

On the biblical-theological front, there is the constant temptation to reify the linguistic analogy in some way such that (or with the result that) the Old Testament (or belief system or sacred text of whatever sort) becomes *unlike* any real language. As chapter 3 makes clear, *every* language—even a freshly invented one—is subject to change, growth, and development.[44] Why shouldn't

---

43. It is not altogether clear to me that the adjective "Old" in "Old Testament" is part of the problem; while it certainly isn't the whole of it, it may well play into it. Christopher R. Seitz has thought hard about the matters of nomenclature and the two-testament form of the Christian Bible; see his *Word without End*, esp. 61–74; Seitz, *Figured Out*, esp. 91–190; and most recently, Seitz, *Character of Christian Scripture*. In any event, the Christian language I employ here (and throughout) is intentional precisely because what I am discussing is largely a Christian issue. The problem is not evident in quite the same way in Judaism, for several obvious reasons. Even so, Judaism also has a kind of NT analogue, a corpus of postbiblical authoritative literature: the rabbinic material (esp. Mishnah and Talmud). Thus Judaism, too, may not be completely immune from the potential death of Scripture. In this regard, notice Tikva Frymer-Kensky's critique of rabbinic "supersessionism" in which the rabbis always trump the Bible ("The Emergence of Jewish Biblical Theologies," in *Studies in the Bible and Feminist Criticism*, esp. 367–68). At least it seems safe to say that certain portions of the Hebrew Bible are more authoritative than others in many segments of contemporary Judaism, representing small deaths of a kind. See, e.g., Sommer, "Scroll of Isaiah as Jewish Scripture"; and the related matters in chaps. 2 and 4–6.

44. Cf. G. Kaufman's review of *Nature of Doctrine*, where he makes the point that "no linguistic grammar ever is unchanging in the way in which Lindbeck's doctrinal 'grammar' is supposed to be" (241); Tanner, *Theories of Culture*, 138–43.

the language that is the Old Testament do the same, especially if and when it is regularly practiced? Indeed, reification of any "cultural-linguistic" system is doubly problematic if (and when) it seems to reflect only a cognitive approach to meaning, belief, and language. Matters of meaning, belief, and language are all best understood as *embodied*,[45] and one must not neglect that crucial insight, nor the importance of *practice* as such in any "language" of whatever sort.[46] A closely related issue is that one must guard against implying that there is (or ever was) a pure, original "language" of "biblical belief" and that all subsequent developments are somehow deficient or substandard.[47] The Old Testament itself bears witness to multiple dialects and diachronic change—whether that is in terms of the Hebrew used within the Bible,[48] in stories about (and data from) ancient Israel and its linguistic realities (e.g., Judg. 12:4–6; cf. Isa. 19:18; Ps. 114:1), or in the analogical sense discussed above (the "Job" dialect vs. "Deuteronomy" dialect). Which dialect was "the original"? Which stage was most "pure"?[49]

I will return to these issues in various ways in the chapters that follow. For now, though, it is enough to point out that since the analogy is imperfect, we shouldn't press it too hard or far. It remains an *analogy*. Even so, despite any and all problems, the analogy remains highly instructive, helping to explain, among other things, why the saints in that church in metropolitan Atlanta

45. See Lakoff and M. Johnson, *Philosophy in the Flesh*; W. S. Brown and B. D. Strawn, *Physical Nature of Christian Life*. For the power of poetry to combine thinking and feeling, see chaps. 8–9.

46. This was, of course, a major critique of Lindbeck; see notes 28 and 44 above. The work of Ludwig Wittgenstein is important at this point. See Sluga, "Wittgenstein," esp. 977–78, 980. Perhaps the most embodied form of language is sign language.

47. Cf. Holm, *Introduction to Pidgins and Creoles*, 1–4. In several of his works, John Mc-Whorter makes a compelling case against any pure, "blackboard" grammar, and the best proof against that is precisely the historical development of the language in question. See, e.g., Mc-Whorter, *Word on the Street*; McWhorter, *Doing Our Own Thing*; McWhorter, *Our Magnificent Bastard Tongue*; McWhorter, "Linguistics from the Left"; McWhorter, *What Language Is*. Even so, the existence of diachronic development does demonstrate change from earlier forms and thus at times highlights more pristine (at least theoretically) linguistic stages. For more on pidgins and creoles, see chap. 3. On the English language, see Crystal, *Cambridge Encyclopedia of the English Language*.

48. See, e.g., I. Young, Rezetko, and Ehrensvärd, *Linguistic Dating of Biblical Texts*, esp. 1:173–200; Kutscher, *Linguistic Background of the Isaiah Scroll*, 62–71; Bauer and Leander, *Historische Grammatik der hebräischen Sprache*; Sperber, *Historical Grammar of Biblical Hebrew*; Rendsburg, "Comprehensive Guide to Israelian Hebrew"; Rendsburg, *Diglossia in Ancient Hebrew*; Miller-Naudé and Zevit, *Diachrony in Biblical Hebrew*; Day, *Recovery of the Ancient Hebrew Language*; Sáenz-Badillos, *History of the Hebrew Language*; Waldman, *Recent Study of Hebrew*; Schniedewind, *Social History of Hebrew*; Sawyer, *Sacred Languages and Sacred Texts*; and more generally, chap. 3 below (with additional bibliography).

49. I mean to avoid, then, giving the impression that "God spoke Hebrew" and also skirt some of the (comparable) critiques raised to Lindbeck's work (see above). See further chaps. 8–9.

didn't know their Psalm 22, and why that (non)telling vignette is, upon further reflection, a very disturbing story indeed.

Second, although I am at pains here to diagnose and prevent the death of the Old Testament, and therefore the talk is everywhere about the Old Testament, I nevertheless believe that the argument also holds true for the entirety of the Christian Bible. If the Old Testament dies, the New Testament will not be far behind it, even if that process takes a bit longer (see chaps. 4–7 for proof of the point). The "linguistic" problems that face the Old Testament also face the New. In the main, then, I believe the data show that it is the language of Scripture *as a whole*—not just that of the Old Testament—that is seriously threatened. Even so, as Christians move further away from Scripture, they surely move furthest away from the Old Testament, since it is at the farthest remove from them in terms of chronology, ideology, ethics, theology, and so on.[50] That is why it is increasingly difficult for Christians to understand and speak "Old Testament." Of course, that is only true for the uninitiated—those who are novices in the language of Scripture. The biblically fluent, by way of contrast, already know that the Old Testament provides the deep structure for the New Testament and thus the Bible's deep language, maybe even its universal grammar.[51] This is further proof of how the death of the Old Testament bears directly and profoundly on the death of the New Testament. After all, the saints who didn't know Psalm 22 also, and as a direct result, didn't know the Gospel of Mark.

50. Cf., inter alia, Gunneweg, *Understanding the Old Testament*.

51. For an example of how the Passion Narratives of the NT depend on the book of Exodus ("deep structure"), see Strawn, "Exodus," esp. 33–34. "Deep language" alludes to C. S. Lewis's *Lion, the Witch, and the Wardrobe*; and "universal grammar" alludes to Noam Chomsky's linguistic theory.

2

Initial Testing

As I admitted in chapter 1, establishing the claim that the Old Testament is dying, if not already dead, for large segments of Christianity in North America faces several problems. According to some polls, 75 percent of American citizens identify themselves as Christian, which, given the present population, would mean that there are approximately 242 million Christians in the United States alone. How might one even begin to get an accurate assessment of such a large population and how "it" views the Old Testament? And what of the diversified nature of such a large population, which is replete with so many groups and subgroups? These are real problems for any attempt to gauge "the health of the Old Testament in North American Christianity," and I confess that I am no pollster. Then again, even pollsters must rely on representative samples, randomly selected, and so must reckon with margins of error. Apart from the U.S. Religious Knowledge Survey, the data I discuss below are not based on polls, and so the results are far more anecdotal than statistical, with the margin for error no doubt far larger than the acceptable +/-2 percent or +/-5 percent.

This important point granted, in what follows I present four pieces of "hard data" that both separately and together constitute empirical (or at least *semi*-empirical) proof supporting my diagnosis that the Old Testament is dying. To continue with the medical metaphor, these four data sets comprise a battery of initial tests of our patient—analysis of the Old Testament's symptoms, as it were—so as to identify the pathology, its causes, and its possible treatment. Chapters 4–6 discuss three additional and especially troubling signs of morbidity, but those are different from the tests found in the present chapter.

For one thing, the material discussed in chapters 4–6 concerns larger, more public, and in at least one case, less Christian realms. It seems appropriate and instructive, then, to delay those topics and begin our testing with areas that are more focused on and concerned with the life of the Old Testament within the Christian church. Even so, I start with a wide-angle lens—the state of religious literacy among the general US populace—before moving to more specialized analyses of the Old Testament in sermons, hymnody, and the lectionary.

The U.S. Religious Knowledge Survey

In September 2010, the Pew Forum on Religion and Public Life released a study on religious literacy in the United States.[1] The survey took its inspiration from Stephen Prothero's 2007 book, *Religious Literacy: What Every American Needs to Know—and Doesn't*, especially his claim that, while Americans are deeply religious, they are equally and simultaneously profoundly ignorant about religion.[2] Prothero cited findings from a number of opinion polls, but in the absence of any nationwide survey, he was forced to rely heavily on anecdotal evidence. As compelling as such anecdotes can be, they are less satisfying than a large-scale empirical analysis. Providing such an analysis was precisely what the Pew Forum set out to do.[3]

To quote from the survey, the Pew study was designed

> to gauge what Americans know about their own faiths and about other religions. The resulting survey covered a wide range of topics, including the beliefs and practices of major religious traditions as well as the role of religion in American history and public life. Based on an analysis of answers from more than 3,400 people to 32 religious knowledge questions, this report attempts to provide a baseline measurement of how much Americans know about religion today.[4]

At best, the survey provides a baseline because no similar survey had ever been conducted. Without a preexisting study, it is impossible to determine

---

1. Pew Forum, *U.S. Religious Knowledge Survey*. The full report is available online.
2. Prothero, *Religious Literacy*.
3. In addition to the U.S. Religious Knowledge Survey, cf. the national study "The Bible in American Life" (March 6, 2014), conducted by the Center for the Study of Religion and American Culture; and the National Study of Youth and Religion, conducted by the University of Notre Dame, along with two books that explicate that study: C. Smith with Denton, *Soul Searching*; and Dean, *Almost Christian*. Cf. also Kinnaman with Hawkins, *You Lost Me*. Finally, Beal's amazing book *Rise and Fall of the Bible*, while not empirically based, deserves careful consideration.
4. Pew Forum, *U.S. Religious Knowledge Survey*, 4.

if US religious knowledge has improved or declined. Regardless, the survey, conducted from May 19 through June 6, 2010, was a nationwide poll of 3,412 Americans, aged eighteen and older, executed in both English and Spanish. The following is from the executive summary:

> Atheists and agnostics, Jews and Mormons are among the highest-scoring groups on a new survey of religious knowledge, outperforming evangelical Protestants, mainline Protestants and Catholics on questions about the core teachings, history and leading figures of major world religions.
>
> On average, Americans correctly answer 16 of the 32 religious knowledge questions on the survey. . . . Atheists and agnostics average 20.9 correct answers. Jews and Mormons do about as well, averaging 20.5 and 20.3 correct answers, respectively. Protestants as a whole average 16 correct answers; Catholics as a whole, 14.7. Atheists and agnostics, Jews and Mormons perform better than other groups on the survey even after controlling for differing levels of education.[5]

Table 1 presents these data, along with those pertaining to the two lowest-scoring groups—Black Protestants and Hispanic Catholics, both of whom scored below the category of people who had no particular religious affiliation.[6]

Table 1. Summary of Religious Knowledge Survey

Atheists and Agnostics, Jews and Mormons Score Best on Religious Knowledge Survey

Average number of questions answered correctly out of 32

Total	16.0
Atheist/Agnostic	20.9
Jewish	20.5
Mormon	20.3
White evangelical Protestant	17.6
White Catholic	16.0
White mainline Protestant	15.8
Nothing in particular	15.2
Black Protestant	13.4
Hispanic Catholic	11.6

Pew Research Center's Forum on Religion and Public Life, May 19–June 6, 2010

5. Ibid., 6.

6. Ibid. The differences among persons of different ethnic backgrounds raise questions about possible cultural bias(es) in the survey, esp. over what "counts" as religious knowledge. See further below.

More information can be gleaned the further one digs into the results. So, for example:

> On questions about Christianity—including a battery of questions about the Bible—Mormons (7.9 out of 12 right on average) and white evangelical Protestants (7.3 correct on average) show the highest levels of knowledge. Jews and atheists/agnostics stand out for their knowledge of other world religions, including Islam, Buddhism, Hinduism and Judaism; out of 11 such questions on the survey, Jews answer 7.9 correctly (nearly three better than the national average) and atheists/agnostics answer 7.5 correctly (2.5 better than the national average). Atheists/agnostics and Jews also do particularly well on questions about the role of religion in public life, including a question about what the U.S. Constitution says about religion.[7]

A few observations should be made about this survey. First, the questions do not strike one as particularly difficult; they are, in the main, rather basic.[8] As a result, even high scores by various groups are not especially impressive. It is clear, nevertheless, that both evangelical and mainline Christians score rather poorly, especially vis-à-vis other groups. It is also noteworthy that atheists/agnostics and Mormons score comparatively highly. In the case of the former, one suspects that, at least in the heavily religious United States, being a "nonbeliever" involves a good bit of study or self-education so as to carve one's position out amid a sea of belief, especially if one is convinced that such belief is largely delusional. In the case of the Church of Jesus Christ of Latter-day Saints (LDS), the impressive and extensive built-in educational system of that church, especially via institutions of higher education and the training in faith that young Mormons receive when they go on their mandatory missions, probably deserves significant credit for the higher scores.[9]

Not to be missed is how the survey data correlate (or don't, as the case may be) with previous work done by the Pew Research Center on levels of

---

7. Ibid., 7.

8. Then again, of the 3,412 people surveyed, only 2% answered 29 or more of the 32 questions correctly, and only 8 individuals scored a perfect 32. On the opposite end of the curve, 3% got less than 5 questions right, including 6 people who missed every single question (ibid., 16). For a listing of the Bible questions, see note 13 below.

9. The survey and previous Pew Forum studies reveal high levels of educational attainment for Jewish and atheist/agnostic groups, which "partially explains their performance" (ibid., 10). That granted, even after the survey controlled for levels of education and other demographic traits (race, age, gender, and region), "significant differences in religious knowledge persist among adherents of various faith traditions" with atheists/agnostics, Jews, and Mormons still having the highest levels of religious knowledge, followed by evangelical Protestants (ibid., 11). For more on the LDS church, see Dean, "Mormon Envy," chap. 3 in *Almost Christian*, 45–60.

religiosity in America. According to the latter, nearly 60% of US Americans indicate that religion is "very important" in their lives, and approximately 40% say they attend worship services at least once a week.[10] But there is surely a major disconnect at this point vis-à-vis the U.S. Religious Knowledge Survey: despite widespread religious belief, or at least *professed* belief, the survey reveals significant deficiencies in that professed belief (if not the belief more broadly), at least with regard to basic content, at least some of which reflects important doctrine. So, for example:

> More than four-in-ten Catholics in the United States (45%) do not know that their church teaches that the bread and wine used in Communion do not merely symbolize but actually become the body and blood of Christ. About half of Protestants (53%) cannot correctly identify Martin Luther as the person whose writings and actions inspired the Protestant Reformation, which made their religion a separate branch of Christianity.[11]

A second observation about the survey is that it does not test for fine points of detail or highly nuanced formulations; it sticks resolutely with large topics that should be, presumably, widely known. To be sure, at only thirty-two questions, the survey doesn't even begin to test for all of the most important things. Conversely, some knowledge that the survey did test for may not be all that important, at least not in terms of the *practice* of the faith—for example, identifying Luther as the founder of Protestantism.[12] Transubstantiation for Catholic theology of the Eucharist would seem to be a very different matter, however! Regardless, the statistics pertaining to knowledge of the Bible and Christianity are shocking:

- Only 55% of the people surveyed know that the Golden Rule is *not* one of the Ten Commandments.
- Only 45% know that the four Gospels are Matthew, Mark, Luke, and John.
- Only 16% know that "Only Protestants (not Catholics) traditionally teach that salvation comes through faith alone."[13]

---

10. Pew Forum, *U.S. Religious Knowledge Survey*, 7–8. Others have put the number closer to 20%. See Hadaway, Marler, and Chaves, "Overreporting Church Attendance in America"; Hadaway, Marler, and Chaves, "What the Polls Don't Show."

11. Pew Forum, *U.S. Religious Knowledge Survey*, 8.

12. See ibid., 15, on how the survey did not necessarily "reflect the most important things to know about religion," even as it was not meant "to test mere trivia." Instead, "the Pew Forum selected questions intended to serve as indicators of how much people know in several areas. . . . The questions included in the survey were intended to be representative of a body of important knowledge about religion; they were not meant to be a list of the most essential facts."

13. Ibid., 8. The seven Bible questions on the survey are as follows (ibid., 19): (1) What is the first book of the Bible? (an open-ended question); (2) What are the names of the first four

To put the last item in different terms: slightly more than eight out of ten people do not know why there is a Protestant movement in the first place as opposed to just the Roman Catholic Church alone. Several, if not most, of those eight people might not even know or understand the term "Protestant." Most disturbing of all: the majority of Protestants themselves don't know this (81%)![14]

The data pertaining to detailed knowledge of the Bible are slightly more positive, but these, too, aren't much to get excited about (see table 2). Some 71% of the people interviewed knew that Jesus was born in Bethlehem, but the number is lower (63%) with regard to knowing that Genesis is the first book of the Bible. Again, the statistics can be further filleted:

> On the full battery of seven questions about the Bible (five Old Testament and two New Testament items), Mormons do best, followed by white evangelical Protestants. Atheists/agnostics, black Protestants, and Jews come next, all exhibiting greater knowledge of the Bible than white mainline Protestants and white Catholics, who in turn outscore those who describe their religion as nothing in particular.[15]

The authors of the study are thus spot-on when they write that, despite the claim of deep religiosity among US citizens, the poll reveals that "large numbers of Americans are uninformed about the tenets, practices, history, and leading figures of major faith traditions—including their own."[16] As proof of the point, consider two final details: First, while 85% of white evangelicals and Mormons know that Genesis is the first book of the Bible, followed closely by Black Protestants (83%) and atheists/agnostics (71%), less than half of Catholics know this fact (42%), with the specific breakdown comprising 47% of white Catholics and 29% of Hispanic Catholics.[17] Second, while 81% of Mormons know that the Golden Rule is not one of the Ten Commandments,

---

books of the New Testament, that is, the four Gospels? (open-ended); (3) Where, according to the Bible, was Jesus born? Bethlehem, Jerusalem, Nazareth, or Jericho? (multiple choice); (4) Which of these is *not* in the Ten Commandments? Do unto others . . . , no adultery, no stealing, keep Sabbath? (multiple choice); (5) Which figure is associated with remaining obedient to God despite suffering? Job, Elijah, Moses, or Abraham? (multiple choice); (6) Which figure is associated with leading the exodus from Egypt? Moses, Job, Elijah, or Abraham? (multiple choice); (7) Which figure is associated with willingness to sacrifice his son for God? Abraham, Job, Moses, or Elijah? (multiple choice).

14. Only 19% of Protestants as a whole got this question right (ibid., 23). Compare the following groups: white evangelical (28%), Mormon (22%), atheist/agnostic (22%), white mainline (14%), Jewish (10%), nothing in particular (10%), Black Protestant (9%), Catholic (9%).

15. Pew Forum, *U.S. Religious Knowledge Survey*, 9, also see 17.

16. Ibid., 8.

17. Ibid., 20. Another troubling statistic: only 47% of the Hispanic Catholics surveyed correctly answered the question about where Jesus was born (ibid., 22).

Table 2. Knowledge of the Bible according to the U.S. Religious Knowledge Survey

Knowledge of the Bible

% who know . . .	Old Testament					New Testament		
	First book in the Bible	Golden Rule is *not* one of the Ten Commandments	Religious Figures					Avg. number correct out of 7
			Moses	Abraham	Job	Birthplace of Jesus	Four Gospels	
	%	%	%	%	%	%	%	
Total	63	55	72	60	39	71	45	4.1
Christian	66	57	71	61	41	74	50	4.2
Protestant	76	56	74	63	48	78	57	4.5
White Evangelical	85	67	80	69	58	83	71	5.1
White Mainline	61	49	68	53	34	79	43	3.9
Black Protestant	83	49	73	61	51	70	50	4.4
Catholic	42	57	65	55	25	65	33	3.4
White Catholic	47	63	71	60	26	74	40	3.8
Hispanic Catholic	29	45	48	40	19	47	15	2.4
Mormon	85	81	92	87	70	83	73	5.7
Jewish	65	62	90	83	47	61	17	4.3
Unaffiliated	54	50	72	56	31	62	28	3.5
Atheist/ Agnostic	71	62	87	68	42	70	39	4.4
Nothing in Particular	48	46	67	52	27	59	24	3.2

Q39, Q40, Q41, Q46, Q47a–d
Pew Research Center's Forum on Religion and Public Life, May 19–June 6, 2010

only 67% of white evangelicals know this, followed by 63% of Catholics and 62% of Jews and atheists/agnostics. Only 49% of white mainline Protestants and Black Protestants get this question right.

Although there are other "hard data" to consider—data pertaining more directly to Christian practices—the U.S. Religious Knowledge Survey, which is far from anecdotal, is already sufficient to confirm the diagnosis offered in chapter 1. In brief, large swaths of religious people—including, let it be noted, Christians of various ethnic and denominational backgrounds—are quite uninformed if not ill-informed (perhaps *mal*-formed would be the better term) about even the most rudimentary details of their religion. In linguistic terms, the vast majority of the religious people surveyed are adherents who, presumably and by their own profession, "speak the language of faith," but who are actually missing huge portions of the most basic vocabulary, syntax, and so forth of their (putative) religious tongue. That sounds like nothing so much as someone who cannot speak the language after all, who is (functionally) illiterate,[18] or who at best speaks a severely reduced idiolect—a few words here and there, baby talk perhaps—or, in linguistic terms, someone who can speak only a pidgin language (see chap. 3). To go back to Marcus Borg's remarks cited in chapter 1, we wouldn't call someone "French" who wasn't fluent in French. Why should it be otherwise if the "language" in question is somehow religious?

One final result from the Pew study should be mentioned. According to the report the "single best predictor of religious knowledge" is

> educational attainment—how much schooling an individual has completed.
> . . . College graduates get nearly eight more questions right on average than do people with a high school education or less. Having taken a religion course in college is also strongly associated with higher religious knowledge.[19]

Lest we think (wrongly) that religious knowledge is solely something gained in a formal classroom, we should note that other factors are also crucial. The survey explicitly mentions

> reading Scripture at least once a week and talking about religion with friends and family. People who say they frequently talk about religion with friends and family get an average of roughly two more questions right than those who say they rarely or never discuss religion. People with the highest levels of religious commitment—those who say that they attend worship services at least once a week and that religion is very important in their lives—generally demonstrate higher levels of religious knowledge than those with medium or low religious commitment. Having regularly attended religious education classes or participated in a youth group as a child adds more than two questions to the average

18. Cf. the United Nations Educational, Scientific and Cultural Organization's (UNESCO) 2003 definition of literacy: "the ability to identify, understand, interpret, create, communicate and compute, using printed and written materials associated with varying contexts" (*Aspects of Literacy Assessment*, 21). On biblical illiteracy, see above and chaps. 4–6 below. A study of German students also revealed that many thought the Golden Rule belonged to the Decalogue: Beyer and Waltermathe, "Good, the Bad and the Undecided," esp. 158n1. My point in this book is less about biblical *literacy* than about the Bible's *mortality*.

19. Pew Forum, *U.S. Religious Knowledge Survey*, 10; see further 37–38, 46.

number answered correctly, compared with those who seldom or never participated in such activities.[20]

Seen via the linguistic analogy, this suggests that people who actually speak the language, who spend time practicing it, and who began to learn it at a young age know it better than those who never use it, who never practice speaking it, and who never had instruction in it at formative periods or stages.[21] This is completely commonsensical and not surprising in the least. If we are surprised by this result, it is proof not that we are religiously ignorant, but that we're just plain ignorant.

The information from the U.S. Religious Knowledge Survey is troubling, to be sure, but given the situation, especially when viewed via the lens of language learning, it is hard not to spread the blame widely—beyond, that is, the individual religious adherents themselves. If individual believers' knowledge is suffering, if they can't speak the language, then at least part of the blame must be laid at the door of the religious systems (and their leaders) to which they belong and to which they adhere (even if only loosely, which is, of course, part of the problem). To be more direct, the failures in religious knowledge reported in the survey appear to reflect massive failures in the religious system(s) in question, especially the educational arm(s) of said system(s), and the leaders responsible for those systems and that education. For Protestant Christianity, that means not only the failure of the "Sunday school" or "Bible study" phenomena (whether for children or adults), but also the failure of the sermon to be an effective tool in disseminating the language that is the Christian faith, not to mention other failures to provide adequate linguistic instruction in the Bible's—and, more specifically still, the Old Testament's—contribution to that faith.

Of course, even in low-church traditions of Protestantism, not to mention other Christian traditions, the burden doesn't lie solely with (1) the sermon but with the worship and liturgy as a whole, which includes matters of (2) music/ hymnody and (3) the public reading of Scripture, the latter sometimes (in "higher" churches at least) organized by the Revised Common Lectionary (RCL). In the balance of this chapter, I address each of these three areas in turn, noting a demonstrable lack of the Old Testament in each case. It thus

20. Ibid., 10 (see also n. 3 on that page). At this point, given the emphasis on embodied and communal practices, the survey seems to evade many of its critics who have deemed it overly cognitive. See, e.g., Kristof, "Test Your Savvy on Religion"; Douthat, "God and the Details"; Plate, "Why Pollsters Still Don't Get Religion"; and a blog from the Social Science Research Council, "Surveying Religious Knowledge." Thanks to Steven M. Tipton for these references.

21. See Pew Forum, U.S. Religious Knowledge Survey, 38, 40, 50.

is not improbable and indeed is highly likely that it is the dying (or death) of the Old Testament in sermon, song, and Scripture reading as much as the lack of a college religion class that has led to the dismal results reflected in the U.S. Religious Knowledge Survey, at least on those matters pertaining to scriptural knowledge.

The "Best"(?) Sermons

Given their oral nature, analyzing sermons is a daunting task. By way of comparison, a great deal of Christian education curricula is in print. One could conceivably gather a large amount of that and assess it. For the purpose of the present study, the main question would not be simply *whether* such studies engage the Old Testament—a little, a lot, or not at all—but also, and equally as important, *how* they engage the Old Testament, if in fact they do.[22]

To be sure, a similar procedure is possible for sermons, though the vast majority of sermons aren't formally published, and this complicates analysis.[23] There is, of course, a massive amount of *informal* publication of sermons on the internet, in both text and multimedia formats. Indeed, there are far too many sermons available in this manner to properly assess, at least en masse. An entrée of some sort is needed.

Happily, there is, or rather there *was*, a series of books, each titled *Best Sermons*, that collected—no surprise here—the purported "best sermons" for a particular year. There were actually three such series of best sermons: one in the first half of the twentieth century (4 vols., in 1924–27),[24] a second in the middle of the twentieth century (10 vols., in 1944–68),[25] and the third toward the end of the twentieth century (7 vols., in 1988–94).[26] With very little digging one is able to determine if the "best sermons" in these series are

22. On the importance of *how* the OT is present, not just *if* it is, see chap. 1 above and chaps. 4–6 below.

23. The same could also be said for much Sunday school curricula, at least in adult education formats, where many classes often do not follow published or denominational materials.

24. Newton, *Best Sermons 1924*; Newton, *Best Sermons 1925*; Newton, *Best Sermons 1926*; Newton, *Best Sermons*, vol. 4 (1927).

25. Butler, *Best Sermons: 1944 Selection*; Butler, *Best Sermons: 1946 Edition*; Butler, *Best Sermons: 1947–1948 Edition*; Butler, *Best Sermons: 1949–1950 Edition*; Butler, *Best Sermons: 1951–1952 Edition*; Butler, *Best Sermons: 1955 Edition*; Butler, *Best Sermons*, vol. 7, *1959–1960 Protestant Edition*; Butler, *Best Sermons*, vol. 8, *1962 Protestant Edition*; Butler, *Best Sermons*, vol. 9, *1964 Protestant Edition*; Butler, *Best Sermons*, vol. 10, *1966–1968 Protestant Edition*. As is clear from the titles, vols. 7–10 are Protestant collections. The earlier volumes are ecumenical and even interfaith insofar as they occasionally include sermons from Jewish rabbis. While most of the authors are North Americans, there are a few from other locations (e.g., Britain, Australia).

26. Cox, *Best Sermons*, vols. 1–3; Cox, *Best Sermons*, vols. 4–7.

taken from the Old Testament or the New, both, or neither by simply looking to see what biblical text(s), if any, is given at the head of each sermon as the (primary) preached text.

Four comments are in order before presenting my findings from these series: First, the selection process(es) for these series is not always transparent. In the case of the volumes edited by Newton, for instance, there is no indication given as to why these particular sermons and not some others were deemed "the best." The volumes edited by Butler and Cox are clearer on this point. Butler reports that over 11,000 sermons were submitted for possible inclusion in the first 2 volumes; he selected the winners with the help of an advisory committee, and only 3 of the 104 sermons included in the first 2 volumes were invited.[27] In Butler's tenth and final volume, he indicates that 8,975 clergy submitted sermons for possible inclusion among the 52 sermons published that year. Cox's volumes operate very differently. For his first volume, 28 sermons were commissioned, and the remaining balance of 24 sermons were selected from a competition of over 2,000 sermons "from around the world."[28] Cox states that the most important criteria for selection were "originality, scriptural and/ or Christian basis, relevance, clarity, and interest."[29]

Despite the subjectivity involved in the selection process, the size of the submission pool for the Butler and Cox series is not insignificant. That said, even 9,000 submissions in one year is barely the tip of the iceberg, especially since many estimates put the total number of congregations in the United States at over 300,000. If that is accurate, it may be multiplied by 52 sermons a year, yielding a minimal total of 15,600,000 sermons per year (not counting multiple, nonreduplicated sermons whether on Sunday or midweek). So 9,000 submissions is just a drop in the bucket of 15.5+ million sermons per year—0.00058 percent if one does the math.

Second, I must admit that I did not read every one of the 879 sermons in these three series of sermon collections, and so I want to be careful not to misrepresent that fact or the sermons themselves. Several sermons give evidence of having been written for lectionary environments, which typically combine or at least include the public reading of texts from both Testaments. I catalogued these as "combination sermons," though it may well be the case that just one of the texts from just one of the Testaments was actually the primary or only text focused on in the sermon. Similarly, there can be little doubt that Old Testament texts are occasionally used in some fashion (e.g.,

27. See Butler, *Best Sermons: 1947–1948 Edition*, xvii.
28. Cox, *Best Sermons*, 1:ix.
29. Ibid., x. These criteria are repeated in other volumes (as in Cox, *Best Sermons*, 3:ix).

allusively or illustratively), even in some of the New Testament–only sermons; and vice versa.

Third, despite the crucial distinction between *if present* and *how present* mentioned above, and because I did not read every sermon, I cannot speak definitively as to how the Old Testament was used in (1) the sermons that are taken exclusively from the Old Testament, (2) the sermons that include an Old Testament text(s) with another (or several others) from the New Testament, or (3) the sermons that may have mentioned the Old Testament even if the preached text was taken exclusively from the New Testament (or no text was identified at all). An exploration of the *how present* question in these sermons would make for a very important and interesting study, but it is not something I do here.[30] For my purposes, with the present data set, it is enough to focus on *if present*. The results, even when considering only this factor, are quite enlightening (though discouraging).

Fourth, the theological inclination of the series and the editors should be kept in mind. Though such inclinations aren't always clear, the three series generally seem ecumenical, mostly mainline Protestant, with some Catholic participation, and occasionally also appear interfaith insofar as a few of the volumes include sermons by Jewish rabbis.

Table 3 presents a summary of the Best Sermons series data (see further apps. 1–3); note that the items mentioned above suggest a margin of error, though I cannot compute that with precision.

As was the case with the U.S. Religious Knowledge Survey, one can dig further into these statistics for more insight, and here, no less than there, the results are revealing. Of the total number of sermons (879), published in 21 volumes over a span of 71 years, no less than 432 (49%) are taken from the New Testament (alone), while only 186 (21%) are taken from the Old Testament (alone). This is a rather telling statistic and, from my perspective, quite disturbing. Equally disturbing, however, and proof of a comment made in chapter 1 that the death of the Old Testament is symptomatic of the death of Scripture as a whole, we might notice that no less than 202 of these sermons (23%) provide no biblical text whatsoever.[31] Indeed, the no-text sermons outnumber the Old Testament–only sermons!

---

30. For the beginnings of such an analysis for the Cox series, see Miles, "Proclaiming the Gospel of God," esp. 113–76.

31. I do not know exactly what to make of the fact that the Newton series has only one (1.1%) no-text sermon, while Butler has 172 (out of 483, or 35.6%) and Cox has 29 (out of 305, or 9.5%) of them. The patterns of the no-text sermons are also curious. Indeed, the 1949–50 volume edited by Butler includes a no-text sermon on Easter Sunday! Guilt for these sermons must be spread around: they are written by Protestants, Jesuits, rabbis, and, in one case at least, by a Quaker Friend. In the latter case, the preached text was a poem by Robert Burns.

Table 3. Summary of Best Sermons Series

Series	Total	OT-only sermons	NT-only sermons	Combination sermons	No-text sermons	Ratio: NT to OT	% OT only	% NT only	% of combined	% of no text	OT books represented (combined)	OT books represented (OT only)
Newton	91	18	67	5	1	3.72	20%	74%	5%	1%	4 out of 39 OT bks.	10 out of 39 bks.
Butler	483	99	206	6	172	2.08	20%	43%	1%	36%	6 out of 39 bks. (cf. next column)	25 out of 40 bks. (including Sirach from OTA)
Cox	305	69	159	48	29	2.3	22%	52%	16%	10%	22 out of 39 bks. (cf. next column)	25 out of 40 bks. (including Wisdom from OTA)
Totals	879	186	432	59	202	2.32	21%	49%	7%	23%		

The news isn't all bad. There are, after all, a number of sermons—approximately one in five—that are taken from the Old Testament, and a smattering of others (59 sermons, or 7%) at least list one or more Old Testament texts along with one or more New Testament ones. And again, as per my earlier comment, it is likely the case that even the New Testament–only sermons occasionally mention the Old Testament. Still the statistics are overwhelmingly skewed toward the New Testament—49% to 21%, or a ratio of 2.32 New Testament sermons to every Old Testament one; this ratio seems odd when one recalls that the Old Testament constitutes 78.1% of the Protestant Christian canon (in terms of number of chapters) and is even more substantial (81.4%) in Roman Catholic and Eastern Orthodox canons, since these latter include the apocryphal or deuterocanonical books (see app. 4 and chap. 7). If size were the only consideration, one should expect sermons from the Old Testament to be at least three times as frequent as those from the New Testament.

Of course things are rarely if ever so straightforward. Moreover, it is easy to imagine someone objecting that it is entirely normal if not altogether right (maybe even righteous) to expect Christian preaching to come mostly (if not exclusively) from the New Testament.[32] This pernicious idea cannot be fully analyzed and refuted here, though much of what is said in chapters 4–6 and 8–9 bears directly on it. For now, I must content myself with saying that, if the New Testament alone were sufficient to the life of Christian faith, then surely the early church would have jettisoned the Old Testament when it had the chance (see chap. 5). The fact that the early church did not do so, even in the face of invitations to do exactly that, remains one of the most serious problems for any who would be too oriented toward the New Testament alone. At this point it pays to remember that it was no less a Christian and, let it be stressed, no less a Christocentric theologian than Dietrich Bonhoeffer who wrote: "In my opinion it is not Christian to want to take our thoughts and feelings too quickly and too directly from the New Testament."[33]

Further insight from the Best Sermons series concerns the specific texts used. What texts from the Old Testament are considered worthy of preaching in the Best Sermons? Table 4 collates the data (see further apps. 1–3).

Once again, the data aren't *all* bad, just *mostly* bad. The majority of the thirty-nine books of the Protestant Old Testament canon are represented at least once, though that isn't much to celebrate considering the nature of these

---

32. This is a not infrequently encountered trope, even in books devoted to the exact subject of preaching *the Old Testament*. See, e.g., Achtemeier, *Old Testament and the Proclamation of the Gospel*; and Greidanus, *Preaching Christ from the Old Testament*.

33. Bonhoeffer, *Letters and Papers from Prison*, 157.

sermons series, the total number of sermons, the lectionary context of many of the sermons, and so on and so forth.

Table 4 also reveals the favorite go-to Old Testament texts for preachers. Most of this information comes as no surprise. The book of Psalms is by far the most popular (76 hits) with Genesis and Isaiah almost tied for second (29 and 28 hits, respectively), but trailing the Psalter by a considerable margin. The next most popular books are Exodus with 20 hits and Jeremiah with 12. More troubling is the significant number of books that are not represented at all and the books that are seriously underrepresented:

- Three hits: Nehemiah, Ecclesiastes, Daniel—3 books.
- Two hits: Leviticus, 2 Kings, 2 Chronicles, Proverbs, Song of Songs, Lamentations, Joel, Habakkuk (and Sirach in the Apocrypha)—8 books; or 9, including the OTA.
- One hit: Judges, Ezra, 1 Chronicles (also Wisdom in the Apocrypha)—3 books; or 4, including the OTA.
- Not represented: Ruth, Esther, Obadiah, Micah, Nahum, Zephaniah, Haggai—7 books; or 24, including what is missing from the OTA.

The non- or underrepresented books total 21 of the 39 books (53.8%) of the Protestant Old Testament; still more for the Old Testament with Apocrypha (40 out of 58 books, or 69%). It bears repeating that *only five books* break into double digits: Genesis, Exodus, Isaiah, Jeremiah, and Psalms.[34]

Furthermore, the texts preached from the Old Testament are rarely, if ever, off the beaten track. Not only do a disproportionate amount of sermons come from the "big three" books of Psalms, Genesis, and Isaiah, but even these sermons typically come from very well-known and, dare one say, overused texts. Little here is unusual or novel—the vast majority of the preached texts are classics. For example, 11 of the 29 sermons (38%) from Genesis come from the first three chapters; but these chapters together constitute only 6% of the entire book!

This preference for the familiar also holds true even for the few sermons that draw from less popular books: the two sermons from Leviticus, for instance, come from (1) Lev. 16:2–3, the famous chapter about the Day of Atonement (Yom Kippur); and (2) Lev. 19:1–2, 15–18, which, in addition to being the only text from Leviticus in the RCL (Seventh Sunday after Epiphany, Year A: Lev. 19:1–2, 9–18), includes the well-known verses about being holy because God is holy (Lev. 19:2, cited in 1 Pet. 1:16 and alluded to in Matt. 5:48) and loving

---

34. Even these are often conjoined with NT texts for "combined sermons."

Table 4. Old Testament Texts Used in the Best Sermons Series

Text	Newton	Butler	Cox	Totals (out of 879; with % of whole)
Genesis	(3) 3:23–24; 3:24; 13:12	(8) 9:11–16; 9:21; 11:7; 13:8; 32:26; 45:8; 45:26–28; 50:20	(18) 1:1–2:3; 1:1–5; 1:26–28; 1:26–27; 1:27–31; 2:18; 2:21–24; 3:1–6; 3:6–12, 16; 4:1–16; 9:8–17; 11:31–12:3; 12:1–9; 15; 22:1–18; 22:1–9; 32:22–31; 45:1–15	29 (3.3)
Exodus	(3) 5:1; 33:23; 39:14	(6) 2:11; 3:5; 16:2, 8; 16:19–20; 25:8; 32:19–20	(11) 1:8–2:10; 3:1–12; 3:6; 3:7–12; 4:10; 20:1–6; 20:1–2, 17; 20:7; 20:14; 33:12–13, 17–23; 33:14	20 (2.2)
Leviticus	0	(1) 16:2–3	(1) 19:1–2, 15–18	2 (0.22)
Numbers	(1) 13:33	0	(5) 13:17–14:2; 13:25–33; 13:1–3, 25–28a, 30–32, 33b; 14:1–4; 22:6, 28, 32	6 (0.68)
Deuteronomy	0	(2) 16:20; 30:14	(4) 6:4–5; 8:1–10; 25:1–6; 34:1–12	6 (0.68)
Joshua	(1) 24:15	(1) 24:15	(5) 1:1–11; 2:1–24; 3:4; 4:1–9; 6:20–26	7 (0.79)
Judges	0	0	(1) 17; 18	1 (0.11)
Ruth	0	0	0	0 (0)
1 Samuel	0	(3) 7:12; 12:7; 27:10	(2) 28–31; 31:1–6	5 (0.56)
2 Samuel	0	(1) 18:31–33	(3) 1:2–4, 11–12, 17–27; 18:24–33; 21:14–22	4 (0.45)
1 Kings	(1) 22:14	(3) 17:3; 19:9; 22:8	(5) 16:19–33; 17:10–16; 17:8–16; 17:17–24; 18:20–29, 36–39	9 (1.02)
2 Kings	0	(1) 20:2, 7	(1) 5:18–19	2 (0.22)
1 Chronicles	0	0	(1) 29:10–25	1 (0.11)
2 Chronicles	0	(2) 12:9–10; 30:8	0	2 (0.22)
Ezra	0	0	(1) 3:10–13	1 (0.11)
Nehemiah	0	(1) 2:18	(2) 3 (selected verses); 8:2–4, 5–6, 8–10	3 (0.34)
Esther	0	0	0	0 (0)
Job	(1) 14:14	(3) 8:7; 16:4; 23:3	(3) 1:20–21; 3:1–4; 3:20–4:6	7 (0.79)
Psalms	(12)[a] 5:3; 9:9; 36:5–6; 36:9 (2×); 46:1; 68:5; 81:5; 84:1; 90:1; 121:1; 142:5	(38) 8:3–4; 8:4a; 8:4–5; 11:3 (2×); 13:1; 22:21; 23:4; 23:5; 24:1–2; 25:1; 30:5; 33:12; 37:1a; 40:3; 42:3 (2×); 46:1; 51:11; 73:17; 77:7–9, 14; 89:16; 90:12; 95:6; 99:1; 103:3–4; 119:18; 119:54;	(26) 1:3; 8 (whole psalm, 2×); 8:4; 23 (whole psalm); 23:6; 24:1–5; 25 (whole psalm); 33:20; 51 (whole psalm); 71 (whole psalm, 2×); 77:3, 6; 84 (whole psalm); 86:11–17; 88 (whole psalm); 90:12; 98 (whole psalm); 100	76 (8.64)

		119:97; 121:1; 121:8; 125:2; 126:5; 127:1; 137:1–4; 139 (whole psalm); 139:1–2, 4–5, 7–8; 139:7; 139:10	(whole psalm); 102:1–12; 119:105; 121 (whole psalm); 138 (whole psalm); 139 (whole psalm); 145 (whole psalm)	
Proverbs	0	(2) 4:7–9; 9:1	0	2 (0.22)
Ecclesiastes	0	0	(3) 2:20–3:15; 3:1; 3:1–15	3 (0.34)
Song of Songs	0	(1) 4:16	(1) 2:8–17	2 (0.22)
Isaiah	(1) 2:4	(16) 1:18; 5:4; 6:1; 25:9; 26:9; 28:24, 26; 31:1; 32:2; 35:7; 40:8; 40:31; 44:17; 49:22–23; 50:2; 52:10; 55:2	(11) 9:2; 11:6–9; 40:1–8; 40:1–11; 40:29–31; 42:1–4; 43:1–5; 46:1–4; 55:6; 60:1–6; 61:1–11	28 (3.18)
Jeremiah	0	(5) 1:9–10; 2:31; 18:1–6; 22:16; 44:4	(7) 1:4–10; 8:8–13; 9:23–24; 14:7–10, 19–22; 15:10–21; 32:1–15; 48:11	12 (1.36)
Lamentations	0	(1) 3:39	(1) 1:1–22	2 (0.22)
Ezekiel	0	(3) 1:1; 47:12; 48:35	(2) 34:11–24; 36:22–32	5 (0.56)
Daniel	0	(2) 7:14; 12:12–13	(1) 3:13–18	3 (0.34)
Hosea	(1) 11:8–9	(1) 11:1	(2) 11:1–4; 11:1–11	4 (0.45)
Joel	0	(1) 3:14	(1) 3:1–2, 9–17	2 (0.22)
Amos	(1) 8:11, 12	(1) 5:18	(2) 3:1–8; 5:18–24	4 (0.45)
Obadiah	0	0	0	0 (0)
Jonah	(1) 1:3	(1) whole book	(2) 3:1–5, 10; 3:10–4:11	4 (0.45)
Micah	0	0	0	0 (0)
Nahum	0	0	0	0 (0)
Habakkuk	(2) 1:16; 3:18	0	0	2 (0.22)
Zephaniah	0	0	0	0 (0)
Haggai	0	0	0	0 (0)
Zechariah	0	0	(2) 4:1–14; 8:1–8	2 (0.22)
Malachi	(1) 2:10	0	(3) 1:1–2, 6; 2:10; 3:13–17 (1 sermon)	4 (0.45)
Wisdom	0	0	(1) 7:27b	1 (0.11)
Sirach	(2) 15:14; 31:10 (1 sermon)	0	0	2 (0.22)

aFour of these texts (Pss. 46:1; 68:5; 9:9; 90:1) come from a single sermon.

your neighbor as yourself (Lev. 19:18, cited in Matt. 5:43; 19:19; 22:39; Mark 12:31, 33; Luke 10:27; Rom. 12:19; 13:9; Gal. 5:14; and James 2:8).[35] Or consider the three sermons from Ecclesiastes, all of which include part of chapter 3, the familiar poem on the times and seasons.[36] Or, similarly, there is one sermon from Ps. 137, the infamous imprecatory psalm, which happily dispenses not only with the infamous cursing section itself (vv. 7–9) but even the slightly unpleasant sentiments in vv. 5–6 in order to focus instead on only vv. 1–4!

One should note, too, that the selected Old Testament texts are often snippets at best, many taken from only one verse or from just a few. Apart from some small psalms (but even these are often selectively used), only a handful of sermons deal with any extended textual unit (note, e.g., the exceptions provided in the sermons on Judg. 17, 18; 1 Sam. 28–31; and the book of Jonah).

Finally, the Old Testament sermons—whether from the Old Testament by itself or in combination with a New Testament text(s), and whether from familiar texts or the few notable exceptions—are often preached by "experts" in the field: biblical scholars who specialize in the Old Testament, professors of homiletics, especially famous preachers, or, the coup de grâce, Jewish rabbis (see apps. 1–3).[37] None of these are the average, run-of-the-mill preachers, which suggests that Old Testament preaching, especially of the off-the-beaten-path variety, is probably very rare indeed among "lesser lights." In my opinion, these considerations effectively offset the unknown margin of error in the sermon analysis that I acknowledged above.

But here one might wish to protest. "Who in their right mind," someone could ask, "*would want* to preach on every book of the Old Testament, let alone on all its obscure passages? And furthermore," the objection could continue, "aren't famous passages famous for good reason?" The answer to the first question is simple. To return to the linguistic analogy, those who are fluent in Scripture are both able and desirous to preach on every nook and cranny of the Old Testament (or New Testament, for that matter) *precisely because* they are fluent, and because of that fluency, every bit of the Old Testament (and New) is part of their language and broader linguistic system. It is neither hard nor especially onerous to preach these parts any more than it is hard or onerous to properly conjugate a particularly difficult irregular verb form. Conversely,

35. Analogically, this could be seen as a kind of linguistic interference—the OT lection may only have been chosen because of its presence in the NT. See chaps. 3, 7–9.

36. Though Ecclesiastes does not appear in the RCL on Sundays, Eccles. 3:1–13 is the OT lesson for New Year's Day in all three years.

37. On the latter, see also the textual dexterity (equivalent to linguistic fluency) evident in the sermons collected in Saperstein, *Jewish Preaching, 1200–1800*.

leaving out any part of the "language" would neglect crucial bits of the grammar and lexicon. Both points are underscored by the fact that so many of the Old Testament sermons in the series are by "experts," since these individuals are (presumably) the most adept in the full language of Scripture. This answer to the first possible objection can be further strengthened by appealing to the great writers and theologians in the history of Christianity, many of whom made it a practice to preach regularly and seriatim through the Old Testament books.[38] Augustine's and Calvin's treatments of the Psalms come immediately to mind, but so does Luther's extensive work on Old Testament texts (he was, after all, a Bible professor for much of his career). Perhaps the most famous example is Bernard of Clairvaux's (1090–1153) series of eighty-six sermons on the Song of Songs, in which he progressed only as far as the first verse of chapter 3![39] Nearer to our own time, one might consider the sermons of the prolific Old Testament scholar Walter Brueggemann, which differ markedly from the Best Sermons series.[40] Only 10.4% of Brueggemann's sermon corpus is composed of New Testament–only sermons. Somewhat surprisingly, Old Testament–only sermons constitute still less, only 5.9%. The vast majority (83.5%) are sermons drawn from *both* Old and New Testament texts. That is largely because Brueggemann is a lectionary preacher.[41] But once again, the *how present* question is important. Even in his combined sermons, Brueggemann often pays extensive, if not exclusive, attention to the Old Testament text(s). That said, he is well known for his penchant and ability to make connections between many texts, including texts that span the Testaments. Another important observation: Brueggemann, too, does not preach on every book of the Old Testament, but for every book he does preach from, his corpus outperforms the other three sermons series combined, despite the fact that his corpus is 6.5 times smaller than the total number of sermons collected in those other series.[42]

---

38. Indeed, it seems safe to say—given the importance of the OT in early Judaism and in the nascent Christianity that emerged from it, not to mention the slow growth, stabilization, and finalization of the NT writings and canon—that for several centuries the OT texts were at least as important if not more important than the NT ones. I am grateful to Anthony Briggman and Ian McFarland for discussions on this matter.

39. See Davis, *Wondrous Depth*, 5. For the sermons themselves, see Bernard of Clairvaux, *On the Song of Songs*.

40. Brueggemann, *Collected Sermons of Walter Brueggemann*; Brueggemann, *Inscribing the Text*; Brueggemann, *Threat of Life*. Appendix 5 presents sermons from the latter two volumes that are not found in the former—a total of seven and six sermons, respectively.

41. C. Campbell (foreword to *Threat of Life*, ix) points out that Brueggemann is "generally a lectionary preacher" but frequently of the intertextual sort, combining two or more lectionary texts.

42. Brueggemann's corpus lacks sermons from Joshua, Judges, Ruth, 2 Samuel, 2 Chronicles, Ezra, Nehemiah, Esther, Ecclesiastes, Song of Songs, Joel, Amos, Obadiah, Jonah, Nahum,

To put matters more theologically and less linguistically, the answer to the first objection regarding who would want to preach (the entirety of) the Old Testament is simply this: those for whom the whole of the material is canonical, which means those for whom the material functions as authoritative Scripture. If we desire yet more proof of the point, we might observe that no less than 11 of the 186 Old Testament–only sermons in the Best Sermons series are by rabbis, and that the only sermons on texts from the Apocrypha come from Catholic priests (for whom these books are not "apocryphal" at all!).[43]

Answering the second objection (Aren't famous passages famous for good reason?) is simple too: Of course such texts are famous for good reason, or for several good reasons, though we do well to remember that the popularity of various texts tends to wax and wane throughout history, and so the reason(s) for a text's popularity are hardly self-evident, essential, or eternal.[44] More to the point, however, is the crucial observation that there is a downside to fame. That downside is simply that many people will end up knowing only these texts and not others—though some of those others may be (and truly are) just as important and significant as "the highlights." So, for example, Gen. 1–3 is certainly an important section of Scripture, but what of Abraham, circumcision, Sarah and Hagar, Isaac and Ishmael? And this is only to mention the neglected parts of Genesis from the Best Sermons series that appear in Paul's Epistle to the Galatians!

The point should be clear: the fame of a few passages comes at a high price. In terms of the linguistic analogy, when people know only a few phrases of a language, it is proof of significant language loss and lack of fluency. So, as will be demonstrated more fully in chapter 3, knowing only bits, even if these bits are "the hits," suggests that the speaker's language facility is on the wane and that the language itself is endangered.[45] Here is yet more proof that a dark cloud surrounds the very thin silver lining of a few "Old Testament highlights." And in this case, the dark cloud is definitely a "cloud of unknowing," though of the worst kind (apologies to Pseudo-Dionysius and his medieval interpreter). What is unknown is the vast majority of the vast majority of the Christian Bible.

Haggai, and Zechariah. The fault here may be less Brueggemann's than the lectionary's, since, as noted above, he is primarily a lectionary preacher, and because, with the exception of 2 Samuel, these books are severely underrepresented in the RCL (see further below).

43. See apps. 1–3 below.

44. See, e.g., Holladay, "How the Twenty-Third Psalm Became an American Secular Icon."

45. This might even explain why so many more NT-only sermons were judged "best"—they stem from more familiar texts, after all, ones known better to the preachers, their audiences, and the judges of the competition.

The Psalms in Mainline Hymnody

In moving from the sermons that are preached in worship to the hymns that are sung there, the work of W. Sibley Towner is instructive. In 2003, Towner wrote a quasi-empirical study of five mainline hymnals published since 1985 and how they treat the Psalms in approximately 211 "psalm-hymns" and paraphrases.[46]

Towner's thesis is not particularly controversial: "The Psalter sung in paraphrase and hymn is both selective and interpretive." Where things start to get interesting is when Towner claims, "In its overall scope as well as in its re-presentation of individual psalms it offers theological communications somewhat at variance with the biblical psalms themselves."[47] He demonstrates this variance by noting how the psalm-hymns sometimes

> redirect or subvert their sources' original intentions; sometimes they distort them altogether. This is true even of the paraphrases, though they attempt to reproduce the original more faithfully than the . . . freely-composed hymns. The truth is, we have in the hymnal a second canon of accepted teaching, less authoritative than the canon of Scripture to be sure . . . but widely accepted, meaningful, and useful in the theological enterprise of the church.[48]

While none of this is particularly surprising, the situation is nevertheless potentially problematic. "What shall we say," Towner asks, "if the time-honored and vital theological medium of hymnody turns out to be conveying messages somewhat at variance with the very texts of Scripture that it purports to transmit?"[49] Towner's ultimate conclusion is that the variation is acceptable as long as no one claims (or thinks) that the two—the Scripture and the song—are identical.[50] But that is precisely the rub, since the ability to differentiate the two is predicated on adequate knowledge (linguistic

46. See Towner, "'Without Our Aid.'" Towner defines "psalm-hymn" as a musical representation of a biblical psalm that intends "to convey [the] meaning of the biblical text without being bound by the strict conventions of simple versification or even of paraphrase" (17n1). The five hymnals he examines are *Psalter Hymnal* (Christian Reformed Church), *The United Methodist Hymnal* (United Methodist Church), *The Presbyterian Hymnal* (Presbyterian Church U.S.A.), *Rejoice in the Lord* (Reformed Church in America), and *The New Century Hymnal* (United Church of Christ). For a much briefer (and earlier) treatment that supports Towner's analysis, see Holladay, *Psalms through Three Thousand Years*, 294.

47. Towner, "'Without Our Aid,'" 19. This re-presentation is accomplished in three ways: (1) via *the tunes*, which are "suggestive of meaning"; (2) via *selectivity*; and (3) via *the texts of the hymns*, which play "the primary interpretive function" (18–19).

48. Ibid., 18. Whether or not this second, sung canon is less authoritative may be doubted. See further below and chap. 7's discussion of Sheppard's work ("Canon," esp. 64–67).

49. Towner, "'Without Our Aid,'" 17.

50. Ibid., 19.

competence, as it were) of the original, scriptural Psalter. Lacking that, one could easily think that the song one just sang that *depends on*, say, Ps. 46, is in fact *the same as* Ps. 46.

As just noted, Towner's analysis highlights two important aspects of contemporary hymnody's use of the Psalms. The first concerns *selectivity*. Towner focuses on (1) which psalmic genres "resonate more vigorously with the contemporary singing church," and (2) which individual psalms "emerge as most meaningful to the contemporary believing community, judged by the number of different settings for each one."[51] He answers the genre question statistically. Table 5 reveals "where the preponderance of hymnic interpretation lies, and thus the functional psalter of today's worshiping Christian community."[52]

What is perhaps most striking about this "functional psalter" is what is absent from it. A lot: "64 of the 150 psalms (43%) have no cognate hymns at all."[53] What *is* present in the functional psalter is thus akin to a canon within the canon. And what is the message of this smaller, highly selective canon? Towner puts it memorably in the words of the wicked witch Evillene from the 1974 Broadway musical *The Wiz*: "Don't nobody bring me no bad news!" "Clearly," Towner writes, "contemporary mainstream American Protestants want to praise God when they sing in worship, not to complain and lament."[54]

It is hymnic selectivity, *and no other factor*, that has produced this functional psalter with its correlate "good news" message. The Hymns of Praise and Songs of Trust that are found in the book of Psalms are no more "lyrical, singable, and communal than . . . the much more numerous Individual Laments," Towner asserts. These laments, too, were evidently "sung in Second Temple worship from the very beginning."[55] In point of fact, "their preponderance in the Psalter and their connection with intercessory prayer, sacrificial offerings, and healing suggest that worship and chant in biblical times may have been substantially devoted to lament and intercession." Hence the contemporary liturgical move away from lament is not supported or recommended by the biblical material itself, as if "lament was meant only to be a prayer whispered in private." No, the modern taste for psalms of praise and trust "surely . . . has something to do with the spirit of our times."[56]

The second important aspect has to do with the *interpretive* nature of the lyrics in the hymns and how those relate to the canonical psalms. Towner finds

51. Ibid., 20.
52. Ibid., 21.
53. Ibid., 21n8.
54. Ibid., 22.
55. Ibid.
56. Ibid.

Table 5. Hymns according to Psalm Genre

Psalm genre	No. of biblical psalms (total = 150)	No. of hymns (total = 211)	Average hymns/ psalm	Psalms with highest number of hymns (total number)
Individual lament (including penitential psalms)	45	33	0.73	130 (6), 51 (5)
Hymn (not including songs of Zion and enthronement hymns; see below)	22	70	3.18	103 (12), 148 (10), 150 (10)
Communal lament	16	10	0.63	90 (5), 89 (3)
Individual thanksgiving	11	15	1.36	118 (5)
Royal psalm	9	7	0.78	72 (6)
Instruction (wisdom)	9	13	1.44	1, 91, 119, 139 (3 each)
Song of trust	8	21	2.6	23 (12), 121 (4)
Prophetic oracle of judgment	7	3	0.33	95 (3)
Song of Zion	6	12	2.0	46 (5), 84 (4)
Enthronement hymn	5	7	1.4	96 (3)
Blessing	3	4	1.33	133 (2)
Communal thanksgiving	3	4	1.33	67 (3)
Historical psalm	3	2	0.67	105 (2)
Liturgy	3	10	3.33	24 (7)

the interpretation offered in the songs to be frequently moralizing, sacramentalizing, and Christianizing—such as transforming Ps. 23 into a text about humans not forsaking God's ways or about the eucharistic table or about Christ the Good Shepherd.[57] By means of very small changes, as minute as the introduction of a conditional clause or an adjectival qualifier, a biblical psalm can become something strikingly new and altogether different. But not all interpretations are dramatically different. Towner points out that Jane Parker Huber's 1988 composition "The Lord's My Shepherd" avoids the theme of eternal life (which many scholars believe to be absent from Ps. 23 itself)[58] and also "neither moralizes, sacramentalizes, nor Christianizes the psalm." Huber's song demonstrates that "a hymnic re-presentation . . . can clarify and vivify without abandoning the canonical communication."[59]

And yet, while it is clearly possible to write a hymn that is "close(r)" to the original, what is wrong with a more (heavily) interpretive composition?

57. See ibid., 25–27.
58. But see Janzen, "Revisiting 'Forever' in Psalm 23:6."
59. Towner, "'Without Our Aid,'" 28.

On the one hand, the answer seems to be nothing per se; interpretation is simply a part of the deal. We are dealing with an *English song*, after all, not the original *Hebrew psalm*—and that means that translation, a major interpretive activity, is already part of the process.[60] Moreover, it is virtually automatic, if not axiomatic, that secondary treatments tend to expand on their primary sources. Scripture itself does the same.[61] But while everything may well be interpretation—hermeneutics all the way down, so to speak— we should also acknowledge that not everything is *good* interpretation. To cite the literary critic Wayne C. Booth, "There are an unlimited number of valid ways to interpret or evaluate any fiction, any historical event or historical account of events, any philosophy, any critical work. And there are even more ways to get it wrong."[62] This, then, is the "on the other hand": yes, interpretation is to be expected and to some degree is "innocent" as an automatic exercise, but we also see that many songs have a way—indeed, songs *are* a way—of codifying and transmitting poor interpretations (not all of them "innocent"!) for centuries, perhaps because of their ability to ingrain their lyrical interpretations in our brains via their musicality (see further chaps. 8–9).

The title of Towner's study drives this point home. It is taken from a line in William Kethe's hymn "All People That on Earth Do Dwell" (1560), which is a re-presentation of Ps. 100.[63] The pertinent stanza reads as follows:

> Know that the Lord is God indeed;
> Without our aid He did us make;
> We are His folk, he doth us feed,
> And for his sheep He doth us take.

The second line, "Without our aid He did us make," reflects a particular understanding of a crux in the underlying Hebrew text of Ps. 100. The present text that is written (*ketiv*) has the negative particle לֹא/*lōʾ* ("not"), but at some point in the Masoretic tradition, scribes indicated that this was incorrect and the word should be read aloud (*qere*) as לוֹ/*lô* ("his"). The *qere* seems to make better sense and is reflected in most contemporary translations (the crux is italicized):

---

60. See, e.g., Eco, *Experiences in Translation*, 13 ("translation is a special case of interpretation") and 39 ("It is on the basis of interpretive decisions . . . that translators play the game of faithfulness").

61. See Towner, "'Without Our Aid,'" 17–18. The classic study on this is by Fishbane, *Biblical Interpretation in Ancient Israel*.

62. Booth, *Company We Keep*, 324.

63. For what follows, see Towner, "'Without Our Aid,'" 28–30.

Know that the LORD is God—
he made us; we belong *to him*.
We are his people,
the sheep of his own pasture. (Ps. 100:3 CEB)

"Without our aid he did us make" appears rather nonsensical—in both Hebrew and English, despite the fact that it is reflected in the KJV ("It is he that hath made us, and *not* we ourselves") and in Kethe's hymn (which predates the KJV by more than fifty years).[64] Indeed, most scholars now believe that "without our aid/not we ourselves" is mistaken, a mistake that has been perpetuated for centuries by public singing in countless congregations.[65] Kethe's hymn has probably done as much to perpetuate the flawed understanding as the KJV itself has.

Towner deems it somewhat ironic that across the ages most singers "probably failed to notice that they were singing nonsense . . . or else . . . thought the psalm and its paraphrase were driving home the point that the Creator's powers are infinitely superior to our own."[66] When the matter is put this way, the flaw in question (if it is one) seems rather minor. What's wrong with singing about the Creator's powers being superior to our own? Surely there is no doctrinal error here; the theology seems quite solid on several levels—even if it be a case of the right doctrine from the wrong text. But it is not just the wrong text; it is also the wrong text wrongly understood. So Towner: "Are we content that one of the most beloved of all church songs should perpetuate a textual error?"[67] If we are not, even in so "benign" a case as Kethe's re-presentation of Ps. 100, then what should we say of less benign cases such as Martin Luther's hymn "Out of the Depths" (1524), which is based on Ps. 130? According to Towner, the second stanza of Luther's hymn makes the psalm

a precursor of the Pauline, and quintessentially Lutheran, doctrine of justification by faith alone. Is this really the direction in which the psalm is going: "Our works, alas! are all in vain"? The psalm does not address itself to "our works," nor does it develop the faith vs. works antithesis.[68]

64. Note that it is found in the Episcopal Church's *Book of Common Prayer* (1979), 45, in the Daily Morning Prayer Rite One, but not in Daily Morning Prayer Rite Two nor in Ps. 100, both of which read "we are his" (83, 729, respectively).

65. A notable exception to this judgment is Janzen, "And Not We Ourselves.'"

66. Towner, "'Without Our Aid,'" 30. On this latter point, see Janzen, "'And Not We Ourselves,'" esp. 126–33.

67. Towner, "'Without Our Aid,'" 30.

68. Ibid., 32.

But once again: What's so bad here? Surely no Protestant would want to call Luther's hymnic theology the opposite of "benign" and thus malicious. (Then again, in light of the U.S. Religious Knowledge Survey, the Protestant in question may not even know who Luther was or what he stood for!) Be that as it may, the issue at hand concerns differences between an original psalmic composition and its later hymnic version, especially if the differences are large and the stakes high. When does the hymn no longer reflect the underlying psalm at all but present a new composition altogether—one that is, despite the advertising (clearly false, in this case), no longer "based on" (or at least not *solely* based on) the original? Using linguistic terminology, when is the hymn no longer a dialect but something further removed than that? When is it something distinct—a different language altogether, perhaps made through language contact or the processes of pidginization or creolization (see chap. 3)? Answering these questions is difficult.[69]

Throughout this discussion, one shouldn't forget the crucial role corporate singing plays in Christian (esp. Protestant) worship. Indeed, singing seems to be more important than ever, even and especially in low-church traditions, and this exacerbates the problems Towner has identified by, on the one hand, valuing sung texts far more than, and to the elimination of, other liturgical aspects (such as the public reading of Scripture); and by, on the other hand, the singing of songs that are lyrically stripped down and/or not much interested in the biblical material but only an inspiring line or thought therein—if such songs are not, in fact, completely disinterested in or uninspired by Scripture altogether. This last-mentioned concern applies to some, though certainly not all, contemporary Christian music, which is more popular than ever—not only in the marketplace, but also in free-church traditions, which tend to sing these sorts of songs *instead* of traditional hymns. Then, too, we must reckon not only with *what* is sung (in terms of underlying biblical genre/text and hymnic lyric) and *how* it is sung, but also with what is *not* sung, which is as important for the question of hymnody as it was earlier with reference to the Best Sermons. Which texts are overrepresented and which underrepresented or absent altogether—and to what effect?

At this point the *problem of selectivity*, favoring certain psalm types over others, could be rephrased as the *problem of neglect*: the massive overlooking of a particular psalm type—namely, the laments. Bad news, as Towner has shown, doesn't make the cut for the canon within the canon of the functional, sung psalter. Lest someone object here that everyone has a canon within the

---

69. It is not wholly unrelated to speciation. Animals are considered different species when they can no longer interbreed. See further chaps. 3, 6, and 9.

canon, whether they admit it or not, I only echo the earlier point from Booth: even if that is so, not every "minicanon" is equally good, and countless ones are really bad and even worse. Towner concurs and puts his finger on the very real problems created when selectivity becomes neglect:

> Our sung psalters do not offer us a range of concept and emotion as wide as that of the biblical Psalter. Except for denominations committed to singing every psalm in chant, paraphrase, or hymn, contemporary hymnists and hymnals prefer to celebrate God as creator and thank God as liberator rather than to lament to the God who listens. To this end, they more often take as their texts the canonical Hymns and Psalms of Trust. Yet, perhaps this is to be expected—singing about sin and suffering sounds like an oxymoron, especially in the communal context of a congregation. [But] perhaps this selection also says something about the theological climate in the mainstream churches in recent decades. Put in commercial terms, in the competitive denominational marketplace of the twenty-first century, somber doesn't sell. We prefer to sin and repent, lament and die in silent privacy.[70]

There can be little doubt that individuals have preferences and tastes. The same is true for corporate "persons"—communal bodies like institutions, denominations, congregations. But at what price does the preference to "sin and repent, lament and die in silent privacy" come? At the very least it seems that we must agree with Towner: "A persistent preference for praise in psalm-singing impoverishes the emotional range of worship, depriving worshipers of access to a source of hope that grows out of suffering."[71] The "praise-preference" *impoverishes* at this point, allowing no hope, because, in the Psalms, a (if not *the*) primary way to get to hope is precisely *through* (never around) lament. One only knows hope, that is—especially the hope that grows out of suffering—if one knows the full Psalter, which is to say if one can "speak Psalms," and do so fluently, not haltingly or with a heavy lisp of praise. But that full knowledge of and full fluency in the Psalms is precisely what the preference for praise opts out of.

The linguistic reduction at work in hymnic selectivity-turned-neglect is thus of dread importance. The problem of the Psalms' presence (or absence) in contemporary hymnody is not, therefore, simply a matter of well-meaning but mostly harmless Christianization of ancient Hebrew texts that predate Christ as well as our smartphones and praise bands. Transformation and

---

70. Towner, "'Without Our Aid,'" 33.
71. Ibid., 33n34, with reference to Billman and Migliore, *Rachel's Cry*; and Brueggemann, "Costly Loss of Praise."

updating are surely inevitable, even laudable in some instances, if it "stays within recognizable parameters."[72] According to Towner, such recognition depends on maintaining "the distinction between what is canonical, quasi-canonical, and ephemeral."[73] He reserves Scripture for the canonical category, believing preaching to be ephemeral and deeming liturgy and hymnody quasi-canonical, though that could be inaccurate for low-church traditions where preaching, too, is quasi-canonical (if not more than that) and where liturgy is often, at best, implicit.

Regardless, Towner is spot on that

> people learn their hymns by heart in church and then draw on them in prison camps and hospitals, while driving in the car and lying in bed, for guidance and consolation in daily lives. Well and good, and may the tradition continue and grow, as new outbursts of hymnody enrich the life of the church! The only question is: How do we know when the float has gone too far?[74]

Once again, answering this last question is not easy: it is akin to the question of determining when a dialect has become a new language. To anticipate some of what will be said in chapters 3–6, however, it seems that things *have* gone too far if we no longer know the original (psalm or language) in all its complexity, nuance, and, yes, difficulty. If it's all *good* news, all the time, then it's probably *not real* news, *nor biblical* news—not, at least, from the Psalms. The float (drift) at this point has indeed gone too far. It is now a new language, a different "psalm"—no longer "the LORD's song" (cf. Ps. 137:4)—and thus no longer a dialect belonging to the language of faith.[75]

Viewing Towner's study through the linguistic analogy that the Old Testament is (like) a language means that a great deal is at stake in the use of the Psalms in contemporary hymnody. It is not solely a matter of exegetical niceties, truth in advertising, and so forth, but a matter of linguistic capacity, competence, and dexterity: the ability to speak the (full) language or not. In the case of the Psalms, it is one thing to ask "How can we sing the LORD's song in a foreign land?" (Ps. 137:4 NASB). It is quite another thing to ask "How can we sing the LORD's song *at all*, especially if (or in light of the fact that) we no longer even know that the LORD has a song, let alone more than one type?"

---

72. Towner, "'Without Our Aid,'" 34. See chaps. 1, 3, and 8–9 on the realities and normalcy of language change.

73. Ibid.

74. Ibid.

75. Cf. chap. 1 on speaking Job or Proverbs or, in this case, the Psalms. I return to matters related to dialectology in chaps. 3, 6, and 7–9.

Ominous evidence of this very possibility may be found in several contemporary Christian music recordings. As one example, consider "Who Am I?" by the singing group Point of Grace, which contains the following lines:

> Who am I
> To give you anything but praise?[76]

The song is not a psalmic re-presentation like Kethe's hymn, but I deem the lyric altogether analogous to "Without our aid He did us make." Yes, it is powerful and evocative theology; it also gives rise to an intriguing and not altogether erroneous by-product (or by-interpretation)—namely, a grand vision of God that cannot help but eventuate in human praise. And yet, in and by itself, the line is profoundly ignorant of the biblical witness, especially and specifically the Psalms, because it is precisely there, perhaps more than anywhere else, that the human being offers God *far more* than praise, a good bit of which is about as far from praise as possible,[77] all of which, however, is somehow sanctioned and allowed for and heard by the God who listens. Let it be underscored that this sanction and authorization is realized

- *canonically*, by the inclusion of the book of Psalms in the canon of Holy Scripture;
- *pedagogically*, given the psalms' connection to Torah, especially as instruction in prayer, which is to say that we *should* pray like the psalmists pray, not just that we are *permitted* to do so;[78]
- and finally vis-à-vis *the dynamics of the psalms themselves*, which often include the psalmist's testimony that God has heard the prayers—a testimony supported by other texts as well (e.g., 1 Sam. 1).

But all that is lost in a single, catchy line on the radio or stereo or music player: "Who am I / To give you anything but praise?" The loss is profound and carries serious consequences—personally, publicly, even politically[79]—especially if the song becomes as theologically authoritative (or *more* theologically authoritative) to a listener as the Psalms themselves. Kethe's version

---

76. Point of Grace, "Who Am I?," released August 5, 1998, on *Steady On*, Word, B00123N74A, released on compact disc July 5, 2005.

77. Cf. Davis, *Getting Involved with God*, 8–9, who speaks of the Psalms as "a kind of First Amendment for the faithful," guaranteeing free speech, "even up to its dangerous limits, to the very brink of rebellion."

78. See Pss. 1, 19, and 119; McCann, *Theological Introduction to the Book of Psalms*; Wenham, *Psalms as Torah*.

79. See Brueggemann, "Costly Loss of Praise."

of Ps. 100 shows that such a scenario is entirely possible, to which I'll add a personal testimony: I am not the first to find myself battling uphill in some teaching context, trying to convince people that grief and disappointment with God are legitimate emotions and part of the life of faith. These people, too, seem to be convinced that they are "nobodies" who cannot and must not offer God anything but praise, even if they didn't learn that on the radio from a contemporary Christian music song.[80]

To sum up, the (non)use of the Psalms in contemporary hymnody represents a death of sorts. The death of the "little Bible" (Martin Luther's term for the Psalter) is a microcosm of the dying of the whole Old Testament. When the full language of the Psalms is no longer spoken, or in this case *sung*, large and rich parts of the wider linguistic system die too.[81] In this, the second test of our patient, the use of the Psalms in contemporary hymnody not only showcases the morbidity of the Old Testament; it also highlights in a powerful way how much is riding on its survival.[82]

The Revised Common Lectionary (and the Psalms)

The picture painted so far is not pretty. Then again, perhaps one shouldn't expect too much from the general populace in terms of knowledge of the Bible generally or the Old Testament specifically (as per the U.S. Religious Knowledge Survey). Preachers, one would hope, should know better on both scores, with their sermons reflecting as much, but the data from the Best Sermons were equivocal at best. Moreover, even if Towner is right about the ephemeral nature of preaching, the treatment of the psalms in quasi-canonical hymnody evinces the same problem besetting the other data sets: loss of basic linguistic competence, not to mention full fluency, in the language that is the Old Testament. When viewed through the linguistic analogy, the loss of lexical items, accompanied by large-scale reductions in nuance and massive simplification of grammar and syntax, sounds like nothing so much as (re)pidginization, which is something that happens to languages that are about to

80. I do not mean to pick on Point of Grace unduly. It is the nature of lyric poetry, including song lyrics, to be episodic. This line I have cited does not reflect the theology of the group's entire oeuvre. There are also wonderfully substantive lyrics to be found all across contemporary Christian music. The existence of good examples, however, does not eliminate the problems posed by the less good.

81. Cf., on the linguistic side, Harrison, *Last Speakers*, and chap. 3 below.

82. A few denominations do sing/chant/read through the whole Psalter. An exceptional example was the community of Little Gidding, which flourished in the early seventeenth century. Its thirty people prayed the entire Psalter every day. See Kingsmill, "Psalms: A Monastic Perspective," esp. 605–6.

die (see chap. 3). As if all that wasn't bad enough, and as yet further proof that my diagnosis regarding the Old Testament's death is accurate, there is one last preliminary test to run on the patient: the public reading of the Bible via the lectionary, which, as part of the liturgy, is another "quasi-canonical" source, to continue with Towner's categories.

By now it should come as no surprise that the trends identified above are also to be found in the Revised Common Lectionary (RCL). The RCL is a useful tool that, in a generous, best-case scenario assessment, is designed to expose a congregation to an extensive and representative sample of the entire Bible across a three-year cycle. The RCL depends on previous lectionaries, including daily lectionaries that, if followed, have a user read the entirety of the Bible (or nearly so) in the course of three years, sometimes less. There are also more specialized lectionaries that lead readers through the entire Psalter in a month, the whole Torah in a year, and so on and so forth, but for present purposes a focus on the RCL is in order since it is the primary lectionary used by many Christian groups, including the Episcopal Church in the United States of America, the Evangelical Lutheran Church in America, the Presbyterian Church USA, the Reformed Church in America, the United Church of Christ, and the United Methodist Church, to name a few.[83] The RCL is also widely used elsewhere in the world, including in Canada, Great Britain, South Africa, Korea, the Philippines, Australia, and New Zealand.[84] This explains the "Common" part of the RCL title, and indeed, use of the RCL (or something quite like it) has been a notable point of ecumenical cooperation in the past few decades.[85] The RCL also enjoys a large support apparatus, which includes everything from studies of its structure, meaning, and significance to a host of exegetical collections focused on the various lections themselves.[86]

The RCL includes four biblical texts for each Sunday—an Old Testament lesson, a psalm or hymnic responsorial, a Gospel lesson, and an epistle lesson. There is a certain balance to these four—two Old Testament lessons and two New Testament lessons—and that is a good thing, but things aren't quite as balanced as they might seem on first blush. For one thing, the second lesson, frequently sung liturgically as a response to the first lesson, is often omitted,

---

83. The RCL is not a solely Protestant phenomenon. Among other things, it depends on pre-existing Catholic lectionaries (esp. the 1969 *Ordo lectionum Missae*), and Catholics participated in the Consultation on Common Texts (CCT) that was responsible for the RCL.

84. H. Allen, "Introduction: Preaching in a Christian Context," esp. 2.

85. See West, *Scripture and Memory*.

86. See, e.g., ibid.; Bower, *Handbook for the Revised Common Lectionary*; Van Harn, *Lectionary Commentary*; Van Harn and Strawn, *Psalms for Preaching and Worship*; and Bartlett and Taylor, *Feasting on the Word*.

such that the first New Testament reading (the third in the RCL) becomes the second reading, with the RCL's second New Testament reading (technically the fourth lection) becoming the third.[87] In this process the previous 2-to-2 balance between Old and New Testaments is skewed to become 1-to-2. The reasons for the omission of the psalmic/hymnic lesson are several, but it is usually due to a lack of liturgical support—no choir to sing the response, for example. According to some, the hymnic responsorials are more a matter of prayer than of preaching anyway.[88] Such a judgment may be correct, and the prayerful use of the psalms is certainly traditional and justifiable, but at the same time such a determination leaves the didactic aspects of the psalmic material at best implicit or inductive (via modeling and practice) rather than explicit and expositional,[89] especially if Bartlett is right that, in the construction of the RCL, "no particular attention [was] paid to the way in which their content may relate to the content of the Gospel texts."[90]

A second way things aren't as balanced as they seem is that, beginning with Easter Sunday and running through Pentecost, the (first) Old Testament lesson gets dropped altogether, being replaced by a lesson from Acts. The Old Testament lesson only returns eight weeks later, on the first Sunday after Pentecost (Trinity Sunday). A third way things are imbalanced is that, even in churches that use the RCL, typically not all the lessons will be read; neither will all serve as the preached text(s). We saw earlier that the Best Sermons series of the twentieth century were inordinately weighted toward the New Testament, and so it seems safe to assume that the Old Testament is getting short shrift, even in RCL-based churches.[91]

---

87. Note, too, that there is one non-OT responsorial (Luke 1), so the category itself is not exclusively an OT one. Luke 1 appears in the RCL cycle no less than six times: once in Year A (Third Sunday of Advent), twice in Year B (Third Sunday of Advent and Fourth Sunday of Advent), and three times in Year C (Second Sunday of Advent, Fourth Sunday of Advent, and Christ the King). In four of these six it is one of two possibilities that might be chosen (the other being an OT text), but in three of the four it is listed first.

88. Bartlett, "Lectionaries," esp. 993, though he admits that the Psalms can provide appropriate texts for proclamation. On this point, note that the first three volumes of Van Harn's *Lectionary Commentary* did not include exegetical treatment of the Psalms. Such treatment had to await vol. 4, published 8 years later (Van Harn and Strawn, *Psalms for Preaching and Worship*).

89. See note 78 above.

90. Bartlett, "Lectionaries," 993.

91. Thomas G. Long (via private communication) informs me that recent decades have witnessed a move from very little lectionary preaching to relatively high use, though that seems to have plateaued and may now be tapering off. Even for churches that follow the RCL, most probably read at most two of the four lessons for the day (one from the OT and one from the NT). Long suspects that the vast majority of lectionary-based sermons (perhaps as high as 85%) focus on only the NT lesson. For more on the OT in the RCL, see Seitz, *Word without End*, 300–318; Ramshaw, "First Testament in Christian Lectionaries"; Bailey, "Lectionary in Critical

Since this last point is just a supposition—though a fairly reasonable one in light of the other data considered in this chapter—perhaps we should give the RCL the benefit of the doubt and instead assume the best about its intentions regarding the Old Testament in Christian liturgical practice. The problem is that even when we assume the best, it is still readily apparent that the RCL is far from foolproof and manifests some significant problems vis-à-vis the full language that is the Old Testament (and thus the full language that is Christian Scripture). One way to analyze these problems is to see them as further symptoms of the death of the Old Testament. Yet another way to think about the matter is to wonder if it is not precisely the flaws in liturgical instruments like the RCL (as well as the flaws in sermons and hymnody) that are contributing directly to the demise of our patient.

A thorough analysis of the Old Testament throughout the RCL would no doubt yield significant findings.[92] It must suffice here to provide an entrée into that larger issue by looking at the use of the Psalms in the RCL; this has the advantage of a more manageable focus but also can serve as a kind of check on Towner's study of the Psalms in hymnody. I have done this work elsewhere and simply cite my conclusions here:

> As helpful as the lectionary is in the task of preaching the Psalms, it is not foolproof. Simply put, the lectionary omits much that the Psalter deems precious. Fifty-one psalms—more than a third of the Psalter—do not appear in the lectionary.[93] While Holladay is correct that "[t]he range of psalms in this [the Common] lectionary is impressive: much of the riches of the Psalter becomes available to the alert listener," it is nevertheless a real concern that so much of the Psalter is missing. The problem of missing psalms is exacerbated in two ways: *first*, even the ninety-nine psalms that do appear in the lectionary are not all intact; some forty-three of these are *excerpted*.[94] While this excerption is sometimes for reasons of space and (liturgical) time, it must be admitted that

---

Perspective," esp. 151–52; and Stookey, "Marcion, Typology, and Lectionary Preaching." Cf. also J. White, "Our Apostasy in Worship."

92. Note the recent assessment by Callen, *Beneath the Surface*, 43–44: "While it [the RCL] is understandably Christ-centered, the Foundational Testament [the OT] is significantly disadvantaged by the choice of passages suggested for consideration in Christian worship. Not including the Psalms, this lectionary contains some 435 readings from the last twenty-seven books of the Bible and only about 270 from the first thirty-nine books. . . . Christian worship is thereby impoverished."

93. The absent psalms are Pss. 3, 6–7, 10–12, 18, 21, 28, 35, 38–39, 44, 49, 53–61, 64, 69–70, 73–76, 83, 87–88, 94, 101–2, 108–9, 113, 115, 117, 120, 129, 134–36, 140–44.

94. The excerpted psalms are Pss. 5, 9, 17, 22, 25, 31, 33–34, 36–37, 40, 45, 50–51, 62–63, 66, 68, 71–72, 77–81, 86, 89–92, 103–7, 112, 116, 118–19, 132, 139, 145, and 147. Four additional psalms that are used more than once appear in both holistic and excerpted fashion: Pss. 27, 85, 96, and 146.

at other points it is hard to avoid the conclusion that this excerption reflects *theological censorship*, which is the *second* worsening of the situation.

Holladay's careful study of the Roman Catholic Liturgy of the Hours and the Common Lectionary has demonstrated that the omitted psalms and/or omitted parts of psalms are either laments or imprecations (curses) contained within psalms (esp. laments). Certainly lectionaries are constantly being revised, and Holladay notes a distinct improvement in the Common Lectionary over the Liturgy of the Hours when it comes to the Psalms. That progressive trend is also found in the Revised Common Lectionary. One notes, for example, that Ps. 137:7–9 is omitted in the Liturgy of the Hours but is given in full in the Revised Common Lectionary (though, admittedly, as an optional text). It is clear, regardless, that lament is typically underrepresented in the lectionaries and that lectionaries have a tendency to omit "some, if not all, of the harsh language regarding enemies." As Holladay has ominously put it, there is a "constant tendency" in the church "to bypass materials with a negative import." Now it must certainly be admitted that the psalms of divine wrath that often include vicious cursing of the enemies of God (and of the psalmist) are among the Bible's most difficult texts. But even these texts are not without merit, nor are they bereft of spiritual help. . . . The point . . . is that censorship of lament (or imprecation) simply won't do: the stakes are too high and the results truly deleterious. Such censorship neglects a significant portion of the real life and real faith of the psalmists. And it neglects a significant portion of the real life of those who pray (or *should* be praying) the Psalms now and their real struggle to correlate their lives with something approaching reality and the real faith of the Psalms. In brief, if the Psalms are censored, one will not get the full anatomy of the soul, but something far less, partial, and grotesque—perhaps even hideous, like a skeleton: strangely attractive in its whitewashed articulations but utterly devoid of the parts that make a human being *alive*.[95]

The main problem facing the Psalms in the RCL is the same as one of the main problems facing the Psalms in hymnody—namely, *selectivity*. In the case of the RCL, this selectivity is not accompanied by overt interpretation—no paraphrases or re-presentation as with contemporary hymnody—but the RCL's selectivity nevertheless contains within itself a correlate "interpretivity," an implicit curriculum, as it were, which explains and justifies the selection process (even if these explanations and justifications have to be

---

95. Strawn, "Psalms: Types, Functions, and Poetics." Apart from the two preceding notes, I have excised the footnotes from the original text, but the three quotations come from Holladay, *Psalms through Three Thousand Years*, 278, 311, and 314, respectively. At the time of Holladay's writing, the RCL was not yet available (released in 1994), hence his focus on the "Common Lectionary."

"reverse engineered" since they are not explicit).[96] It seems both natural and reasonable that readers would deduce that what is lacking from the RCL is simply less important—and that holds true not only for the psalms omitted from the Psalter but also for the entire books (!) of the Old Testament that are omitted from the RCL altogether (7 out of 39 books, or 18%),[97] as well as for those Old Testament books that are severely underrepresented (13 books, or 33%, are found only once in the three-year Sunday cycle).[98] Moreover, it seems quite likely that, for many Christians, what is lacking from Sunday's readings (and from sermons and hymns) will go unknown, precisely because it is unheard and unread. Here too someone might argue that such a situation isn't all bad. Maybe it's even better than that: maybe it's "quite good" or at least "good enough." Some Old Testament is better than none, after all. Furthermore, there were presumably good reasons for the selectivity of the RCL in the first place. Maybe, then, what is not represented in the RCL isn't known because it *ought* not be known. Perhaps it is dangerous in some way, or off-putting and offensive, maybe even non-Christian. That could well be the message, intended or otherwise, of the RCL's selectivity; that could be the effect of its "censorship," unintended or otherwise.

I've clearly moved from giving the RCL the benefit of the doubt to treating it in the worst-case scenario. Surely that isn't entirely fair—at least not with regard to the original purpose of the RCL and its crafters. But this skeptical assessment may not be too far off target when it comes to the reception of the RCL; and from where we stand in the twenty-first century, long after the New Criticism, Poststructuralism, and Reader Response approaches, we should be prepared to reckon as seriously with a work's reception and interpretation as we reckon with its presumed "original intent." Part of that reception/interpretation is the effect produced by the (original) design. So, whatever the original (best) intent of the RCL, its selectivity or censorship is more than obvious. And that selectivity comes with significant interpretive baggage, which is to say, it comes at a high price.

Not all the news on the lectionary front is bad, however, and even the points that are problematic are not without some balance. So, for example, many agree that the RCL selects Old Testament lections on the basis of "a kind of typological relationship to the NT text; that is, for Christians the OT text can be read in conversation with the Gospel text, either as a kind of foreshadowing

96. There is also a "null curriculum" composed of the psalms completely omitted.

97. The Sunday readings of the RCL omit any lessons from 1–2 Chronicles, Ezra, Ecclesiastes, Obadiah, Nahum, and Zechariah.

98. Leviticus, Numbers, Judges, Esther, Nehemiah, Song of Songs, Lamentations, Joel, Jonah, Habakkuk, Zephaniah, Haggai, and Malachi.

or as a promise whose fulfillment is found in the Gospels."[99] That is good as far as it goes, though in my judgment that isn't nearly far enough (see chap. 9), and those responsible for the RCL concur. According to Bartlett,

> Those who designed the Revised Common Lectionary were concerned that the typological constraint limited both the range and meaning of OT texts that could be read. Therefore in the season from Pentecost to Advent (so-called "Ordinary Time") the Revised Common Lectionary is more apt to go through one OT book at a time, in a kind of continuous reading.[100]

But, since not everyone likes *lectio continua*—or attends church during Ordinary Time[101]—one should observe that alternative Old Testament readings between Pentecost and Advent are given for "those churches that want to maintain the close thematic connection between OT and Gospel texts."[102] Happily, the opposite is also true. The *Feasting on the Word* series originally neglected the Old Testament readings from Ordinary Time that are more sequentially based, but due to popular demand, the publisher decided to add treatments of these lections as well.[103]

To summarize: the RCL is more balanced than what we saw in the Best Sermons series and in contemporary hymnody, but the results are still rather mixed. On the one hand,

> the use of the lectionary can broaden the range of texts that the preacher preaches and the congregation hears. The lectionary provides a protection against the tendency of preachers to recycle favorite texts and favorite themes week after week and helps to ensure that, for instance, justice and mercy will be balanced

---

99. Bartlett, "Lectionaries," 993, notes that, by way of contrast, there is no operative assumption "that the epistle text will have any particular thematic connection with the Gospel text for that Sunday."

100. Ibid.; e.g., in Year A, the OT lessons for the thirteen Sundays after Pentecost are all taken from Genesis in a sequential ordering: (1) Gen. 1:1–2:4a; (2) Gen. 6:9–22; 7:24; 8:14–19; (3) Gen. 12:1–9; (4) Gen. 18:1–15; (21:1–7); (5) Gen. 21:8–21; (6) Gen. 22:1–14; (7) Gen. 24:34–38; (8) Gen. 25:19–34; (9) Gen. 28:10–19a; (10) Gen. 29:15–28; (11) Gen. 32:22–31; (12) Gen. 37:1–4, 12–28; (13) Gen. 45:1–15. Even so, as Fleming Rutledge has noted: "There is no opportunity in the lectionaries currently in use to preach through any Old Testament book" (*And God Spoke to Abraham*, 12). One might compare the Torah cycle in synagogue reading: the whole Torah (not just parts of it) is covered in one or three years, often with the Haftarot (non-Pentateuchal readings) as well (though the latter are selective).

101. This is tongue-in-cheek, but the more serious correlate is the significance of the readings on the high holy days and during major liturgical seasons.

102. Bartlett, "Lectionaries," 993.

103. The *Feasting on the Word* series is published by Westminster John Knox Press. I thank Thomas G. Long for bringing this fact to my attention. The vignette demonstrates that a NT, Gospel-driven lectionary can do only partial justice to the full language of Scripture.

not only among the attributes of God but [also] among the sermons preached to honor God.[104]

In this way, by using the RCL, Christians gather around a common table and a common set of texts.

Yet, on the other hand, the problem remains that this common table of texts offers a greatly reduced menu. As Bartlett notes, "The decision about which verses to include and which to omit from a particular pericope sometimes seems arbitrary and oddly anti-canonical."[105] So, while the RCL protects against some problems—the penchant to produce an even more reduced selection of pet texts, an imbalanced understanding of divine attributes, and so forth—it nevertheless introduces others. Perhaps the most important point to make here is that the introduction of (new) problems directly and adversely affects the avoidance of other problems. The prophylactic that is afforded by the "fuller" (or more truthfully, "less reduced") complement of texts from the RCL would presumably be even more effective if the selection of texts was yet fuller still—which is to say, if it comprised the *whole language* of Scripture. Thus the RCL would be better if it contained *no* excerption or selectivity at all.[106] Of course, at that point the RCL would no longer be the RCL—at least not in its present form. It would simply be the entire Bible.

In his excellent book on the lectionary, Fritz West has argued that the three-year lectionary cycle uses the memory of the church to interpret the Bible and uses the Bible to structure the memory of the church.[107] West's argument is another "best-case scenario" and a generous reading of the lectionary. The proof, however, is always in the pudding, and it is quite telling to correlate this fourth and final test involving the RCL with the first test about the U.S. Religious Knowledge Survey. Historically, it has been the Roman Catholic Church, more than Bible-centered Protestant congregations, that has employed lectionaries for worship, liturgy, and preaching. In the U.S. Religious Knowledge Survey, however, Catholic groups often scored very poorly in terms of Bible knowledge (see above, esp. tables 1–2). Somewhere along the way, it seems, the Bible is failing to structure the memory of the church—perhaps because

104. Bartlett, "Lectionaries," 993.

105. Ibid., 994. Bartlett supports his critique with NT data: John is "seriously underrepresented," and no Gospel or Epistle, save for Philemon, is fully represented in the RCL. So, as per chap. 1, the problems besetting the OT also face the NT, even if not to the same degree.

106. Note J. Smith, "Scriptures and Histories," esp. 34–35, on lectionaries being "syntagmatically unreadable"—"unreadable serially," which results in "an unacknowledged fifth gospel," but one that "in this case . . . [is] heard by more individuals than have ever read the full New Testament text."

107. West, *Scripture and Memory*, passim.

the lectionary simply isn't cut out for the job.[108] The memory of the church, in turn, is failing, which means that it has precious little to go on in terms of interpreting the Bible (to complete West's feedback loop). And it isn't just the church's *memory*. It is also the church's *language*, if only because so much memory is encoded in language and correlate linguistic systems.[109]

Conclusion

The preliminary tests of our patient are now complete, and the results are not encouraging for the following areas of concern:

1. how well the Old Testament (or parts of it) is known and how broadly;
2. how often and how much of it is present in the very "best" of sermons;
3. how much and what parts of it (including what is often touted as its "dearest part," the Psalms) are reflected in musical worship; and
4. how much and what parts of it are present in the liturgical instrument that is the RCL.

Thus our patient shows serious signs of morbidity. The Old Testament is very, very sick. Indeed, as I said from the outset, my own diagnosis puts matters much more strongly: the Old Testament is dying. The four "tests" presented above are proof of the point. Even more troubling, the last three tests not only showcase symptoms of the disease; they may actually reveal contributing factors to the patient's demise. The first test clearly demonstrated that a language must be practiced in order to thrive; the last three tests, which in principle revealed distinct opportunities for such linguistic practice, fail definitively at exactly this point.

To spell this out further: the U.S. Religious Knowledge Survey reveals that the most knowledgeable individuals spent time "speaking the language," as it were, practicing that language in various ways, listening to it, learning it, and so on and so forth—and they typically did this from a young age, as children, or at a formative period in life, as college students taking a religion course. Sermons, hymns, and the lectionary—which together form a significant

---

108. Cf. Rutledge, *And God Spoke to Abraham*, 11: "The Old Testament has fallen into the background and, in some poorly informed circles, has even become suspect. This may or may not be the result of lectionary use, but it has happened concurrently with its widespread adoption"; ibid., 13: "The present lectionary-based system is not improving the knowledge and understanding of the Bible among Christians."

109. Again, see Harrison, *Last Speakers*; also D. Wheeler, "Death of Languages"; and further chap. 3.

percentage of regular Christian worship, even in low-church traditions—are, analogically, primary opportunities where Christians speak (or don't speak), practice (or don't practice), hear (or don't hear), and learn (or don't learn) the language of Scripture. These are also where Christians do these things (or don't do them), or at least *can* do them, from young ages (if they were exposed to such as children) or at formative periods (via worship at its best).[110] Sermons, hymns, and lectionary thus constitute a major part of the Christian "educational curricula," even without the formal instruction that the U.S. Religious Knowledge Survey suggests is so crucial. (If such education is crucial for the very small and minimal base of knowledge tested by that survey, how much more for full linguistic fluency!) But running the last three tests after the first one reveals serious problems with this language training. The educational system is failing, not in terms of available material—the Old Testament is there, after all, at least for now (but see chaps. 4–7)—but *in terms of practice.* Indeed, the cold hard fact is that, thanks to large swaths of sermons, hymns, and liturgy, Christians are learning precisely how *not* to speak the language, practice the language, hear the language, or learn the language that is the Old Testament, whatever their age—from smallest tyke to octogenarian and everything between and beyond. The Old Testament is dying, and it seems that the Christian practices of sermon, song, and lectionary are at least partly to blame.

Additional testing is in order, especially if we are to gain some access on how best to treat the patient, if it isn't already too late. But before proceeding on these points, we need greater clarity on two fronts: First, we need to know more about the specific pathology (or pathologies) that our patient is suffering from. This is the concern of chapter 3, which focuses on linguistics so as to discuss the problem of language demise and death in greater detail.

Second, we need to know what is at stake. In the preceding discussion I noted several possible objections to my argument, but these can be focused more bluntly as follows: What difference does it make if parts of the Old Testament disappear (e.g., the psalms not represented in hymnody), or large

---

110. To be sure, the formative power of Christian worship, whether in liturgy, song, or sermon, can be (and has been) doubted. See, e.g., among many others, Hunter, "Ministry—or Magic?"; and Witten, *All Is Forgiven.* Perhaps people hear (only) what they want to hear in worship, perhaps ministers and songwriters and liturgists don't care much for (comprehensive) biblical content, and/or maybe people simply don't change in these ways via these instruments. There is, however, at least some empirical evidence to the contrary. See, inter alia, Fawcett and Linkletter, "Bible Reading and Adolescents' Attitudes," whose sample showed "a significant relationship between frequent Bible reading . . . and . . . disapproval of the use of some illicit substances and some sexual activities" (418). Many similar studies are available, but much work remains to be done; such "empirical" studies are hardly foolproof even though social-scientific.

parts (e.g., the books not reflected in the RCL) wither away, or even the whole thing dies off? Answering that question would take many tomes; the *testimonia* used as epigraphs to the present volume and what has already been said so far should, I hope, make it clear that one pays a high price indeed if one loses the Old Testament, or even just some of its constituent parts. Chapters 4–6 cast still more light on this matter, but to anticipate that material, we will see there (1) that the early church deemed the Old Testament absolutely essential to Christian faith; (2) that devastating results happen when Christians sever their connections to the Old Testament and, correlatively, the Judaism with which they share this material; (3) how Christians are incapacitated to answer severe and significant criticisms of the Old Testament (and the Bible as a whole) if they lack full fluency; and (4) how Christians are bamboozled into thinking life is mostly a zero-sum game about prosperity if they do not know what should be, but no longer is, their mother tongue.

3

On Language Growth and Change, Contact and Death

Throughout the preceding chapters, I have been employing the metaphor (or simile) that the Old Testament is (like) a language, and have been relating that idea analogically to various linguistic processes. It is now time to speak more directly and extensively about the linguistic side of this metaphor. Given my diagnosis—that the Old Testament, which is (like) a language, is dying—it will prove both illuminating and instructive to discuss the most important moments in the language life cycle, including how languages grow and change, how they atrophy, and ultimately, how they die. Although the death of a language is of special concern to my argument, the other moments in the life cycle are also crucial, and so deserve some treatment, even if that is relatively brief. In truth, each stage in a language's life cycle is a large topic, and here I cannot do justice to any one stage, much less all of them. Even so, given the importance of pidgins and creoles (and the related processes of [re]pidginization and creolization), especially for the signs of the Old Testament's morbidity that are on display in chapters 4–6, special attention is given to these topics.

Language Change and Language Contact

Like any other human artifact, languages change through time, especially via repeated and extensive use. The changes human languages experience are legion and can vary a good bit among different language groups because a large number of social, political, economic, and geographical factors (to name a few) play significant roles in linguistic change. That granted, the most basic principle of linguistic change is that languages *do* in fact change and do so *through the course of time*.[1] As a closely related second principle, it can be asserted that, while language change comes about through a number of ways or is the result of a myriad of influences, much change comes about simply through *repeated use*. Such changes can *simplify* a language, as in the dropping of case endings, plural markers, or irregular verb forms; but they can also make a language *more complex*, as when languages develop new material even as they lose other material—indeed, both processes can happen within the same language through the course of time and repeated use.[2] Languages can also *expand* by the internal development of grammatical rules or by external influence (e.g., the adoption of loanwords), even as they can *contract* in yet other ways (e.g., elimination of archaic forms or obsolete definitions).

Changes such as those mentioned above and many others have been carefully documented by linguists, especially those who work in historical and comparative linguistics. To give but one simple example of an apparently universal cause of language change, we cite the phenomenon of "lazy mouth" syndrome and its impact on phonology.[3] Complicated phones are often simplified through the course of time as people stop bothering to pronounce them correctly. For example, one can frequently hear—even find the spelling—*prolly* for the word *probably*, simply because the former is easier to say and is acceptable in informal settings, even in certain informal written contexts (say, on the internet). The most ancient of languages, by contrast, are often marked by very complicated phonologies: the most famous examples are the so-called click languages of southern Africa (Nama, Xhosa, etc.).[4] These languages are deemed the oldest still in existence because complicated phonological elements are typically dropped over time. The preservation of such in the click

---

1. For a useful overview, see Aitchison, *Language Change*.

2. Ibid., 55–130; McWhorter, *Power of Babel*, 177–215. McWhorter (*Language Interrupted*, 11) states that all grammars eventually reached "a high degree of complexity. . . . Then, short of an intervention of some kind, all grammars remained highly complex *in perpetuo*." Grammatical simplification, in this light, "suggests that there has been an interruption in the regular transformation of the grammar."

3. McWhorter, *Power of Babel*, 18–22; Aitchison, *Language Change*, 84–97. The importance of spoken language cannot be overestimated. Only about 200 of the world's 6,000 languages are written; hence language is very much a spoken phenomenon far more than it is a written one. Indeed, some claim that if written language was placed on a 24-hour clock, it would fall *after* 23:07 (i.e., 11:07 p.m.) in the "day" of human language. See, e.g., McWhorter, *What Language Is*, 145–50.

4. McWhorter, *Power of Babel*, 50–51.

languages testifies to the antiquity of that complicated phonology. Be that as it may, whatever the cause of the specific linguistic change, phonological or otherwise, the fact that languages change through the course of time through repeated use means that each language encodes a history and has a memory; thus much can be learned by studying a language's historical development, looking for traces of its past that are still remembered here and there, now and then.[5]

A third important principle of linguistic change is that languages often change through *contact with other languages*.[6] Loanwords or loan phrases are an example of such contact. Without contact with French, there would never be an English speaker who said, after a hard day of work, "Well, that's how it goes, I guess. C'est la vie." In point of fact, English is a complex mishmash of other languages, replete with borrowed words and phrases but also other aspects of grammar, morphology, and syntax.[7]

Rare indeed are languages that exist in complete isolation from all others—not in the sense that they are unrelated to other well-established language families (i.e., linguistic isolates like Basque, Burushaski, and Sumerian, among others),[8] but in the sense that their speakers have never encountered someone from another linguistic group. Moreover, even in those unusual instances when a newly discovered people group has never had contact with the "outside world," that pristine situation is immediately despoiled, to some degree at least, at the moment of first contact. Contact with other people groups means contact with their languages, and language contact often brings with it linguistic change, not only in the borrowing and replacement of specific words (e.g., note the contemporary German preference for the loanword *Telefon* rather than the earlier *Fernsprecher*) but also in terms of phonology, morphology, syntax, and so forth.[9]

The topic of linguistic change via language contact is a large one, but for reasons that will become clear momentarily, it is especially important for my diagnosis that the Old Testament is dying. So, for present purposes, despite

---

5. On the phonological level, an example of such memory from Biblical Hebrew is how the original short vowels of the so-called segholates return when these words are suffixed (e.g., *melek*, "king" > *malkî*, "my king"). This vowel is not spontaneously generated but is a trace of earlier forms when these words were monosyllabic (*qatl*, *qitl*, *qutl*), if not, at a still earlier period, bisyllabic due to case endings, as one finds in Ugaritic (nominative *qatlu*, genitive *qatli*, and accusative *qatla*). See, e.g., Joüon and Muraoka, *Grammar of Biblical Hebrew*, 1:242–43 (§88C.a*).

6. For an extensive treatment, see Matras, *Language Contact*.

7. For more on English, see McWhorter, *Our Magnificent Bastard Tongue*; and Crystal, *Cambridge Encyclopedia of the English Language*.

8. For a listing of isolates, see *CEL* 328–29.

9. Again, see Matras, *Language Contact*, passim; Aitchison, *Language Change*, passim.

the breadth of this topic, it suffices to focus on two particular examples of contact languages—pidgins and creoles—and the associated processes of pidginization (and repidginization) and creolization (and decreolization).

Pidgins and Creoles, Pidginization and Creolization

Although the etymology is debated, the term *pidgin* probably derives from Chinese *pei tsin*, "business," which is what Canton traders named the language they used to communicate with English-speaking traders from the seventeenth century to the twentieth.[10] Speaking generally, pidgins can be described as greatly abbreviated languages that facilitate the bare minimum of communication needs between people who do not share a common language but who must nevertheless interact for some reason—trade, for instance, or residence in highly traveled areas, military defeat, colonization, or the like.[11] Pidgins are, therefore, contact languages.[12] Linguists call the process by which a pidgin is created *pidginization*.

Pidgins emerge out of the interaction of two (or more) groups of people, each with their respective and native language(s) that contribute to the pidgin's construction; nevertheless, pidgin languages are typically based primarily on just one of the two languages, that of the dominant group. The dominant language is called the *superstrate* and contributes the lion's share of the material that makes up the pidgin; the language of the weaker group is called the *substrate* and contributes far less. John Holm explains this imbalance as due to the fact that "usually those with less power (speakers of *substrate* languages) are more accommodating and use words from the language of those with more power (the *superstrate*)," but, he continues, "the meaning, form, and use of these words may be influenced by the substrate languages."[13] So, while both the superstrate and substrate languages contribute to the construction of the pidgin—the former more so than the latter for sociolinguistic reasons[14]—*both* languages are changed in the process of pidginization, which creates a new

10. See Holm, *Introduction to Pidgins and Creoles*, 9, for a discussion of the etymology. Also *CEL* 336; and Hancock, "On the Origins of the Term Pidgin."

11. See *CEL* 336–41; and Holm, *Introduction to Pidgins and Creoles*, 71–105, for extensive, but still partial, listings of the world's many pidgin languages. A few are discussed in further detail below. For discussion of contact between languages, pidginization, and related issues in ancient languages, see, among others, Vita, *Canaanite Scribes*, 1–3.

12. Matras, *Language Contact*, 275–88.

13. Holm, *Introduction to Pidgins and Creoles*, 5.

14. McWhorter, *Power of Babel*, 134–35: "Usually . . . sociohistorical realities are such that one group has its foot on the other's neck, and the subordinate group is compelled to make do as best it can with the dominant group's language, rather than the two groups mutually

language, the pidgin, out of two. Most important and pronounced above all of these changes is the fact that the superstrate and substrate languages undergo profound simplification—the former perhaps less so than the latter, since it predominates—to produce, as it were, a least common denominator that facilitates communication between the two language groups. The result is

> a make-shift language to serve [the speakers'] needs, simplifying by dropping unnecessary complications such as inflections (e.g., *two knives* becomes *two knife*) and reducing the number of different words they use, but compensating by extending their meanings or using circumlocutions. By definition the resulting pidgin is restricted to a very limited domain such as trade, and it is no one's native language.[15]

In addition to the Chinese-English *Pei tsin*, well-known pidgins include the Melanesian-English Tok Pisin ("talk pidgin") used in Papua New Guinea (PNG), and the Norwegian-Russian pidgin called Russenorsk, now extinct, which was used by Norwegian and Russian traders in the 1700s and 1800s. In terms of its lexicon, Russenorsk employed some three hundred words taken from Norwegian and Russian, a massive and stunning reduction of two rich and complicated languages. But the reduction was not restricted to vocabulary: Russenorsk lacked articles, gender, markers for tense and case, and verb conjugations. It had but one preposition (*po*) that was forced to do the work of all others.

While Russenorsk may seem to be an extreme example (though in truth it isn't), it is no exaggeration; neither is it intended pejoratively to assert that, in the main, pidgins lack the nuanced vocabulary and complex grammar needed to render the most sophisticated speech, thinking, and writing.[16] This is not to say that those who use pidgins are themselves incapable of the highest levels of speech, thinking, and/or writing—both superstrate and substrate languages are no doubt capable of such; it is simply the case that the contact language itself, the pidgin, is not. It would be impossible, for example, to execute the novels of the great Russian writer Fyodor Dostoyevsky in Russenorsk! That granted, it should be emphasized that pidgins are not simply lists of random words strung together: they have at least some loose rules (e.g., the use of *po*

---

accommodating to each other's. As such, in most pidgins, the bulk of the vocabulary is drawn from the dominant group's language."

15. Holm, *Introduction to Pidgins and Creoles*, 5.

16. See McWhorter, *Power of Babel*, 132–33. In many cases, pidgins exist solely in oral forms, and spoken language, by definition, tends to be simplified compared to written language (see ibid., 88–92, 235–51).

in Russenorsk). Even more to this latter point, that pidgins are real languages is demonstrated by the fact that pidgins can *grow*.

In their most "pure" form, pidgins are constructed for particular communicative needs, thus have short life spans, and are specifically focused. Long-lasting pidgins like Tok Pisin in PNG are the exception, not the rule. Such exceptions are called "expanded pidgins" because they have outgrown their original, more reduced forms and have extended beyond their original purposes. Pidgins become expanded pidgins when they are used among speakers of different substrate languages over an extended period of time.[17] When this happens, "the simpler structure of the earlier pidgin is elaborated to meet more demanding communicative needs."[18] This is precisely what has happened with Tok Pisin, which is spoken by many different people groups in PNG, where it functions as the language used in mass media and government contexts.[19]

It is not difficult to see that, with enough time, enough speakers, and enough expansion, a pidgin could become the dominant, if not only, language of a people group or area. In such a scenario, the language in question would no longer be called a *pidgin*, not even an *expanded pidgin*, but something else altogether, something new and different: a *creole*.[20] The process by which a pidgin becomes a creole is called *depidginization* or, more properly, *creolization*.[21]

In certain cases, then—but perhaps above all others when a pidgin survives long enough so that children born to pidgin-speaking parents acquire the pidgin as their first or primary language—pidgins can become creoles. A creole language

> has a jargon or a pidgin in its ancestry; it is spoken natively by an entire speech community, often one whose ancestors were displaced geographically so that

17. Holm, *Introduction to Pidgins and Creoles*, 5.
18. Ibid.
19. For more on Tok Pisin, see ibid., 96–101; *CEL* 336–37. McWhorter, *Power of Babel*, 140–46, prefers to call Tok Pisin a creole, rather than a pidgin or expanded pidgin, and not without good reason. See further below.
20. See Holm (*Introduction to Pidgins and Creoles*, 9) for the etymology of *creole*: the term goes back to Latin *creāre*, "to create," which became Portuguese *criar*, "to raise (a child)," with the past participle *criado* meaning "raised; a servant born into a household," and then *crioulu*, meaning an African slave born in the New World, in Brazilian use. This term was used of Europeans born in the New World and then of the customs and speech of Africans and Europeans who were born in the New World.
21. Or *nativization*, a term that highlights how, via the process, the pidgin acquires native speakers (see further below). Creolization/nativization is the exact opposite of pidginization: the former is a process of expansion and the latter one of reduction (ibid., 7).

their ties with their original language and sociocultural identity were partly broken. Such social conditions were often the result of slavery.[22]

Since the preexisting pidgin now enjoys native speakers, it quickly takes on a life of its own and behaves like any other language, growing and changing as other languages do. Hence linguists describe this process as one in which the pidgin is depidginized and becomes an altogether new language, a creole, created via creolization. The creole develops new phonological rules (e.g., assimilation) and adds or creates (often via combination) more vocabulary items, because, unlike the earlier pidgin, it is now being used for all aspects of life, not just the specific and limited task the pidgin was originally created for (e.g., lumber trading).

Once they've been created, creoles—no less than any other language—participate fully in the language life cycle, growing, changing, and developing in terms of grammar, syntax, and lexicon,[23] with one exception: since they are new, freshly created languages, creoles are marked by extreme grammatical regularity vis-à-vis their predecessors and other, older languages. In many ways, a creole is a language starting over again,[24] almost as if (but not really) by scratch, and why would one start over with a host of difficult, irregular verb forms?[25]

Eventually, then, a creole will be indistinguishable from any other "full" language. Although they developed from pidgins, creoles are no longer reduced, abbreviated languages suitable only for momentary purposes. They are, rather, *full* languages, indeed *new* languages that are just beginning, and which, because of that, provide important information about what languages are like in their infancy and how they grow and develop.[26] In any event, the only

22. Ibid., 6. In what follows, I leave aside explicit mention of jargons since they are somewhat different from pidgins, though linguists often treat them as equally important progenitors of creoles. I return to jargons briefly in chap. 8.

23. Although debate will no doubt continue, acquisition of native speakers and increased grammatical complexity are the primary ways that a creole differs from an expanded pidgin (Holm, *Introduction to Pidgins and Creoles*, 7–8). Even so, many linguists prefer to speak of a creole continuum or, even more precisely, creole continua. See, e.g., McWhorter, *Power of Babel*, 159–67; McWhorter, *Language Interrupted*, 253–54. For the complexity of creoles, see, inter alia, McWhorter, "Linguistics from the Left," 187.

24. I am dependent on McWhorter for the language of "starting over," specifically his course "The Story of Human Language" for the Teaching Company mentioned in the preface. See also the next two notes.

25. The regularity that marks creoles can be illustrated more minutely whenever one creates a new verb like "to Google: to use the search engine Google on the internet." Thus "I Googled, I Google, and I will Google" is in a fully regular pattern, rather than "I Geegled, I Google, and I will Gogogle." The latter type of irregularity marks many old languages or, at least, old forms of a language.

26. McWhorter, *Power of Babel*, 138: "Because as a rule any language spoken on earth traces back to unbroken development from a former full language (or languages), when we see

way to discern the difference between a creole and any other "full" language is to know the history of the creole's development—namely, that somewhere in its past, there was a linguistic ancestor that was a pidgin.[27]

Even if a native creole speaker lacks such knowledge of their language, it remains the case that, both historically and descriptively, the creole in question is quite distinguishable and at a significant remove from the original languages that led to the construction of the pidgin, which was, in turn, the creole's most immediate ancestor.[28] Diagram 1 represents these processes of pidginization and creolization, demonstrating that the creole is at least two steps removed from the original languages that lie in its past. In truth, since pidginization is a process of massive reduction, and since creolization is a process of equally significant expansion by means of many new developments that are not necessarily based on either the pidgin or its two parents, the creole is actually very different from its predecessors, even though it often contains recognizable or recoverable traces of them, especially of the superstrate. The existence of such historical traces, or linguistic memories, is exactly what we would expect of a creole, since it is a new and full language and all languages preserve traces and memories of their pasts, largely because every language developed from one or more others.

Many pidgins and creoles are documented among the world's languages, making clear that pidginization and creolization are not infrequent happenings but, instead, part and parcel of language growth and change, especially via language contact. Pidgins and creoles occur in various contexts (not just Louisiana), among various languages (not just French and English), and for various reasons, though most of the latter involve a limited range of historical, political, and economic realities (esp. trade, colonialism, and slavery).

Pidginization and creolization are no doubt intrinsically important and interesting, linguistically speaking, but both are also crucial for understanding the death of the Old Testament when that is seen via the linguistic analogy that the Old Testament is (like) a language. Pidginization is crucial because, when languages die, they tend to revert to pidgin-like forms in a process known

---

pidgins transformed into creoles we come closest to witnessing the birth of a human language." See further, ibid., 137–51.

27. Hock, *Principles of Historical Linguistics*, 527; Holm, *Introduction to Pidgins and Creoles*, 6; but see 8, on early or abrupt creolization. Also see the next note.

28. See McWhorter, *Defining Creole*, for an extended discussion of whether the category "creole" is synchronic and not just sociohistorical. If it is, then there are ways to distinguish creole languages from other "full" languages that have not descended from pidginized ancestors. Note also McWhorter's earlier treatments: *Towards a New Model of Creole Genesis*; McWhorter, *Missing Spanish Creoles*.

Diagram 1

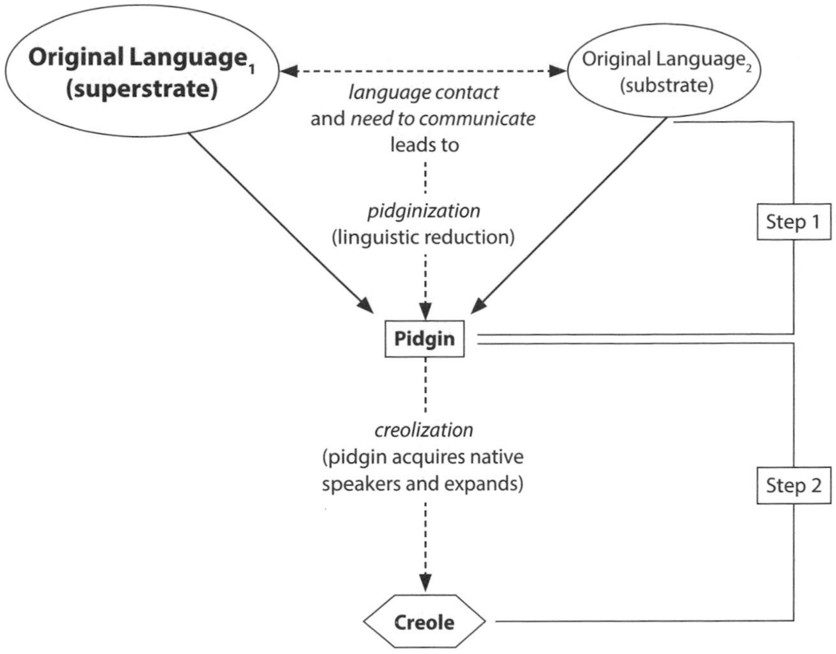

as *repidginization.*[29] When people first learn languages, they tend to learn pidgin-like versions. Further, while pidgins are usually birthed for specific reasons and thus have short life spans, it isn't necessarily the case that every pidgin must die. Pidgins can expand, depidginize, and ultimately, creolize, whereby some pidgin languages survive and even thrive, though in new and distinct forms as creoles. In chapters 4–7 I will return to these various aspects of pidgins and creoles, pidginization and creolization, and their analogical application to the Old Testament. First, however, some discussion of the end of the language life cycle is in order.

Language Death

Linguists posit that there may have been as many as 150,000 languages throughout the course of human history; today there are about 6,000, give or take a few.[30]

29. See further below.
30. See *CEL* 287, who lists the 150,000 number as a plausible middle-of-the-road figure, with conservative estimates being around 30,000, and more radical ones over 500,000.

This significant attrition indicates that it is by no means uncommon for languages to die.[31] That granted, the crisis of language extinction seems to have reached new levels in recent years, if only due to the fact that, with fewer languages, each loss becomes more costly, or perhaps because the problem of endangered languages has finally reached general public awareness.[32] Whatever the case, most linguists believe that languages are dying at an alarming rate, a minimum of one every two weeks, and it is even possible that (in an accelerated scenario), by the year 2100, only 600 of the 6,000 languages currently in existence will survive.[33] That represents a net loss of 90 percent of the world's languages in less than a century—a stunning and unprecedented tragedy.

Not unrelated to the fact of language death is, for lack of a better term, *language concentration*. Some 96 percent of the world's population speaks one or more of the top twenty most spoken languages: Chinese, English, Spanish, Hindi, Arabic, Bengali, Russian, Portuguese, Japanese, German, French, Punjabi, Javanese, Bihari, Italian, Korean, Telugu, Tamil, Marathi, and Vietnamese.[34] A corollary to the growth and success of these large-scale languages is the failure and death of the smaller ones.

The loss of any language is not simply a loss to professional linguists (data, for instance, for some general theory of grammar); it is far more a profound cultural loss since languages abound in information about the world, history, human culture, even medicine and science.[35] Great effort is now being exerted in preserving if not reviving dying languages, or at the very least documenting them before they become fully extinct. In chapter 7 I will return to attempts at language preservation and the documentation of dying languages; in what follows here I offer further remarks on *how* languages die, *why* they die, and *what is lost* when they do so.

31. See McWhorter, *Power of Babel*, 253–62; Dorian, *Investigating Obsolescence*. If human language developed as long as 30,000 years ago (see *CEL* 290–93), the reduction from 150,000 to 6,000 languages would represent an average loss of 4.8 languages per year. Language death does not happen at a uniform pace, however.

32. See, e.g., Harrison, *Last Speakers*; D. Wheeler, "Death of Languages"; McWhorter, *Power of Babel*, 260–61, 280.

33. For both statistics, see Crystal, *Language Death*, 11–19.

34. McWhorter, *Power of Babel*, 257; cf. *CEL* 288–89.

35. See Harrison, *Last Speakers*, passim; Crystal, *Language Death*, 27–67; McWhorter, *Power of Babel*, 281–86; Hagège, *Death and Life of Languages*, 3–10. More briefly, see D. Wheeler, "Death of Languages," on linguists who, remaining in descriptive modes, refuse to say that language death is tragic or bad: it isn't necessarily bad, it just is. McWhorter observes scholarly "advocacy as well as curiosity" in the study of creoles (*Defining Creole*, 4), which is proof that linguistics, no less than other fields, often traffics in the prescriptive even when it prefers or protests not to do so.

How Languages Die

The answer to the question of how languages die would seem rather simple: they die when the last living speaker of the language dies, but in truth the death in question can be a long and protracted process. Moreover, as with any other death, especially one that is drawn out over the course of many years, the precise moment of death is preceded by many other moribund moments along the way. In terms of language death, the most telling and deadly of these—indeed, the moment that eventually produces the situation where only one speaker survives—is when a generation of speakers stops communicating its language on a regular basis to its children. At this crucial juncture the language is no longer a productive, spoken language. Any language learning that is done after this moment—whether by the second, third, or fourth generation (if the language lasts that long)—is minimal at best and seriously incomplete. The same judgment obviously holds true for any language learning that is done after the final speaker dies: there will be pockets of the language, some quite large, that will simply be irrecoverable without a living speaker.

As a language dies, it goes through a process of *repidginization*. It reverts to a pidgin-like form as it undergoes massive simplification and reduction, losing complicated inflections, huge swaths of vocabulary, and virtually all other nuances that mark a vibrant language as a full-orbed, living, and productive tongue, and not just a pidgin.[36] Once the language in question is not communicated extensively and regularly—that is, *productively*—to the next generation, the result is that any language learning done by that generation (and all subsequent ones) is not really "learning the language" at all, but at best learning only bits and pieces, maybe just an isolated word or phrase here and there—in other words, a (re)pidginized form of the language.[37] But, in contrast to the pidgins that are born through language contact, repidginized languages are on their way to death. Since they are no longer productive lan-

36. See, e.g., McWhorter (*Power of Babel*, 262) for how the once vibrant Native American language Cayuga, by atrophy, retained words for *leg*, *foot*, and *eye* but lost its words for *thigh*, *ankle*, and *cheek*. Similarly, the full language once had a word for "enter," but it had been forgotten and was no longer used, the verb "go" taking its place. So, instead of "Come into the house," the reduced Cayuga used "Go into the house." "The nuance of where the speaker was in relation to the house—determining whether one would say from the porch *Come in* or say from a hill up yonder *Go in*—was left to context" (emphasis original). It *had* to be left to context since the atrophied form of the language had lost that nuance.

37. Hagège (*Death and Life of Languages*, 97–98) rightly notes that a dying language is not exactly the same as a pidgin. The destruction of the former is far more random than the latter: so, e.g., "underusers [of a dying language] often retain elements that have no function or clear meaning, and that are residue, surviving amid the decay of the language. This phenomenon has not been noted in forms of pidgin, where every element responds to a specific function."

guages, they will not be spoken to subsequent generations, because they *cannot* be spoken: there is no longer anyone left with sufficient facility to generate sentences.[38] At most, then, a few stock phrases or lexical items will be passed on to the third generation and beyond: speakers of those generations might be able to identify themselves and their names in the language or ask a simple question or two (probably by rote memorization), perhaps be able to utter a few random words, but they will be unable to carry on a conversation (active knowledge of the language) or understand much of anything else (passive knowledge). The telltale sign in language morbidity, then, is when only the elderly speak a language, but no middle-aged persons of childbearing years regularly employ it or teach it to their children. At that point the language is severely endangered and is in threat of total extinction. Much hangs, then, on the children. In the words of David Wheeler, child speakers are "an essential factor in any language's survival."[39]

Why Languages Die

The question of why languages die also seems to have a fairly straightforward answer: they die because no one speaks them. But why a language should want for speakers is a more complicated question, admitting of several responses. All of the speakers might have been killed in war, for instance. More often than not, however, the situation is not the result of a military defeat; neither does it depend on total annihilation of the speaking population. Instead, the "defeat" (or linguistic end) is due to sociopolitical and socioeconomic reasons: a less powerful group adopts a more powerful group's language—again, for a whole host of reasons. The processes of pidginization and creolization, as described above, can take place in such a scenario, via language contact, but that need not be the case. The subordinate group might just abandon their native tongue altogether and switch to the dominant language. If so, the first generation would obviously retain knowledge of their original language, but it would be lost almost immediately and in toto by all others. Usually language death isn't quite so abrupt, though once a language is not spoken by children, it can die as quickly as one generation, perhaps about twenty years.[40]

38. This is unlike true pidgins, which are in use among groups for particular purposes and thus spoken and productive, some on their way to expansion if not creolization. See above and cf. Hagège, *Death and Life of Languages*, 97–98.

39. Wheeler, "Death of Languages," 2; cf. Hagège, *Death and Life of Languages*, 79: "in most known cases, the absence of young speakers can be considered a gloomy prognosis for the survival of the language."

40. CEL 286; Hock, *Principles of Historical Linguistics*, 530; cf. Hagège, *Death and Life of Languages*, 92–93.

Again, why a language would lack for young learners is a complicated question. Second and third generations do not speak their ancestors' language for a host of complex political-cultural and socioeconomic reasons. Younger generations might feel ashamed of their parents' language: it might seem backwater or somehow less official, especially if it is exclusively oral and lacks a written form.[41] In today's world, much of the dynamic of language death is caught up in larger economic processes, including that of urbanization, globalization, and so on. Indeed, these latter factors lie behind the phenomenon of language concentration, mentioned above, which in turn relates directly to the death of smaller languages.[42] John McWhorter puts it directly and poignantly: many next-generation individuals do not want to continue with the old language, because it proves to be "a lesser option than the world of tall buildings," ultimately "incompatible with the upward mobility they seek."[43]

What Is Lost When Languages Die

Every language "has a dual character: it is both a means of communication and a carrier of culture."[44] When a language dies, a great deal is thus lost—and on more than one level. Languages are repositories of life: "They . . . contain our history."[45] "The stakes are not low," writes Claude Hagège. "It is the cultures built by human societies that are in danger of being lost forever" whenever a language dies.[46]

To begin with, then, large amounts of raw information are lost when a nguage perishes. Among a virtually endless list of things, this information ;ht concern, say, the medicinal qualities of vegetation in a region. Those medicinal qualities will persist in the plants, of course, but without native speakers to direct others to the right plants for the right reasons and at the right times, it would be an incredibly costly and time-consuming process of trial and error to determine such things, even if one has access to the latest testing facilities.

In many cases the information contained by a language encodes significant cultural aspects of its speakers (and vice versa). K. David Harrison describes Tuvan, a language spoken in Siberia that encodes an extensive "landscape awareness" in its verbs of motion:

41. See McWhorter, *Power of Babel*, 271; cf. Crystal, *Language Death*, 138–41; and note 3 above.
42. Cf., inter alia, McCrum, *Globish*; Hagège, *Death and Life of Languages*, 106–68.
43. McWhorter, *Power of Babel*, 271; cf. Aitchison, *Language Change*, 235–36.
44. Ngũgĩ wa Thiong'o, *Decolonising the Mind*, 13.
45. Hagège, *Death and Life of Languages*, 7.
46. Ibid., 74.

It turned out that learning to say "go" in Tuvan is much more complex than I'd imagined. It requires not only an internal compass but also an acute awareness of the local landscape, even parts of it that may not be visible. . . . I was amazed to find that my hosts always seemed to know the exact locations of migrating friends and relatives many miles distant. . . . People would answer me with absolute confidence anytime I inquired as to the location or migration date of almost any member of the community.[47]

This impressive ability on the part of the Tuvans is made still more amazing by how their verbs of motion work:

> Tuvans live in a land where level spaces are unusual. Nearly every patch of ground slopes in one direction or another. This provides a framework for orientation—the directions of watersheds and river currents. Though Tuvan does have a general word for go, it is less often used. Most of the time, Tuvans use, as appropriate, verbs meaning "go upstream" (còkta), "go downstream" (bàt), or "go crossstream" (kes). You'd rarely hear, "I'm going to Mugur-Aksy" (the nearest town to the Mongush family camp), but rather "I'm upstreaming [or downstreaming] to Mugur-Aksy." Being a visitor rather than a lifelong resident, I was clueless as to what rivers were nearby and in which directions they flowed, so I could never confidently select the correct "go" verb. The Mongushes, on the other hand, could not explain to me the invisible orientation framework that was all around them and underfoot. No one ever said to me, "To say 'go,' you must locate the nearest river, ascertain its direction of flow, then locate your path relative to the current." They simply knew all this information without knowing that they did.[48]

Things are even more complex since Tuvan speakers can refer to different rivers that flow in different directions! Competent communication thus depends in no small degree on intimate knowledge of the local landscape and all its rivers and streams.

Tuvan is not alone in thus encoding local knowledge within language, even in verbs of motion. The larger point here, however, is not how various languages orient movement from a speaker's perspective, but how all such encoded knowledge is immediately lost when a language dies. Dying with that knowledge are a particular culture's ways of viewing, seeing, and living in the world. In the case of Tuvan, an unparalleled knowledge of the geography of the region would be lost if it were to perish.

This type of information loss comes at a high price: beyond the things already mentioned, the loss of information means a loss of problem-solving

---

47. Harrison, *Last Speakers*, 49.
48. Ibid., 50–51.

ability—whether that concerns the medicinal qualities of certain plants or navigation of the local countryside. In the Old Testament, the story of the Tower of Babel (Gen. 11:1–9), while ultimately about the multiplication of languages, shows that when one (common) language is lost, information processing and problem solving shut down . . . definitively.

The Babel story also touches on another problem of language death: when a language starts to die, specifically when it begins to repidginize, ease of communication and communication efficacy are impeded simply because the full language is no longer known or fully operative. Imagine for a moment that "mechanic-ese" was a language (and it is certainly a kind of trade jargon) that was dying out and repidginizing in the process. Next, imagine that the word "carburetor" and several other technical terms relating thereto were no longer known, not having been transmitted to the current generation of speakers. Imagine, finally, how complicated it would be for a mechanic to communicate to an assistant (or a customer) what was wrong with a vehicle, what needed to be fixed, and so forth. This information could be eventually communicated through circumlocutions of various sorts, long descriptions, pointing and gesturing, but things would be a whole lot simpler and quicker if the mechanic could simply say, "The carburetor needs fixing," and if the assistant (or customer) immediately understood what he was talking about. Barring effective and efficient communication, the broken carburetor may not get fixed at all or (equally bad) fixed incorrectly—all because of the dying of language.

Could the mechanic simply make up a new word for the carburetor? Certainly. It doesn't matter what the carburetor is called, but the likelihood that the mechanic would create a new word, should the old one be lost, is simply proof of the point that effective and efficient communication is facilitated by speakers knowing the (same) language and that, should pieces or the entirety of a language die, serious problems result. The fact that carburetors are now things of the past, having been replaced by fuel injectors, is equally germane: if enough time passes and this portion of "mechanic-ese" dies out, there may be no one left who knows what a carburetor does, how it works, or how to fix it. And this is a rather simpleminded example about one straightforward word. Imagine if the "word" that is lost is not so straightforward but a complex metaphor, like the connection of anger and patience to the nose in Biblical Hebrew (see chap. 1), or, to return to Tuvan, how verbs of motion relate to the surrounding countryside.[49]

49. I am grateful to Ryan P. Bonfiglio for discussions on these points and what follows in this section.

If we come back to the linguistic analogy of the Old Testament as (like) a language, it is clear that the matter is obviously not one of medicinal qualities of plant life, or of motion verbs and direction, or of fixing mechanical parts. Even so, when "the Bible is no longer venerated, a massive religious resource has been lost."[50] That massive religious resource encodes a massive amount of (religious) cultural information, as does any language. And so, should that information be lost, it would lead directly to an incapacity for problem solving—a point that is on display in the signs of morbidity discussed in chapters 4–6. Or, as another example, consider the process of repidginization, which leads to a loss of nuance and efficiency in talking about Scripture. Sure, people can still talk about Scripture with a reduced linguistic inventory, but it will be significantly harder, it will take far longer, and the likelihood of misunderstanding is greatly increased.[51] Finally, as in the case of any language death, if the Old Testament dies, it would mean the loss of a particular (religious) culture's ways of viewing, seeing, and living in the world (cf. chap. 1).

Three citations demonstrate what is riding on the death of scriptural language. The first is from Karl Barth's *Dogmatics in Outline*; it is one of the *testimonia* of the present book (see also chap. 1). Barth writes that biblical language is essential for the proper and precise expression of key aspects of Christian faith, many of which "can be uttered directly in this language alone." He continues:

> One thing is certain, that where the Christian Church does not venture to confess in its own language, it usually does not confess at all. Then it becomes the fellowship of the quiet, whereby it is much to be hoped that it does not become a community of dumb dogs.[52]

If Barth is right—and such confession is often, in his terms, "bitterly necessary" but only possible in the language of Scripture[53]—then the loss of that language would mean no confession at all, "the fellowship of the quiet," and finally, "a community of dumb dogs." The stakes, in Barth's time, were high, with much riding on confessing (or not). He knew what it meant to confess (or not) in Nazi Germany (see chap. 5). To not confess, in the language of Scripture,

---

50. R. Morgan with J. Barton, *Biblical Interpretation*, 60.
51. Cf. Rutledge, foreword to Miller, *Stewards of the Mysteries of God*, xi: "The problem remains . . . that without total and continual immersion in 'the strange new world of the Bible,' the preacher will only be able to tell stories from his or her personal human perspective, relating them almost incidentally to the readings for the day—thereby failing to transmit the world-overturning, *kosmos*-re-creating nature of the Voice of God."
52. Barth, *Dogmatics in Outline*, 31.
53. Ibid.

was equivalent to the death of the church's way of life—its ways of viewing, seeing, and living in the world—which is to say, it was the death of the gospel.[54]

Second, Robert W. Jenson, in his *Systematic Theology*, has pithily captured the varied understanding(s) of the atonement in Scripture in one paragraph:

> Christ's death was our "ransom" from sin; it was a sacrifice, more explicitly of Passover or to seal covenant or for atonement; Christ "bore our sins," somehow instead of us; the death was a victory over the powers that maintain the wall of alienation. As with central trinitarian and christological matters, none of this becomes a problem requiring theoretical resolution *until the mission moves into a world whose discourse is not shaped by the Scriptures.*[55]

Jenson's concern is the meaning(s) of Christ's death, specifically the various theories of atonement that have been offered in Christian theology across the centuries. What Jenson observes is that several different perspectives on the atonement are found in Scripture, where they coexist happily, inform one another mutually, and, taken together, are greater than the sum of their individual parts. This linguistic complexity is not a problem for the native speakers of Scripture, but it becomes problematic exactly when that scriptural language encounters (which is to say, comes into linguistic contact with) another language that operates with a fundamentally different grammar—one not shaped by Scripture. Suddenly there are communication problems, ones that require "theoretical resolution" of whatever sort—typically a reduction by means of favoring one or another aspect of the atonement to the neglect (functional death) of all others. If the language of Scripture dies in this moment of language contact, or somehow becomes pidginized in the process (whether as superstrate or substrate need not concern us right now), the loss is profound: a great host of understandings, metaphors, and meanings of the central event in Christian faith will be lost, presumably forever. Large swaths of the vocabulary would suddenly become unintelligible, such as the entire book of Hebrews and its dependence on Leviticus or, more specifically, 2 Cor. 5:21: "God caused the one who didn't know sin to be sin for our sake so that through him we could become the righteousness of God" (CEB). What would such books and verses mean without an understanding of the larger linguistic system?

---

54. Inspired by Barth's verbiage, Eller, in his somewhat clever but equally odd little book *Language of Canaan* (48), captures this point: "Unless we first go to the Bible for some language training, there is no chance of the gospel's being truly spoken or heard among us." See chaps. 4–6 for more on this general point.

55. Jenson, *Systematic Theology*, 1:185, emphasis added.

To be sure, the significance of Christ's death, the importance of the cross, an understanding(s) of the atonement—all these would still be possible and communicable without the full range of images and metaphors Jenson catalogues, but without the full language of Scripture everything is considerably thinned down, as if a language speaker woke up and could suddenly use only present tense verbs, having lost all other tenses. The person could continue speaking, but that language would never again be the same. On this point, it is sobering to realize that the "other world" (or language) that Jenson speaks of—the one not shaped by Scripture—is now our world. Worse still, that other world is now the church itself, if my diagnosis that the Old Testament is dying is accurate.

Finally, Luis Alonso Schökel has conducted an intriguing thought experiment:

> Let us imagine these two possibilities: A community of monks knows all the Psalms by heart and recites them every day; then during a persecution, they are deprived of any written exemplar of the Psalter. A Christian has a lovely bound copy of the Psalms in a deluxe edition, but he never reads it. In the first instance, the inspired words are not lost; in the second, they never existed.[56]

This passage is not exactly about language death proper, but it is nevertheless applicable to the linguistic analogy and the death of the Old Testament. In Alonso Schökel's scenario, it is precisely the generative power of a living language—knowing it "by heart," using it "every day"—that secures its survival (cf. chap. 2). The never-opened book, on the other hand, is effectively already dead. It is revealing that the most frequently encountered icon of the Bible is, in fact, that of a closed black leather-bound book.[57] That closed book, like a closed casket, may symbolize the death of the language of Scripture, with all that means for its raw information, for its encoded cultural knowledge, for the ability to problem-solve by means of it, and for the capacity to communicate effectively and efficiently while using it.

Conclusion

Although much more could be said about the topics touched on above, this chapter may already include more from linguistics than the reader cares for! Yet it should be clear, especially from the immediately preceding paragraphs, that the specific items I have focused on here have direct bearing on the language of

56. Schökel, *Inspired Word*, 75.
57. See Beal, *Rise and Fall of the Bible*.

the Old Testament—or better, the *languages* (plural) of the Old Testament. We might begin with the observation that the Old Testament is itself bilingual, including both Hebrew and Aramaic. Moreover, scholars have detected different dialects within Biblical Hebrew,[58] including, perhaps, differences between the written Hebrew of the Bible and the Hebrew apparently spoken on the ground, with some scholars going so far as to argue that Biblical Hebrew is a made-up language—something like Esperanto.[59] While that is certainly going too far, it is nevertheless clear that the Hebrew language has a history and that some of that history is already reflected in the Hebrew of the Old Testament.[60] Hebrew has *changed* such that, regardless of ongoing debates about chronology or dialectology, most scholars agree that the language of something like Exodus 15 is quite different from that of Ecclesiastes.

Hebrew also *changed via contact* with other languages. Biblical Hebrew knows of Akkadian loanwords, Aramaic loanwords, Persian loanwords, and Greek loanwords.[61] Beyond loanwords, Aramaic has left its trace on Biblical Hebrew in several ways, and not solely in those parts of Genesis, Jeremiah, Daniel, and Ezra that are composed in Aramaic.[62] Biblical Hebrew, in turn, has influenced other biblical languages like Biblical Aramaic,[63] or via substrate interference, the Greek of certain books of the Septuagint and its revisions (e.g., the translation of Ecclesiastes)[64] as well as certain passages in the New Testament (perhaps most famously in the infancy narrative in Luke).[65] Or, to jump to the modern period, mention could be made of the role various pidgins or creoles have played in Bible translation,[66] or, even further afield, the way knowledge of Biblical Hebrew (though often in a pidgin-like form) played a role

58. See, e.g., Rendsburg, *Diglossia in Ancient Hebrew*; Kutscher, *History of the Hebrew Language*, 45–55, 70; see also chap. 1 and the works cited there.

59. See North, "Could Hebrew Have Been a Cultic Esperanto?," which ultimately refutes this "artificial" position.

60. See, e.g., Sáenz-Badillos, *History of the Hebrew Language*; Waldman, *Recent Study of Hebrew*; W. Chomsky, *Hebrew*; and other works cited in chap. 1.

61. See, e.g., Sáenz-Badillos, *History of the Hebrew Language*, 75, 115, 146; Waldman, *Recent Study of Hebrew*, 57–61; Mankowski, *Akkadian Loanwords in Biblical Hebrew*; and M. Wagner, *Die lexikalischen und grammatikalischen Aramaismen*.

62. See M. Wagner, *Die lexikalischen und grammatikalischen Aramaismen*; Sáenz-Badillos, *History of the Hebrew Language*, 55, 114–15; Waldman, *Recent Study of Hebrew*, 79–83; Kutscher, *History of the Hebrew Language*; Kutscher, *Linguistic Background of the Isaiah Scroll*, 23–29. Cf. Schniedewind, "Aramaic, the Death of Written Hebrew."

63. See Blake, *Resurvey of Hebrew Tense*; M. Wagner, *Die lexikalischen und grammatikalischen Aramaismen*; Fassberg and Hurvitz, *Biblical Hebrew in Its Northwest Semitic Setting*.

64. See, e.g., Seow, *Ecclesiastes*, 6–9.

65. See, e.g., Fitzmyer, *Gospel according to Luke*, 1:114–27.

66. E.g., Winedt, "Case Study in Creole Bible Translation"; Wycliffe Bible Translators, *Da Jesus Book*; Smit, "On Translation and Transformation."

in early America, including the selection of many place names, the adoption of Hebrew loanwords and phrases, and so forth.[67] Then, too, there is the role of Biblical Hebrew in the resurrection of Modern Hebrew (see chap. 7), which in turn continues to develop through (among other things) language contact.[68]

Although all of that is quite interesting and not altogether off the subject, it is not why I've spent time presenting the linguistic material of this chapter. Instead, the primary point is that these insights from linguistics are pertinent to the Old Testament when it is understood analogically as (like) a language. While this chapter has focused on the linguistic side of the analogy in order to flesh it out further, the ramifications of the linguistic insights should be obvious not only for the Old Testament specifically but also for the entire Bible more generally. Indeed, I have not hesitated to make the connections explicit in the preceding pages. Even so, for the sake of clarity, the most important points may be summarized as follows:

1. If the Old Testament is (like) a language, then, like any language, it can be learned and spoken, or, conversely, can be forgotten and die.

2. As languages near death, the only fluent speakers left are the elderly. At this point the dying language reverts to a pidgin-like form since the younger, nonfluent people who know anything of the endangered language know precious little of it, having picked up only bits and pieces, and/or have forgotten the rest.[69] In terms of the Old Testament, this scenario helps to explain not only why so many Christians know so little of it in the first place (because it is an endangered language), but also why they typically "mispronounce" the few parts that they do know, whether those parts are especially bright and happy or particularly dark and brutal. It also explains why so many Christians cannot "carry on a conversation" by using the language of the Old Testament. Their language facility is no longer active; at best it is passive, and often far less than that. At most they may know only a few words of "Old Testament"; the capacity to generate new and accurate sentences is impossible once those fluent in the language are no longer around (or once the next generation is unwilling to learn).

3. Pidgins can become creoles, so a language that is pidginized (or repidginizing) could reverse direction and become creolized instead, whereby

---

67. See Katsh, *Biblical Heritage of American Democracy*.

68. See, e.g., Zuckermann, *Language Contact and Lexical Enrichment in Israeli Hebrew*.

69. Cf. Ilan Stavans's personal account of forgetting his childhood Hebrew in *Resurrecting Hebrew*; see further chap. 7 below.

the greatly reduced pidgin version of the Old Testament (or Bible) would become an entirely new language—one related to, but distinct from, the earlier pidgin, which in turn is related to, but distinct from, the Old Testament itself.[70] Whether this creole is for weal or for woe (or *about* weal or *about* woe) matters little: either exclusive option reveals itself to be deficient precisely because of its overly dichotomized all-or-nothing nature. A crucial point, regardless, is that this new language (or perhaps better, set of new languages, since one suspects a host of new creoles) contains a large number of linguistic elements, which, due to the nature of the language as a creole, were not part of its immediate biblical predecessor, which wasn't the Old Testament anyway, but only a pidginized form of the Old Testament. Still further, given the way the pidginization process works, it can be seen that the underlying pidgin, too, was based not solely on the Old Testament but on another language (or languages) as well, even though it remains to be seen what that other language is and *which* language—the creole, the pidgin, or the Old Testament—is dominant (the superstrate) and which is subordinate (the substrate). In either case, it is clear that both the Old Testament-as-pidgin and Old Testament-as-creole are far indeed from the "original language" and the "native speakers" who once spoke the Old Testament fluently.

Chapters 4–6 will have more to say about how pidgins, creoles, "mispronunciations," and the like relate to the Old Testament as (like) a language. But before turning to those subjects, it is instructive to consider the question of *cause*: why is the Old Testament dying in the first place? Or, to put it more strongly in terms familiar from the many Old Testament despisers (not all of them cultured): Isn't it the case that there are good reasons why the Old Testament is dying? "Isn't the Old Testament dying, in no small measure"—so the logic might run—"because of the many and major problems it poses to modern sensibilities, whether those sensibilities are specifically Christian, more broadly 'religious,' or even none of the above?"[71] One thinks immediately of the problems that priestly law, violence and war, the wrath and judgment of God, and the issue of cursing one's enemies (a stand-in for problematic ethics writ large) pose for contemporary minds, not to mention specifically

---

70. Cf. diagram 1 above for the way a creole is two steps removed from the original language. Note also Hagège, *Death and Life of Languages*, 57: "A recognized genetic origin is not sufficient to conclude that the ancestor and descendant are one and the same thing"—quite the opposite!
71. Cf. Gunneweg, *Understanding the Old Testament*, 3: "The hermeneutical problem of the Old Testament . . . arises from the very content of the Old Testament itself."

Christian reflection.[72] None of these four issues are easily addressed, and many more could be added to the list. In light of significant problems like these, some might say that the death of the Old Testament is well deserved and, if anything, should be accelerated if at all possible. Call it canonical-linguistic euthanasia.

Such an argument has been advanced by a number of people—both ancient and modern—who have asserted that it is high time for the Old Testament to be permanently retired. That these arguments are not insignificant is demonstrated by the fact that more than a few people have made them over the years, and many more than a few have agreed. But, when seen via our linguistic analogy, these arguments can be seen as deeply flawed, reflecting serious deficiencies in language facility if not, in fact, the presence of (re)pidginization. Indeed, the next two chapters will argue that most of these anti–Old Testament arguments are thoroughly pidginized insofar as they reflect and argue against what is at best a pidgin Old Testament. Chapter 6 will then consider creolized versions of the Old Testament (and Bible as a whole). Both the pidgins that give rise to pidginized critiques and the creolized versions are, each in their own ways, on the road to language death. This is more immediately apparent in the pidgin forms than the creoles (though they, too, depend on pidginization), if only because languages revert to pidgin-like forms as they die. And yet, while the creole versions may still be spoken and are thus productive, their drastic differences from the original language may actually make them a more insidious threat to the survival of the Old Testament than the pidginized forms.[73] They are, after all and by definition, *new* languages.

---

72. These issues (along with others) have generated a truly massive literature, a small selection of which is cited and discussed in chap. 5.

73. Here one might compare Harry G. Frankfort's argument, in his book *On Bullshit*, that bullshit is a greater threat to truth than lying because, while liars intentionally misrepresent the truth, they at least know what the truth is; they agree it exists. Bullshitters, by contrast, don't care about the truth at all but only about how good they look to others.

Signs of Morbidity

4

The New Atheism

The initial testing of the Old Testament in chapter 2 led us to fear the worst. Chapter 3 then provided further diagnostic tools drawn from the linguistic side of the analogy that I am employing here. Armed with these tools, we can return to the Old Testament proper, broadening our view to realms of discourse and arenas (in some cases, quite literally) that are larger and consequently more public, to see if these, too, manifest telltale signs of the Old Testament's morbidity. This chapter and the next two, which together comprise part 2, focus on three areas that, sadly, confirm the existence of our patient's disease and, what is still more worrisome, demonstrate just how far along it really is.

The three areas on display in part 2 are not unrelated, though they are by no means identical. There is a good bit of overlap between the first two particularly, but, in a strange way, so also with the third. When seen through the lens of chapter 3, the interrelationship among all three comes as no real surprise: the first two reflect the process of (re)pidginization, while the third manifests creolization. Pidgins and creoles are closely related in the language life cycle, after all, and both are—each in their own way—on the road to language death, at least when it comes to the original language(s) that now lies in their distant past. So, seen in this linguistic light, the overlap of the three areas I take up below comes as no significant surprise.

These three areas of discourse are the New Atheism (chap. 4), Marcionites Old and New (chap. 5), and the New Plastic Gospels of the "Happiologists" (chap. 6). Each of the three shows telltale signs of the disease, manifesting a very curious (and in truth, pathological) understanding of the Old Testament (and the Bible as a whole). My argument throughout part 2 is that the understandings of the Old Testament found in these three cases are in fact profound *mis*understandings—nothing less than proof of (re)pidginization and creolization, each in its own way a sign of morbidity, and thus proof that the Old Testament is dying in very large, very public ways. Along with my analysis of these three morbid signs, I hope to demonstrate that the full language of Scripture not only reveals the nature of the pathologies present but also points the way toward their remedy—a topic that will be discussed more extensively in chapters 7–9.

Dawkins and the New Atheists on the Old Testament

Early in his best-selling book, *The God Delusion*, the Oxford biologist Richard Dawkins throws down the gauntlet:

> The God of the Old Testament is arguably the most unpleasant character in all fiction: jealous and proud of it; a petty, unjust, unforgiving control-freak; a vindictive, bloodthirsty ethnic cleanser; a misogynistic, homophobic, racist, infanticidal, genocidal, filicidal, pestilential, megalomaniacal, sadomasochistic, capriciously malevolent bully.[1]

If, after reading this characterization, one is still uncertain how Dawkins *really* feels (!), further clarity can be gained by observing how he calls God "the Old Testament's psychotic delinquent" and "the cruel ogre of the Old Testament," and so, ultimately, "an easy target" for his criticisms.[2] And let us not forget "God's maniacal jealousy"![3] Dawkins finds the Lord "an appalling role model" and is flabbergasted at those who would "try to force the same evil monster (whether fact or fiction) on the rest of us."[4] He goes so far as to boast that the problem of evil is "childishly easy to overcome" by "simply postulat[ing] a nasty god—such as the one who stalks every page of the Old Testament."[5] He summarizes the Old Testament as an "ethical disaster area."[6]

I could go on, but Dawkins's position is already more than clear. Why does he take this view? On what does he base this vicious disdain for the Deity—all theistic notions thereof, let it be remembered, not just Christianity, since

1. Dawkins, *God Delusion*, 51.
2. Ibid., 59, 283, and 51, respectively.
3. Ibid., 279.
4. Ibid., 281–82.
5. Ibid., 135. See chap. 5 below on how the same move is anticipated in Marcion already in the second century.
6. Ibid., 284. Cf. Hitchens, *God Is Not Great*, 103, who speaks of "the horrors and cruelties and madnesses of the Old Testament."

Dawkins is an equal-opportunity offender against any and all theists—but especially for Yahweh, whom he calls the "most unlovely instantiation" of the "God Hypothesis"?[7] The answer to these questions is, of course, the Old Testament itself. It is because of the Old Testament, on the basis of it, that Dawkins promotes his vitriol. In his own words:

> To be fair, much of the Bible is not systematically evil but just plain weird, as you would expect of a chaotically cobbled-together anthology of disjointed documents, composed, revised, translated, distorted and "improved" by hundreds of anonymous authors, editors and copyists, unknown to us and mostly unknown to each other, spanning nine centuries.[8]

This comment is "fair" in the same way any backhanded compliment is fair, but it is nevertheless quite instructive to note the implicit valorization of consistency in Dawkins's remark and to observe that the facts of the Bible's historical development mixed with a smidgeon of knowledge (always a dangerous situation) about the Bible's composition history stoke the flames of his disaffection with Scripture.

But it isn't just the Bible's redaction or its nature as an anthology that bothers Dawkins; it's the content. As telling examples illustrating why the Bible should not—indeed *cannot*—be used as a source for morals or rules for living, Dawkins zeroes in on the classic "texts of terror":[9] the flood story, the story of Sodom and Gomorrah, the incest between Lot and his daughters, the story of the rape of the Levite's concubine, the endangering of Sarah by Abraham, the near sacrifice of Isaac,[10] the sacrifice of Jephthah's daughter, God's jealousy over idolatry, the holy war practice of *ḥērem* ("the ban," or utter destruction), and pentateuchal legislation regarding capital punishment.[11]

This is not the place to attempt a refutation of all the criticisms of theism, let alone Christian theism, that Dawkins and others have leveled. In fact, that is the first thing to acknowledge: Dawkins is not alone; a number of other writers—Christopher Hitchens, Sam Harris, and Daniel Dennett, to name a

---

7. Dawkins, *God Delusion*, 51–52. He defines the "God Hypothesis" as follows: "*There exists a superhuman, supernatural intelligence who deliberately designed and created the universe and everything in it, including us*" (emphasis original).

8. Ibid., 268. Cf., similarly, Hitchens, *God Is Not Great*, 104, 110 (on the NT).

9. The phrase goes back to Trible's classic work *Texts of Terror*. Dawkins himself does not refer to the texts as such, nor does he cite Trible.

10. Dawkins does not call the story "the near sacrifice of Isaac," but "the infamous tale of the sacrificing of . . . Isaac" (*God Delusion*, 274). The misnomer is telling. See further below.

11. See ibid., 269–83.

few—have written similar books and made similar points.[12] Not all of these books are composed in the same full-throttle, polemical, antagonistic style of Dawkins, and yet, for that very reason, they may be even more compelling since several are written by journalists with religious backgrounds and excellent senses of humor, who are often writing directly or exclusively about religion, the Bible, even the Old Testament itself, and their experience of reading it.[13] Again, this is not the place to review all of that work, let alone engage it in dialogue, especially because there has been no shortage of competent responses to the New Atheism (as the movement has come to be called) exemplified by Dawkins, Hitchens, and Harris.[14]

I do, however, feel the need to address what the New Atheists say about the Bible, especially the Old Testament, because that hasn't received as much attention in the literature responding to the New Atheism.[15] Why that is the case, I cannot say—perhaps because the respondents thus far have not been biblical scholars. Perhaps a respondent or two even worries that the New Atheists have scored a victory here and there, maybe even several, against the Bible—especially against the Old Testament—so there's nothing much that can be said in reply. Maybe it's a sign that the Old Testament is already dead, not worth defending any longer. Whatever the case, a response of some sort is necessary because it has become almost pro forma for every New Atheist book to include a section, if not a full chapter or two, debunking the Bible as a whole and the Old Testament in particular.[16] A response is also in order because the New Atheists' take on the Bible—and, again, the Old Testament specifically—is seen in a very different light when one views it through the lens of the linguistic analogy I am employing here. While any of the New Atheists would serve as a suitable example of my points, in what follows I focus on Dawkins, partly because I would like to pick up the gauntlet he has

12. Hitchens, *God Is Not Great*; Harris, *Letter to a Christian Nation*; Harris, *End of Faith*; Dennett, *Breaking the Spell*. Note also Boyer, *Religion Explained*.

13. See, e.g., Plotz, *Good Book*, esp. 299–305 and the afterword available only in the paperback ed. (P[ost].S[cript]., 5–11). Plotz himself is Jewish, and his book covers only the OT. Note also Auslander, *Foreskin's Lament*.

14. See esp. Eagleton, *Reason, Faith, and Revolution*; Hart, *Atheist Delusions*. Note also Haught, *God and the New Atheism*; Garrison, *New Atheist Crusaders*.

15. But see, among others, Haught, *God and the New Atheism*, esp. 31–33, 100–101; as well as Lamb, *God Behaving Badly*; Copan, *Is God a Moral Monster?*; and C. Wright, *God I Don't Understand*. Note also Moberly, *Theology of the Book of Genesis*, 57–65, who has engaged Dawkins's earlier book *River out of Eden*.

16. See, e.g., Dawkins, *God Delusion*, 268–316; Hitchens, *God Is Not Great*, 97–122. The biblical research that no doubt goes into writing such chapters, thin though it ultimately is (see below), is an example of how atheists can score so well on an instrument like the U.S. Religious Knowledge Survey (see chap. 2 above).

so forcefully thrown down, and partly because his critique serves as suitably representative of others.[17]

Answering Dawkins

We might begin with the fact that Dawkins, expert biologist that he is, is no Bible scholar. Upon reading his remarks, one is immediately struck by obvious deficiencies in his understanding of the field of biblical studies, the methods and tools of biblical criticism, and so on and so forth. To cite a few examples: he seems completely unaware of form criticism as well as specialized treatments of intertextuality, allusion, or inner-biblical exegesis, which, among other things, biblical scholars frequently employ when dealing with closely similar texts like those concerning the endangered ancestress or Sodom and Gomorrah and Judg. 19.[18] As another example, Dawkins betrays a lack of rudimentary knowledge regarding ancient Israel when he states that it is not surprising that Jephthah's daughter is the first to come out of the house after his rash vow in Judg. 11:30–31.[19] The standard architecture of the Israelite four-room house, with one entrance used by both humans and animals,[20] is precisely what makes Jephthah's vow understandable (he was expecting an animal, not his daughter, to emerge), as well as what makes that vow potentially so stupid and tragic—as confirmed by the subsequent narrative (Judg. 11:34–40).

To be fair (to borrow Dawkins's phrase), on these and other points Dawkins is (to borrow again from his terminology) "an easy target" precisely because he isn't an expert in the biblical material nor the methods of biblical criticism. And yet these points are nevertheless quite significant, not just persnickety, because I am quite confident that, if I were to weigh in on evolutionary and biological matters with a similar level of (in)expertise in Dawkins's own discipline—say, having read only bits and pieces of Darwin's *Origin of Species* a time or two but little else, and then weighing in on, for example, the silliness of this or that aspect of the latest in evolutionary theory—Dawkins would be quick to point out my lack of credentials as well as my massive ignorance on the details, on which so much depends and wherein the devil (if you believe in one) resides. Simply put, I'm not expert in Dawkins's disciplinary language.

17. Eagleton finds Dawkins and Hitchens sufficiently similar that he reduces them "for convenience to the single signifier 'Ditchkins'" (*Reason, Faith, and Revolution*, 2).

18. See Dawkins, *God Delusion*, 272–74.

19. Ibid., 276.

20. Stager, "Archaeology of the Family in Ancient Israel"; also King and Stager, *Life in Biblical Israel*, 28–35.

But the opposite is equally true. Much of Dawkins's critique falls wide of the mark and fails miserably due to simple lack of expertise.[21]

The biggest problems do not emerge from the niceties of the guild of biblical studies, however, so much as from Dawkins's general manner of reading the Bible. I do not call this reading style a "method," as I doubt that it is self-reflective enough to be categorized as such. In any event, and in a word, Dawkins reads the Bible flatly. *Very* flatly. Almost always "literally"—whatever that means[22]—in a way not unlike and indeed altogether similar to those with whom he most disagrees.[23] That is to say, Dawkins doesn't read the Bible any differently or more sophisticatedly than his opponents; he simply delights in pointing out the Bible's contradictions, or its immoral or submoral aspects, which, presumably, his interlocutors—flatfooted, literal types to a fault—are unable to account for.

Consider, for example, Dawkins's comment on Gen. 19 and Lot's offering of his daughters: "Whatever else this strange story might mean, it surely tells us something about the respect accorded to women in this intensely religious culture."[24] Well, no, not exactly. Or at least not nearly as straightforwardly as Dawkins implies. Lot is hardly a laudable character in this narrative, and the citizens of Sodom are portrayed negatively. In Gen. 18:20, God says, "The cries of injustice from Sodom and Gomorrah are countless, and their sin is very serious!" (CEB). Later in the same chapter we discover that God is willing to spare Sodom if even only ten (!) righteous people could be found therein (Gen. 18:22–33). One is hard pressed, then, to say that the conduct of either Lot or the Sodomites is something the narrator wishes to commend. And, if that conduct is not commendable with regard to their treatment of women, is it impossible to think that a different ethic, one more positive toward women, might be commended, at least implicitly, by this "intensely religious culture," if not even this disturbing story itself? Of anyone in the story, it is the divine visitors who are the most likely "role models"—the good guys, as it were—and

---

21. See Eagleton (*Reason, Faith, and Revolution*, 1–46) on how Dawkins's critique is unfair since it is predicated on the worst examples and an ungenerous reading.

22. To be clear: I can deduce what Dawkins and others *think* reading "literally" means, but I doubt very much that this is what it really does mean or should mean, which is no small point. See further below and Strawn, "Jonah and Genre." For an example of "literalism," note Dennett's remark: "The Old Testament Jehovah [*sic!*] is definitely a sort of divine man (not a woman), who sees with eyes and hears with ears—and talks and acts in real time. (God *waited* to *see* what Job would do, and *then* he *spoke* to him.)" (*Breaking the Spell*, 9, emphasis original, cf. also 206). While the Bible is certainly full of anthropomorphisms, it is also a good bit more subtle than that. See, inter alia, Sommer, *Bodies of God*.

23. Cf. Haught, *God and the New Atheism*, 30–35.

24. Dawkins, *God Delusion*, 272.

they strike the Sodomites with blindness before anything can be done to Lot or his daughters (Gen. 19:11). True, the story implies that in ancient Israel, women were denigrated and mistreated—at least by *some*, though not necessarily *good*, people and certainly not by *all* people (see Ruth 2:8–17)—and this is a significant and sad point, confirmed many times over by ancient texts and data but also by our own present-day circumstances. Dawkins is not the first modern commentator to highlight such facts; indeed, feminist interpretation drew attention to such items long ago. Even before feminism, however, the narrative qualities of stories like Gen. 19 showcased such details. By "narrative qualities" I mean to say, once more, that in no way does the narrative present the behavior of Lot or the citizens of Sodom as exemplary; nor is their behavior ever tied in the narrative (that is, by the narrator) to these characters being "intensely religious." Quite the contrary, as Gen. 18:16–33 makes clear! This is a city full of injustice and sin; you'd be lucky to find ten righteous people in it. (And the fact that the city is destroyed in Gen. 19 indicates there were less than that number.)[25] Still further, neither Lot nor the Sodomites mention God once in this story: they are hardly portrayed, then, as "intensely religious." The only characters who mention God are God's messengers, who announce the destruction of the city precisely because "the LORD has found the cries of injustice so serious" (Gen. 19:13 CEB). Even a dull reader will probably eventually understand the scene, deducing that the way the Sodomites wished to treat these guests, Lot, and/or his daughters is exactly such an example of unrighteous behavior, what the Hebrew text (Gen. 18:20) calls "outcry" (צעקה/זעקה, ṣəʿāqâ/zəʿāqâ).[26] To sum up: Dawkins's moral outrage at Gen. 19 is not entirely wrongheaded in theory, just wrongheaded about Gen. 19. His fatal faux pas is that he presents his outrage as being about this specific text; as such, his critique fails rather miserably due to poor reading.

Two other examples from Dawkins deserve mention. First, here is Dawkins's take on Gen. 22, the near sacrifice of Isaac: "By the standards of modern morality, this disgraceful story is an example simultaneously of child abuse, bullying in two asymmetrical power relationships, and the first recorded use of the Nuremberg defence: 'I was only obeying orders.'"[27] To be sure, Gen. 22 is a very difficult text, and exactly on the moral points that Dawkins invokes.

25. In my view, the saving of Lot has more to do with Abraham than with Lot's own righteousness (see Gen. 18:16–19). That the city is destroyed implies a lack of even ten righteous people (Gen. 18:32) according to the narrative's perspective. In terms of Lot's own family, we hear of only four such persons—Lot himself, his wife, and his two daughters—and even they had to be forcibly removed.

26. CEB: "cries of injustice." For more on this term and its importance in the OT, see Boyce, *Cry to God in the Old Testament*; and Kim, "'Outcry.'"

27. Dawkins, *God Delusion*, 275.

But here too Dawkins seems out of his depth in reckoning with the story's complexity or demonstrating the kind of interpretive dexterity that such a complex story demands of would-be interpreters. For starters, competent readers of Gen. 22 must wrestle with the significance of the narrative introduction to this story: "After these events, God tested Abraham" (Gen. 22:1 CEB).[28] Now, Abraham might not know this is a divine test, but the reader does. That doesn't "fix" the story by any stretch of the imagination, but it is a crucial detail at a crucial moment of the story—the very introduction to all that follows—that must be taken into consideration.[29] But Dawkins is happy to ignore it altogether.

We might next consider how Dawkins's critique of "this appalling story" rests almost entirely on it being "a literal fact" and how, according to him, many real people read the story as "literal fact" and thus live their lives accordingly.[30] I myself am highly dubious of this assertion without some empirical studies of such real people (e.g., how many are there?) and their lives that are modeled (in what way?) on Gen. 22. Does that imitation include also God's miraculous deliverance of their loved ones, I wonder? In any event, at this point in his "interpretation," Dawkins is as simpleminded as it gets. It is certainly *possible* for someone to read the Gen. 22 story and go out and kill their child, saying that God told them to do so. That has in fact happened.[31] But such an actualization is by no stretch of the imagination a logical or appropriate interpretation of the biblical narrative where, in fact, *no child dies*

28. See, e.g., Childs, *Biblical Theology of the Old and New Testaments*, 325–36, who speaks of the text as a "patriarchal temptation" that has a "unique, unrepeatable quality" (327, cf. 334).

29. Indeed, the verbal syntax of Gen. 22 depends entirely on the main verb of v. 1. Said differently, the narrative sequence—the ordering and meaning of the verbs that follow—does not happen (not in the way that it currently does) without v. 1's verb, "God tested." That sets up all that follows, and it is syntactically impossible to read the chapter without v. 1.

30. Another case of sloppy reading: Hitchens characterizes the beginning of the Decalogue as containing "a stern reminder of . . . limitless revenge" (*God Is Not Great*, 99). Indeed, Exod. 20:5 (cf. Deut. 5:9) may be stern (though how would one know?), but biblical scholars are agreed that this sentiment puts a rather firm limit on punishment (just to "the third and the fourth generation"), esp. in light of the seemingly limitless beneficence promised ("to the thousandth generation," in Exod. 20:6; Deut. 5:10; see Strawn, "Yhwh's Poesie"). Not surprisingly, the latter bit goes uncommented on (unnoticed?) by Hitchens, whose offense stems from "the moral and reasonable idea that children are innocent of their parents' offenses" (ibid.). But Hitchens does not comment on the debate concerning individual retribution evident from Deut. 24:16; Jer. 31:29–30; and Ezek. 18:1–32; 33:1–20. If by "limitless revenge" Hitchens is speaking of the third commandment (Exod. 20:7; Deut. 5:11) rather than of the second commandment, the adjective *limitless* may apply, but the noun *revenge* is surely wrong. One would hope for better accuracy from Hitchens, who made his living as a journalist. Unfortunately, the errors and misrepresentations continue in the pages that follow.

31. See the discussion in Moberly, *Theology of the Book of Genesis*, 196; depending on Delaney, *Abraham on Trial*.

at all. Such an actualization is *not* good reading at all but a manifestation of psychosis, in the same way that it would be psychotic for someone to kill the elderly or infirm after reading a book on the survival of the fittest. "But Darwin told me to," such a person might plead to the authorities at trial, but who would believe that person, and who would blame *The Origin of Species* for such violent actions?

Dawkins anticipates a response like this to some degree, but deems it proof of a larger anti-Bible point. The only way we guard against the worst parts of the Bible, Dawkins asserts, is by a random strategy of picking the nice bits from the nasty. But, he quickly asserts, we can only do that by "some independent criterion for deciding which are the moral bits: a criterion which, wherever it comes from, cannot come from scripture itself."[32] But this simply isn't true; neither is it a logical necessity. Once again, it is more than obvious from the very start of Gen. 22 *itself* that God does not want Abraham to kill Isaac. It is, after all, a test (22:1), and, lest any doubt remain, the child is rescued (22:13–14). I repeat that these details do not fix all of the difficult and troubling aspects of the story,[33] but one thing is absolutely certain, contra Dawkins: they do not in this case come *ab extra*, from outside the narrative. They are, instead, a matter of *simply reading the story*, of reading it *closely and carefully*, and—perhaps most important—the habit of *continued reading*. There is, after all, far more to God and Abraham and Isaac and child sacrifice than simply, merely, or only Gen. 22.[34] If one simply keeps reading, one learns a lot more about all of that (and more), and what to do about all of that (and more), in the same way that one learns more as one continues to read a science textbook—for example, that survival of the fittest in its most brutal form doesn't apply to Savannah, Georgia, like it does to the savannah of Africa. One needs, in sum, a comprehensive knowledge of the book that one is reading. That may not suffice in every instance, but it may suffice in a large number of them, and it is entirely system-intrinsic such that Dawkins's "outside the Bible hence anti-Bible" point is neither a logical nor a necessary sequitur. Let us return to the linguistic analogy: to adequately understand and use a language, one needs fluency. Knowing little bits here and there simply

---

32. Dawkins, *God Delusion*, 275, similarly 298: "The holy books do not supply any rules for distinguishing the good principles from the bad." See further below.

33. E.g., many interpreters have observed that Isaac and Abraham are never portrayed as speaking to each other directly again after Gen. 22. Is this an implicit indication of the long-lasting effects of trauma? Of course, Gen. 22 is among the most (in)famous of texts in the history of biblical interpretation. Among a virtually endless sea of options, see esp. Kierkegaard's *Fear and Trembling*.

34. See Moberly, *Theology of the Book of Genesis*, 179–99, esp. 196–99; further Moberly, *Bible, Theology, and Faith*; Levenson, *Death and Resurrection of the Beloved Son*.

won't do. Snippets definitely don't count as the full language. They also can't count as serious criticism.

As my second example, Dawkins is similarly out of his depth in the New Testament when, in continuing his extra-Bible–anti-Bible argument, he asserts, "Jesus was not content to derive his ethics from the scriptures of his upbringing. He explicitly departed from them. . . . Since a principal thesis of this chapter is that we do not, and should not, derive our morals from scripture, Jesus has to be honoured as a model for that very thesis."[35] Dawkins is thus proud to be an "Atheist for Jesus" and to have a T-shirt bearing that motto. But any New Testament scholar worth their salt would say that Dawkins's statement seriously underestimates Jesus's indebtedness to and embeddedness within the Judaism of his day, not to mention how deeply the New Testament writers—every one of them, evidently—are indebted to and embedded within the symbolic world of the Old Testament.[36] And this is not even to mention how deeply the New Testament writers root Jesus himself in the Old Testament.[37] If Dawkins means by Jesus's departure from the Old Testament to refer to the so-called antitheses of the Sermon on the Mount, we might note that the departure there is hardly "antithetical" at all: Jesus makes the Ten Commandments harder than ever. The Decalogue is no longer just about murder but about being angry, not just about committing adultery but about lusting. Furthermore, insofar as the book of Deuteronomy itself expands on the significance of the Decalogue, clarifying its brief, almost poetically spare injunctions with fuller case law,[38] one could make the case that Jesus not only derived his morals from Scripture but also, evidently, his exegetical method. But of course Dawkins is in the dark about all such matters.

The examples outlined above demonstrate Dawkins's penchant for flat reading and signal other problems as well—the biggest of which is how poorly he understands hermeneutics writ large, especially in his repeated insistence that readings of Scripture that are not as flat as his are arbitrary:

We pick and choose which bits of scripture to believe, which bits to write off as symbols or allegories. Such picking and choosing is a matter of personal decision, just as much, or as little, as the atheist's decision to follow this moral

35. Dawkins, *God Delusion*, 284.
36. See Johnson, *Writings of the New Testament*, 2; more extensively, R. Hays, *Echoes of Scripture*; E. Sanders, *Jesus and Judaism*; Charlesworth, *Jesus within Judaism*.
37. See, e.g., Juel, *Messianic Exegesis*.
38. See, inter alia, Olson, *Deuteronomy and the Death of Moses*, 62–125; S. Kaufman, "Structure of the Deuteronomic Law"; Braulik, "Sequence of the Laws in Deuteronomy"; and Walton, "Decalogue Structure of the Deuteronomic Law."

precept or that was a personal decision, without an absolute foundation. If one of these is "morality flying by the seat of its pants", so is the other.[39]

In light of what I've already said above, it comes as no surprise to hear that I deem this to be far from accurate, and here I invoke the massive juggernaut of the history of biblical interpretation as proof of the point. To be sure, there is no small amount of willy-nilly interpretation contained therein, but there is just as much, if not far more, that is marked by careful rules—whether explicit or implicit—regarding how best to interpret the Bible, even and especially its most difficult and problematic parts, that is about as far from "flying by the seat of its pants" as is Dawkins's own careful research in evolutionary biology. But, since Dawkins is largely ignorant of that history of interpretation (if not of interpretation, generally), he continues to insist that our picking of good bits and rejection of bad is completely arbitrary, completely unjustified by the biblical text itself, and only warranted by external, nonbiblical, and nonreligious criteria.[40] (By the way, the contested nature of biblical interpretation—that not everyone agrees—is no different at precisely that point than the contested nature of scientific discovery: in the latter realm, too, there is often widely divergent opinion on this or that matter, but that does not mean that scientists are randomly or arbitrarily picking and choosing.)

A further and more specific word should be said about Dawkins's tirade against writing parts of the Bible off as symbols or allegories. Here again Dawkins seriously misjudges and underestimates (or simply under-*knows*) the rules of figural interpretation, a hermeneutical approach that has a long and venerable history and is already manifest within the Bible itself.[41] Because Dawkins appears to know nothing about any of that, he is content to caricature it as "that favourite trick of interpreting selected scriptures as 'symbolic' rather than literal. By what criterion do you *decide* which passages are symbolic, which literal?"[42] The answer to that question is "By *several criteria*, certainly never just *one criterion*," though there is not space to do justice to all that here.[43] It must suffice to gesture toward one possible strategy

39. Dawkins, *God Delusion*, 269. Harris's preferred term is "cherry-picking" (e.g., *Letter to a Christian Nation*, 18, 105).

40. See Dawkins, *God Delusion*, 275.

41. Instructive studies include Fishbane, *Biblical Interpretation in Ancient Israel*; Kingsmill, *Song of Songs and the Eros of God*; Dawson, *Christian Figural Reading*; Seitz, *Figured Out*, esp. 13–88; Steinmetz, "Superiority of Pre-critical Exegesis"; Stone, "Ethical and Apologetic Tendencies."

42. Dawkins, *God Delusion*, 280, emphasis original.

43. For a beginning, see the works cited in note 41 above.

of "picking and choosing" with reference to the particularly disturbing (to many people) issue of "holy war" (*ḥērem*).[44] When one reads *slowly* (which is to say, carefully) and *widely* (which is to say, one continues to read)—even, let it be stressed, *only* within the Old Testament itself—one finds that the Old Testament largely contains and constrains the holy war tradition to the period of conquest and settlement (Deuteronomy–Judges). The motif is not found extensively elsewhere, which means that it is not enjoined as a dominant metaphor for the religious life or, more to the point, for religious practice(s).[45] That situation could and should be immediately contrasted with the way the Old Testament everywhere and repeatedly evokes the exodus tradition as a root metaphor of its life with God.[46] So, as problematic as the holy war tradition is—and it is *very* problematic, to be sure—there is nevertheless within the Bible itself a kind of textual "containment strategy" that limits the damage from being even worse than it is. Noticing that textual logic, then building out from it toward an ethic that is peaceable and ultimately nonviolent,[47] is hardly an arbitrary picking and choosing on the basis of an external non- or irreligious criterion of morality. It is rather, and quite simply, a close and careful reading of the whole Bible, or, put differently, it is a case of knowing the full language, perhaps including its diachronic development (see chap. 3), not just little bits and pieces of it here and there. It seems that it is Dawkins, in the end, who is the one picking and choosing.

Now I seriously doubt that any of this would satisfy Dawkins. In his estimation it is too little, too late. The damage has already been done to the "poor slandered, slaughtered Midianites" and company.[48] Of course, one needn't be an atheist to be upset about the conquest tradition; a lot of Christians are upset by it too, and although many of these may not know the Bible very well (and so are just bothered in general, perhaps in the same way Dawkins

44. The Hebrew Bible never uses the adjective "holy" to describe or modify the noun "war," a few translations of Joel 3:9 notwithstanding (where a verbal form of the root *qdš* is employed; cf. CEB: "Prepare a holy war"). See Chapman, "Martial Memory, Peaceable Vision." Chapman suggests "Yahweh war" or "divine war" as more suitable terms. See also Kang, *Divine War in the Old Testament*; Smend, *Yahweh War and Tribal Confederation*.

45. While divine war/warfare imagery is found elsewhere in the OT, outside Deuteronomy–Judges it is not presented via the specific issue of taking land from the Canaanites. See Chapman, "Martial Memory, Peaceable Vision," 60–61. For more on God as warrior, see Miller, "God the Warrior." The violent imagery of Revelation or at Qumran in the *War Scroll* (1QM/4QM) is resolutely eschatological, which actually strengthens the point made above.

46. See, famously, B. Anderson, *Understanding the Old Testament*, 9–14. For an extensive listing of traces of the exodus theme throughout the Bible, see Houtman, *Exodus*, 1:190–218.

47. See esp. the excellent treatment by Chapman, "Martial Memory, Peaceable Vision."

48. Dawkins, *God Delusion*, 278. Cf., similarly, Hitchens, *God Is Not Great*, 101.

is), many do know the text well.[49] But the point is that the Bible *itself* may be upset with the conquest tradition. Better: the Bible itself *is* "upset" with the conquest tradition—insofar as it contains and constrains it—but only a careful and sophisticated understanding of the entirety of the Bible knows that. Dawkins doesn't have such an understanding, and therefore what Dawkins knows of the Bible—the biblical "language" that he speaks—is neither full nor fluent, but, in the end, little more than a pidgin. There is no doubt that Dawkins gets some of the lexemes right—divine war, violence, killing, moral outrage, and the like—but he lacks the full vocabulary or a syntax that can appropriately relate the different words to one another. Put slightly differently, every language has "bad" words in it, but no language is comprised solely of the "bad" words.[50] Critiquing a language's "bad" words as if it had no "good" words in it is pure silliness, the epitome of linguistic ignorance. That this is not special pleading (no doubt what Dawkins would say it is) can be demonstrated by one final example drawn from his work.

Dawkins is quite taken with a paper written by a physician and evolutionary anthropologist, John Hartung, which argues that the famous injunction to "love your neighbor" in Lev. 19:18 applies only to one's fellow Israelites.[51] Dawkins takes great delight in the fact that this ethical "highpoint" in the Bible is, in his (Hartung's) view, originally and therefore evidently only (though this last part is assumed rather than argued) exclusivist, which is to say that it refers only to one's own in-group. In Dawkins's words: "'Love thy

49. Indeed, the recent literature on this and related points is rather voluminous. See, e.g., (alphabetically) Brueggemann, *Divine Presence amid Violence*; Chapman, "Martial Memory, Peaceable Vision"; Copan, *Is God a Moral Monster?*; Cowles, Merrill, Gard, and Longman, *Show Them No Mercy*; Creach, *Violence in Scripture*; Earl, *Reading Joshua as Christian Scripture*; Earl, "Deuteronomy 7"; Earl, *Joshua Delusion?*; Garber, "Amalek and Amalekut"; Jenkins, *Laying Down the Sword*; Lamb, *God Behaving Badly*; Moberly, *Old Testament Theology*, esp. 53–71; Moberly, "Toward an Interpretation of the Shema"; Seibert, *Disturbing Divine Behavior*; Seibert, *Violence of Scripture*; Sparks, *Sacred Word, Broken Word*; Stone, "Ethical and Apologetic Tendencies"; Strawn, "Canaan and Canaanites"; Strawn, "Teaching the Old Testament"; C. Wright, *God I Don't Understand*; plus the essays in Bergmann, Murray, and Rea, *Divine Evil?*; Thomas, Evans, and Copan, *Holy War in the Bible*; and *Interpretation* 66, no. 2 (April 2012), devoted to Joshua. Among others, classic studies include von Rad, *Holy War in Ancient Israel*; Craigie, *Problem of War in the Old Testament*; Lind, *Yahweh Is a Warrior*; and Miller, *Divine Warrior*. Not all of this literature is of equal value or reflects the same viewpoint, but Dawkins et al. seem entirely ignorant of it, even of the classic studies.

50. I use scare quotes around "bad" and "good" for two reasons: (1) to indicate that these terms are not necessarily the best descriptors; (2) to indicate that the particular items in question may not be simplistically so defined. For more on the "bad" parts, see further on Tertullian in chap. 5.

51. Dawkins, *God Delusion*, 287–97; Hartung, "Love Thy Neighbor," plus forum discussion thereon.

neighbour' didn't mean what we now think it means. It meant only 'Love another Jew.'"[52]

A reply: this observation is hardly as "devastating" as Dawkins would make it seem because it is, in fact, *nothing new*. Any decent commentary on Leviticus, whether written by a Christian or Jewish scholar, will dutifully report that Hebrew רֵעַ/*rē(a)ʿ* refers to a nearby neighbor and thus not a citizen of a far distant country.[53] The same holds true for much of the kin language found in the Bible. Thus far, then, Dawkins and Hartung are quite right, though again, this is hardly a novel insight, and religious people, not just atheists, have made the point—indeed long before Hartung wrote his paper or Dawkins read it![54] That is to say that one doesn't need a PhD in Bible to make this observation about "neighbor" language (hence Hartung), but people with PhDs in Bible (and without them) have made the same observation, in contrast to how Dawkins would make it seem.[55]

But the biggest problem in all this is that Dawkins seems completely ignorant of the fact that there is more than just this one "exclusivist" text in the Bible concerning the love of others (or rather, *non*others: in-group members). Only a few verses later *in the very same chapter* (Lev. 19:34), one finds the very same injunction as Lev. 19:18: וְאָהַבְתָ . . . כָּמוֹךָ/*waʾāhabtā . . . kāmôkā*, "and you must love . . . as yourself," only this time the object of love is not the in-group "neighbor" (רֵעַ/*rē[a]ʿ*) but the גֵר/*gēr*, a sojourner or "immigrant" (CEB)—a designation that without doubt refers to an *out-group*.[56] If Lev. 19:18 is "exclusively exclusivist," then Lev. 19:34 must be considered every

---

52. Dawkins, *God Delusion*, 287. Dawkins's delight is at root historicist, yet most scholars would deem his language of "another Jew" to be historically *inaccurate* before the Greco-Roman period, and perhaps before the end of the second century BCE. See S. Cohen, *Beginnings of Jewishness*, esp. 69–106. Note also that even (presumably, in Dawkins's opinion) "benign" and "moral" injunctions like Lev. 19:18 can be lived out or not lived out. For a poignant vignette of how this text and the Golden Rule played out in the death of a neighbor two doors down in an apartment hall, see Jacobs, *Year of Living Biblically*, 321–25.

53. In 2001 I made this very point myself (Strawn, "Leviticus 19:1–2, 9–18," esp. 119), well before I read Dawkins's book (2006), precisely because of the mentions of the immigrant in Lev. 19:10, 34. See also *NIDOTTE* 3:144–49; *TLOT* 3:1243–46.

54. For just one example that predates Hartung, see Hartley, *Leviticus*, 317–18, and the even earlier literature cited there.

55. A similar silliness is found in Hitchens's (*God Is Not Great*, 120–22) exposé of the story of the woman caught in adultery in John 7:53–8:11 and its secondary textual status, with a little help from the NT scholar Bart Ehrman. Once again, this situation has been known for centuries (note, e.g., Euthymius Zigabenus already in the twelfth century[!] or the many Greek manuscripts that mark the passage as uncertain), has not been covered up, and is hardly deleterious to belief. See, e.g., Barrett, *Gospel according to St. John*, 589–92; Beasley-Murray, *John*, 143–47; and R. Brown, *Gospel according to John*, 1:332–38.

56. Especially given the contrast with אֶזְרָח/*ʾezrāḥ*, "citizen." See Levine, *Leviticus*, 134; Hartley, *Leviticus*, 322; more extensively, *NIDOTTE* 1:836–39; *TLOT* 1:307–10.

bit as "inclusively inclusivist." Alas, Dawkins seems blissfully unaware not only of Lev. 19:34 (if only he had kept reading for sixteen more verses!) but also of the many other texts that offer a strong counterperspective to the exclusivist strain that he delights in uncovering and that, admittedly, do cause problems for some people and some perspectives.[57] To put things directly: there is far, far more in the Old Testament than just holy war or only intratribal loyalty ("love") when it comes to the foreign nations. There's the story of the Moabitess Ruth and her incorporation into Israel; or the streaming of the nations to Zion in Isa. 2:2–4//Mic. 4:1–3 (the repetition of the oracle itself is noteworthy); or God's equal care for Egypt and Assyria, whom God calls by pet names typically reserved only for Israel (Isa. 19:19–22); or God's concern to liberate other people groups (Cush, Israel, Philistia, Aram—perhaps a merism for "all people") via exoduses, just like God did in bringing Israel out of Egypt (Amos 9:7);[58] or Deuteronomy—the theological home of the holy war tradition!—which speaks of Israel's nearest neighbors, often deep political enemies, as "relatives" (אחים/'aḥîm, "brothers") who should not be bothered or engaged in battle in part because God performed conquest-like and land-giving activities on their behalf just as God did for Israel (Deut. 2:4–5, 9–12, 19–23).[59] This listing is just the tip of the iceberg in the Old Testament proper and doesn't yet invoke the New Testament and Jesus's careful definition of "who is my neighbor" in the good Samaritan story—a definition that is anything but exclusivist and, seen in the light of the Old Testament texts I've cited, hardly a *re*definition of "neighbor" either.[60]

Now perhaps this is unfair to Dawkins. After all, he is an easy target since he is no biblical scholar—nor is Hartung—so how can he be expected to know all that? But this is precisely the larger (linguistic) point: Dawkins doesn't know "all that," and so what he is critiquing is not the full story at all but a massive reduction of "all that"—taking just a part, just a bit, and the worst bit at that. Linguistically, what this means is that Dawkins only knows and only speaks an "Old Testament pidgin," and therefore what he is critiquing

57. Particularly around the issues of election and covenant, which are frequently railed against in the New Atheist literature. For serious theological treatments of the issue, see Kaminsky, *Yet I Loved Jacob*; Kaminsky, "New Testament and Rabbinic Views of Election"; and Moberly, *Old Testament Theology*, 41–74.

58. See Brueggemann, "'Exodus' in the Plural (Amos 9:7)"; Strawn, "What Is Cush Doing in Amos 9:7?"

59. See Miller, "God's Other Stories"; Strawn, "Deuteronomy," esp. 66–67.

60. See, e.g., Wenham, *Book of Leviticus*, 269. For the same reasons, Dawkins's interpretation of the sixth commandment (*God Delusion*, 288) as applying only to killing other Jews, an exclusivistic interpretation that again depends on Hartung, is to be rejected. Cf., e.g., 2 Sam. 12:9 and Matt. 5:21–22.

is only an Old Testament pidgin, not the full Old Testament itself. His pidgin critique of a pidgin Old Testament is quite effective as far as it goes (we would have to agree with much of it), but it doesn't go very far simply because the full language includes all of Dawkins's "bad" parts but also many other "good" ones that he doesn't treat at all, and which he certainly doesn't treat *together*.[61] But the coexistence of both kinds of discourse in the full language means that critiquing the "bad" bits alone simply won't do. Dawkins scores points, surely, but only vis-à-vis the pidgin language, not against the real, full language. To quote Eagleton, "Critics of the most enduring form of popular culture in human history [i.e., Christianity] have a moral obligation to confront that case at its most persuasive, rather than grabbing themselves a victory on the cheap by savaging it as so much garbage and gobbledygook."[62]

Still further on this point, the coexistence of both "good" and "bad" parts—the binary presentation doesn't begin to do justice to the linguistic complexity (see further below)—doesn't mean that one is permitted to pick one part, whether "good" or "bad," willy-nilly. Dawkins is spot on here, even though he is wrong in characterizing all such picking as willy-nilly. Instead, the coexistence of both parts (and yet still others) means one must be fluent in and attempt to understand the whole linguistic complex, which, like any language, can be exceedingly complex. That is difficult work indeed, involving language facility and dexterity won over long stretches of time—a sense of the whole system and the functionality of its constituent parts—all of which Dawkins doesn't have or is unwilling to give. In its place, he himself is guilty of picking and choosing, which is a cardinal error in his book! Moreover, analogically speaking, Dawkins is content to critique a sentence like "Dick and Jane ran"—or, in biblical terms, "God is love" (1 John 4:16)—as "utterly simplistic." Who beyond five years of age wouldn't agree?

Unfortunately, Dawkins's own sentences are equally simplistic when considered via the linguistic analogy. Consider the following, for example: "We . . . (and this includes most religious people) as a matter of fact *don't* get our morals from scripture. If we did, we would strictly observe the sabbath and

---

61. Cf. Lamb, *God Behaving Badly*, 17: "Dawkins . . . simply avoids texts that speak of God favorably."

62. Eagleton, *Reason, Faith, and Revolution*, 33. Cf. Haught, *God and the New Atheism*, who says of Friedrich Nietzsche, Martin Heidegger, Ernst Bloch, Karl Marx, Jacques Derrida, Jacques Lacan, and Jürgen Habermas: "At least the atheists on this list had enough understanding of theology to make conversation interesting and productive. In marked contrast, the level of theological discernment by the new atheists is too shallow and inaccurate even to begin such a conversation" (93). Among other things, Haught points out that none of the New Atheists seem "remotely aware of the biblical prophetic tradition" (94), and the same is true for the theme of liberation (100–101).

think it just and proper to execute anybody who chose not to."[63] Such a remark is tired and tiring; it hardly warrants a response. Suffice it to say that such a sentiment could only be voiced by someone who doesn't know the full language of Scripture, is horribly simplistic about hermeneutics, is rigidly literalistic in the worst sense of the term, and is evidently completely unaware that (speaking within our analogy) *languages change* (see, e.g., Matt. 12:1–14; Mark 2:23–28; 3:1–6; Luke 6:1–11; 13:10–17; 14:1–6; John 5:1–18; 7:14–24; 9:1–34; cf. 1 Sam 21:6; Acts 15:22–29). Surely Dawkins would scoff at anyone who told him we should give up our smartphones and use Oldowan stone tools from the Lower Paleolithic period because, well, that's the way humans *used* to do it, and for heaven's sake (or some other entity's sake), we must be consistent!

Pidgin versus Pidgin

Let me reiterate that Dawkins isn't all wrong: he gets several things exactly right. But that is what we would expect with a pidgin: greatly reduced, lacking significant vocabulary, largely devoid of nuance and sophistication, but not entirely distinct from the original languages (whether superstrate or substrate) that went into its production.[64] To go even further, I believe Dawkins is completely correct when he asserts that many religious people do *not* get their morals (solely) from the Bible, for whatever reason (and some of those reasons should be thoughtfully considered—not all of Christianity or Christian theology is coterminous with what is found in Scripture). At one point Dawkins paints the situation starkly: "Do those people who hold up the Bible as an inspiration to moral rectitude have the slightest notion of what is actually written in it?"[65] His implied answer is "No, they don't," and here I

---

63. Dawkins, *God Delusion*, 283. Similarly, Harris, *Letter to a Christian Nation*, passim.

64. The judgment holds true for other New Atheists as well. See Haught, *God and the New Atheism*, esp. 34: "If biblical truth cannot be *reduced* to scientific truth [as per the New Atheists], then it does not qualify as truth in any sense"; and 101: "Dawkins . . . wants his readers to join him in *reducing* the Bible to moral education" (emphases added). Cf. Copan, *Is God a Moral Monster?*, 23: "In many cases, the New Atheists aren't all that patient in their attempts to understand a complex text, historical contexts, and the broader biblical canon." In this regard it is telling that Harris, in his afterword to the 2008 edition of *Letter to a Christian Nation*, proves himself (1) incapable of distinguishing linguistic dexterity from cherry-picking and/or bowdlerization when it comes to Scripture; and (2) incapable of delineating differences in religious belief systems (or thinkers), as he ultimately lumps what he calls "moderate religion" together with "religious extremism," on the one hand, and contrasts that with complete disavowal of faith, on the other (104–7). Everything is *either* this *or* that. Nothing, it would seem, can be anything other than just one, narrowly defined "simple" thing, largely, or so it seems, because that is how scientific rationality would have it. So then, is light a wave or a particle?

65. Dawkins, *God Delusion*, 281.

find myself in general agreement with Dawkins—though I agree for different reasons than his and with far different outcomes.

In my judgment, most people don't have the slightest idea of what is actually written in the Old Testament because they, like Dawkins himself, cannot speak the language. The Old Testament is dying. If it isn't already dead, it is at least reverting to a pidginized form, and those who do know anything of it, whether friend or foe, typically know only snippets: a phrase or two here, a word or three there. Dawkins himself is one of these second-, third-, or fourth-generation speakers who lack fluency; he just happens to be an unreligious one. Dawkins's preferred interlocutors apparently are similarly impaired, however, which is further proof of my point that his pidgin critique is, in turn, only of (and therefore only valid for) another pidgin. Dawkins is fond of citing the most extreme examples of religious rhetoric: everything from "rapture" websites to the television evangelist Pat Robertson.[66] With respect to the latter, Dawkins cites the following statement Robertson made after the citizens of Dover, Pennsylvania, removed members of their public school board who were trying to enforce the teaching of intelligent design in science classes:

> I'd like to say to the good citizens of Dover, if there is a disaster in your area, don't turn to God. You just rejected him from your city, and don't wonder why he hasn't helped you when problems begin, if they begin, and I'm not saying they will. But if they do, just remember you just voted God out of your city. And if that's the case, then don't ask for his help, because he might not be there.[67]

Perhaps Dawkins is correct when he writes that Robertson is "typical of those who today hold power and influence in the United States,"[68] though I find that an incredible and unsubstantiated claim. Regardless, his is a critique of Robertson, not the Bible. And Robertson is speaking a pidgin here, no less than Dawkins himself. Since when, per Robertson's syntax, is "intelligent design" equivalent to "God"? Or when is voting down the teaching of intelligent design equivalent to "voting" or "rejecting" God "out of a city"? Nowhere in the Old Testament, that's for sure. Or the New Testament, for that matter. So while Dawkins may have scored one against Robertson, it is at best a case of pidgin versus pidgin. Neither is satisfying if we care about the full language. If anything, both are equally troubling because they manifest repidginization—the language *on its way to death*—because when a language

66. See ibid., 271, 288.
67. Cited in ibid., 271.
68. Ibid.

reverts to pidgin form, it means that it is seriously threatened, imminently in danger of becoming extinct. To make matters still worse, lack of fluency among the faithful leaves them completely incapacitated to answer the likes of either Dawkins or Robertson. Without knowing more, the pidgin in question sounds sufficient if not altogether compelling, whether the result is that one is somehow bowled over by Dawkins's *intellect* and walks away from faith forever, or one is overcome by Robertson's *piety* and sends in a large contribution to the web address or 1-800 number on the screen.

This incapacity is exactly the kind of failure in problem solving that accompanies the death of a language (see chap. 3). One might also observe that church leaders have warned about such situations long before the twenty-first century. Already in "An Address to the Clergy" (1756), John Wesley makes the same argument I have, though he bases his plea on knowing the Bible in Greek and Hebrew:

> Do I understand Greek and Hebrew? Otherwise, how can I undertake . . . not only to explain books which are written therein, but to defend them against all opponents? Am I not at the mercy of every one who does understand, or even pretends to understand, the original? For which way can I confute his pretence? Do I understand the language of the Old Testament? critically? at all?[69]

Let me reiterate that Dawkins is not alone in mounting his considered and cantankerous critique of the Old Testament. The work of other incisive minds (and pens!) could easily be cited on his behalf. Here again one thinks of such brilliant minds and sharp pens as Hitchens, Harris, and Dennett, to name a few.[70] In my judgment, however, these other works offer little in terms of substantive critique beyond the ringing rhetoric that Dawkins has already offered. These other works are, in the main, variations on the same theme, each writer, of course, bringing a particular area of expertise to bear. But the substance of the atheistic critique is rather similar, and so I think the responses offered to Dawkins above can largely stand in for these others as well.[71] In each

---

69. John Wesley, "Address to the Clergy," 491. A highly similar argument can be found still earlier in Martin Luther's 1524 address "To the Councilmen of All Cities in Germany."

70. Within the field of biblical studies proper, one might include Avalos (*End of Biblical Studies*) and Carroll (*Wolf in the Sheepfold*), who by dint of their training are obviously far better informed about biblical matters than those who work only in the hard sciences. For an adroit reply to Carroll's work, see Moberly, *Old Testament Theology*, 112–16; Brueggemann, "Sometimes Wave, Sometimes Particle." For a furthering of some of Carroll's points, see Pyper's fascinating collection in *Unsuitable Book*.

71. I do not mean to paint all critiques as identical to Dawkins's, nor my own brief responses as sufficient to answer all opponents. I leave full treatments to others (esp. Eagleton, *Reason, Faith, and Revolution*; and Hart, *Atheist Delusions*), given the more specific focus of the present study.

case, some crucial piece or fairly large swath of the language that is the Old Testament (or Christian Scripture) seems to be woefully lacking, perhaps ignored but more likely completely, maybe even willfully, unknown. Nevertheless, this particular "company of scholars" is not solely of recent vintage (despite the "new" in the New Atheism) but is truly ancient insofar as the virulent anti–Old Testament polemic of the New Atheists has a heritage that long antedates the relatively recent coinage of the word *atheism*.[72] As chapter 5 on the next sign of morbidity makes abundantly clear, there is a good bit of family resemblance between recent characterizations of the Old Testament by New Atheists and the famous second-century arch-heretic Marcion and the legacy he bequeathed to (Christian!) posterity.[73]

72. The English word *atheist* dates to 1571, with *atheism* dating to 1587 according to *OED* (online ed.). For more on these terms and yet others, see Schweizer, *Hating God*, esp. 6–20.
73. Haught (*God and the New Atheism*, 102) also links Dawkins and Hitchens to Marcion.

5

Marcionites Old and New

For those with some knowledge of early church history, the antagonistic posture and disparaging attitude that the New Atheists adopt toward the Old Testament and its portrayal of God are strikingly similar to Marcion and the heresy that bears his name. The similarity is not limited to the surface—what the Old Testament says (at times) about God—but is also found in the deep structure of the New Atheists' argument, since among other things, Marcion too was profoundly troubled by contradictory presentations of God in the Bible.[1] One of his main works, the *Antitheses*, appears simply to have set biblical statements side by side that, in Marcion's view, simply could not coexist. Here is a sampling:

- Joshua conquered the land with violence and cruelty, *but* Christ forbade all violence and preached mercy and peace.
- The prophet of the Creator-God, when the people were locked in battle, climbed to the top of the mountain and stretched forth his hands to God, that he might kill as many as possible in the battle; [*but*] our Lord, the Good, stretched forth his hands (namely, on the cross) not to kill men but to save them.

---

1. To the sentiments offered in chap. 4, one might add Hitchens, *God Is Not Great*, 97: "Since . . . these revelations, many of them hopelessly inconsistent, cannot by definition be simultaneously true, it must follow that some of them are false and illusory"; and Harris, *Letter to a Christian Nation*, 10: the "teachings of the Bible are so muddled and self-contradictory that it was possible for Christians to happily burn heretics alive for five long centuries."

- In the law it is said, "An eye for an eye, a tooth for a tooth," *but* the Lord, the Good, says in the Gospel, "If anyone strikes you on one cheek, turn to him the other also."

- The prophet of the Creator-God, in order to kill as many as possible in battle, had the sun to stand still that it might not go down until the adversaries of the people were utterly annihilated; *but* the Lord, the Good, says, "Let not the sun go down upon your wrath."

- The prophet of the Creator-God commanded the bears to come out of the thicket and to eat the children; *but* the good Lord says, "Let the children come to me, and do not forbid them, for of such is the kingdom of heaven."

- *Maledictio* characterizes the law, and *benedictio* characterizes faith (the gospel).

- In the law the creator of the world commands us to give to our brothers, *but* Christ simply says to give to all who ask.[2]

It is revealing that this (partial) listing of contradictions includes topics that the New Atheists also find so off-putting, such as divine violence and divine election.[3]

These parallels between what the New Atheists say about the Old Testament (and its God) and what Marcion said about the same suggest that further discussion of the great arch-heretic, his heresy, and his opponents may prove instructive. In the present chapter, then, I focus especially on those aspects of Marcion's second-century thought that resonate most closely with the death of the Old Testament as represented in the New Atheism of the twenty-first century. In the process, we will have occasion to take a notable detour into the early twentieth century to examine the work of Marcion's greatest interpreter, Adolf von Harnack.[4]

2. The preceding points come from von Harnack, *Marcion: The Gospel*, 60–62, emphases added. See further there for no less than thirty such antitheses. A more extensive treatment appears in von Harnack, *Marcion: Das Evangelium*, 238*–319*. See also May, "Marcion in Contemporary Views," esp. 140–41; Lebreton and Zeiller, *History of the Primitive Church*, 523.

3. See chap. 4 for violence; for Marcion on election, see Blackman, *Marcion and His Influence*, 118.

4. Von Harnack, *Marcion: The Gospel*; von Harnack, *Marcion: Das Evangelium*, esp. apps. on *1–*358. Although I rely heavily on von Harnack's classic work in what follows, it has been surpassed in many areas. See, e.g., Blackman, *Marcion and His Influence*; Balás, "Marcion Revisited"; May, "Marcion in Contemporary Views"; Rumscheidt, *Harnack: Liberal Theology*, 28; Williams, "Reconsidering Marcion's Gospel"; May and Greschat, *Marcion und seine kirchengeschichtliche Wirkung*, esp. the essays by May, "Marcion ohne Harnack," and by Kinzig, "Ein Ketzer und sein Konstrukteur"; and most recently, Moll, *Arch-Heretic Marcion*. For reasons

The Old Marcion

Although certainty remains elusive on many of the details, it seems that Marcion (d. ca. 160 CE) was born in Sinope, in Pontus, and was a well-to-do shipowner.[5] By 140, Marcion was in Rome and in the church there, but when he presented his ideas to the church in a formal meeting in 144, he was excommunicated and deemed a heretic because of them.[6] Unfazed, Marcion continued to promulgate his ideas and attracted much attention, especially from the orthodox heresiologists (including Justin Martyr, Irenaeus, Tertullian, Clement of Alexandria, Ephraem the Syrian, and Eznik of Kolb). He gained numerous converts, apparently because he was an effective preacher and organizer.[7] As E. C. Blackman put it, "Marcion was the founder not of a school, but of a church."[8] Marcion won many to his cause and established communities that lasted as late as the fifth century.[9] Indeed, the fact that so many of Marcion's positions are reflected not only in the New Atheism, but also among many contemporary Christians' experience of the Old Testament, indicates that his influence is still felt to this day. Perhaps Marcion wasn't the very first to identify the problem he addressed, though he is clearly the most (in)famous. Regardless, his perduring legacy demonstrates that he put his finger on a problem that *was*—and *still is*—widely felt.[10]

---

that will become clear below, my reliance on von Harnack is less historical than it is theological and rhetorical.

5. Most scholars discount the tradition that Marcion was the son of a bishop who excommunicated him on the grounds of sexual immorality. The term for Marcion's occupation, *nauklēros*, which seems reliable, may mean only that he worked for a shipowner (May, "Marcion in Contemporary Views," 136). In any event, his significant donation to the church at Rome, which May, at least, accepts as historically reliable (ibid., 137), indicates a certain degree of financial success. Many appeal to his later success as proof of a business-savvy individual with excellent organizational skills.

6. Seibert, *Disturbing Divine Behavior*, 59.

7. See Clabeaux, "Marcion," esp. 515, for the possibility that Marcionites outnumbered non-Marcionites in the 160s and 170s. For summaries of the heresiologists mentioned above, see May, "Marcion in Contemporary Views," 137–43.

8. Blackman, *Marcion and His Influence*, 1; also see ix, 1–14, for the Marcionite church's organization, which included, among other things, catechumens, elders and bishops, worship buildings, and the observation of holy days and sacraments.

9. See *ODCC* 1033–34; Klassen, "Marcion"; Hall, "Marcion"; Clabeaux, "Marcion," 515; May, "Marcion in Contemporary Views," 151; E. Evans, *Tertullian*, 1:ix; Lebreton and Zeiller, *History of the Primitive Church*, 531.

10. See von Harnack, *Militia Christi*, 46, who writes that by 200 CE "there had already existed within Christianity for several decades an active and widespread movement which declared itself against the Old Testament and rejected the God of Israel because he was warlike and thereby contradicted the gospel." Seibert, *Disturbing Divine Behavior*, 54–57, tracks the problem of God's disturbing behavior already in the text of Chronicles, *Jubilees*, and in the emendations of the scribes (*tiqqune sopherim*). Gunneweg, *Understanding the Old Testament*, 143, notes

What was (is) that problem? In many ways it is no different than what bothers Dawkins or other New Atheists: the problem of portrayals of God that seem anything but sublime, and which are, to boot, if not also at root, contradictory (esp. vis-à-vis the New Testament). Apparently taken with Paul's law/gospel dichotomy—or rather, a particular version of that dichotomy[11]—Marcion argued that the Christian gospel was completely a gospel of love, to the absolute exclusion of law. He equated the gospel of love with Jesus Christ and the previously unknown ("alien") God that sent him, while identifying the law with the god of the Old Testament. These were at odds, according to Marcion, with the differences irreconcilable.[12] He thus completely rejected the Old Testament as a valid expression of the gospel.[13] For Marcion, the god of the Old Testament from Genesis 1 forward was not the true God but an evil, creating god (demiurge) who had absolutely nothing to do with the God of Jesus Christ. This "Jewish [*NB!*] God constantly involved himself in contradictory courses of action; . . . he was fickle, capricious, ignorant, despotic, cruel"[14]—a judgment that could have come as easily from Dawkins or Hitchens in the twenty-first century as from Marcion in the second century. Indeed, in Winrich Löhr's opinion, "Marcion's defamatory comments on the god of the Old Testament" have much the same function as the New Atheism, since they "can be read as an attempt at character assassination."[15]

"Utterly different" from the Old Testament god was "the Supreme God of Love whom Jesus came to reveal. It was His purpose to overthrow the Demiurge."[16] According to Marcion, the apostle Paul was the only one who

---

similar dynamics in the Gospel of John. For more on the problem of the OT in later periods, see ibid., passim; and Kraeling, *Old Testament since the Reformation*, passim. For discussion of some modern "functional Marcionites," see Seibert, *Disturbing Divine Behavior*, 67–68.

11. See Blackman (*Marcion and His Influence*, 103–12) for Marcion's "Paulinism," esp. 111: "It must be pointed out that Paulinism is not the Gospel itself, but an interpretation of the Gospel." Further, cf. Löhr, "Did Marcion Distinguish?," esp. 144–45. May ("Marcion in Contemporary Views," 147) speaks of "an ontologizing of the Pauline juxtaposing of old and new, law and grace." For a pioneering volume in what came to be called the New Perspective on Paul, see E. Sanders, *Paul and Palestinian Judaism*.

12. Seibert, *Disturbing Divine Behavior*, 58.

13. But see Moll, *Arch-Heretic Marcion*; von Harnack, *Outlines*, 71; Hall, "Marcion," 423; and Blackman, *Marcion and His Influence*, on Marcion accepting the OT in some ways. "It was possibly the only history book he knew, and he accepted it as a reliable account of the past, of the earliest history of mankind, that is, and of the Jewish race in particular, since the time of Moses" (Blackman, *Marcion and His Influence*, 113).

14. *ODCC* 1034.

15. Löhr, "Did Marcion Distinguish?," 145.

16. *ODCC* 1034. Note Tertullian's summary of Marcion: The OT god is "a judge, fierce and warlike," but the God of the NT is "mild and peaceable, solely kind and supremely good" (*Against Marcion* 1.6; cited in Seibert, *Disturbing Divine Behavior*, 58); and Irenaeus's summary:

fully understood the difference between the Old and New Testament deities. The rest of the apostles and evangelists were still too "Old Testament-ish" for him, so he threw them out along with the Old Testament.[17] But even some of his beloved Paul's corpus had to go: the Pastorals in toto, and from the other Epistles many bits and pieces that Marcion deemed to be corruptions of the apostle's original work.[18] As one can suspect by now, one of the main criteria for Marcion's editing had to do with the relationship of the particular text at hand to Old Testament materials or themes. As a result of this process (so say some scholars), Marcion should be credited as the first person to create a canon of Scripture.[19] Marcion called that construction "the Gospel"—which is as telling in its singularity (just one Gospel) as it is in its content (sans law). Marcion's Gospel was limited to a severely edited version of Luke (lacking, among other things, chaps. 1–2)[20] and his redacted version of ten of the Epistles of Paul.[21]

Debate continues over whether Marcion's Bible was a catalyst in the construction of the orthodox one.[22] Whatever the case, it is clear that Marcion's canon was a *singular*, quite *reduced* canon: "only one Gospel and one Apostle."[23] Later canons recognized by the church catholic are, in contrast, *plural*: made up of both the Old and New Testaments. The inclusion of the Old Testament stands against Marcion, of course; yet it is equally important to recognize that the full Christian Bible is pluralistic *within* each of its Testaments, not offering a single, monochromatic, univocal voice even within one Testament, let alone across both of them.[24] Marcion didn't care for such "Technicolor": proof of this is found not only in his preference for just one

---

Marcion declared God "to be the author of evils, to take delight in war, to be infirm of purpose, and even to be contrary to himself" (*Against Heresies* 1.27.2; ANF 1:352).

17. Here is proof that the death of the OT also involves the death of the NT. See chap. 1 and further below.

18. See von Harnack, *Outlines*, 71; Lebreton and Zeiller, *History of the Primitive Church*, 527.

19. See, e.g., Blackman, *Marcion and His Influence*, 23–41. For arguments supporting the view that Marcion produced his canon rather than simply received it (the point is debated), see Clabeaux, "Marcion," 516. See also Grant, "Marcion, Gospel of"; and Clabeaux, "Marcionite Prologues to Paul."

20. Arguably the most "Jewish" part of Luke. For the relationship between the infancy narratives and the OT, see R. Brown, *Birth of the Messiah*; also E. Evans, *Tertullian*, 1:xiii.

21. For Marcion's version of (what came to be) the NT, see Blackman, *Marcion and His Influence*, 42–60; von Harnack, *Marcion: Das Evangelium*, *157–*237; and E. Evans, *Tertullian*, 1:xiii; 2:643–46.

22. See, e.g., J. Barton, "Marcion Revisited."

23. Clabeaux, "Marcion," 515.

24. Note, e.g., Gillingham, *One Bible, Many Voices*; Knohl, *Divine Symphony*; cf. Clabeaux, "Marcion," 516: "A conscious step in the direction of diversity was taken by anti-Marcionite Christians of the 2d through 4th centuries."

"Gospel," as opposed to the later canonical four, but also in his inability to accept the full Pauline corpus. It was the opinion of the second-century heresiologist, Irenaeus, that Marcion "mutilated the Gospel of Luke" and "dismembered the Epistles of the Apostle Paul," with the result being that Marcion did not give his disciples the full gospel, "but merely a fragment of it."[25] More recently, John J. Clabeaux has described Marcion's Gospel as "a summary dissolution of the tensions that characterized Pauline thought, namely, continuity with Judaism vis-à-vis discontinuity and freedom vis-à-vis obligation."[26]

It was Marcion's dislike of or inability to reckon with (if not both) the rich diversity of the preexisting tradition, above all else the difficulties posed by the variegated Old Testament, that led to his radical redaction. In von Harnack's words:

> Marcion saw himself as called to liberate Christianity from this crisis. *No syncretism, but simplification, unification, and clarity of what bore the Christian label.* . . . A plain religious message was to be set in opposition to the immense and ambiguous complex of what was handed down in tradition. Here, however, Marcion not only stands with Paul, but also together with the Gnostics and over against the church; and just so he most sharply rejects, in opposition to the Gnostics, the new syncretism which they introduced in the mistaken opinion that the material brought in from the mystery-speculations was adequate to the true Christian idea and hence worthy of admiration. Thus here also, as is true in his ruthless carrying through of the *paradoxical* character of religion, Marcion is the consistent one; *true religion must be plain and transparent, just as it must also be alien and absolute-paradoxical.*[27]

To put all this in terms of the linguistic analogy, Marcion didn't like the full language of Scripture. It was too difficult for him, too complex, too irregular (as all languages, especially ancient ones, are). In its place, Marcion opted for something new and different—something far more reduced, compressed, and simple; something far more consistent, coherent, and logical (cf. Dawkins and the New Atheists). What Marcion preferred, linguistically speaking, was nothing less than a pidginized form of Christian Scripture. Or, perhaps better, what he preferred and produced was an *abbreviated language artificially constructed* from the full language of Christian Scripture.

25. Irenaeus, *Against Heresies* 1.27.2 (ANF 1:352).
26. Clabeaux, "Marcion," 514. Von Harnack (*Outlines*, 71) describes Marcion's system as "a Paulinism without dialectics."
27. Von Harnack, *Marcion: The Gospel*, 12, emphasis original. See below for how von Harnack's assessment of Marcion is colored by his own theology.

But more must be said. Pidgins are contact languages, which means that more than one language is at work in their genesis. The Marcionite pidgin clearly favors the Pauline corpus, and the New Testament more generally, to the absolute eradication of the Old Testament.[28] Is that the end of the matter, the Old Testament as the infinitesimally small substrate (or rather, *non*-strate), with the New Testament the predominant if not exclusive superstrate (*mono*strate)? Put differently, is Marcion here (as some would have it) nothing more than a "biblical theologian," an ancient iteration of more recent New Testament–only Christians?[29] The situation is not that simple, if only for the rather obvious fact that in the case of Marcion, cutting the Old Testament meant cutting a good bit of the New Testament as well: even his beloved Paul had to be edited and trimmed. As Fleming Rutledge quips, "It has been said of Marcion that he understood Paul so well that he misunderstood him."[30]

In this light, the guiding principle in Marcion's editorial work, in his *Antitheses*, and in his theology was not biblical at all but *extra*biblical: it was the principle of consistency, logic, or noncontradiction, as he, Marcion, judged those things.[31] According to von Harnack, Marcion was completely flummoxed

28. Though Marcion was unable to eliminate all traces of the OT in the NT, as demonstrated by, among others, Tertullian (see E. Evans, *Tertullian*, 1:506–7, and further below). Somewhat ironically, this demonstrates the marriage of the Testaments, despite Marcion's best efforts to divorce them.

29. Hall ("Marcion," 422–23), e.g., calls the arch-heretic "a radical Biblicist" who encouraged Bible study among his followers; von Harnack (*Outlines*, 70–74) argues that Marcion should not be classed with the gnostics since he didn't employ philosophy, "at least not as a main principle," but rather was guided by "a purely soteriological interest" emphasizing "the pure Gospel" and "the true Pauline Gospel." But whence comes this purity, truth, and soteriology? Even if it is based on internal data, it is still ruled by an *ab extra* principle. Cf. May, "Marcion in Contemporary Views," 129, who queries von Harnack's portrait as "a modern ideal picture, a projection into history," and concludes that Marcion's

> philological work, by means of which he wants to free the texts of his Bible from all supposed adulterations, is anything but unbiased. It is based on dogmatic postulates and a totally unhistorical view of early Christianity. Similarly, his exegesis is dependent on massive dogmatic presuppositions. One calls him a biblical theologian only inasmuch as for him his scripture canon represents the only standard of faith. . . . However, the standard theology of the church was in almost every regard closer to the biblical texts than Marcion's doctrine was. (ibid., 147, and further there)

See also Clabeaux, "Marcion," 515; and Blackman, *Marcion and His Influence*, 66–97, on Marcion's dualism and relationship to gnosticism. While Marcion's dependence on the Syrian gnostic Cerdo continues to be debated, dualistic thinking is more than manifest, as is a docetic and modalist Christology (ibid., 86, and further 98–102). Such positions were not yet "officially" condemned in Marcion's day (Clabeaux, "Marcion," 515).

30. Rutledge, *And God Spoke to Abraham*, 5. Cf. Grant and Tracy, *Interpretation of the Bible*, 41: "While Paul was Marcion's hero, hero worship and comprehension are not the same thing."

31. Blackman, *Marcion and His Influence*, believes Marcion "started with a plain contrast of good and bad gods" (67) and that this "fundamental dualism," along with his "literalist"

in the face of the complexity of the scriptural tradition, especially that of the Old Testament but equally so with that of the New Testament taken in *ipse* (hence the editing of his "Gospel"). Using the linguistic analogy, this means that it was the language of consistency (or some such thing) that served as the superstrate and thus took precedence in the construction of Marcion's linguistic pidgin. It was contact between that "language" and the (substrate) language of the Bible that led to Marcion's greatly reduced, pidginized idiolect.

In this regard Marcion shares much indeed with the New Atheists, who are altogether bewildered by irregularities in the linguistic system that is the Bible more generally and the Old Testament more specifically. The New Atheists, too, have a different superstrate drawn from elsewhere: in the case of writers like Dawkins and Dennett, it is from the realm of science or "scientism." This superstrate becomes the critical determinant in judging the biblical language; it is the latter that must accommodate to the superstrate's power. Such power imbalance marks all contact languages, but the problem in this particular case is that the scientific method simply isn't the best judge of a linguistic system. Why, for example, should the German word for "knife" (*Messer*) be neuter, with "fork" (*Gabel*) feminine, and "table" (*Tisch*) masculine? Such a system is remarkably odd, hard to replicate in the lab, and not entirely rational.[32] Or if it is rational, the rationale is not completely transparent, at least not any-more, or at least not *scientifically*, meaning empirically. As John McWhorter puts it, the existence of three different genders for nouns in German "is not indication that Germans are mentally sophisticated, but rather that their language drags along an unnecessary complication, now meaningless, that arose via a series of accidents."[33] These types of oddities and irregularities are (empirically!) part and parcel of languages, especially ancient languages, which are, let it be stressed once more (and not for the last time), usually very complicated ones.[34]

The insufficiency of this "scientific-logical superstrate" (to coin a term) to assess language can also be demonstrated with reference to poetry. An example is found in Hitchens's book. After stating that many of Jesus's say-ings in the New Testament are "flat-out immoral," Hitchens writes, "The analogy of humans to lilies, for instance, suggests—along with many other

---

treatment of the Bible, "led him to textual falsification, as the only way to make Scripture in all places support his theories" (86–87). For more on Marcion's extrabiblical theological principles, see May, "Marcion in Contemporary Views," 147–49.

32. As John McWhorter asserts, the goal of language is not logic but clarity; see his *Myths, Lies, and Half-Truths*, 78–87; and his *What Language Is*, 61–92. Note Hitchens's odd equation of "biblical consistency or authenticity or 'inspiration'" (*God Is Not Great*, 122)!

33. McWhorter, "Linguistics from the Left," esp. 188.

34. See chap. 3 and McWhorter, *Power of Babel*, 15–52.

injunctions—that things like thrift, innovation, family life, and so forth are a sheer waste of time. ('Take no thought for the morrow.')"[35] It is hard not to laugh out loud at this point. Certainly other things Jesus says suggest quite the opposite or at least put things differently (e.g., Luke 9:62), and the same holds true for other parts of the Bible. Hitchens's failure here stems from the fact that he doesn't know how to read a parable or an image or a poem (despite his correct identification of the lily statement as an analogy)—or perhaps he has simply forgotten how to do so. What would Hitchens say about the opening lines of Robert Burns's poem, "Oh, My Love Is Like a Red, Red Rose"?

> My love is like a red, red rose
> That's newly sprung in June.
> My love is like the melody,
> That's sweetly played in tune.[36]

Would Hitchens say Burns is somehow insane, thinking his love to be a flower; but worse still, Burns must be a schizoid, because he immediately states that his love is now a musical composition? And how terrible that Burns only loves her in the month of June! What of the other eleven months? And what of Burns's promise later in the poem to love his beloved "Till a' the seas gang dry." "An impossible proposition, to be sure, Mr. Burns!" Hitchens would no doubt protest. "No one lives *that* long!" Now *that* much is true; people don't outlive their own lives, though great poetry can and often does.

The point of this brief foray back to the land of New Atheism is to underscore that (1) in terms of the linguistic analogy, there is another language or linguistic system that has gone into the construction of the pidgin that Marcion speaks and shares, to no small degree, with more recent despisers of the Old Testament; and that (2) the critical criterion that he and they bring to bear may be ill-suited to the task at hand or, more properly, to the subject matter under discussion, which in this case is the Old Testament. The criterion is ill-suited because the Old Testament is an ancient, dense, and highly literary—even poetic—linguistic system. It too has its fair share of neuter knives, feminine forks, and masculine tables, not to mention irregular verb forms and complex moods and modalities. Of course contact languages don't have to gel. The dominant group imposes their will on the weaker group. The pidgin that results from the language contact favors the former; the latter are not asked if the shoe fits. Linguistically speaking, then, it doesn't matter if Marcion's or the New Atheists' superstrate "fits" the Old Testament, and

---

35. Hitchens, *God Is Not Great*, 118.
36. Widely available; see, e.g., Kennedy and Gioia, *Introduction to Poetry*, 137–38.

that is true. But it is equally true from a linguistic perspective that the pidgin that has resulted in both scenarios is far from an accurate reflection of the full language of Scripture before its rather brutal subordination.

Historically, Marcion's pidgin resonated with many; it still does, with the New Atheists a recent case in point. But the church catholic overruled Marcion in the matter of a reduced canon sans Old Testament (and so much of the New). The orthodox response to Marcion is informative in this regard and casts light on the problem with other Marcions of more recent vintage.

Tertullian contra Marcion

As previously noted, many tried their hand at refuting Marcion. Irenaeus and Ephraem are notable examples, but no one stands out like Tertullian (ca. 160–ca. 225 CE), who wrote no less than five books "against Marcion."[37] The full range of Tertullian's arguments in *Against Marcion* cannot be engaged here, so I will focus on two significant points that have direct bearing on both the linguistic analogy of the Old Testament as (like) a language, and the critique of the Bible offered by the New Atheism. Before doing so, however, it is worth observing that Tertullian took great delight in pointing out the inconsistency of Marcion's system—a point that has also been mentioned by scholars of early Christianity.[38] In other words, Marcion was unable to attain to his own standard of consistency![39] So, as dominant as Marcion's superstrate was, it appears to have failed both him and his followers. In the words of Jules Lebreton and Jacques Zeiller, it was "not sufficient to act as a basis for a doctrine."[40]

First, then, Tertullian takes up the challenge of Marcion's distinction between "the just Old Testament god" and "the good Alien God"—a distinction

37. The version of Tertullian's work that we now have is the third edition, completed "between April 207 and April 208. . . . The first edition appeared perhaps as early as 198" (E. Evans, *Tertullian*, 1:xviii).

38. E.g., Tertullian, *Against Marcion* 1.5, 14, 15, 19, 25–26, etc. E. Evans notes that in books 4 and 5, Tertullian argues that Marcion's edited Gospel and epistles "will not bear the construction put upon them, but present a Christ who is in all respects such a one as the Creator's law and prophets have given reason to expect" (*Tertullian*, 1:xvii). Note also Blackman, *Marcion and His Influence*, 119: "Let Marcion be given credit for that insight characteristic of the creative thinker who sees certain truths very clearly. But he can hardly be acquitted of the charge of arbitrariness in refusing to take account of complementary truths. The Catholic Church at that time was less arbitrary and more appreciative of the wealth of its heritage." More briefly, Lebreton and Zeiller, *History of the Primitive Church*, 523: "[Marcion's] Bible was a mutilated one, and his theology feeble and inconsistent."

39. Here again are points of contact between Marcion and the New Atheists.

40. Lebreton and Zeiller, *History of the Primitive Church*, 527.

predicated on a sharp division between law and gospel. Tertullian argues that Marcion's good god is actually not so good after all. Indeed, by the time Tertullian is through, Marcion's god has all the same qualities that made Marcion so upset with "the Old Testament god":

> What would your opinion be of a physician who by delaying treatment should strengthen the disease, and by deferring remedy should prolong the danger, so that his services might command a larger fee and enhance his own repute? The same judgement will have to be pronounced upon Marcion's god, for permitting evil, favouring wrong, currying favour, offending against that kindness which he did not immediately exercise when cause arose. Evidently he would have exercised it if kind by nature and not by afterthought, if good by character and not by rule and regulation, if god since eternity and not since Tiberius, or rather—to speak more truly—since Cerdo and Marcion.[41]

Even more striking than Tertullian's satirical prose, however, is that he goes on to discuss "whether a god is to be accounted such by virtue of goodness alone, to the exclusion of those other adjuncts, those feelings and affections, which the Marcionites deny to their god and attach to the Creator, but which we recognize in the Creator as no dishonour to God."[42] Since the true God does, in fact, have other attributes, Marcion's "simplistically good god" (who is not so good after all) is *not* the true God.[43]

The problem with Marcion's "simply good" deity is that he is, in the final analysis, entirely devoid of justice. In this regard, Marcion's god is weak and decidedly *un*-godlike; he may *dislike* evil, but he *does nothing* to put a stop to it:

> For if he displays neither hostility nor wrath, if he neither condemns nor distrains, if, that is, he never makes himself a judge, I cannot see how his moral law, that more extensive moral law, can have stability. To what purpose does he lay down commands if he will not require performance, or prohibit transgressions if he is not to exact penalties, if he is incapable of judgment, a stranger to all emotions of severity and reproof? Why does he forbid the commission of an act he does not penalize when committed? It would have been much more honest of him not to forbid an act he was not going to penalize, than to refrain from penalizing what he had forbidden. In fact he ought openly to have allowed it: for if he was not going to penalize it, he had no reason to forbid it. . . . So this [god] is exceptionally dull-witted if he is not offended by the doing of that which

41. Tertullian, *Against Marcion* 1.22 (E. Evans, *Tertullian*, 1:60–61). The reference to Tiberius is because Marcion's Gospel began with Luke 3:1 and the descent of God to Capernaum in the fifteenth year of the reign of Tiberius Caesar.

42. Tertullian, *Against Marcion* 1.25 (E. Evans, *Tertullian*, 1:68–69).

43. See further below.

he dislikes to see being done. . . . But as he does not punish, it is plain that he is not offended. . . . There is nothing so unseemly for a god as to abstain from prosecuting an act he has disapproved of, an act he has forbidden. . . . For a god to be merciful to evil is more unseemly than for him to punish it, especially if he is a god supremely good: *for he can only be completely good if he is the enemy of the bad, so as to put his love of the good into action by hatred of the bad, and discharge his wardship of the good by the overthrowing of the bad.*[44]

Marcion's "better god," Tertullian observes, is thus one "who is neither offended nor angry nor inflicts punishment," but one who forgives evil "by not avenging, and excuses it by not punishing." The result, he continues, is a divine

defaulter against the truth, one who annuls his own decision. He is afraid to condemn what he does condemn, afraid to hate what he does not love, allows when done that which he does not allow to be done, and would rather point out what he disapproves of than give proof of it. Here you will find the ghost of goodness, discipline itself a phantasm, casual precepts, offences free from fear.[45]

Unfortunately, there is not space here to engage the full range of Tertullian's work or the subtleties of his positions. There can also be little doubt that many today would take issue with a goodly number of Tertullian's points. His strict insistence on the rather stern justice of God, for example, does not fully solve the problem of divine wrath that occasioned Marcion so much difficulty, so much as show the deficiency of Marcion's solution. Tertullian does this, in part, by justifying or accounting for God's wrath—no mean feat. But what is crucial is how Tertullian insists with equal strength on God's justice and not only God's goodness. These two must *proceed together*. God's justice is fully compatible with God's goodness; indeed, the combination of God's goodness with God's justice *enhances* the perfection of God's character.[46] This is part of what it means to speak of the oneness of God: God's goodness is God's justice is God's love. Marcion's notion of God's goodness is anything but divine, since it is devoid of God's justice. As a result, Marcion's god is simplistically and solipsistically "good," meaning "nice" and "without judgment." That is why Marcion's god is a false god.

When Tertullian is assessed through the lens of the linguistic analogy and Marcion's pidginized idiolect, what one sees is that the great heresiologist is going to great lengths to understand the *entire* linguistic system, not just

44. Tertullian, *Against Marcion* 1.26 (E. Evans, *Tertullian,* 1:72–75, emphasis added).
45. Tertullian, *Against Marcion* 1.27 (E. Evans, *Tertullian,* 1:74–77).
46. Tertullian, *Against Marcion* 2.11–12 (E. Evans, *Tertullian,* 1:118–23).

part of it.[47] "How does the goodness of God go together with God's wrath?" is a legitimate question. Rather than adopt Marcion's arbitrary favoring (a *true* case of what Dawkins et al. would call "picking and choosing") of the former and complete discounting of the latter, Tertullian is at pains to show how they function *within one and the same language*. Yes, God is angry in the Bible, but angry *at what*? To *what end*, which is to ask, *for what purpose*? Is the object of God's wrath and its telos sufficient to somehow understand it, to even warrant it as good? If so, there is no contradiction at all in God's presentation in the Bible, let alone God's character; instead, God's wrath would be completely understandable within the larger grammar of Scripture. This is, of course and in fact, exactly what Tertullian argues in pointing out that God's goodness was not met with any severity until the inauguration of sin and disobedience. Thus "the goodness of God came first, as his nature is: his sternness came afterwards, as there was reason for it. The former was ingenerate, was God's own, was freely exercised: the latter was accidental, adapted to need, an expedient,"[48] though Tertullian is quick to point out that "since the beginning . . . the Creator is both good and just, both just and good."[49]

To put the matter in slightly different terms taken from the twentieth-century Jewish scholar Abraham J. Heschel, there is a great difference between "the wrath of God" (*ira Dei*) and "a God of wrath" (*Deus irae*).[50] The latter suggests a kind of stative verb: God *is* wrathful, perhaps even always.[51] The former suggests that God's wrath is a transitive verb: it takes an object; God is wrathful *about something*.[52] When that something changes, so also does the verb; God is now something else altogether—no longer wrathful, perhaps even happy.[53] According to Heschel, this transitivity is the whole point behind the prophet's preaching of repentance: it is not yet too late to turn (שׁוּב/*šûb*; cf. Greek μετανοέω/*metanoeō*). Such turning may, in turn, turn the judgment of God (see, e.g., Jer. 3:12–14; 18:7–10; Jon. 3:10). What Marcion and so many

47. Cf. Holmes, "Five Books against Marcion," esp. 474: "[Tertullian] illuminates the Scriptures and glorifies them as containing the whole system of the Faith."

48. Tertullian, *Against Marcion* 2.11 (E. Evans, *Tertullian*, 1:118–19).

49. Tertullian, *Against Marcion* 2.12 (E. Evans, *Tertullian*, 1:120–21).

50. Heschel, *Prophets*, 358–92.

51. See ibid., 371–74, for a discussion. Note Ps. 7:11 and the rabbinic speculation that the length of time God is angry every day lasts for only 0.06 seconds (*b. Ber.* 7a). See Patton, *Religion of the Gods*, 272 and 444n96.

52. Heschel (*Prophets*, 352–53, 367, 370, 381) uses "instrumental," "transitive," and "transient" (but not "stative"). The above sentiments would also hold true about God "being" or "having" love.

53. For God's happiness, see Fretheim, "God, Creation, and the Pursuit of Happiness."

others dislike, seemingly above all else—God's anger—could in the end be salutary, even therapeutic.[54]

Absolutely not to be missed here is that what God is typically mad about, according to both Tertullian and Heschel, is *injustice*. In Heschel's memorable words, "The wrath of God is a lamentation. All prophecy is one great exclamation: God is not indifferent to evil! He is always concerned, He is personally affected by what man does to man. He is a God of pathos. This is one of the meanings of the anger of God: the end of indifference!"[55] Equally memorable is Tertullian's identification of the problem with Marcion and Marcion's god when one is missing this concern to end injustice:

> You will be forced, no question of it, to lay accusation against justice itself—for this it is that causes any man to be a judge—classing it as one of the varieties of evil: which means that you will have to include injustice among the subheadings of goodness. Justice is an evil thing only if injustice is a good one. But since you are compelled to pronounce injustice one of the worst of things, by the same method of reckoning you are forced to rank justice among the best things: for everything hostile to evil is good, even as nothing that is hostile to the good can help being evil. Consequently, in so far as injustice is an evil thing, to the same extent justice is a good thing. Nor is it to be reckoned as merely a variety of goodness, but as the safeguard of it, because unless goodness is governed by justice so as itself to be just, it cannot be goodness: for it will be unjust. Nothing that is unjust can be good, and everything that is just is bound to be good.[56]

Or back to Heschel, "Man's sense of injustice is a poor analogy to God's sense of injustice. The exploitation of the poor is to us a misdemeanor; to God, it is a disaster. Our reaction is disapproval; God's reaction is something no language can convey. Is it a sign of cruelty that God's anger is aroused when the rights of the poor are violated, when widows and orphans are oppressed?"[57]

To put this more explicitly in the terms of the linguistic analogy: Tertullian and Heschel know the full language, not just the pidgin, and as experts in the language, they are able to account for the "bad" parts within the larger linguistic system.[58] It turns out these "bad" parts aren't so "bad" after all!

54. See Tertullian, *Against Marcion* 2.15 (E. Evans, *Tertullian*, 1:128–29).

55. Heschel, *Prophets*, 365; cf. 367: "The call of anger is a call to cancel anger. . . . For all its intensity, it may be averted by prayer. There is no divine anger for anger's sake"; and 374: "The secret of anger is God's care." See further ibid., 379–82.

56. Tertullian, *Against Marcion* 2.11 (E. Evans, *Tertullian*, 1:120–21).

57. Heschel, *Prophets*, 365, cf. 392: "His anger is aroused when the cry of the oppressed comes into His ears" (citing Exod. 22:21–24).

58. Even if that is only by holding them together, in tensive juxtaposition—it is exactly such "contradiction" that Marcion and the New Atheists cannot endure. Note Heschel, "The Lord is

Tertullian's exposé of Marcion's failure at precisely this point is, to my mind, rather compelling—especially when seen within the linguistic analogy.[59] But Tertullian's is not simply a reclamation project, salvaging a few words left in the trash by Marcion. In a deft passage in book 2, he supplies a catena of passages drawn from the Old Testament (esp. from Isaiah and the Psalms) that demonstrate, in stark opposition to Marcion's blunt amputation, that it is replete with the "same goodness of God" and teaches "godly conduct."[60] He summarizes, in a rhetorical flourish, "These few sentences have I adduced out of all the Creator's scriptures, and I suppose nothing is now lacking for testimony to a God exceedingly good: for this is well enough certified by his precepts of goodness and by its rewards."[61] Note well, "out of *all* the . . . scriptures," and "out of all *the Creator's* scriptures," which is to say from the Old Testament (and its God) as well as the New.[62]

The second significant point is to consider Marcion's rejection of figural reading, another disposition he shares with the New Atheists.[63] Not unlike

---

long-suffering, compassionate, loving, and faithful, but He is also demanding, insistent, terrible, and dangerous" (*Prophets*, 366). But Heschel also knows about something beyond simple tension: "Yet, beyond justice and anger lies the mystery of compassion" (368). On the other side of the equation, Tertullian admits to differences or discontinuities, one could even say antitheses, between the Testaments, "provided that all these differences have reference to one and the same God, that God by whom it is acknowledged that they were ordained and also foretold" (Tertullian, *Against Marcion* 4.1; E. Evans, *Tertullian*, 2:256–57). Note also *Against Marcion* 4.11:

We admit this separation, by way of reformation, of enlargement, or progress. . . . So also the gospel is separated from the law, because it is an advance from out of the law, another thing than the law, though not an alien thing, different, though not opposed. Nor is there in Christ any novel style of discourse. . . . If you had wished to prove a man was of a foreign nation, perhaps you would do so by his idiomatic use of his native speech.
(E. Evans, *Tertullian*, 2:308–11)

Quite apart from the fact of whether one agrees with Tertullian's argument here, or with his language of "reformation, enlargement, progress, advance," the point is that his full linguistic system is complex, not simplistic.

59. Heschel (*Prophets*, 383–92), too, engages Marcion.

60. Tertullian, *Against Marcion* 2.19 (E. Evans, *Tertullian*, 1:138–39). Cf. Lebreton and Zeiller, *History of the Primitive Church*, 529: Marcion has to ignore all the texts in the OT "in which God promises good things to the poor" in order to "see in this preaching of Jesus the opposite of the preaching of the Demiurge" (cf. Tertullian, *Against Marcion* 4.14). Further dexterity is on display in book 4, where Tertullian sets out to disprove Marcion by means of the Gospel of Luke alone (with constant reference to the OT), since it was the one that Marcion preserved (portions of). In book 5, Tertullian also counters Marcion with the Epistles of Paul, and for the same reason.

61. Tertullian, *Against Marcion* 2.19 (E. Evans, *Tertullian*, 1:140–41).

62. A further observation: Tertullian is aware (also contra Marcion) that Christ, too, has stern attributes (*Against Marcion* 4.29) and judicial character (4.35, 37; 5.9; also attested in Paul: 5.12), just as the Creator God has plenty of tenderness (4.35) and mercy (5.11). See further below.

63. See von Harnack, *History of Dogma*, 1:269–70; von Harnack, *Outlines*, 71; Blackman, *Marcion and His Influence*, 114–15; Lebreton and Zeiller, *History of the Primitive Church*, 525–26.

Dawkins and Hitchens (see chap. 4), Marcion's "bent of mind was literalist and prosaic."[64] Blackman deems Marcion's rejection of allegorical exegesis an indication of that "literal-mindedness," and believes that his "lack of imagination was bound to misinterpret much of the prophetic literature," among other things.[65] Indeed, "it is patent that with his rigid exegetical rules he was precluded from perceiving some of the deepest truths of Scripture."[66]

At this point too Tertullian proves the more dexterous reader and fluent language user. An illuminating example is found in his consideration of martial imagery in the Psalms and the New Testament and its application to Christ. The following passage is worth quoting in full:

> *Gird thee with a sword upon thy thigh,* says David [Ps. 45:3]. But what do you find written of Christ just before this? *Thou art timely in beauty more than the sons of men, grace is poured forth on thy lips* [Ps. 45:2]. It is ridiculous to suppose that he was flattering, in the matter of timeliness of beauty and grace of lips, one whom he was girding for war with a sword. So also, when he goes on to say, *And stretch forth and prosper and reign,* he adds [the reason], *because of truth and gentleness and righteousness.* Who is going to produce these results with a sword? Will not that rather produce the opposites of these, guile, and severity, and unrighteousness? These are surely the particular purpose and effect of battles. Let us inquire then whether there is a different meaning for that sword, which has so different an activity. Now the apostle John in the Apocalypse describes a sharp two-edged sword as proceeding from the mouth of God, exceeding sharp: and this has to be understood as the divine word. . . . But if you refuse acknowledgement of John, you have Paul, . . . who girds our loins with truth, and with the corselet of righteousness, and shoes our feet with the preparation of the gospel of peace—not of war—and bids us take to us the shield of the faith, that by it we may be able to quench all the fiery darts of the devil, and [to take] the helmet of salvation, and the sword of the spirit, *which,* says he, *is the word of God* [Eph. 6:14ff.]. This is the sword which our Lord himself came to cast on to the earth [Matt. 10:34], not peace. If this is your Christ, then he too is a warrior. If he is not a warrior, but advances an allegorical sword, then it was permissible for the Creator's Christ in the psalm, without warlike intent, to be girt with the figurative sword of the word—and in keeping with this is the above-mentioned timeliness and grace of lips—the sword with which he was at that time girt upon the thigh, as David puts it, but was afterwards to cast upon the earth. . . . This is how the Creator's Christ is a warrior and an armed man, this is how he is even today taking the spoils, not of Samaria only but of all the nations. . . . Admit then that his spoils are

64. Blackman, *Marcion and His Influence,* 113.
65. Ibid., 115.
66. Ibid.

figurative. As then our Lord speaks, and the apostle writes, figuratively of these matters, we do then with good confidence make use of those interpretations of his, instances of which even our adversaries acknowledge: and so the Christ who has come will be Isaiah's Christ, for the very reason that he was not a warrior, because he is not by Isaiah described as such.[67]

Here again not all contemporary readers (let alone critics) will be convinced by Tertullian's reading; nevertheless, there are at least three main takeaways from a passage like this: as an expert in the full language of Scripture, Tertullian is able to (1) weave and interweave the two Testaments of Scripture together into a unified whole—a whole that (2) is more than the sum of its parts because it uses the whole to make sense of the parts. This leads, finally, to the third point, that (3) flatfooted, overly "literal" reading of the Old Testament—a reading "without criticism and spiritual insight"—"leads to the destruction of the N[ew] Testament" as well.[68] It was Marcion, not Tertullian, who threw large portions of the New Testament out of his "Gospel."

Tertullian did not create figural reading; it was practiced in Christian and Jewish circles long before him.[69] Indeed, the Bible itself has allegories and many other types of figures and tropes. Neither is it only the arch-heretic Marcion or the New Atheists who denigrate figural readings. For centuries figural reading has been out of fashion due to the dominance of historical-critical methodology. Although historical criticism's dominance in the field of biblical studies, along with its rejection of figural reading strategies, has begun to loosen in recent years,[70] there are many who still think readings like Tertullian's above to be substandard in some way. Interestingly enough, the criticism comes not only from those committed to a strict historicist understanding of original authorial intent, but also from those deeply concerned with somehow accounting for or assessing problematic depictions in the Old Testament.

The work of Eric Seibert might be mentioned at this point. According to Seibert, a figural reading strategy like that of typology (which relates the Old Testament in various ways to Christ or the church) is wrongheaded because it "evades problems related to the characterization of God in the Old Testament." In his judgment, "troubling questions about God's character . . . are completely ignored by the typological approach, which passes

---

67. Tertullian, *Against Marcion* 3.14 (E. Evans, *Tertullian*, 1:210–15). A similar passage, with reference to martial imagery in Paul, is found in 5.18 (ibid., 1:622–29).

68. Hall, "Marcion," 424.

69. See the works cited in chap. 4, note 41.

70. See Steinmetz, "Superiority of Pre-critical Exegesis," 27–38; also Davis, *Wondrous Depth*.

over the grittier aspects of the text. Instead, this approach creatively uses Old Testament passages, even ones with problematic portrayals of God, to provide positive lessons about Christ and the church."[71] Seibert's remark is only partly accurate. Figural readings can certainly be "creative," with the lessons drawn "positive," but such creativity is not entirely fanciful (as opposed to deeply rooted in the textual details);[72] neither is it true that difficult problems or "grittier aspects" of the text are "completely ignored" by figural reading. To the contrary, it is *precisely* the difficulties and grittiness that give rise to the need for subtler and defter interpretation, as seen in the passage on Christ's militancy from Tertullian.[73] The most important thing to stress, however, is that figural reading strategies, whether of ancient or recent vintage, are not just simplistic attempts at "salvaging" the Old Testament (or New) or at rendering it harmless in some way by "neutralizing" its most offensive parts.[74] Figural readings are far more than that. They should not be viewed primarily as a *defensive* posture but rather as a *proactive* and *generative* strategy that "enabled Christians to use the whole Bible as the church's book."[75] But even this way of putting things isn't fully satisfying because, in a very real sense, the church *already had* (and has) the whole Bible as its book—or at least the whole Old Testament.[76] Tertullian, Irenaeus, Origen, and all the rest are not, therefore, performing some sort of herculean feat of interpretive magic by which the Old Testament is saved (and without which it is doomed), so much as they are making sense of the entire linguistic system they inherited, which they had mastered, and which they were able to speak—and speak better and more fluently than Marcion and more recent critics of figural readings.[77] It was Marcion, not these church fathers, who

71. Seibert, *Disturbing Divine Behavior*, 60–61.

72. Cf. ibid., 64, which complains about "lack of controls governing how correlations are made between details in the texts and the meaning assigned to them"; or ibid., 68, which states that figural readings are "too subjective and they fail to deal seriously with the plain meaning of the text." This sounds much like Dawkins, and in more than one way.

73. As Seibert himself notes, Origen thought difficulties in Scripture "had been placed there intentionally by the Spirit and were meant to lead the mature reader to deeper insights" (ibid., 62).

74. Cf. ibid., 59–64.

75. Trigg, *Origen*, 60, cited in Seibert, *Disturbing Divine Behavior*, 63.

76. Though certainly not yet in its final canonized order and certainly not yet together with the NT in its final canonical order—developments that took place only later. See McDonald, *Biblical Canon*. The point is primarily that the church had the full complex, "syncretistic" tradition (von Harnack's term) that Marcion found so hard to stomach.

77. Note May, "Marcion in Contemporary Views," 147: "Since the Old Testament is not sufficient for [Marcion's] theological demands, he traces it back to a God of low rank. The rejection of allegorical interpretation is the *consequence*, not the presupposition, of criticism" (emphasis added).

was dumbfounded in facing the complexity of the Old Testament and who simply couldn't master its grammar.

Von Harnack pro Marcion, or the New Marcion(ism)

Like any good heresy, Marcion's never fully died out. It is no exaggeration to say that Marcion's ghost animates many people's continued problems with the Old Testament (both within the church and without), which in turn contributes to the Old Testament's slow and steady demise. One can find Marcionite traces or inclinations in a host of places. It can be too easy, if not tempting, to accuse any anti–Old Testament issue of being "Marcionite." While that isn't always accurate, what are we to say about the phenomenon of New Testament–only Bibles?[78] or "New Testament Churches"? or hermeneutical approaches that always and invariably favor the New Testament as the final judge and jury of all matters pertaining to the Old Testament?[79] These presenting problems, and thousands like them, are not necessarily shackled with all of Marcion's gnostic- or docetic-like tendencies, but they do smack of his fundamental proclivities regarding the relationship of the two Testaments.

A stunning example of modern Marcionism is found in the work of his greatest biographer, Adolf von Harnack (1851–1930). Much of what was said above about Marcion stems ultimately, if not directly, from von Harnack's groundbreaking historical work, though scholarly debate and discussion of the arch-heretic continues and will persist for years to come. For present purposes, what is most important about von Harnack's work on Marcion is how the great church historian found himself in rather marked agreement with the arch-heretic and his position on the Old Testament.

Von Harnack's fascination with Marcion was long-standing. Indeed, he called Marcion "my first love in church history,"[80] since his first award-winning paper was on the arch-heretic, written when he was only nineteen as a university student at Dorpat.[81] Although he frequently had occasion to discuss Marcion in his many writings, von Harnack did not return to round out his early work on Marcion into a full and mature monograph until late in life. The first version of *Marcion: The Gospel of the Alien God* was published in

---

78. Even these often feel compelled to include the Psalms!

79. So Seibert, *Disturbing Divine Behavior*. I will return to this last matter in chap. 9. For now, note Lamb (*God Behaving Badly*, 102), who accuses Seibert of "rejecting major sections of the Old Testament, a bit like Marcion."

80. Von Harnack, *Marcion: The Gospel*, ix. May ("Marcion in Contemporary Views," 129n2) speaks of "Harnack's personal relationship with Marcion."

81. Von Harnack, *Marcion: The Gospel*, ix.

1920; von Harnack released a second edition, his last published book, in 1924, at the age of 73.[82] In this now-classic work, von Harnack makes the following, now infamous, remark:[83]

> The thesis that is to be argued in the following [pages] may be stated thus: *the rejection of the Old Testament in the second century was a mistake which the great church rightly avoided; to maintain it in the sixteenth century was a fate from which the Reformation was not yet able to escape; but still to preserve it in Protestantism as a canonical document since the nineteenth century is the consequence of a religious and ecclesiastical crippling.*[84]

Lest there be any confusion about the force of this statement, von Harnack goes on to summarize his position a few pages later, "[Marcion] was obliged to *reject* the Old Testament as a false, anti-godly book in order to be able to preserve the gospel in its purity, but rejection is not in the picture today at all. Rather this book will be everywhere esteemed and treasured in its distinctiveness and its significance (the prophets) only when the *canonical authority* to which it is not entitled is withdrawn from it."[85] Rejection is not an option today, von Harnack says, but one thinks he "doth protest too much" since what he advocates is exactly and explicitly a *withdrawal* of canonical authority from the Old Testament. And what is withdrawing canonical authority if not, in fact, a *rejection* of the Old Testament's canonical status as Christian Scripture?[86] Pressing his point, von Harnack is so bold as to state that the Old Testament is *not entitled* to such canonical authority. It is impossible to imagine how such denigration and withdrawal will eventuate (so von Harnack) in *universal and ubiquitous esteem* for the Old Testament, though here too von Harnack's gloss is revealing. Apparently the Old Testament's "distinctiveness" and "significance" comes down to just this: "the prophets."[87]

Gerhard May is no doubt correct in observing that "Harnack's book [on Marcion] is not only a historical study; it represents also a document of the theology of its author."[88] Such a judgment is true of every study, in one way or the other, to greater or lesser degrees—even supposedly "objective" or "dispas-

---

82. See Rumscheidt, *Harnack: Liberal Theology*, 28; Rumscheidt, "Harnack, Karl Gustav Adolf von."

83. Rumscheidt (*Harnack: Liberal Theology*, 29) calls it "notorious."

84. Harnack, *Marcion: The Gospel*, 134, emphasis original.

85. Ibid., 138, emphasis original.

86. This is almost exactly how I describe my diagnosis of the OT's death in chap. 1.

87. Cf. von Harnack (*Outlines*, 48), stating that the OT contribution to the faith of early Christians comes down largely to the Psalms and "prophetical fragments."

88. May, "Marcion in Contemporary Views," 129.

sionate" historiography. The problem is not, therefore, that von Harnack was somehow personally invested in his study of Marcion; the problem is rather that von Harnack's personal investment—his own "theology," according to May—is aligned with the arch-heretic's! Indeed, von Harnack's Marcionism is on display elsewhere in the corpus of his work. One example from his book *Militia Christi* (1905) can suffice: "Marcion undoubtedly understood the Christian concept of God in an essentially correct way. . . . It will always be to the glory of the Marcionite church . . . that it would rather cast away the Old Testament than tarnish the image of the Father of Jesus Christ by mixing in traces of a warlike God."[89]

It is not hard, given von Harnack's location in Berlin and the specific dates of his book on Marcion (1920, 1924 [2nd ed.]), to see how his affirmation of the arch-heretic's position on the Old Testament slides easily into a Christian supersessionism laced with anti-Semitism.[90] Note, for example:

> As Christianity is the only true religion, and as it is no national religion, but somehow concerns the whole of humanity, or its best part, it follows that it can have nothing in common with the Jewish nation and its contemporary cultus. The Jewish nation in which Jesus Christ appeared, has, for the time at least, no special relation to the God whom Jesus revealed. Whether it had such a relation at an earlier period is doubtful (cf. here, *e.g.*, the attitude of Marcion, Ptolemaeus the disciple of Valentinus, the author of the Epistle of Barnabas, Aristides and Justin); but certain it is that God has now cast it off, and that all revelations of God, so far as they took place at all before Christ, (the majority [of Christians] assumed that there had been such revelations and considered the Old Testament as a holy record), must have aimed solely at the call of the "new people," and in some way prepared for the revelation of God through his son.[91]

This passage is epitomized in a later abridgement as follows:

> Since Christianity is the only true religion and is not a national religion, but belongs to all mankind and pertains to our inmost life, it follows that it can have no special alliance with the Jewish people, or with their peculiar cult. *The Jewish people of today*, at least, stand in no favored relationship with the God whom Jesus has revealed; whether they formerly did is doubtful; this, however, is certain, that God has cast them off, and that the whole Divine

---

89. Von Harnack, *Militia Christi*, 47.

90. It is debated if Marcion himself was anti-Semitic. E. Evans (*Tertullian*, 1:xii) thinks not, but contrast Lebreton and Zeiller, *History of the Primitive Church*, 528. See May, "Marcion in Contemporary Views," for the possibility that Marcion himself was Jewish.

91. Von Harnack, *History of Dogma*, 1:148; cf. 1:101: "[Apocalyptic literature] was an evil inheritance which the Christians took over from the Jews."

revelation, so far as there was a revelation prior to Christ (the majority believed in one and looked upon the Old Testament as Holy Scripture) had as its end the calling of a "new nation" and the spreading of the revelation of God through his Son.[92]

The different formulation (italicized above) is chilling. Although it may be the result of a different translator making different translation choices (the German originals are highly similar and the specific phrase in question, *zur Zeit*, identical), one sees clearly that this passage, too, in both editions, reflects the theology of its author—and horribly so. In this section of his history of dogma, von Harnack is supposedly summarizing "common beliefs" held by "the great majority of Christians" during the first century,[93] but his accent betrays him. The dispassionate objectivity of a historian is lost; in its place and more than evident are the fraught judgments of a modern-day Marcionite supersessionist.[94]

I do not mean to imply that the early church did not struggle with the Old Testament, nor that the early church was somehow guiltless when it came to the problem of anti-Judaism or anti-Semitism. The examples to the contrary are all too well known. Neither is von Harnack wrong when he states that the Old Testament was often used by early Christian writers to

refut[e] Judaism as a nation, *i.e.* to the proving that this people had been cast off by God, and that they had either never had any covenant with him (Barnabas), or had had a covenant of wrath, or had forfeited their covenant; that they had never understood the Old Testament and were therefore now deprived of it, if, indeed, they had ever been in possession of it (the attitude of the Church as a whole toward the Jewish people and their history appears to have been originally as indefinite as the attitude of the Gnostics toward the Old Testament). . . . Attempts to correct the Old Testament and to give it a Christian sense were not wanting; in the formation of the New Testament there were rudimentary efforts toward this end.[95]

But not all of these "refutations" are of a piece, nor are they all of equal merit. Here again, then, von Harnack reveals a Marcionite preference for

92. Von Harnack, *Outlines*, 42, emphasis added.
93. Ibid., 39–40.
94. Cf. ibid., 74–75, where von Harnack narrowly defines "Jewish-Christianity" as applicable "exclusively to those Christians who really retained, entirely or in the smallest part, the *national* and *political* forms of Judaism and insisted upon the observance of the Mosaic Law without modification as essential to Christianity . . . or who indeed rejected these forms, but acknowledged the prerogative of the Jewish *people* also in Christianity" (emphasis original).
95. Ibid., 48–49.

coherent logic above all else. The New Testament certainly does a lot more (and much less!) than "correct" the Old Testament and "give it a Christian sense." Indeed, as Robert Jenson has noted, it is more accurate to say that the Old Testament accommodated the Christian church than it is to say that the church accommodated the Old Testament.[96] Moreover, the efforts made in the New Testament vis-à-vis the Old Testament may not be "rudimentary" at all, but altogether necessary, if not also sufficient, such that newer attempts at "refutation" or "correction" like Marcion's and von Harnack's are both *un*necessary and *in*sufficient (see chap. 9). Options like those offered in *The Epistle of Barnabas* are, at any rate and at the very least, noncanonical.[97]

To be as fair as possible, one should admit that von Harnack has better moments. As a historian, von Harnack admits that even if "nearly all Gentile Christian groups that we know, are at one in the detachment of Christianity from empiric Judaism," it is still true that "the greater part of Christians did not" detach themselves from the Old Testament.[98] Elsewhere he acknowledges that early Christian opinion differed on the history of Israel and its relation to God,[99] and he remarks that at least some statements in the Old Testament "were too exalted for any caviling, and intelligible to every spiritually awakened mind."[100] And yet von Harnack indicates that "this treasure" that is the best of Scripture was "handed down to the Greeks and Romans," without so much as mentioning the Jewish community.[101] Finally, von Harnack seems aware of Marcion's problems here and there, speaking at one point of the arch-heretic's "crass dualism" that reflected "a Paulinism without dialectics."[102] He even invoked the specter of Marcion in his debate with Karl Barth, when von Harnack accused the Swiss theologian of a Marcionite move, by severing "every link between faith and the human."[103]

But all that is prior to or outside von Harnack's final, culminating monograph on Marcion, with its notorious affirmation of the arch-heretic's views on the Old Testament. That affirmation lines up with the generally negative tenor one sees in von Harnack's assessment of the Old Testament (and Judaism). In the disparaging passages, while von Harnack frequently makes recourse

96. Jenson, *Canon and Creed*, 6, 19–26.
97. See Grant and Tracy (*Interpretation of the Bible*, 41) for Barnabas's closeness to the "heretical Gnosticism of the second century."
98. Von Harnack, *History of Dogma*, 1:148–49n1.
99. Ibid., 1:178.
100. Ibid., 1:177.
101. Ibid.
102. Von Harnack, *Outlines*, 71.
103. See Rumscheidt, *Harnack: Liberal Theology*, 92–93; for Barth's response, see ibid., 101–2.

to the New Testament, he does not, as far as I can see, ever cite Rom. 9–11, a unit where, among other things, Paul says things like this:

> So I ask you, has God rejected his people? Absolutely not! (Rom. 11:1 CEB)

> So I'm asking you: They [God's people, Israel] haven't stumbled so that they've fallen permanently, have they? Absolutely not! (Rom. 11:11a CEB)

> God's gifts and calling can't be taken back. (Rom. 11:29 CEB)[104]

Only an egregious oversight like that enables von Harnack to make a statement like this: "Israel was thus at all times the pseudo-Church."[105]

Again, the majority of von Harnack's work on the history of Christian doctrine preceded his last, most mature and considered statements on Marcion, found in his biography of the arch-heretic. It is there that von Harnack concurs with Marcion, recommending that we do away with the Old Testament altogether in a move that previous generations of Christians, for various reasons, didn't have the nerve to make. Rumscheidt puts it bluntly, but altogether accurately: "Harnack was anti-Judaistic in his interpretation of the Old Testament: for him it was an anachronistic work."[106] The accusation is irrefutable but becomes all the more disturbing in light of the publication of the Marcion monograph in the 1920s and contemporaneous events in Germany, both before and after its two editions.[107]

Contra von Harnack, or the Deadly Ramifications

Perhaps the most important of the events preceding the publication of von Harnack's *Marcion* was the Babel-Bibel controversy, in which the noted Assyriologist Friedrich Delitzsch, in a highly public venue, argued that the Old Testament was little more than a secondary derivation from Babylonian culture.[108] Delitzsch followed his two public lectures with the publication of his

---

104. Romans 9–11 is among the densest collections of OT citations to be found in the entire NT. See J. Wagner, *Heralds of the Good News*; cf. also chap. 9 below.

105. Von Harnack, *History of Dogma*, 1:179; but cf. von Harnack, *Outlines*, 75, where, by his definition, Paul is a Jewish Christian "because of Romans XI." This is not a larger comment on the OT or Judaism proper, however.

106. Rumscheidt, "Harnack, Karl Gustav Adolf von," 506.

107. Cf. Detmers, "Die Interpretation der Israel-Lehre Marcions."

108. See Delitzsch, *Babel and Bible*. See, inter alia, Arnold and Weisberg, "Centennial Review of Friedrich Delitzsch's 'Babel und Bibel' Lectures"; Arnold and Weisberg, "Babel und Bibel und Bias"; Arnold and Weisberg, "Delitzsch in Context."

Die grosse Täuschung (The great deception), the great deception in question being the Old Testament itself, particularly its claim to reveal the true God.[109] In this book, Delitzsch asserts that Germans would receive better help from their own national myths than from the Old Testament, which he recommended setting aside altogether and forever. Delitzsch's reasoning in the early twentieth century reminds one of Marcion's in the second and the New Atheists' in the twenty-first: "The more deeply I immerse myself in the spirit of the prophetic literature of the Old Testament, the greater becomes my mistrust of Yahweh, who butchers the peoples with the sword of his insatiable anger; who has but one favorite child, while he consigns all other nations to darkness, shame, and ruin."[110] While Delitzsch's lectures preceded the publication of von Harnack's *Marcion*, Emil Kraeling is correct when he states that, in Delitzsch, von Harnack got what he wished for: someone who did, for all intents and purposes, withdraw canonical authority from the Old Testament.[111]

The comparison between Delitzsch and von Harnack was not lost on observers at the time,[112] such that von Harnack himself felt the need to address the issue in the second edition of *Marcion*: "Hereby I object to the classifying of my arguments with those of Friedrich Delitzsch (*Die grosse Täuschung*), which has happened several times. The latter are as outdated from a scholarly standpoint as they are objectionable from a religious standpoint."[113] But with all due respect to von Harnack, it is exceedingly difficult to see how one could *not* relate his comments to Delitzsch's work. On the status of the Old Testament, both scholars are nothing if not Marcion redivivus.[114] What is more disturbing than their rhetoric, however, is the dating of the same to that particular moment of German history. It is hard to believe that such sentiments did not have a profound effect on, and were thus partially culpable for, the anti-Semitism of Germany, which came to its most horrific result in the Final Solution of the Nazis.[115]

109. Delitzsch, *Die grosse Täuschung*.

110. Cited in Seibert, *Disturbing Divine Behavior*, 64–65. Marcion, too, had problems with the prophets; contrast von Harnack's valorization of the same (noted above).

111. Kraeling, *Old Testament since the Reformation*, 162–63.

112. See, e.g., the critical comments by Jules Lebreton in his review of von Harnack's second German edition (1924): "Bulletin d'histoire des origines chrétiennes," esp. 360–61.

113. Von Harnack, *Marcion: The Gospel*, 177n6. The note accompanies the statement he makes in ibid., 138.

114. Cf. Seibert (*Disturbing Divine Behavior*, 64), who calls Delitzsch and von Harnack "two modern-day Marcionites" and Hector Avalos a "contemporary quasi-Marcionite." In my judgment, Seibert's own solution to difficult texts in the OT has its own Marcionite elements, as does Stark's *Human Faces of God*. Once again, as per the *testimonia* of the current book, the OT poses a master problem for Christian theology.

115. See Bright, *Authority of the Old Testament*, 67, 79; Gunneweg, *Understanding the Old Testament*, 156–57.

The problem of pidginization of the Old Testament, therefore, is pressed upon us not only by Marcion in the second century, but by the Holocaust in the twentieth. Like any heresy worth its salt, Marcionism has endured. According to church historians, its effects lingered for centuries, and von Harnack, a church historian himself, is proof of the point. So is Delitzsch, and so are, I would argue, the New Atheists (New Marcionites of a sort), not to mention many others.

But Marcion's ghost is also seen in other, less conspicuous ways as well—say, in the way the New Testament is favored and the Old Testament neglected week in and week out, not just in the "best sermons" but also in the hymns and the readings of the church at worship (see chap. 2). In light of Marcion, von Harnack, and the Holocaust, the pidginization reflected in Christian liturgy takes on an increased and dread significance. It is no longer a matter of simple liturgical preference or inclination; it is far more serious than that.

One final proof of the point: According to Doris L. Bergen, the Nazis were able to enjoy success among German Christian groups in part because of widespread biblical—and here one should be specific: Old Testament—illiteracy.[116] The Nazi movement succeeded, at least to some degree, among German Christians because they didn't know their Bibles, especially their Old Testaments. Bergen has chronicled the Nazi's systematic elimination of the Old Testament—how that began with denying the canonicity of the Old Testament and then moved to censorship of liturgical elements and church hymnody.[117] This type of censorship is nothing if not forced language death,[118] executed (literally) within a linguistic community wherein the language is supposed to be practiced and so flourish—in worship.[119] But once the community of faith no longer sings the Old Testament, it is a short step to removing it altogether, from pulpit, prayer, and liturgy. The ontological connection that exists between Israel and the church is thus severed. It is no wonder—though at the same time it is simply unfathomable—that when the death squads came for the Jews, the "German Christians" looked the other way . . . and worse.[120]

We saw in chapter 3 that when languages are dying, they revert to pidgin-like forms. A language undergoing repidginization is a language on its way to death. In the light of Marcion—both the Old and New varieties, from

---

116. Bergen, *Twisted Cross*, 142–71.
117. Ibid., 26, 126, 142–71.
118. See Hagège, *Death and Life of Languages*, 106–8, on violent language death.
119. Cf. the demise of the OT in preaching, hymnody, and the RCL as detailed in chap. 2. Note also Stookey, "Marcion, Typology, and Lectionary Preaching," which is pertinent.
120. See further Bergen, *Twisted Cross*; cf. also Goldhagen, *Hitler's Willing Executioners*.

the second century to the Holocaust in the twentieth, even up to the present day—the repidginization of the Old Testament and its movement toward death become even more ominous and far more deadly. It is no longer simply a matter of language learning or biblical literacy, certainly not of the trivial kind. It is a matter of *life and death*—death of the most physical and horrific kind. The stakes are nothing less than the lives of human beings, not solely the health of a human language.

In this light, the anti–Old Testament sentiments of more recent vintage from the New Atheists take on a rather deathly pallor.[121] Sadly—and this is Marcion's legacy within Christianity—it is not only atheists who make such comments. As Fleming Rutledge has observed, "Many Christians continue, unthinkingly, to speak of 'the God of the Old Testament' as though this supposedly wrathful and judgmental God had been supplanted by an endlessly tolerant and indulgent Jesus. This ill-formed attitude is not exactly anti-Semitic, but it can be called into the service of anti-Semitism."[122] The death of the Old Testament is one example of such anti-Semitism, but it is equally also a contributing factor to the same.

121. See, e.g., Hitchens, *God Is Not Great*, 101: "One mutters a few sympathetic words for the forgotten and obliterated Hivites, Canaanites, and Hittites, also presumably part of the Lord's original creation, who are to be pitilessly driven out of their homes to make room for *the ungrateful and mutinous children of Israel*"; 102: "[The OT] was put together by *crude, uncultured human mammals*"; 107: "None of *these provincials*, or their deity, seems to have any idea of a world beyond the desert, the flocks and herds, and the imperatives of nomadic subsistence" (emphasis added throughout). Note Herman Rauschning's report of a meeting in which Adolf Hitler railed against the OT, esp. the Decalogue:

"There is much more behind this," Hitler began fanatically. . . . "We are fighting against the most ancient curse that humanity has brought upon itself. We are fighting against the perversion of our soundest instincts. Ah, the God of the deserts, that crazed, stupid, vengeful Asiatic despot with his powers to make laws! . . . That devilish 'Thou shalt, thou shalt!' And that stupid 'Thou shalt not.' It's got to get out of our blood, that curse from Mount Sinai! That poison with which both Jews and Christians have spoiled and soiled the free, wonderful instincts of man and lowered them to the level of doglike fright." . . . "Thou shalt not steal? Wrong!" Hitler's voice was loud in the small room. "All life is theft." . . . "I am the Lord thy God! Who? That Asiatic tyrant? No! The day will come when I shall hold up against these commandments the tables of a new law. And history will recognize our movement as the great battle for humanity's liberation, a liberation from the curse of Mount Sinai, from the dark stammerings of nomads who could no more trust their own sound instincts, who could understand the divine only in the form of a tyrant who orders one to do the very things one doesn't like. This is what we are fighting against, . . . the masochistic spirit of self-torment, the curse of so-called morals, idolized to protect the weak from the strong in the face of the immortal law of battle. . . . Against the so-called ten commandments, against them we are fighting."

(Robinson, *Ten Commandments*, xii–xiii)

Note that both Christopher Hitchens and Sam Harris are of Jewish heritage.

122. Rutledge, *And God Spoke to Abraham*, 6; cf. also 97.

6

New Plastic Gospels:
The "Happiologists"

The previous two signs of morbidity (chaps. 4–5) showcased the phenomenon of repidginization—the process by which a language (like that of the Old Testament) reverts to a pidginized form on its way to extinction. It cannot be doubted that in both of the preceding examples—as is true for all cases of repidginization—some (but very little) of the lexical stock from the original Scripture language remains in place; a bit is accurately preserved. Of course that is precisely what one expects from a pidgin language (see chap. 3). It is equally unsurprising that so much of even the little that is retained in the repidginized forms is, as it were, "mispronounced," which is to say, either misunderstood altogether or (re)understood in fundamentally different ways. This too is part of the pidginization process and thus also part of repidginization.

Whatever the case, it is clear that the largest problem facing the linguistic systems offered by the New Atheists and by "Marcion and friends" is that each is inherently deficient because they are massive reductions of the original (substrate) language of Scripture, whether that deficiency is due to duplicity, ignorance, or (superstrate) influence from "logic" or "consistency." The huge loss in terms of phonology, grammar, and lexicon (analogically understood) is the most important proof that the persons advocating these positions, as intelligent and eloquent as they may be (and oftentimes are), are actually nothing of the sort when it comes to the large, rich, and complex linguistic system that is the Old Testament at full stretch. In the face of that fulsome reality, these persons are babblers in the nursery, not Shakespeare and not Einstein.

Repidginization is a sign of imminent language death because it shows there are no fully fluent speakers left, or, just as likely (and consequently), that there is no one left who is interested or willing to learn the full language. It was mentioned in chapter 3 that once a pidgin exists, regardless of the details of its creation, different things can happen to it. Most pidgins are created for some specific and momentary purpose (e.g., trade between cultures), and thus die out quickly. But if a pidgin is spoken for a long enough time—long enough that there are second-generation individuals who grow up with the pidgin as their mother tongue—then it is possible for the pidgin to grow up as well, expanding and developing into a full-blown language, which linguists call a *creole*.[1]

The third and final sign of the Old Testament's morbidity that will be treated in this chapter fits this latter linguistic phenomenon. It concerns preachers of the so-called prosperity gospel,[2] whom I will also refer to as the "happiologists."[3] In what follows I focus on Joel Osteen, but he is just one representative—though a highly influential and successful one—of a much larger movement. To anticipate what follows, I will argue that when it comes to the Old Testament (and the Bible as a whole), the happiologists offer us the equivalent of a modern plastic invention: they do not speak a pidgin but a brand-new creole. That is, they speak a language that began as a pidgin but that has now become a full-blown language, replete with all the linguistic items a creole must create on its way to developing into a full language. These new items include linguistic rules not found in the pidgin or further development of rules already at work in the pidgin; above all other considerations, however, creoles are marked by full regularity in the creation of new grammar. So, while it is clear that the happiology creole is alive and kicking—which is to say, selling well—when assessed vis-à-vis the original language that is the Old Testament, the existence of a creole is a dire situation, indicating that the Old Testament is facing a death that is no less imminent than in the cases of the two repidginized signs of morbidity discussed previously. Indeed, insofar as creoles are even further removed from the languages that birthed their most immediate ancestor, the pidgin (see diagram 1 in chap. 3), the happiology creole is ultimately even more dangerous and troubling than the (re)pidginized Old Testament.

1. See chap. 3 for the fact that there are very few expanded, long-term pidgins.
2. Bowler, *Blessed*, uses the terms "faith movement," "prosperity movement," "prosperity theology," and "prosperity gospel" interchangeably (see 205n2), as will I.
3. As explained in chap. 1, I use "happiologists" and "happiology" to differentiate such prosperity theology and positive thinking from the authentic happiness studied in Positive Psychology. The former two are not the same as the latter, which I deem a legitimate branch of psychological study. See Peterson, *Primer in Positive Psychology*, 7–8; and S. Lewis, *Positive Psychology at Work*, 2–6. For an application of Positive Psychology to the Bible, see Strawn, *Bible and the Pursuit of Happiness*.

The Bible and Your Best Everything Right Now!

Early in the very first chapter of his book *Every Day a Friday: How to Be Happier 7 Days a Week*, Joel Osteen, the pastor of Lakewood Church in Houston, Texas, America's largest megachurch, writes the following:

> We prepare for victory or defeat at the very start of each day. When you get up in the morning, you have to set your mind in the right direction. You may feel discouraged. You may feel the blahs, thinking, *I don't want to go to work today.* Or *I don't want to deal with these children.* Or *I've got so many problems.*
>
> If you make the mistake of dwelling on those thoughts, you are preparing to have a lousy day. You're using your faith in the wrong direction. Turn it around and say, "This will be a great day. Something good will happen to me. God has favor in my future, and I'm expecting new opportunities, divine connections, and supernatural breakthroughs."
>
> When you take that approach, you prepare for victory, increase, and restoration. God says to the angels, "Did you hear that? They're expecting My goodness. They're expecting to prosper in spite of the economy. They're expecting to get well in spite of the medical report. They're expecting to accomplish their dreams even though they don't have the resources right now."
>
> When you begin each day in faith, anticipating something good, God tells the angels to go to work and to arrange things in your favor. He gives you breaks, lines up the right people, and opens the right doors.[4]

This passage is similar to others found in *Every Day a Friday*, not to mention the other books that compose Osteen's lot of bestsellers, and so can serve as a representative example suitable for analysis. Several observations can be made about the passage, especially in light of the linguistic analogy I am employing here.

What is perhaps most obvious is the *full regularity* of Osteen's description. There is no room for flexibility or freedom here, let alone anything surprising, whether that is from the divine or human side of the equation. People may feel one way, but they are entirely able to "turn it around and say" something else. It's either all negative (*the blahs*) or all positive (*This will be a great day*)—one or the other, but nothing in-between and certainly nothing admixed. When people do "turn it around" and "anticipate something good," God—or so it seems from Osteen's language—has no option but to bless in response. God's action is fully regularized: fully contingent, and directly so, on what a human being says or does or thinks. One way to put this is that God, in Osteen's scenario, is decidedly *un*free. Another, less flattering way to put it is

4. Osteen, *Every Day a Friday*, 6–7.

that God is little more than a lapdog, subject to every human whim, as long as that is positive ("Come here, boy! Good dog!"). Either way you put it, the human is the master, not God—a complete reversal of the biblical witness to the power, freedom, and sovereignty of God. The possibility that such full regularity could ever be broken—upset as, for instance, in the biblical case of Job—is not imagined by Osteen, at least not here. Then again, Job is an ancient book, from an ancient collection, and ancient languages are full of irregularities that new languages like creoles simply will not tolerate.

Not only is there full regularity in the citation above, there are also new lexical items, new definitions, and new grammatical rules—all of which one expects in creoles, which are an instance of "language starting over" from scratch.⁵ In terms of *new definitions*, notice how Osteen's "beginning each day in faith" is immediately defined (via apposition) as "anticipating something good." Just a bit earlier "using your faith" in the right direction is defined as expecting goodness, prosperity, health, and the realization of one's dreams (which go unspecified, though achieving them evidently has to do with sufficient "resources"), along with a smidgen of religiosity ("divine connections . . . supernatural breakthroughs," which again go unspecified). As for *new rules*, Osteen's full grammatical regularity—that faith leads directly to God's telling the angels to get to work and favor the faithful individual—is a primary example. How Osteen knows that rule, how he knows what God says to the angels, and so on, is never indicated, only declared.

"Declare" is a most apt word, and an example of a *new lexical item* in the happiology creole. It is, in fact, the main verb (declined in first person, of course) used in the title of one of Osteen's popular volumes: *I Declare: 31 Promises to Speak over Your Life*. There are thirty-one promises to correspond to each day of the month, so that each day, every month, and the entire year can be blessed. Day 1's declaration is illustrative and, again, representative:

I DECLARE God's incredible blessings over my life. I will see an explosion of God's goodness, a sudden widespread increase. I'll experience the surpassing greatness of God's favor. It will elevate me to a level higher than I dreamed of. Explosive blessings are coming my way. This is my declaration.⁶

The use of all capital letters for the initial verb phrase is indicative, not simply typographical. Everything depends on the power of speech in Osteen's work: positive speech, to be precise, and the positive thinking that lies behind it. Some remarks from the introduction to *I Declare* are instructive:

5. See McWhorter, *Power of Babel*, 137–59; see also discussion and bibliography in chap. 3.
6. Ibid., 1.

Our words have creative power. Whenever we speak something, either good or bad, we give life to what we are saying. Too many people say negative things about themselves, about their families, and about their futures. . . . They don't realize they are prophesying their futures. The Scripture says, "We will eat the fruit of our words." That means we will get exactly what we've been saying.

Here is the key; you've got to send your words out in the direction you want your life to go. You cannot talk defeat and expect to have victory. . . . You will produce what you say. If you want to know what you will be like five years from now, just listen to what you are saying about yourself. . . .

[Negative] thoughts may come to your mind, but don't make the mistake of verbalizing them. The moment you speak them out, you allow them to take root. . . . When you [say something positive], you are blessing your future.[7]

Here again the new rules, especially that of full regularity, are on clear display with very little demonstration of how they operate or how Osteen knows they are true. "Scripture" is mentioned but without a reference provided. Presumably the text is Prov. 13:2, but Osteen underquotes it. The full verse reads as follow:

> People eat well from the fruit of their words,
>> but the treacherous have an appetite only for violence. (CEB)

Osteen not only underquotes the verse; he also misquotes it. In addition, he does not explain how he knows that this verse "means we will get exactly what we've been saying." Not all Proverbs commentators would put it that way.[8]

Further along, Osteen continues in his habit of misquoting and underquoting—or is this simply evidence of the broken substrate that lies behind the pidgin that lies behind his creole? In any event, he misrepresents two other "bits" (equally revealing) from the book of Proverbs:

Prov. 6:2	Osteen: "We are snared by the words of our mouth" (only v. 2a) CEB: "You will be trapped by your words; you will be caught by your words."
Prov. 18:21	Osteen: "Life and death are in the power of our tongue" (only v. 21a) CEB: "Death and life are in the power of the tongue; those who love it will eat its fruit."

7. Ibid., v–vi.
8. See Fox, *Proverbs 10–31*, 561; McKane, *Proverbs*, 459–60; Toy, *Book of Proverbs*, 261–62. For more on how the moral self is shaped in Proverbs, and in complicated, poetic ways, see Stewart, *Poetic Ethics in Proverbs*.

Osteen takes these verse fragments—notice that he cites only the first half of both poetic couplets[9]—as proof of his metaphysical rule that "when you speak it out, you're giving life to your faith."[10] But these snippets from Proverbs, especially in Osteen's prose, are nothing more than that: quick, nonsubstantive, and unexplained appeals to, presumably, some sort of authoritative religious text—a text that is, furthermore, seriously misunderstood.[11]

The real support for Osteen's argument, and the predominant part of his rhetoric, are the three illustrations he provides in fairly extensive detail (esp. vis-à-vis the ultra-brief biblical asides): First, the successful renovation of the Compaq Center in Houston for Lakewood Church, despite the fact that the projected cost was millions more than originally expected. Second, the story of a professional baseball player who went from being a winning pitcher to being a losing one when, after moving to a new field, he "prophesied his future" by making "the mistake of speaking out" negative thoughts about the fence in left field being too close.[12] Third and most troubling of all, a maintenance man who "always had a negative report," "was prophesying defeat, . . . cursing his future," and "didn't realize he was being snared by the words of his mouth."[13] Despite Osteen's protestations that he is "not making light of his situation," his version of the story ends with the man getting sick at fifty-five years of age, and dying a "very sad and lonely death": "I couldn't help but think that he had been predicting this sad end his entire life because he was always talking about how he would never make it to his retirement years. He got what he was calling in."[14]

By Osteen's own account, this maintenance man isn't the only one with negative thoughts. Osteen's surmise about the man's untimely and unfortunate death is a negative thought as well, one which, now verbalized, "prophesies"—not only about this man, but also about any and all similarly "negative reports." This is no longer, then, just "a thought" Osteen had in passing as he recalled this man. It is now a metaphysical rule: that is the way Osteen's language works—or rather, the way *language itself* works according to Osteen. You get what you call in. The implication is clear: the man's death is his own fault.

---

9. For the importance of both halves of the line in making a single poetic predication, see the classic study by Kugel, *Idea of Biblical Poetry*.

10. Osteen, *I Declare*, viii.

11. Note how, in Scripture, it is *God's* words that have creative, generative power whereas Osteen attributes all of that to *human* speech. Every instance in the OT of the Hebrew Qal verb ברא/*bārā'*, "to create," has God alone as the subject.

12. Osteen, *I Declare*, viii.

13. Ibid., viii–ix.

14. Ibid., ix.

In light of this new linguistic rule—that verbal articulation makes reality happen—there is nothing to do but to "Declare health. Declare favor. Declare abundance," because "you give life to your faith by what you say."[15] Hence,

> You should send your words out in the direction you want your life to go. . . .
> Your declaration should be, "I know when one door closes, God will open up another door. What was meant for my harm, God will use to my advantage. I'm not only coming out, I will come out better than I was before."
> *Have a report of victory.* . . .
> On a regular basis we should say, "I'm blessed. I'm healthy. I'm strong. I'm valuable. I'm talented. I have a bright future." Those words go out of your mouth and come right back into your own ears. Over time they will create the same image on the inside.[16]

Osteen illustrates this principle by "a doctor in Europe who had some very sick patients" that he read about (unfortunately, he provides no documentation); this doctor (Émile Coué perhaps?) had his patients recite three or four times an hour the mantra, "I am getting better and better, every day, in every way."[17] Despite lack of improvement through the use of traditional medical methods, this new prescription "all of the sudden" produced better feelings in the patients: "What happened? As they heard themselves saying over and over, 'I'm getting better. I'm improving. My health is coming back,' those words began to create a new image on the inside. . . . Once you get a picture of it on the inside, then God can bring it to pass on the outside."[18] "Don't talk about the problem," Osteen concludes, "Talk about the solution."[19] His scriptural "proof" here is taken from Joel 3:10 (though, again, he does not provide the reference, nor does he quote the verse in full):

> The Scripture says, "Let the weak say, 'I am strong.'" Notice it doesn't say, "Let the weak talk about their weakness. Let the weak call five friends and discuss their weakness." "Let the weak complain about their weakness." No, it says in effect, "Let the weak say exactly the opposite of how they feel."
> In other words, don't talk about the way you are. Talk about the way you want to be.[20]

The result of this positive self-talk is, not surprisingly, axiomatic. Osteen avers,

15. Ibid.
16. Ibid., x.
17. Ibid., x–xi.
18. Ibid., xi.
19. Ibid., xii.
20. Ibid.

It will not only change how you feel, it also will change your attitude. You won't go out with a weak, defeated, victim mentality. You will go out with a victor mentality. . . . You are one of a kind. You are a masterpiece. You are a prized possession. When you wake up in the morning and look in the mirror, instead of getting depressed, instead of saying, "Oh, man. Look how old I look. Look at this gray hair. Look at these wrinkles," you need to smile and say, "Good morning, you beautiful thing. Good morning, you handsome thing. Good morning, you blessed, prosperous, successful, strong, talented, creative, confident, secure, disciplined, focused, highly favored child of the Most High God." Get it on the inside. Speak faith over your future![21]

Assessing Osteen "and Company"

It is hard to know where to begin when assessing the problems besetting so much of Osteen's linguistic system, but one shouldn't overlook the fact that many of the thoughts he encourages us to have are downright sugary sweet, not merely "positive."[22] At root, these thoughts (analogically, words and/or sentences) come across as fundamentally narcissistic: individualistic to the core and consistently about the personal betterment of one's own (!) immediate life circumstances, especially in the realms of finance, health, even beauty. Throughout his corpus, from the first breakout volume, *Your Best Life Now*, Osteen's examples are regularly taken from these areas, and seem to center around fiscal matters: the selling of real estate, the purchase of a business, getting out of debt, and so on and so forth.[23]

Not all of that is necessarily bad. Nor is all of it completely wrong. Language does have constitutive power, after all, and there is something known as cognitive-behavioral psychology. It is also the nature of pidgins and creoles to retain a bit of their underlying linguistic ancestors (one can't deny the presence of texts like Matt. 18:18–19 in Scripture). Those points granted, all of Osteen's linguistic system *is* necessarily bad and completely wrong *as a (linguistic) system, all by itself*, to the extent that he and other happiologists claim to be speaking the language of Scripture (note, at the very least, that they are not psychologists). Their language is all bad and completely wrong at this point because it is exactly the full language of Scripture that is so obviously missing from Osteen and other prosperity gospel preachers. So, to

21. Ibid., xii–xiii.
22. For the "unusual" and "distinctive" language that is found in the prosperity gospel, see Bowler, *Blessed*, 251–54, esp. 253.
23. Osteen, *Your Best Life Now*, passim, but esp. x, 11, 41. For further critical remarks, see Strawn, "Triumph of Life," esp. 296–98.

return to an earlier example, Osteen's linguistic system cannot account for someone like Job. Then again, Job's friends couldn't account for Job! But at the end of the book, it is they, not Job, who are put in their place by none other than God. Job, the man and the book, apparently breaks the regularity—if not the act-consequence retribution theology of the ancient Near East itself, then certainly the creole-like regularity of the new plastic gospels peddled by the happiologists. Throughout the book that bears his name, Job "speaks out" a whole lot of what Osteen would no doubt label "negative prophecy," but, in the end, God twice indicates that "my servant Job" has "spoken of me what is right" (Job 42:7–8 NRSV). It is Job's friends who have *not* spoken rightly—his friends, who, among other things, commanded him to shut his mouth about these matters (see, e.g., Job 8:2; 33:31–33). They sound like Osteen: "Don't speak the negative, Job! Tune in to the positive, Job!" But Job knows better:

> But I won't keep quiet;
>> I will speak in the adversity of my spirit,
>>> groan in the bitterness of my life. (Job 7:11 CEB)

And again, it is that kind of speech—*Job's* painful speech, not that of his friends—which is commended by God as being *right* speech, firm and true (Hebrew נכונה/*nəkônâ*).

In my judgment the book of Job all by itself is enough to put the lie to Osteen's entire system, but perhaps using Job as a counterexample is too easy. While Osteen posits a hypersimplistic and superregular system of "If *x*, then *y*," Job seems to posit the exact opposite: "If *x*, then, at least at times, -*y*." But perhaps Osteen might counter that this is the proverbial exception that proves the rule. What, then, of Ecclesiastes? That book seems to posit an equation like "If *x*, then *???*" A few examples suffice to counter happiology definitively:

> It is better to go to a house in mourning
>> than to a house party,
>>> because that is everyone's destiny;
>>> and the living should take it to heart.
> Aggravation is better than merriment
>> because a sad face may lead to a glad heart.
> The wise heart is in the house that mourns,
>> but the foolish heart is in the house that rejoices. (Eccles. 7:2–4 CEB)

Consider God's work! Who can straighten what God has made crooked? When times are good, enjoy the good; when times are bad, consider: God has made the former as well as the latter so that people can't discover anything that will come to be after them. (Eccles. 7:13–14 CEB)

I observed all the work of God—that no one can grasp what happens under the sun. Those who strive to know can't grasp it. Even the wise who are set on knowing are unable to grasp it. (Eccles. 8:17 CEB)

I also observed under the sun that the race doesn't always go to the swift, nor the battle to the mighty, nor food to the wise, nor wealth to the intelligent, nor favor to the knowledgeable, because accidents can happen to anyone. (Eccles. 9:11 CEB)

And perhaps the most stunning piece of advice in all of Scripture for all would-be theologians and preachers:

Don't be quick with your mouth or say anything hastily before God, because God is in heaven, but you are on earth. Therefore, let your words be few. (Eccles. 5:2 CEB)

Via the linguistic analogy, Ecclesiastes might be viewed as an irregular verb form. A *highly* irregular verb form—far too irregular to fit into Osteen's system, which is entirely regular . . . to a fault. There is not space here to unpack these verses from Ecclesiastes—and it must be admitted that this book poses problems for many preachers and theologians, not just those of the prosperity stripe—but the very existence of the book, its inclusion in the canon of Holy Scripture, and its strong countertestimony to happiology suffice to make the point that the linguistic system of Osteen and others is in no way identical to the linguistic system that is the whole Old Testament. The language of happiology does not include all of the language that is the Old Testament; happiology is a massive reduction.

Not just Ecclesiastes or Job makes this point. It is also made in the book of Psalms, with the backbone provided to that book by the individual laments,[24] and it is in every other piece of Scripture that reckons with the dark and down sides of life. For Osteen and company, those parts of life—and also, evidently, of Scripture—are "the blahs," which must be "tuned out." Instead, one should "tune in" to positivity, changing one's mind, so as to think and declare something else.[25] At that point all will be well, and all *must* be well, because the linguistic system is entirely regular. If you do not change your

24. For the importance of the lament psalms in the Psalter, see, inter alia, Westermann, *Praise and Lament in the Psalms*.

25. See, e.g., Osteen, *Your Best Life Now*, passim, but esp. 113–20, 144–45.

thoughts or declare something else, . . . well, it is likely that you will end up unsuccessful in professional sports, failing in business, old-looking and wrinkly, and/or dead at an early age. The exact opposite scenario is found in Scripture. If there is a linguistic rule in the language of the Old Testament, it is one that does *not* exclude lament: "Praise can retain its authenticity and naturalness only in polarity with lamentation."[26]

More should be said contra happiology. In his exhortation to positive self-talk, Osteen sometimes advocates replacement language: instead of saying "I *have* to do this or I *have* to do that" (go to work, drive in traffic, etc.), one should say "I *get* to do this."[27] The shift in language signals a shift from necessity to opportunity, from negativity to positivity. What's so wrong about that?

Again: only everything. It is dead wrong by ignoring all evidence to the contrary, in the world and in the Word. The shift from "have to" to "get to" is clever, but it simply doesn't work in every situation in the real world (e.g., terminal illness, clinical depression, natural disasters). It also doesn't reflect the language of Scripture. It is a new grammatical rule that bears no recognizable relationship to the dynamic of the lament psalms. The psalmists do not reach a place of new life by means of denying their very real, very difficult, and often very unjust circumstances, *but precisely by voicing them.* To operate in denial of these real, often volatile emotions—which is what Osteen recommends ("Don't talk about the way you are"; "say the opposite of how [you] feel")—is not only untrue to the Psalms; it is downright duplicitous, if not pathological. It may even be evil since, according to the Psalms, the only people to enjoy a life free of pain are the wicked (see Ps. 73:3–5, 12).[28] Or, in the words of Tal Ben-Shahar, a prominent voice in Positive Psychology, "the only people who don't experience . . . normal unpleasant feelings are psychopaths. And the dead."[29] Finally, in terms of actual empirical research—not just the one unnamed European doctor that Osteen once read about—there is a large amount of data that shows it is precisely the articulation of painful emotions that facilitates healing and health, whereas inhibition of those emotions leads to disease and dysfunction.[30] This insight is well attested in, if

26. Westermann, *Praise and Lament in the Psalms*, 267. See further Brueggemann, "Costly Loss of Lament."

27. Osteen, *Every Day a Friday*, 9.

28. See W. P. Brown, "Happiness and Its Discontents in the Psalms," esp. 96–97.

29. Ben-Shahar, *Being Happy*, 15.

30. The work of James W. Pennebaker is of paramount importance here. See his *Opening Up*; Pennebaker, "Writing about Emotional Experiences"; Pennebaker, "Effects of Traumatic Disclosure"; Pennebaker, "Telling Stories"; Pennebaker, "Social, Linguistic, and Health Consequences." See also the following multiauthor works: Pennebaker and O'Heeron, "Confiding in Others"; Pennebaker, Hughes, and O'Heeron, "Psychophysiology of Confession"; Pennebaker

not anticipated by, the dynamic of lament in the Psalms, but not only there: "Any survey will show that laments pervade the entire Old Testament and that they are an essential part of what the Old Testament says happened between God and [hu]man[ity]."[31]

Let us shift to the New Testament for a moment since happiology does just as much damage to the New Testament as it does to the Old. Osteen's "have to–get to" switch ultimately makes a mockery of Jesus at Gethsemane. "I don't *have to* drink this cup, I *get to*!" is what Jesus *should* have prayed in the garden, according to Osteen's logic. One thinks immediately of Monty Python's motion-picture parody of the New Testament, *The Life of Brian*, which ends with a song-and-dance routine during the crucifixion with everyone singing, "Always look on the bright side of life." As ridiculous as that number is, it is actually an instantiation of Osteen's linguistic rule when placed in the mouth of Jesus at Gethsemane, let alone Golgotha. If the rule in question doesn't apply to Jesus, if even Jesus can't get out of life without "sweating blood" (Luke 22:44) and worse, who is Osteen to say or think (positively no doubt!) that *we* can?

Or we might consider Matt. 16, where Peter makes "the great confession" identifying Jesus as "Messiah, the Son of the living God" (Matt. 16:16). Jesus blesses him for it, but, Matthew writes,

> From that time Jesus began to show his disciples that he had to go to Jerusalem and suffer many things from the elders, chief priests, and legal experts, and that he had to be killed and raised on the third day. Then Peter took hold of Jesus and, scolding him, began to correct him: "God forbid, Lord! This won't happen to you." But he turned to Peter and said, "Get behind me, Satan. You are a stone that could make me stumble, for you are not thinking God's thoughts but human thoughts." (Matt. 16:21–23 CEB)

According to Osteen's language, Peter is doing the right thing: telling Jesus to get over the "blahs." Jesus shouldn't verbalize such negativity since it could come true! Instead, Jesus should talk positive: "This won't happen to you." But it is Jesus who sets Peter straight: human thoughts aren't God's thoughts, *certainly not always*. God's thoughts sometimes include suffering

---

and Susman, "Disclosure of Traumas and Psychosomatic Processes"; VandeCreek, Janus, Pennebaker, and Binau, "Praying about Difficult Experiences"; Gortner, Rude, and Pennebaker, "Benefits of Expressive Writing"; Pennebaker and Chung, "Expressive Writing, Emotional Upheavals, and Health." For a brief application of Pennebaker to the Psalms, see Strawn, "The Psalms and the Practice of Disclosure." See also Strawn, "Poetic Attachment"; and Strawn, "Trauma."

31. Westermann, *Praise and Lament in the Psalms*, 263.

and death. Not according to happiology, however, which is all shine and no sweat, a theology of glory without a theology of the cross, all Easter Sunday but without Good Friday. Hence the new plastic gospels are, in the end, not the gospel of God. Jesus recognizes what is at stake: "Get behind me, Satan."

These comments on the New Testament are not because I have forgotten the purpose of this book and its focus on the Old Testament. They are intended as further proof of what was asserted in chapter 1 and was equally on display in the two previous signs of morbidity: if the Old Testament dies, the New Testament is not far behind. The language of happiology faces just as much resistance from the New Testament as it does from the Old. It is the full language of Scripture, in its parts and as a whole, that reveals the problems of the prosperity gospel; it is also only the full language that can redress those problems.

Another way to put matters is that the full language of Scripture can account for the happiology creole, at least broken fragments of it, but the reverse is not true. Little bits and pieces of the Bible are found scattered throughout the lexicon of prosperity theology, to a greater or lesser degree, but they are nothing more than that: mere traces surviving from a substrate language that was at some point combined with a superstrate to create a pidgin, which subsequently developed into a creole. The original, full language of Scripture is now far back in the linguistic ancestry and was never the dominant language in the linguistic contact anyway. Can pieces of the "good news" of the prosperity gospel be found here and there, now and then, in bits and pieces of the Bible, whether Old Testament or New? Of course! There is no doubt about that. But the full complexity of the language that is Scripture is not captured by happiology: Job, Ecclesiastes, the Psalms, and even Jesus and his cross simply don't fit. In brief, the happiologists do not speak the language of Scripture, but a fully regular creole that emerged from a pidgin, produced after the Bible came into contact with some other language. That other language must be considered the superstrate, given the damage Scripture has suffered in the construction of the pidgin-turned-creole. Simply put, little of the Bible is left.

It is worth delving deeper into the nature of the language contact that produced this creole in order to pinpoint the original superstrate that has prevailed over the language of Scripture. To begin with, it may be best to posit more than one superstrate, since "the roots of the modern prosperity gospel," according to Kate Bowler, "are long and tangled."[32] In her insightful and sensitive history of the movement, Bowler traces it back to "certain ways

---

32. Bowler, *Blessed*, 11.

of thinking about spiritual power that emerged and competed for attention early in the twentieth century," the core of which was the conviction that

> *adherents, acting in accordance with divine principles, relied on their minds to transform thought and speech into heaven-sent blessings.* It focused on the individual rather than groups and emphasized the power of the individual's mind. . . . We might envision the prosperity gospel as composed of three distinct though intersecting streams: pentecostalism; New Thought (an amalgam of metaphysics and Protestantism . . .); and an American gospel of pragmatism, individualism, and upward mobility.[33]

Bowler carefully unpacks each of these streams in her study. For my purposes it is enough to recognize that each of these streams are, in my linguistic analogy, languages that have now come into contact with the language of Scripture. A contact language is the result: a pidgin that facilitates communication between the different systems but which is, in the process, a reduction of the superstrate and substrate. While pidginization reduces both languages, the language of the more powerful group predominates, meaning that more of that group's language (the superstrate) survives than does that of the other (the substrate).[34] If the linguistic analogy holds water, we should be able to determine not only which language is the superstrate and what is the substrate (by the comparative analysis of what survives in this pidgin-turned-happiology-creole) but even, if we are lucky, the identity of the superstrate itself.

On the basis of what has already been said above, it seems abundantly clear that it is the Bible that has been most severely reduced—far more than the "mind-power" that was a hallmark of the late nineteenth-century New Thought movement.[35] It is the Bible, then, that is the substrate, with the superstrate being New Thought mind-power. This explains why Job doesn't fit within Osteen's language system and why Job ultimately doesn't have any part in it, but it also explains why Osteen's system couldn't survive without positive thinking.

Bowler highlights three crucial presuppositions of New Thought: "a high anthropology, the priority of spiritual reality, and the generative power of positive thought."[36] In happiology, it is especially the last-mentioned item that proves to be the superstrate, surviving—in this case—virtually intact vis-à-vis the language of Scripture, which takes a beating. It is the Bible, after all,

33. Ibid., 11, emphasis original.
34. See chap. 3; also McWhorter, *Power of Babel*, 135: "In most pidgins, the bulk of the vocabulary is drawn from the dominant group's language."
35. For a discussion of "mind-power," see Bowler, *Blessed*, 12–15.
36. Ibid., 14.

that highlights the necessity and benefits of *both* "negative" and "positive" thought and speech.

One should not imagine too direct of a line from New Thought to the prosperity gospel of the happiologists. Indeed, an early twentieth-century prosperity preacher, E. W. Kenyon, "flatly rejected the 'religion of healthy-mindedness' as counterfeit," arguing that it was "a substitution of gospel truth with abstract 'principles.'"[37] And yet, working when and where Kenyon did—"in areas of New Thought's greatest influence"—he ended up producing a pidgin of his own, combining his understanding of "divine principles" to unlock "God's treasury of blessings" through what he called "dominating faith."[38] According to Bowler, Kenyon's "foundational works on spiritual power articulated a set of universal laws that electrified late-nineteenth-century evangelicalism and its offspring, pentecostalism, with confidence in human capabilities."[39]

What one can see in Kenyon, then, is a contact language produced by New Thought encountering Scripture (though the situation is probably more complex still), with one adding more to the mix than the other. So, for example, "though the priority of spirit," one of New Thought's key presuppositions, "seemed a peripheral theological detail, Kenyon drew it into every beginners' course on the gospel."[40] Once this new lexical item is in place, and leveled through the system, the pidgin has become expanded: the high anthropology of New Thought now trumps all counterevidence in Scripture (linguistic antonyms, as it were) so that union with God became, for Kenyon, the starting point, not the eschatological goal.[41] It is a short step from expanded pidgin to full creolization, replete with new and fully regularized rules. So, for example, "faith," as defined by Kenyon, "was the 'confident assurance based on *absolute knowledge* that everything is already provided through *the operation of certain immutable laws.*' . . . 'Faith-filled words' not only brought the universe into being but also governed the world as an invisible force."[42]

Bowler summarizes Kenyon's thinking: "New Thought employed the right process with the wrong theology."[43] Assessed linguistically, this is nothing other than saying that in the contact between Scripture and New Thought, it is New Thought that proves dominant. Not only is that so, but the little that survives

---

37. Ibid., 15; for more on Kenyon, see ibid., 15–20.

38. Ibid., 15.

39. Ibid.

40. Ibid., 17.

41. Ibid., 18, cf. also 25.

42. Ibid., 19, emphasis added; citing Simmons, *E. W. Kenyon and the Postbellum Pursuit of Peace*, 150; and Kenyon, *Two Kinds of Faith*, 20. On other spiritual "laws" and Kenyon's influence on pentecostalism, see Bowler, *Blessed*, 20–22.

43. Bowler, *Blessed*, 20.

of the substrate is fundamentally qualified and altered by the superstrate.[44] Kenyon's theology in the pidgin and, even more so, in the theology of the pidgin-turned-creole that he helped to create is made up of Scripture dominated by something else that *isn't* Scripture—or at least not fully Scripture, not the full warp and woof of Scripture. As troubling as that might be, especially to Kenyon's theological heirs (assuming they care about Scripture), it is the normal situation (exactly what we expect) with contact languages like pidgins and with the creoles that can result. The process at work here, then, is exactly the same as what was observed with the morbid signs provided by the New Atheism or the Marcionites Old and New, the only variable being the different superstrates involved.

While more might be said, the most important point is obvious: the prosperity gospel of happiology is a contact language, at the very least one step removed (as a pidgin) from the language of Scripture. That's why so much of Scripture doesn't "fit" in the prosperity gospel and why the gospels of the happiologists are new plastic ones, not identical to the "old-time religion," which in addition to being ancient, has a lot of twists and turns that cannot be stomached by those who prefer a different language—one that is simpler, cleaner, and more regular, whether they be atheists, anti-Jewish preachers and theologians, or contemporary mind-power spiritualists.

The result of this language contact is, first, massive reductionism via pidginization. Just one example among a cast of thousands, if not millions, is the pastor described by Kate Bowler, who referred to "Jesus' resurrection as the moment when 'He couldn't stand being [financially] broke any longer!' . . . Jesus rose from the grave as the redeemer of poverty's curse."[45]

But again, *pidginization* is just the first step. Insofar as the prosperity pidgin has been around for some time now, it seems better to describe it as an *expanded pidgin*. Given the existence of so many new grammatical rules— "absolute knowledge," for example, and the "immutable laws" (so Kenyon) of faith, speech, power, health, and so forth—it is more accurate to say that what current happiologists speak is not a pidgin nor even an expanded pidgin, but *a fully regularized creole*. If this is accurate, it would indicate that someone like Osteen—or similar second-generation happiologists (and those following them)—acquired the (expanded) prosperity pidgin natively, from their

44. Cf. ibid., 23, on the pentecostal preacher Fred F. Bosworth, who borrowed from Kenyon: "Though he would have despised the association, his own methods 'sanctified' aspects of New Thought mind-power for pentecostal audiences." Also ibid., 24, on John G. Lake, another pentecostal, who preached "suprahuman abilities": "Lake's . . . stronger claims to spiritual power suggest that New Thought lit the fuse of pentecostalism's psychological dynamite."

45. Ibid., 96.

forebears, and developed it further into a full-blown creole: an entirely new language. In truth, the creolization may have taken place before Osteen and the current crop of prosperity preachers; regardless, the speakers of the happiology pidgin or pidgin-turned-creole are many and several, with perhaps the most notable being Norman Vincent Peale (1898–1993). Peale's *The Power of Positive Thinking* was a *New York Times* bestseller for what was at that time a record-breaking three years, selling over a million copies.[46] When Osteen's language is compared with earlier versions, there is little that is new. Peale, too, advocated a way "by which we can control and even determine" life's circumstances.[47] "Declaring a blessing" is Osteen's slightly updated version.

Four final observations should be made on this last sign of the Old Testament's morbidity, which may be the most troubling of all. First, it is not hard to see the influence of American civil religion in the prosperity gospel movement.[48] Bowler speaks of that religion as prosperity theology's "nationalistic alter ego," and argues that the prosperity gospel "was constituted by the deification and ritualization of the American Dream: upward mobility, accumulation, hard work, and moral fiber."[49] While Bowler speaks of American civil religion and prosperity gospel theology as *sharing* various elements such as high anthropology and the like, the linguistic analogy suggests that it is just as likely that the prosperity gospel is *derived* from American civil religion, not a completely independent development. That is to say, linguistically, that it is American civil religion that constitutes (a large part of) the superstrate.

Bowler also makes a good case for seeing the prosperity gospel as "an account of globalization."[50] In both perspectives—the global world and the more localized, American slice of it—one can trace the important role of individualistic consumeristic capitalism. Bowler makes the point succinctly: "A marketplace ethos prevails" in prosperity gospel thinking.[51] A memorable example is the preacher chronicled by Bowler who argued that "God's laws and the laws of business were one and same, as sowing and reaping yielded financial as well as spiritual harvests."[52] Ecclesiastes 11:6 and Mark 4:26–27 would seem to nuance this "immutable law(s)," however.

46. Peale, *Power of Positive Thinking*, still in print (e.g., New York: Touchstone/Simon & Schuster, 2015). For more on Peale, see Bowler, *Blessed*, 55–60.

47. Bowler, *Blessed*, 57.

48. Note that Bowler's conclusion in *Blessed* is titled "An American Blessing" (ibid., 226–37). For more on the topic, see Laderman, *American Civil Religion*.

49. Bowler, *Blessed*, 226; cf. 7: "Countless listeners reimagined their ability as good Christians—*and good Americans*—to leapfrog over any obstacles" (emphasis added).

50. Ibid., 229; see further 229–32.

51. Ibid., 262.

52. Ibid., 200.

Once the marketplace in question—whether fiscal or spiritual or both if these are "one and the same"—is of any size, there is increased pressure toward upward mobility, fitting in, urbanizing, and leaving old-fashioned and antiquated habits of the past behind, past habits such as ancient and native tongues. So, as I pointed out in chapter 3, one of the main reasons for language death is precisely the kinds of pressures brought on by globalization, urbanization, and economic considerations.[53]

The desire for economic success is patently a major cog in the machinery of Osteen and company. Indeed, the "and company" is especially appropriate at this point because the prosperity gospel is big *business*. Osteen's best-selling books (is there one that hasn't been a hit?) are quickly followed up with an entire apparatus of accessories: journals, daily reading books, and so forth, which, if nothing else, increase the profit margin. Consider, for example, the small-sized library that was published to support the success of *Your Best Life Now*:

1. *Your Best Life Now Journal: A Guide to Reaching Your Full Potential*
2. *Your Best Life Now Study Guide: 7 Steps to Living at Your Full Potential*
3. *Daily Readings from Your Best Life Now: 90 Devotions for Living at Your Full Potential*
4. *Scriptures and Meditations for Your Best Life Now*
5. *Your Best Life Begins Each Morning: Devotions to Start Every New Day of the Year*
6. *Your Best Life Now for Moms*

There's even a board game,

7. "Your Best Life Now: The Game!"[54]

As if all that wasn't proof enough of the economic engine driving happiology, one might consider the fact that the specific day of the week celebrated in Osteen's *Every Day a Friday* is not Sunday, the day of Christian worship. Neither is it the Jewish Sabbath. It is Friday, but not Good Friday, the day of Jesus's crucifixion. Instead of these religiously important days, the day Osteen writes about is the day that marks the end of the workweek. The good feeling that one has when one ends work and starts the weekend is the feeling that can, and should, mark every day (note the regularity!). An instructive

53. McWhorter, *Power of Babel*, 271; cf. also McCrum, *Globish*.
54. Made by Endless Games.

comparison is offered by the prayer for Fridays in the Book of Common Prayer: "Almighty God, whose most dear Son went not up to joy but first he suffered pain, and entered not into glory before he was crucified: Mercifully grant that we, walking in the way of the cross, may find it none other than the way of life and peace; through Jesus Christ your Son our Lord. *Amen.*"[55]

The contrast could hardly be more pronounced. In The Book of Common Prayer, Fridays are marked by a remembrance of Christ's crucifixion and the fact that one doesn't go up to joy without first suffering pain, or enter into glory before experiencing death. The Book of Common Prayer has the advantage of being far more scriptural than Osteen's end of the workweek, "Thank God It's Friday" feeling. The Book of Common Prayer is also superior insofar as it acknowledges that it is God—not us and our mind-power, positive thinking, or faith words—who has the power to transform the way of the cross to a way of life and peace. And note these key details: that acknowledgment is made in the midst of *prayer*, not in a command to a lapdog; it is predicated on *divine mercy*, not on the efficacy of the pray-er's own speech power; and it is performed in the subjunctive mood, "Mercifully grant that we *may*." Those small, but altogether crucial, linguistic details demonstrate that what is happening in the prayer is *not* automatic, not universal, not invariable. But these subjunctive expressions are rare these days and altogether absent from happiology's immutable laws of positive thinking and prosperity theology.[56] It is, after all, only a very thick definition of "happiness" that could call the Friday of Jesus's death "good," and the "good" of "Good Friday" is certainly *not* the kind of "good" feeling one has when five o'clock rolls around at the end of the workweek. Neither is it the kind of "good," let alone "great," that goes with "Have a good day" or "I'm feeling great!"[57]

A second observation: it is the omnipresence of optimism, victory, and triumphalism in happiology—a syrupy sweet and thin definition of the good

55. Episcopal Church, *Book of Common Prayer* (1979), Morning Prayer II, p. 99.

56. Such moods are also among the more complex and tricky parts of a grammar. See, inter alia, Palmer, *Mood and Modality*. For the automaticity of prosperity speech, which is deemed to "force" God to "move accordingly," functioning "not as requests but as contracts, guaranteeing miraculous results," see Bowler, *Blessed*, 22–23.

57. According to Bowler, only one prosperity church in Houston held a Good Friday service; the other churches avoided gloomy occasions. That one church was Osteen's Lakewood Church. Bowler recounts that she was greeted no less than six times with a chipper "HAPPY GOOD FRIDAY!" on her way in (*Blessed*, 193, emphasis original). She describes how Jesus was resurrected by the second song of the service and that Osteen's wife, Victoria, took the stage pumping her fist and shouting "Isn't it great we serve a Risen Lord?" effectively "preempting Easter by two days" (194). For more on a thick definition of happiness in biblical perspective, see the essays in Strawn, *Bible and the Pursuit of Happiness*; esp. Strawn, "Introduction: The Bible and . . . Happiness?"; and Strawn, "Triumph of Life."

life—that led Eric G. Wilson to call Christian denominations in North America "basically happiness companies."[58] He did not intend it as a compliment. At this point, so much of the New Atheism's critique of contemporary Christianity finds an appropriate target. Consider Terry Eagleton, who earlier defended Christianity against the New Atheism's unfair and foul (in the linguistic analogy, pidginized) presentation, who nevertheless believes that much of contemporary Christianity has "betrayed the revolution."[59]

In the case of the prosperity gospel, no less than with the New Atheism or the Marcionites Old and New, the problem is not simply *theoretical*, limited to some arcane or obsessive concern to be absolutely thorough with regard to the language of Scripture. It is equally and every bit a *pragmatic* problem—one of practice, ethics. There are very real, very deleterious downsides to happiology. To "speak only positively and believe for the best"—what Bowler calls "the message of cultivated cheerfulness"—is the prosperity gospel's "greatest gift and heaviest burden."[60] It is a heavy burden in light of so many counterfactuals: death, sickness, failure—yes, even among the faithful, and yes, in the flesh, not just in the pages of Scripture, but also there! For some prosperity preachers observed by Bowler, "death meant failure, the failure of the believer to win the spiritual battle against illness," a notion that forced believers to choose "a once-and-for-all Savior and silence in illness rather than face public shame."[61] D. R. McConnell, whom Bowler cites at this point, puts it even more strongly: "The time when a dying believer needs his faith the most is when he is told that he has it the least. . . . Perhaps the most inhuman fact revealed about the Faith movement is this: when its members die, they die alone."[62]

The full language of Scripture highlights the theoretical and theological problems with all happiology creoles and also redresses their practical problems. Note, at this point, how Bowler chronicles the existence of some believers amid prosperity churches who "quietly concluded that illness could

58. E. Wilson, *Against Happiness*, 20. In my judgment, Wilson errs too far in the opposite direction. In his next book, *Mercy of Eternity*, Wilson is candid about his own struggle with bipolar depression.

59. Eagleton, *Reason, Faith, and Revolution*, 47–108.

60. Bowler, *Blessed*, 232.

61. Ibid., 176.

62. McConnell, *Different Gospel*, 166. By way of contrast, note the data on what constitutes a good attachment between a parent and a child: children in distress vocalize it to their parents. Poor attachment is marked by silent suffering. See Strawn ("Poetic Attachment," 408–9) with reference to the Psalms. On the parent-child metaphor in Scripture, see further Strawn, "'Israel, My Child.'" Cf. chap. 2 and W. Sibley Towner's remark there on the dearth of lament in contemporary worship: "We prefer to sin and repent, lament and die in silent privacy" ("'Without Our Aid,'" 33).

portend righteous suffering" and who did so, frequently, with reference to Job![63] Vignettes like that demonstrate that, while the prosperity gospel may *sell*, it can't *save*.

But, for now, the new plastic gospels are selling very well indeed. The success of happiology in the prosperity gospel mode is undeniable. The bottom line of "Brand Osteen" includes 38,000 people in attendance every Sunday, with seven million television viewers weekly, and millions of books sold.[64] While Osteen's Lakewood Church may be the largest of its kind, the average congregational size in a prosperity gospel church is 8,577 members.[65] In point of fact, the phenomenal success of the prosperity gospel, when viewed through the linguistic analogy, may suggest a process of *decreolization*—the process by which a creole is made more and more similar to the standard, dominant language.[66] I have already indicated my belief that the superstrate in the pidgin-turned-happiology-creole is exactly the dominant language already "spoken here"—both in North America and worldwide. If correct, the happiology creole is now coming full circle, back home where it started.

A third observation is that however happiology is analyzed, which depends somewhat on the speakers and their placement in the history of the movement—whether, that is, prosperity theology is deemed an expanded pidgin, a pidgin-turned-creole, or a creole in the midst of decreolization—the language of Scripture within the prosperity gospel is well on its way to extinction, if it isn't dead already. In chapter 7 I will have occasion to say something slightly more positive about preachers like Osteen, but I do not want to soften too much the severity of my judgment here: a substrate in a pidgin-turned-creole is at least two significant steps removed from the original language (see chap. 3 and diagram 1 there). The new, regularized creole may survive—it might even thrive—*but it is not the original language*. Far from it. The original has been reduced, then subsumed, then transformed, and then eventually and entirely forgotten. The prosperity gospel, no less than the New Atheism, is a deathly serious sign of the Old Testament's morbidity.

The reason for this severe judgment is that creoles are, by definition, new languages. Creoles are not dialects of a language, but entirely new ones.[67] Analogically, the prosperity gospel is not simply a new language: *it is a new*

---

63. Bowler, *Blessed*, 176.
64. See ibid., 5, 239; cf. 6 and 9.
65. Ibid., 183, fig. 5.3.
66. See *CEL* 338, 424.
67. See McWhorter, *Power of Babel*, 145–46.

gospel. That is a cause for real concern, if, that is, Gal. 1:8 is still in our lexicon. There Paul says that "even if we or an angel from heaven should proclaim to you a gospel contrary to what we proclaimed to you, let that one be accursed!" (NRSV). Admittedly Paul elsewhere writes that "the important thing is that in every way, whether from false motives or true, Christ is preached" (Phil. 1:18 NIV). But, in light of my analysis above, the very real question facing happiology—quite apart from the question of motives—is whether it is "Christ" that is being preached (linguistically considered) or if the admonition of Galatians 1 is in effect.

A fourth and final point is worth making: historically creolization is largely associated with colonization. According to McWhorter,

> . Most creoles formed during the so-called "exploration" of the world by a few European powers from the 1400s through the 1800s, in which cultivation of food and material goods to enrich the coffers of the "exploring" country required large crews of manual laborers to do work that whites back home were only fitfully willing to do. Namely, the slave trade and its contractual aftermath under a different name in the 1800s gave birth to several dozen creoles.[68]

"The tragic truth," he continues, "is that most creoles have arisen amid conditions of unthinkably stark and ineradicable social injustice."[69] The majority of creoles, that is, began in contexts of slavery. It was the native languages of the slaves that suffered most in the construction of the contact languages (pidgins) that eventually became creoles.[70] When seen through the linguistic analogy, this indicates that the language of Scripture now subsumed in the prosperity gospel creole has been enslaved to a more dominant master—the master of individualistic, narcissistic, consumeristic, zero-sum economics. If that analysis is correct, what the prosperity gospel offers us is no good news at all, but only a new form of slavery. A slavery, furthermore, that is inescapable since prosperity theology depends on a high anthropology wherein everything depends on us, where God's agency is altogether lacking or entirely dependent on our "faith words" and positive thoughts, and where faith is commodified such that you have to have enough of it to buy what you need. In Scripture, however, it is God who delivers Israel from Egypt, without them even asking,

68. Ibid., 146–47; see further 149–50; McWhorter, *Missing Spanish Creoles*; McWhorter, *Language Interrupted*, 252; Holm, *Introduction to Pidgins and Creoles*, 6, 68–71.

69. McWhorter, *Power of Babel*, 150n5.

70. Ibid., 134–35: "Usually . . . sociohistorical realities are such that one group has its foot on the other's neck, and the subordinate group is compelled to make do as best it can with the dominant group's language, rather than the two groups mutually accommodating to each other's."

let alone doing anything (Exod. 2:23–25).[71] In Scripture, it is Christ who died for us, even while we were still sinners (Rom. 5:8).

Conclusion to Part 2

Despite the length of the three chapters that compose part 2, more could be said about each of the three signs of the Old Testament's morbidity, but much would be simple variation on the themes already identified. For example, one could note the extreme reductionism (pidginization) that turns into regularized grammar (creolization) in Bruce Wilkinson's *The Prayer of Jabez: Breaking through to the Blessed Life*, in which an entire system of prosperity is built on a rather obscure snippet in 1 Chron. 4:10. The stunning success of the Jabez volume (over 8 million copies sold) was not lost on the author and publisher, who quickly capitalized (!) on that by accessorizing (!) the initial book with a host of companion volumes, including devotionals, journals, Bible studies (inspired by one verse?), and versions of Jabez's prayer (or rather the book by that name) for women, teens, kids—even babies![72] Here again, no less than in Osteen's Best Life library, the driving force (the superstrate) in the Jabez-language juggernaut is big business, with any and every possibility to turn a buck fully engaged. Meanwhile, the substrate, the Old Testament itself, has dwindled to almost nothing: Jabez's prayer is only thirteen words in Hebrew, and all that the Old Testament says *against* prosperity understood solely via individualistic, narcissistic, consumeristic business seems completely neglected, forgotten, lost. The word on the street is that Multnomah Books, the press that published *The Prayer of Jabez*, evidently "enlarged its borders" a bit too much in the wake of the phenomenon, and when the wind left the Jabez sails, the publisher, too, had to cut back. That seems ironic, in terms of the biblical content, but insofar as the happiology creole is more dependent on the economy than on Scripture, it just seems like the ups and downs of the market. You win some, you lose some. Where's the next moneymaker?

The Prayer of Jabez is not alone. The "capitalization" of theological phenomena is now everywhere, thoroughly widespread. Creflo Dollar's *The Holy Spirit, Your Financial Advisor*, comes to mind, as does Laurie Beth Jones's

---

71. See further Lind, *Yahweh Is a Warrior*.

72. B. Wilkinson, *Prayer of Jabez: Devotional*; B. Wilkinson, *Prayer of Jabez: Bible Study*; B. Wilkinson, *Prayer of Jabez for Teens*; B. Wilkinson, *Prayer of Jabez Journal*; B. Wilkinson, *Prayer of Jabez for Kids*; D. Wilkinson, *Prayer of Jabez for Women*; Carlson and Natchev, *Prayer of Jabez for Little Ones*, a baby board book. How infants "enlarge their borders" is unclear: perhaps more diapers or pacifiers?

several publications, *Jesus, CEO*; *Jesus, Inc.*; *Jesus, Entrepreneur*; *Jesus, Life Coach*; and *Jesus, Career Counselor*. These are but a few examples. Once again, the prosperity gospel is big business. Its language, too, is (that of) big business. How could it be otherwise? Business is the superstrate, business drives the creolization, business is leading to decreolization so that the happiology creole, in the end, won't be a creole at all but just the same language that everybody else is already speaking.

And it's not just the prosperity gospel that knows how to turn a profit. Bible publishing is stronger than ever but, as Timothy Beal argues, is in its own way contributing to Scripture's rapid demise with the never-ending repackaging of biblical content to suit the consumer's felt needs.[73] The end result, according to Beal, is a profound simplification (read: pidginization) of the Bible that ultimately leads to "a different cookie" altogether[74]—or in my terms, an entirely different language. Beal goes so far as to describe the incredible rate of Bible publishing (in 2005 alone, no less than 6,134 different Bibles were published) as like unto a distress crop: when a plant puts out all its seeds right before it dies.[75]

These and the other examples that could be added to the mix only underscore the points made about the three signs investigated here in part 2, offering additional and definitive evidence that the Old Testament is dying, dying fast, and that the results of this death are devastating on many different levels. And yet, close analysis of each of the three signs also revealed that recourse to the full language of Scripture can redress their problems—remedy their pathologies, as it were. The full language is a way to counter the disease, prevent its spread, perhaps even cure the patient altogether. This means that there may yet be some hope despite what seems to be the imminent if not already realized death of the Old Testament. There may yet be hope that the Old Testament is still alive, even if only barely, and that something might be done to impede its demise, undo its sickness-unto-death, and return it to a state of health and vibrancy. That is the work of the three chapters in part 3.

Before doing so, one final remark: the three arenas of discourse that were examined here in part 2 are, like the initial tests run on the Old Testament in chapter 2, not just signs of the disease but also contributing factors to the

73. Beal, *Rise and Fall of the Bible*.
74. Ibid., 68–69.
75. See ibid., 49, 80–83. Beal cites research indicating that "the average Christian household owns nine Bibles and purchases at least one new Bible every year" (ibid., 36). For a sampling of odd Bible publications, see ibid., 133–36. See also essays by Metzger, "Curious Bibles," 143–44; Marini, "Family Bible," 224–25; and Bentley, "Illustrated Bibles," 298–300—all in Metzger and Coogan, *Oxford Companion to the Bible*.

patient's demise. They reflect the spread of the disease but are also causing the same, even accelerating it. The New Atheists along with the Marcionites Old and New are up front about that: they advocate for linguistic euthanasia—the quicker the Old Testament can be put out of its (and our) misery, the better. The happiologists' contribution is far more insidious insofar as they pretend or actually think (it matters little either way) that they are actually speaking the original language. So, too, then, do their willing adherents, babbling away in their new tongue, without the foggiest idea that the language they speak can no longer crossbreed with the original.[76]

76. See Hagège (*Death and Life of Languages*, 53) on how communication impossibility is a sign of language death or a new language, esp. his chaps. 1 and 3 on dialectology and speciation.

PART 3

Path to Recovery

7

Recommended Treatment

The language that is the Old Testament is in dire straits. It is very, very sick. Its death seems imminent. The coldest, hardest fact about language death is that once a language dies, it is virtually impossible to bring it back. This ups the ante significantly with regard to saving the Old Testament. If it is not saved while there is still time—while there are still some who can speak the language fluently, as it were—bringing it back will be nothing short of miraculous, perhaps impossible. For some linguistic communities, it may already be too late.

In this chapter I return to the linguistics side of the linguistic analogy in order to discuss some of the strategies that linguists adopt in their attempts to save dying languages. I then turn to what most consider to be the only victory in what is a history of failed attempts to do just that. The sole success story is Hebrew. How Hebrew was saved leads directly to a discussion of language learning, in terms of both learning a first language (as children do) or learning a new (but perhaps very old) language as a second tongue (as adults often do). The latter situation indicates that some attention should be paid to diglossia and bi-/multilingualism, which is when (respectively) a speech community or a particular language speaker operates in two or more dialects or languages.[1]

1. The terms *dialect* and *language* should be carefully distinguished. Diglossia is often discussed in terms of high (H) and low (L) dialects of a language or language group (e.g., Standard German and Swiss German), which are sometimes correlated with written and oral forms. Bi-/multilingualism designates the ability to operate in more than one fully distinct language—say, Italian and Arabic, or English and Spanish. See McWhorter, *Power of Babel*, 87–92. For diglossia in ancient Israel, see Rendsburg, *Diglossia in Ancient Hebrew*; Young, Rezetko, and Ehrensvärd, *Linguistic Dating of Biblical Texts*; and further bibliography in chap. 1. In actual practice, it is

This, in turn, raises the issue of what linguists call *code-switching*, which is when (and why) a multilingual speaker switches from one language (or dialect) to another, often in midstream. Each of these linguistic phenomena, no less than the others explored to this point, has profound ramifications for the Old Testament understood analogically as (like) a language. Each will prove instrumental if that language is to be saved.

On Saving Dying Languages

Thousands of the world's languages have died out over the course of human history (see chap. 3). Language death continues to this day, with a large number of languages dying at what seems to be an unprecedented rate.[2] Language death is thus a not uncommon part of the language life cycle, but it is not invariable: it need not take place and indeed will not take place as long as there are living speakers of a language who are actively teaching it to a younger generation that is actively learning it.

Numerous movements are underway to save contemporary languages that are dying or in danger of doing so. These include attempts to revive languages like Welsh, Irish Gaelic, Maori, and Hawaiian. While these efforts are laudable, some linguists are of the opinion that, once a revival movement for a language is launched, it is already too late for that language. That is largely because so many of the dying and endangered languages are old ones, which means they are especially complex and very hard to master, especially if a user (or would-be user) wasn't raised in the language since childhood. It has been said, for example, that some especially difficult Algonquian (Native American) languages like Cree and Ojibwa (both endangered) are so complex that even children born into these languages are not deemed fully competent in them until the age of ten.[3]

Not only are so many dying languages archaic; they are also typically arcane, quite different from the other (often Western European) languages that dominate the globe.[4] As McWhorter states, "Rare is the threatened language whose

not always easy to determine where one dialect leaves off and a new language begins. In what follows I focus primarily on bi-/multilingualism. For more on dialects, see also chaps. 8–9.

2. On language death and various attempts to stop it, see, inter alia, Hagège, *Death and Life of Languages*, esp. 169–238, 328–33; Dorian, *Investigating Obsolescence*; Crystal, *Language Death*, esp. 11–26; Aitchison, *Language Change*, 235–48; Harrison, *Last Speakers*; Harrison, *When Languages Die*; Nettle and Romaine, *Vanishing Voices*; Grenoble and Whaley, *Saving Languages*; Kroskrity, *Telling Stories in the Face of Danger*; and Abley, *Spoken Here*.

3. McWhorter, *Power of Babel*, 200, cf. 205.

4. As noted in chap. 3, 96 percent of the world's population speaks one or more of the top twenty most-spoken languages. See McWhorter, *Power of Babel*, 257; cf. *CEL* 288–89.

grammar requires only the effort that Spanish or Dutch would to master."[5] The most difficult languages are often the most complicated phonologically and grammatically. So, for example, there isn't a single regular verb in Navajo.[6]

Chapter 3 has already noted the great losses that accompany the death of any human language. Two brief citations reinforce the point: "Just as the extinction of any animal species diminishes our world, so does the extinction of any language."[7] "With every language that dies, another precious source of data about the nature of the human language faculty is lost."[8] Alongside these sad truths is another: It is extremely unlikely that all of the world's currently spoken 6,000 languages will survive. It seems equally unlikely that all will die save one, with humanity returning to a pre-Babel state, when "the whole earth had one language and the same words" (Gen. 11:1 NRSV). But saving the languages that can still be saved is hard work and must overcome a number of obstacles. These obstacles include the fact that many speakers of the non–top twenty languages think their native tongues are less significant, maybe even somehow less real—especially if they are exclusively spoken languages or, even if written, are not used widely in written form or in other "official" communication.[9] Massive redistribution of people to urban contexts also complicates the survival of many languages if only because the children in these scenarios are typically required to speak the city's lingua franca, which is usually one of the top twenty languages.[10] These children may acquire their parents' language as their first language (L1), but it is quite likely that they, with the linguistic pressure caused by the urbanization-cum-lingua-franca, will become underusers of L1 and increasingly expert in the second language (L2) of the city.[11] Or they may only partially acquire their parents' language, never achieving full, native fluency for the same reasons. Either way, the L1 will not be fully productive, and so whatever is passed along to the next generation

5. McWhorter, *Story of Human Language*, 3:37.

6. McWhorter, *What Language Is*, 65.

7. Hale et al., "Endangered Languages," 8.

8. Crystal, "Death of Language," 58.

9. See D. Wheeler, "Death of Languages," 4. He notes that indigenous speakers sometimes feel shame about their native languages. This feeling can be exacerbated (for immigrants) by governmental policies concerning language use since nationalistic fervor is often couched in linguistic terms. In the United States, for instance, there are occasional attempts to somehow legislate the use of English and no other language. Obviously the reasons for language death are many and varied, and I focus on only certain aspects of the phenomenon. See further and more extensively Crystal, *Language Death*; and Hagège, *Death and Life of Languages*.

10. Stavans, *Resurrecting Hebrew*, 92–93: "Exile and polyglotism are synonymous."

11. On the problem of underuse in language, including language death, see McWhorter, *Language Interrupted*; also Hagège, *Death and Life of Languages*, 80–81; Dorian, "Problem of the Semi-Speaker"; and Aitchison, *Language Change*, 243.

will be even more deficient. This is nothing other than the way languages revert to pidginized forms as they die (see chap. 3). And if this repidginization process is too far along, the reclamation or revival efforts face insurmountable difficulties because key parts of the language may simply be irrecoverable.

What can be done? At a bare minimum it is possible to record a dying language before its last speaker dies, and many linguists spend their careers doing just that. Such an endeavor documents the language and thus "saves" it to some degree, but only on paper for posterity. Whether the published grammar of something like Ubuh,[12] for example, will be read by anyone three hundred years from now is hard to say, but even if so, that grammar will not do full justice to the whole language or the speakers who once spoke it, though it probably earned the linguist in question tenure at a respectable university.

At best, then, documentation is an exercise in antiquarianism, not equivalent to (nor adequate for) preservation.[13] Even so, documenting a dying language is not without significant merit, for it means that the language—or some version of it—could be taught and learned (again) in the future, even once it becomes completely extinct, with no productive speakers left and no revival possible. Some languages fit this description: functionally dead but preserved and taught regularly.[14] Latin comes immediately to mind,[15] but so do the many languages mentioned in chapter 1 that are pertinent to studying the Bible: everything from Akkadian to Sumerian to Ugaritic to Middle Egyptian, and so forth, not to mention the Koine Greek of the New Testament and the Classical Hebrew of the Old Testament. All of these languages are appropriately described as "dead";[16] they will never be spoken like safe and viable, robust and living languages.[17] If spoken versions of these dead languages exist, they are only of the recorded-and-taught variety (e.g., Latin) or much, much later

12. Ubuh (or Ubykh) was a West Caucasian language that died with its last speaker, Tevfik Esenç, on October 8, 1992 (see Crystal, *Language Death*, 1–2). There are several published analyses of Ubuh.

13. Recall the point made in chap. 3, that language is more a spoken phenomenon than a written one. Only about 200 of the world's 6,000 languages are written; if plotted on a 24-hour clock, written language would fall after 23:07 (or 11:07 p.m.) on the "day" of human language. See, e.g., McWhorter, *What Language Is*, 145–50.

14. For Hagège, *Death and Life of Languages*, such languages are not completely dead and so have at least a theoretical chance of coming back to life. See further below.

15. See ibid., 52–57, deeming Latin one of the languages "not alive nor completely dead" (57).

16. For definitions of what constitutes a dead language, see Crystal, *Language Death*, 1–26; and Hagège, *Death and Life of Languages*, esp. 51–74.

17. For levels of danger, from safe through endangered to extinct (often with further subclassification, e.g., potentially endangered, endangered, seriously endangered, moribund, extinct), see Crystal, *Language Death*, 19–23. Hagège (*Death and Life of Languages*, 29–30) distinguishes between "living" languages and "existing" ones.

versions, which are often at significant remove from their ancestors, and as a result, for all intents and purposes, different languages.[18]

A language that is exclusively a taught one isn't a living one precisely because it is no longer spoken by a living language community. It isn't productive, and it can't be practiced—not outside of very narrow bounds (like a classroom or a field of study like Classics). For a dying language to survive, it needs speakers—preferably a lot of them—and it needs good reasons for being spoken.

Resurrecting Hebrew

There is, however, one solitary success story in a history of failed attempts to revive dead languages. That sole exception is Hebrew. The story is not without controversy. Some people, not without reason, argue that Hebrew never fully died, and to some degree that seems accurate.[19] Hebrew continued to be used in the synagogue and was the language of the Torah, specifically, and Tanakh (Scripture), more generally—not to mention some rabbinic literature. Hebrew was also sometimes used in secular writings in the mid-nineteenth century. But as Lewis Glinert notes, after Hebrew ceased to be spoken in the second or third century CE, it was "apparently never a mother tongue," even though it continued to be used, particularly in written texts.[20] It is the fact that Hebrew was no one's native tongue, no one's first language, that has led most linguists to say that Hebrew—at least of the classical, biblical variety—did die. Amazingly, it was reborn some seventeen or eighteen centuries later.[21] This stunning turn of events was largely, though not exclusively, the work of Eliezer Ben-Yehuda (1858–1922).[22]

Ben-Yehuda and (Modern) Hebrew

Ben-Yehuda became obsessed with Hebrew and with making Hebrew a full language, the national language of the land of Israel and the spoken language

18. Syriac, e.g., and ancient Aramaic (more closely); or Modern English and Old English (more distantly). See Kutscher, *History of the Hebrew Language*, 296.

19. See, e.g., W. Chomsky, *Hebrew*, 206–27. For Hagège, Hebrew is one of the languages that died in terms of losing native speakers but that continued to survive: no longer living but not quite dead (*Death and Life of Languages*, 268–69).

20. Glinert, *Grammar of Modern Hebrew*, 2.

21. Cf. ibid., xxv: Hebrew is "the only known case of a mother tongue reborn"; and the judgment of Chaim Rabin: "Hebrew is the only case of a language which had completely ceased to be spoken and had no administrative status, and yet was successfully revived" (cited in Kutscher, *History of the Hebrew Language*, 294; cf. further 296).

22. See Glinert, *Grammar of Modern Hebrew*, 2; more extensively, Stavans, *Resurrecting Hebrew*.

of all Jews even beyond Israel. In a manner not unlike ancient child-language experiments,[23] Ben-Yehuda and his wife raised their first child in a Hebrew-only environment—speaking no other language to him; he was, therefore, the first person in almost two thousand years to acquire Hebrew as his L1. This was no small feat, if only because the Hebrew the child learned was not yet extensively expanded but was still mostly a version of Biblical Hebrew, which lacks much of the vocabulary necessary for life in the modern world (e.g., "antibiotic," "coffee," "telephone," "train," "car").

The circumstances that permitted the successful rebirth of Hebrew—its wide-scale adoption from one family to an entire nation and language community—are unique and should not be missed. At least four factors are crucial: (1) First, there was the newly constituted state of Israel, (2) along with a massive influx of Jewish immigrants from all over the world, even before 1948, who needed a lingua franca.[24] (3) Hebrew had been richly and continuously preserved in written form, particularly in sacred writings and in liturgical contexts. Partly because of that, (4) the rebirth of Hebrew was associated with a strong religious impulse, though Ben-Yehuda himself was not observant and many Orthodox Jews resisted the use of Hebrew as a vernacular.[25] These four items are not true for any of the many human languages that are dying today, but they are replicated in the case of the Old Testament. This serendipity is a positive piece of news amid a sea of bad news (see chaps. 2 and 4–6). Ultimately it should come as no great surprise, however, since the Old Testament was originally written in Hebrew (and Aramaic) and in its Hebrew form played a direct role in several of the factors mentioned above. Even so, the "resurrection of Hebrew"[26] is nevertheless a sign of hope for the possible resurrection of the Old Testament as a language.

Admittedly, there is no one piece of geographical territory or a nation-state (factor 1) to speak of in terms of the language that is the Old Testament,[27]

23. See Lust, *Child Language*, 101; *CEL* 230.

24. See, among others, Kutscher, *History of the Hebrew Language*, 193. Glinert (*Grammar of Modern Hebrew*, 2) notes that, even before 1948, the Balfour Declaration (1917) and Great Britain's recognition of the official status of Hebrew "secured its place as a spoken vernacular and as an all-purpose written medium."

25. See Stavans, *Resurrecting Hebrew*, 42–45; Hagège, *Death and Life of Languages*, 287–89; cf. Kutscher, *History of the Hebrew Language*, 185, for earlier attempts to restrict or eliminate Hebrew.

26. This phrase marks an extensive section in a chapter on Hebrew by Hagège (*Death and Life of Languages*, 241–310, esp. 269–308), which in turn belongs to the third part of that book, titled "Languages and Resurrection." Note also the title of Stavans's book, *Resurrecting Hebrew*. Others (e.g., Glinert, *Grammar of Modern Hebrew*, xxv) prefer the language of rebirth. See also note 30 below.

27. But see the reflections of Brueggemann, *Land: Place as Gift, Promise, and Challenge*.

but there is nevertheless a large community of faith that needs a lingua franca (factor 2),[28] and there is the rich and continuous preservation of the Old Testament (and the Bible as a whole) in written form, if not also—at least in theory if not also occasional practice—in liturgical and devotional use (factor 3). There is also the long tradition that these books are important, authoritative, even sacred, and so there are good religious reasons (factor 4) to revive the Old Testament so that it is once again "spoken here," and so it doesn't remain a dying or altogether dead language that exists only in written form for antiquarian or academic purposes.[29] Perhaps the Old Testament, like Hebrew itself, can come "back from the page," if not actually back from the dead.

Despite the successful rebirth of Modern Hebrew, and the confluence of circumstances facilitating that success with circumstances suggesting the possible revival of the Old Testament, the task remains daunting. Both the initial testing of chapter 2 and the serious signs of morbidity in chapters 4–6 show just how sick the Old Testament is, how close it is to extinction. In some circles, it seems to be altogether too late; revival of the language appears impossible. Then again, those who still retain a bit of that ancient tongue know that nothing is impossible with God (Gen. 18:14; Job 10:13 LXX; 42:2; Zech. 8:6; cf. Matt. 19:26; Mark 10:27; 14:36; Luke 1:37; 18:27), so perhaps the Old Testament, like the Hebrew language itself, can be resurrected, and not solely through human effort. Indeed, those who know the language know that resurrection does not depend on human effort at all.[30] Here too is a contrast with the happiologists of chapter 6, whose creole posits that everything depends on anthropology, not theology.

The Hebrew Language and (Jewish/Christian) Identity

The importance of the Hebrew language, particularly its nature as the language of sacred texts like the Bible, and therefore also the significance of its resurrection for Jewish identity is a significant point that also pertains to the

28. Of course this community already has a lingua franca; it just tends *not* to be Scripture. See further chaps. 1–2, 4–6, and 8–9.

29. See Hagège (*Death and Life of Languages*, 3), who thinks languages are only truly dead if they have no speakers and "beyond that, if they have left no living traces in the cultures of the descendants of those who died speaking them." Call it the second (linguistic) death.

30. For resurrection in theological perspective, see Madigan and Levenson, *Resurrection: The Power of God*; Levenson, *Resurrection and the Restoration of Israel*. A primary point of these works is that resurrection is a new and unexpected thing—the raw transformative power of God. For the position that resurrection is more pronounced and earlier in the OT and ancient Israel than frequently thought, see esp. Levenson, *Resurrection and the Restoration of Israel*; and C. Hays, *Death in the Iron Age II and in First Isaiah*.

resurrection of the Old Testament. The following remarks by the celebrated Hebrew scholar E. Y. Kutscher are worth citing in full:

> We can safely say that there would have been no Israel and no consciousness of Jewish-Israeli nationality without Modern Hebrew. For the Israeli, Hebrew is the language of the Bible, of the Mishna and other classical sources. It is this consciousness that creates the feeling of continuity between our generation and the previous generations, especially those who had lived in Eretz Israel and spoke Hebrew.
>
> The Bible is a fundamental element of the consciousness of all Israeli Jews, believers and nonbelievers alike. . . . The very fact that an Israeli can go back to the Bible without having recourse to a translation creates a feeling of immediacy. Every reader can be his own interpreter. . . . This is possible only if we ensure that the linguistic chasm between BH [Biblical Hebrew] and IH [Israeli Hebrew] does not become unbridgeable. The day the Bible will have to be translated into IH will mark the end of the special attitude of the Israeli toward the Bible. . . . A native speaker of IH has practically no difficulty in reading the Bible, the Mishna and other creations thousands of years old, which is impossible in any other language. And it is this capability which creates the vital historical consciousness in the Israeli. The vast majority of Israeli Jews feels that it is essentially a member of the people which created this language, both within Israel as outside it, and which employed it as a sacred language especially during the past two thousand years.[31]

The (analogical) application of Kutscher's sentiments to Christians and their Old Testament should be obvious, especially since his comments are replete with references to the Bible, which for him is the Hebrew Bible or Old Testament (in Christian parlance) itself. After the tests and analyses found in chapters 2 and 4–6, we can, borrowing Kutscher's words, "safely say that there would have been no" church "and no consciousness" of Christian identity without the Old Testament.[32] For the Christian, the Old Testament "is the language" of Scripture (or the vast majority of it), the language of the Christian tradition, and the language of Christian theology, at least in theory. "It is this consciousness that creates the feeling of continuity" between present-day Christians and previous generations (the communion of saints), including those who lived in Jerusalem, in Judea and Samaria, and at the very ends of the earth (cf. Acts 1:8) and spoke the language of Scripture, if not natively, then certainly with greater fluency than is typically the case today. So it is that the Bible is—or *should be*—"a fundamental element of the consciousness"

31. Kutscher, *History of the Hebrew Language*, 298–99.
32. See also Jenson, *Canon and Creed*, 19–26; also chap. 5.

of all Christians, and the day when Christians can no longer understand the Bible for themselves but must have it "translated"—not in terms of Hebrew or Greek to English but in terms of it being refracted through (re)pidginized or (de)creolized forms—"will mark the end of the special attitude" of Christians toward the Bible. It will, among other things, mean that Christians will no longer have "a feeling of immediacy" or intimacy toward the Old Testament and will be unable to be their own interpreters thereof. To prevent that, we must "ensure that the linguistic chasm" between us and the Old Testament "does not become unbridgeable." Other "languages" (esp. pidgins and creoles, in my analogy) will *not* suffice and are not the same thing as "a native speaker" understanding the Old Testament, the whole of Christian Scripture, or the massive edifice of Christian theology, which depends on all that. Native speakers have "practically no difficulty" in understanding such things, but understanding them natively is (by definition) "impossible in any other language" than the original. It is, then, this native linguistic capacity, dexterity, or fluency "which creates the vital historical" and theological "consciousness" of Christians such that they feel "essentially a member of the people which created this language . . . and which employed it as a sacred language especially during the past two thousand years."

The burden of the present book has been to describe how all of this is on the brink of being lost forever. That loss, if it happens, would be inestimable—devastating to virtually every part of what Christianity holds dear. It would be the end of Christianity as we know it. We have, sadly, already become witnesses to this death, this dismal end, in various ways in our own time.

Learning First, New, and Very Old Languages

The situation is dire, to be sure, but the resurrection of the Hebrew language offers a sliver of hope, perhaps even more than a sliver given the shared factors facilitating its revival and those that might permit the same for the Old Testament. While Hebrew remains the sole success story in the history of dead languages never to have returned, its revival was far from easy. Other languages were proffered as the possible lingua franca, and the battle was won, in no small measure, at the level of preschool instruction.[33] This signals the importance of early language learning, among the very youngest speakers,

33. There were, of course, additional factors, but elementary education was a principal one. See Hagège, *Death and Life of Languages*, 279–80, 285; Stavans, *Resurrecting Hebrew*, esp. 41–45; W. Chomsky, *Hebrew*, 231–44; Waldman, *Recent Study of Hebrew*, 221–22; Kutscher, *History of the Hebrew Language*, 193; Sáenz-Badillos, *History of the Hebrew Language*, 269–72.

and several important insights can be gained from first-language (L1) as well as second-language (L2) acquisition for the task of saving dying languages like that of the Old Testament.

Child Language Acquisition, or There Is Hope for a Pidgin (Less for a Creole)

Since the pioneering work of Noam Chomsky, many linguists believe that the human brain has some hardwiring for language acquisition if not, in fact, a built-in "universal grammar."[34] While universal grammar remains a hotly contested area, it is undeniable that children learn language initially and extensively from their caregivers, especially their primary caregiver, who, for most children, is their mother. Children go a long time before they are able to speak, though they learn to communicate in various ways long before they ever utter a word. Children also begin to understand communication and language, both verbal and nonverbal, before they begin to vocalize words for themselves.[35]

Children learn language from their caregivers by extensive exposure, repetition, and imitation, all typically within some sort of communal context (family unit, tribe, village, etc.).[36] At first, children can say only the briefest of utterances, a word or two, but slowly over time they expand their vocabulary and the complexity of their syntax. Caregivers (and others in the language community) are crucial here because they often (and repeatedly) expand a child's language via dialogue. The following exchange is typical:

> Child: Go car.
> Mother: Yes, Daddy's going in his car.[37]

Caregivers also use special language with children. This special language, sometimes called "motherese" (or "Baby Talk Register") by linguists, is marked

34. Noam Chomsky's works are legion, but the classic is N. Chomsky, *Syntactic Structures*. For more on Chomsky, see, inter alia, Aitchison, *Linguistics*, 30–32, 191–229. Important works include Garman, *Psycholinguistics*; and Pinker, *Language Instinct*. For Chomsky and language acquisition, see L. White, *Universal Grammar and Second Language Acquisition*; L. White, *Second Language Acquisition and Universal Grammar*.

35. For child language acquisition, see Lust, *Child Language*, esp. 101–241; Elliot, *Child Language*; Lightbown and Spada, *How Languages Are Learned*; and Meisel, *First and Second Language Acquisition*.

36. Note the importance of the social unit for education more generally in Lave and Wenger, *Situated Learning*.

37. See CEL 233; expansions tended to increase when observers were present, however, suggesting that glossing may be meant for the observers more than (instead of) the children. See Elliot (*Child Language*, 90–93) on holophrases, where children say one word and the adult is able to interpret accurately the force of the utterance.

by extensive amounts of repetition, frequent use of diminutive forms (*doggy, bunny, kitty*) and rhyme (*itsy-bitsy*), and comparatively short and simple sentences that are often constructed with recurrent frames (e.g., *Where's the doggy? Where's the kitty? Where's the . . . ? Yes, that's a blanket, that's a pillow, that's a . . .*) and that usually refer to the immediate context wherein the child and mother are interacting.[38] As they begin to learn, children are not worrying about the future imperfect or past pluperfect tenses. Here and now suffices.

In many ways—and this is a most important point for the linguistic analogy—the initial states of a child's language acquisition and thus aspects of the motherese used to facilitate that, *resemble a pidgin language.*[39] Children can't learn a language in toto, in one fell swoop, and so they first learn bits and pieces, very small, very fragmentary bits and pieces. Mothers accommodate themselves and their own knowledge of the language to the child's stage of learning and ability with the express purpose of teaching the child the language.

A second point, equally as important as the preceding one, is that while children begin to learn languages by learning something akin to a pidgin—a significantly reduced form of the full language—caregivers are, as a rule, *not content to leave things there.* So it is that motherese also includes consistent and recurrent habits of clarification, the addition of information that would be unnecessary with an adult speaker, the expansion of the child's speech (as in the example above), the paraphrasing of sentences, and the repetition of material over and over again, often very slowly and on more than one occasion. Finally, there is an affective or expressive quality to motherese, as seen already in the diminutive forms, but also in the special use of sound and tone (e.g., rounded lips or a high, wide pitch-range: *Oooooo!!! What a good baby!!!*). It is also evidenced in the frequent elicitation of feedback from the child, asking questions with high rising intonation (*Okay, sweetie? Are you alright, honey?*).

Once a child learns to speak, it becomes possible to next learn how to read and write. The most effective method for teaching children how to read has been the one developed by Siegfried Englemann and his Project Follow Through. This is the well-known system of phonics-based teaching methods that employs systematic drilling on what is being learned.[40] In this process, the child speaks out loud what she reads on the page, until eventually the reading aloud can be dropped, replaced by silent reading.

---

38. See *CEL* 237; Elliot, *Child Language*, 149–63; and Lust, *Child Language*, 110–22, though the latter challenges its use in language teaching per se.

39. See Klein, *Second Language Acquisition*, 30–32.

40. See McWhorter, "Linguistics from the Left," 185; *CEL* 210–13.

There is nothing particularly earth-shattering about the above: it seems rather commonsensical for the most part, though the experience of watching one's own children learn to speak, then develop greater language facility, and finally learn how to read and write are sources of perennial parental wonder and delight. Be that as it may, when seen within our linguistic analogy, we might say that, in a very real sense, it is not so bad if people speak a pidgin version of the Old Testament or Bible as a whole *as long as they don't stay there*. Motherese and a child's baby talk are similar to pidgins, but the key difference is that the caregivers know the full language and intend to take their children all the way to full fluency. The pidgin-like form is a step toward that but is certainly not the final stage in the child's journey toward full fluency and linguistic dexterity. "Go car" is cute in a toddler's mouth, but it will not inspire much confidence when uttered by a teenager in a job interview in response to the question "How will you be getting to work?"

Still, there is hope for a pidgin (cf. chaps. 4–5) as long as these pidgins are employed as steps toward mastery of the full (original) language. Language learners who go no further than the pidgin form are, in this light, little more than baby-talkers, stuck in a highly abbreviated linguistic stage that will simply be inadequate if they wish to "grow up" into the full riches, insight, and uses of the language. A similar point can be made for the "mothers" (and "fathers"!) who speak such pidgins to various groups. Put more directly, insofar as some happiologists speak a pidgin, even an expanded pidgin, it is possible that what they are preaching may be of great use *as long as the language instruction doesn't stop there*, but instead uses the abbreviated form as a step toward full fluency. If so, then there is hope that the pidgin-like language learning might grow into something far larger and far better. It could be even better than that: the abbreviated presentation could be an intentional and highly effective pedagogical device to move "children" (that is, people, whatever their age, who are learning a language like the Old Testament) to full fluency. Of course it is far from clear that most happiologists view their "product" (I use the term intentionally) as but a first step in the larger project of biblical fluency. I very much doubt it. It is even possible that happiologists and their "clientele" (again, I use the term intentionally) are completely innocent of the fact that the language they speak is not coterminous with the original. In many instances, they speak a new language (a creole) and are blissfully unaware of its distance from the old one. At least Marcion and the New Atheists are up front about their pidginization (see chaps. 4–5).

What, then, about the creoles? Here too I am not particularly sanguine. Creoles are, after all, at even further remove from the original (substrate) language than is a pidgin. There is no straight line from a creole back to that original, and so, unlike less creolized forms, one can't build on (or from) a creole so as to learn that original. So, while there is hope for a pidgin, there is far less hope for a creole. The extent to which happiologists like Osteen speak a pidgin-turned-creole will have direct bearing on whether or not their flocks can learn the original, full language of Scripture or not. In the worst-case scenario—perhaps even in the best—most people will have to start all over from scratch.[41]

Either way, pidgin or creole, whatever hope might exist quickly evaporates if the language learners stop moving forward in their learning. At that point the case is one of arrested development, the equivalent of saying "Go car" at a job interview.[42] The same judgment obtains for those language teachers who refuse to speak anything but the most basic motherese to their "children." Teachers (or preachers!) who are content to teach only baby talk infantilize those who are depending on them to provide instruction in the full language.[43]

To make the point as clear as possible: baby talk is okay for a time—for example, when one is actually, biologically a child or, to quote Paul, when people are "infants in Christ" (1 Cor. 3:1 NRSV) and, according to Hebrews, they need to learn "the basic elements of the oracles of God" (Heb. 5:12 NRSV)—but there comes a time when childish things must be put away (1 Cor. 13:11), when milk is insufficient and one must mature and move on to solid food (Heb. 5:14; cf. 1 Pet. 2:2). Hebrews indicates that such maturity, the solid food that comes after breast milk, is marked by the ability to distinguish good from evil—and, one might add, a pidgin/creole from the full language—with the goal being to leave basic teaching behind, moving on to a more advanced curriculum (see Heb. 5:14–6:3). One example of basic teaching, of a childish thing that must be put away, is infantile, baby-talk pidgin languages. There may be hope for a pidgin, but a pidgin will not do. That is, it will not do

41. See above for problems with underuse. In the case of creoles like that of happiology, the language that is the OT is not just forgotten; it is *mis*-remembered if not *dis*-membered. As in the case with so many pidginized forms, many speakers don't even know they are speaking a creole.

42. Incomplete language acquisition can cause problems and/or lead to major differences in later stages of a language—just as pidginization and creolization. See McWhorter, *Language Interrupted*. Even closer to the point, see Dennett, *Breaking the Spell*, 328: "If you have to hoodwink—or blindfold—your children to ensure that they confirm their faith when they are adults, your faith *ought* to go extinct."

43. Cf. Beal, *Rise and Fall of the Bible*, 27; also C. Smith, *Bible Made Impossible*. Note also, more generally, Dean, *Almost Christian*; Bergler, *Juvenilization of American Christianity*; Bergler, *From Here to Maturity*. To return to one of the figures from chap. 5, it is chilling to note that Marcion apparently came before the elders in Rome with questions regarding important Gospel texts like Luke 6:43 but received no satisfying answers. See Lebreton and Zeiller, *History of the Primitive Church*, 524, 526.

for long if one wants to reach "God's goal . . . for us," which is "to become mature adults—to be fully grown, measured by the standard of the fullness of Christ" (Eph. 4:13 CEB). And "one crucial way that we grow up into the full stature of Christ," according to Carolyn Sharp, is precisely through "the spiritual process of wrestling with God's Holy Word."[44]

By now it should be clear that, when seen through the linguistic analogy, the phenomena of motherese and pidgin-like child language acquisition raise important issues to consider with regard to the Christian education of children. Among other things, these suggest that repetition, affective communication, and so on are highly useful strategies to introduce children to the language of the Old Testament (and the Bible as a whole). All that is well and good and seems to be widely known and practiced. The idea of recurrent frames also seems particularly important. This is where children learn, via repeated framing devices, that, for example, at the end of the sentence "There's a . . ." will be an animal of some sort (rabbit, bear, monkey, elephant)—at least when they are looking at a book about mammals that Daddy is reading to them.

Recurrent frames of a certain sort seem to be employed widely in Christian education, especially for the young. This is why—to use an old joke—church kids know that the answer to the question "What is furry and grayish brown, climbs trees, and eats nuts?" is "Jesus" even if, by all other lights, it would seem to be a squirrel! The frame that has been learned in this case is that every "sentence" somehow ends with (or points toward) Jesus or God.

More seriously, the recurrent frames children learn with regard to the Old Testament seem to stem primarily from the biblical stories that are most colorful and memorable: Noah and the flood, Daniel in the lions' den, David and Goliath, and the like. These "sentences" tend to be carefully framed such that the stories children learn are almost always accompanied by some sort of moral, which is (no surprise here) almost always simplistically moralistic. "Noah was righteous" (*never mind all the drowned bodies*), "Daniel survived" (*never mind the enemies who are devoured by the lions*), "David beat Goliath" (*don't pay attention to the beheading*). Insofar as abbreviation, simplification, recurrent frames, and so forth are part of pidgin-like child language acquisition, this is all fine and good, but only for four-, five-, and six-year-olds, maybe ten- and eleven-year-olds. But by middle-school and high-school age (not to

44. Sharp, *Old Testament Prophets for Today*, 20. Note also the thoughtful remarks of Moberly on Job and how its "axiom" that "piety is wisdom," which sounds "unsuited to 'real life' beyond the nursery or Sunday school," is significantly thickened up by Job's "displaying and maintaining fear of God and departing from evil amid utter dereliction" (*Old Testament Theology*, 271, cf. 277).

speak of college and adulthood), and for some children even before that, such devices are no longer adequate. The phrases "Go car" or "Noah righteous," while not entirely incorrect, are both in need of appropriate development. More syntax, more vocabulary, more nuance is necessary.[45] The same is true for the sentence "God is love" (1 John 4:16) or, for that matter, "God is mean" (esp. in the OT; cf. chaps. 4–5 above).

Unfortunately, many Christians—whatever their age—appear to experience arrested development at precisely these points. Without further language training, practice, and instruction, such individuals are left with a primary-school-level capacity to engage with the Old Testament, including its moral dilemmas. Obviously, this will not suffice in the adult world wherein they must eventually live (we hope). With such a limited capacity, they are easily convinced by Dawkins's and others' intellectual critiques. For inspiration and moral engagement, they eventually look to places other than the Bible. Practically any television show or movie or song will provide more substantive engagement with the full reality of life than recurrent frames learned in second-grade Sunday school. The end results are finite in number (three), but altogether predictable. Lacking any training in higher levels of the language, stunted language learners: (1) leave faith behind altogether; (2) remain Christian but, for all intents and purposes, look elsewhere for the "authoritative literature" to live their lives by (see below); or (3) balkanize in communities that prefer to speak only baby talk—a pidgin-like form of the Old Testament and Bible as a whole—or, still worse, some sort of creole. As I have argued throughout the preceding pages, these three results are not entirely unrelated but exist on a continuum or sliding scale.[46] But whichever option is chosen, the invariable end is that the language of Scripture dies.

Second-Language Acquisition (SLA), or Practice Makes Perfect

Acquiring the language that is Christian Scripture is difficult because it is no one's mother tongue. Recall Stanley Hauerwas's remark, cited in chapter 1, that "to learn to be a Christian, to learn the discipline of the faith, is not just similar to learning another language. It *is* learning another language."[47] What that means is that, for many people, they must acquire this second language as adults, if they do so at all.

Adult acquisition of a second language (L2) differs from a child's acquisition of a first language (L1), because the adult is no longer a child and already has

---

45. Once again, cf. Beal, *Rise and Fall of the Bible*; C. Smith, *Bible Made Impossible*.
46. On the linguistic side of the analogy, see McWhorter, *Language Interrupted*.
47. Hauerwas, *Working with Words*, 87, emphasis original.

(at least) one language in place.[48] Even so, there are some striking similarities.[49] While there is usually no biological mother present speaking motherese to the adult who is acquiring a second language (that would be embarrassing for all concerned), L2 learners nevertheless also acquire their new language in bits and pieces, just as children do with their first languages. Adults too begin to learn the L2 in a pidgin-like form. Once again the crucial point is that L2 learners are not content to stay in the pidgin-like stage but are intent on mastering the full language. The same holds true for their L2 instructors, who, while not caregivers proper, do speak a kind of motherese when teaching. So, according to David Crystal, "To facilitate learning, in the early stages, teachers need to keep their input relatively simple, interesting, comprehensible, relevant to the learning task, sufficiently repetitive to enable patterns to be perceived, and capable of providing appropriate feedback."[50] Several of these strategies sound like nothing so much as L2 "motherese" being spoken to adult "children."

Despite the similarities, it is much harder for an adult to master an L2 than it is for a child to acquire L1, in part due to the increased plasticity in a child's brain and the limited time an adult has to learn the L2.[51] Unlike children, adults typically do not have years to immerse themselves in a language environment, with all that that offers—above all, the extensive, incessant feedback from fluent, native speakers. So, according to "some estimates, . . . it takes well over a year to accumulate as much L2 experience as a young child gets from the L1 in a month."[52] And not all adult L2 learners succeed, or succeed equally. Certain personal qualities seem to help in second-language acquisition. These include empathy and adaptability, assertiveness and independence, good drive and powers of application.[53] Additionally, "people need to be capable of assimilating knowledge in difficult conditions. They should have a good memory, and be good at finding patterns in samples of data."[54]

48. In what follows, I focus on adult SLA, though children, too, can and do acquire L2s. For SLA more generally, see Klein, *Second Language Acquisition*; Meisel, *First and Second Language Acquisition*, esp. 191–99; Matras, *Language Contact*, 68–86.

49. For both similarities and differences, see Meisel, *First and Second Language Acquisition*, passim, esp. 240–46.

50. *CEL* 377. For more on language teaching, see Richards and Rodgers, *Approaches and Methods*; Lightbown and Spada, *How Languages Are Learned*.

51. Note also the idea of a critical period that is ideal in human development for language learning (generally speaking, before puberty). On this matter and brain plasticity, see Lust, *Child Language*, 92–96. For the critical window, see also Klein, *Second Language Acquisition*, 8–10; Meisel, *First and Second Language Acquisition*, 202–39.

52. *CEL* 377.

53. Ibid., 375; further, Lightbown and Spada, *How Languages Are Learned*, 76; Matras, *Language Contact*, 69–72.

54. *CEL* 375.

Strong motivation is a huge issue in both the student and the teacher, as is a positive attitude because a "negative attitude is likely to influence language learning achievement—and conversely."[55] Finally, output is as important as input. The language must be taken outside the classroom and practiced in the real world. One cannot simply sit in class and absorb the language: one must use it in real life, in real situations, or at least in the language lab. Practice makes perfect is true in language learning, perhaps like nowhere else. Among other things, this means that exposure to the L2 must be regular, and the most effective instruction will be frequent, even if it must remain brief.[56]

Bilingualism and Code-Switching

In the case of second-language acquisition, there is already an L1 in place, which means that the successful student will become bilingual—even multilingual if there is an L3 and beyond.[57] Bilingual individuals can revert, becoming functionally monolingual if one of their languages becomes dormant through nonuse or underuse. The un(der)used tongue could even be lost altogether. Normally, though, the term "bilingual" is reserved for those people who have native-like fluency in two languages, and as long as that fluency is exercised, it is unlikely to disappear.

Even among bilinguals, it is rare to encounter someone who is equally good in both languages. "The vast majority of bilinguals do not have an equal command of their two languages: one language is more fluent than the other, interferes with the other, imposes its accent on the other, or simply is the preferred language in certain situations."[58] This notion of language interference is important and has bearing on second-language acquisition, since one's L1 can cause errors in one's acquisition and use of L2.[59] One language is always dominant and takes precedence over the other, even among those fully fluent in both.

There are some interesting points of similarity between the dominance of one of the two languages a bilingual speaks and the way one of two languages dominates in the creation of a pidgin, and thereafter how a language can

55. Ibid.
56. See chap. 2 for the correlation between regular religious practice and higher scores on the U.S. Religious Knowledge Survey.
57. See above on the difference between diglossia and bilingualism. Again, the precise delineation between two dialects of the same language and two entirely different languages is not always clear and sometimes somewhat arbitrary, both linguistically and sociopolitically. See, e.g., CEL 362–65. For more on diglossia, see further below and chap. 9.
58. CEL 364; similarly, Klein, *Second Language Acquisition*, 13.
59. CEL 376.

dominate a pidgin-turned-creole, even leading to its ultimate decreolization.[60] For the person who is (or becomes) bilingual, then, the question is which language dominates and why.

A fascinating and not unrelated question concerns when and why a bilingual speaker shifts from one language to another. This can take place even in midsentence and is called "code-switching" in linguistics.[61] There are numerous reasons why bilingual speakers switch languages: everything from the sudden need to accommodate a monolingual interlocutor, to symbolizing one's national identity, to signaling solidarity with a social group. It seems that, in most cases, code-switching is not random but motivated by *something*, even if the cause in question isn't always obvious to observers or conscious on the part of the speakers.

Let me be clear about how the preceding considerations relate to the linguistic analogy of the Old Testament as (like) a language. It should be obvious, first, that to keep the Old Testament alive, to prevent it from total eradication, will require a goodly number of fully fluent language users, and that means, if Hauerwas is right, their acquisition of a second language.[62] Learning to speak Christian involves, in no small part, learning to speak Scripture, both Old and New Testaments; here, too, that isn't just similar to acquiring another language: it *is* acquiring another language—a *second* one.

Several things follow from this. One is that language acquisition is easiest when one is young (on the crucial role of religious education for children, see chap. 9). A second item is that many people will need to acquire the language of the Old Testament much later, as adults. That, in turn, means a lot of hard work, since adult language acquisition is far more difficult than child language acquisition. And again, acquiring an ancient language is even more difficult, much harder than acquiring a newer, comparatively easier one.

A third item, logically prior to the others, is that learning an L2 means that another language (L1) is already in place. Whatever that first, mother tongue may be, it is not impossible and indeed quite likely that it will cause interference in the acquisition and deployment of L2.[63] In my judgment, that is what has happened in the creolization process of the happiologists, who

60. See chaps. 3 and 6 on creolization and decreolization, and further, Holm, *Introduction to Pidgins and Creoles*.

61. See, among others, Bullock and Toribio, *Cambridge Handbook of Linguistic Code-Switching*, esp. Gardner-Chloros's essay, "Sociolinguistic Factors in Code-Switching"; Gardner-Chloros, *Code-Switching*; Kellman, *Switching Languages*; and Matras, *Language Contact*, 101–45.

62. Hauerwas, *Working with Words*, 87.

63. See, e.g., Lightbown and Spada, *How Languages Are Learned*, 93–96; Matras, *Language Contact*, 72–74, 91–99.

manifest errors in their knowledge of and use of L2 precisely because of the predominance of their L1.[64] (The L1, in other words, can also be understood analogically, just like the L2 of Scripture.) I believe the happiology pidgin-turned-creole to be comprised of a dominant superstrate that is not the Old Testament at all, but something else altogether (see chap. 6). The superstrate of prosperity theology seems entirely similar to the cultural-linguistic forms of twenty-first-century individualistic, narcissistic, consumeristic big business. Quite apart from the question of whether every nook and cranny of that superstrate is bad, it should be clear that not every bit of it is good either, and it is irrefutable that not every bit of it is the same as the language of Scripture. And since the two are not the same, if that (modern) L1 is dominant, it can easily cause interference with the (ancient) L2, especially if the L2 in question is not even Scripture at all but a pidgin or a creole that is already dependent on or dominated by the L1. Accurate retrieval errors are just one of the many problems that can result in such a situation, leading to confusion of the two languages, hybrid forms, erroneous syntax, misuse of vocabulary, and so forth. All that is to say that the L2 will not be "spoken here," and it certainly won't be spoken accurately.

The existence of an L1, of whatever sort (good or ill), means that people who learn the L2 of the Old Testament (and the people who teach them) will need to contemplate what it means to be bilingual—how they can avoid L1–L2 problems like those mentioned above; and how, when, and why they will code-switch. As a rudimentary beginning on these questions, I want to simply point out that L2 learners and teachers must come to terms with the fact that the L2 in question (whether it is the OT, the Bible, or the Christian faith writ large) is *not* identical to their L1. This seems obvious—why else would *second*-language acquisition even be necessary?—but it is made far less than obvious or is otherwise hidden altogether by the pidginization and creolization processes. Those acquiring this particular L2 will therefore need to cultivate (at the very least) a hair's breadth of difference between the language of Scripture (L2) and the native language of their culture (L1).[65]

Much rides on this critical distance. According to the great literary critic George Steiner, "*Language is the main instrument of [hu]man[ity]'s refusal to*

---

64. For several examples, see chap. 6, but note esp. the following two that are cited there: (1) the preacher who identified the laws of God and the laws of business as "one and the same" (Bowler, *Blessed*, 200); and (2) Osteen's curious metaphor of "explosion" or "explosive" to describe God's goodness and blessing (*I Declare*, 1).

65. Not unrelated, perhaps, is the need to differentiate a low dialect (L) that is somehow more pervasive, say, at the spoken level, from a high dialect (H) that is somehow more official. Just as L1 ≠ L2, so also H ≠ L. See further below on the additional distinction between canon 1 and canon 2. Note also Dean, *Almost Christian*, 112–15.

accept the world as it is."[66] Walter Brueggemann, an Old Testament scholar, declares that it is the task of prophetic ministry *"to nurture, nourish, and evoke a consciousness and perception alternative to the consciousness and perception of the dominant culture around us."*[67] Combining Steiner and Brueggemann, we can say that the Bible provides us with the language or script to resist what needs to be resisted: the dominant culture around us, the nefarious aspects of our L1. *L1 is not L2*: that is the first, most basic, foundational point to make in the acquisition of L2. To put it in familiar language from Christianity: "This world is not our home" (see John 17:11, 14–16; cf. 1 John 2:15–17; 3:1; 4:4). And because of that fact, it is even more important that L2 be acquired so one can test the spirits—and the tongues—to see if they are of God (see 1 John 4:1; Acts 2:1–4).

But a qualifier must be quickly added: L2 is not just a matter of *resistance* vis-à-vis L1 and "the dominant culture around us." L2 also allows us to *recognize* what is right and good about that culture, what truths may reside there, in L1, and beyond. We know, after all, and thanks to Scripture itself, that God is at work both within Israel and outside of Israel, both within the church and beyond the church, and thus working in "the world" more broadly, where Christ is at work and "on the loose."[68]

In sum, the L2 of Scripture offers nothing less than *the power to resist* and *the ability to recognize* in the face of all that surrounds us. To add a third "R" to the mix: Scripture gives us the means by which we can *redescribe* the world.[69] What could possibly be more important than the full acquisition and correct usage of that L2?

It Could Happen to You (Us)

In this chapter, no less than in the others, the linguistic analogy of the Old Testament as being (like) an endangered language has proven to be both insightful and evocative. The implications of the linguistic data are obvious, even apart from the rather direct relationship that exists between the imperilment of the Old Testament and the successful resurrection of Hebrew. It remains

66. Steiner, *After Babel*, 228, emphasis original.
67. Brueggemann, *Prophetic Imagination*, 3, emphasis original. See further Strawn, "On Walter Brueggemann."
68. For outside Israel, see esp. Gen. 1–11; Isa. 2:1–4; 19:23–25; Amos 9:7; Ps. 87; and more generally Moberly, *Old Testament of the Old Testament*. For outside the church, see, e.g., Acts 10. For the language of Christ being "on the loose," see Juel, "Disquieting Silence."
69. See Brueggemann, "That the World May Be Redescribed"; also, more generally, Ricoeur, *Rule of Metaphor*; Goodman, *Ways of Worldmaking*.

to draw out several of these implications more directly and offer some further concrete suggestions on how the Old Testament might be saved from total extinction (see chaps. 8–9). Before doing that, however, a possible objection must be acknowledged and addressed.

The possible objection is that the linguistic analogy seems to go awry on the subject of language death because the Old Testament has canonical status as sacred writ. How could anything as sacred as canonical literature—the Holy Bible, in this case—be lost? How could something like that "die"? After all, didn't Hebrew itself continue to exist, in some form at least, until its full revitalization?

This objection seems quite reasonable, at first blush, and no doubt people mean well by appealing to (and trusting in) the special place that the Bible holds in Christian thought and practice. Unfortunately, the objection is otherwise seriously uninformed, for several reasons. First, one should remember that the Hebrew language, which according to most scholars did suffer linguistic death, was also deemed sacred. The rabbis taught that Hebrew was God's own language, the language God used to create the world.[70] But even *ha-lāšôn ha-qōdeš* (the holy tongue) died. Yes, Hebrew eked out a slim existence, preeminently by means of its use in written sacred texts, but it was lost as a spoken vernacular, which means that most Jews did not understand Hebrew, could not read the sacred texts written in it, and could not converse in Hebrew, which means they could not think in its idiom, compose in its cadences, resist and recognize and redescribe the world and God's work in the world through its lens—at least not in its precise linguistic form.[71]

Second, the objection operates with a facile understanding of the meaning and significance of "canonical status" and "canonical literature." Long ago Gerald T. Sheppard identified the existence of at least two types of canon.[72] The first type (canon 1) is whatever is widely authoritative for people. This

70. See Stavans, *Resurrecting Hebrew*, 72, 93; cf. *Jubilees* 12.25–27 but contrast *b. Sanh.* 37b.

71. Though of course Jews could (and did!) draw on the Hebrew Bible, analogically understood, in all these ways, exactly as I am arguing via the linguistic analogy (see Kutscher, *History of the Hebrew Language*, 183–96). Thus I am not arguing that people be fluent in the *biblical languages* per se (Greek, Hebrew, Aramaic, and so forth) but in *biblical language* (singular). See further chaps. 1 and 8–9. There can be no doubt, regardless, that the continued existence of Hebrew in written form played a crucial role in its revival—a situation that the OT shares and that could be drawn on for its successful "resurrection" (see above).

72. Sheppard, "Canon," esp. 64–67. See also McDonald, *Biblical Canon*, 55–58. Note also J. Sanders ("Canon: Hebrew Bible," 847) on the difference between *norma normans* (functionally authoritative texts) and *norma normata* (sacred texts with unchangeable shapes); and the brief discussion in Strawn, "Authority: Textual, Traditional, or Functional?" Barr (*Holy Scripture*, 75–79) speaks of three canons, but in a very different sense (see McDonald, *Biblical Canon*, 55n40).

may be or include the sacred literature of their religious community, but, within the linguistic analogy, could just as well be composed of someone's favorite literature, music, political pundits, and so forth. Whatever is impinging on people, guiding and informing their lives somehow—*that* is what is authoritative for them, and so, functionally at least, canonical. There's always a *scripture* of some sort; the question is whether or not it is *Holy Scripture*.

Canon 2 refers to that subset of canon 1 that a religious body (or individual) selects and deems authoritative in a special way, distinct from and more important than (at least officially) the rest of canon 1. Canon 2, then, refers to what most people tend to identify when they think of "canon" or "canonical literature" or "the Bible." In the process of canon formation, canon 2 is constructed or selected from a larger body of religious writings that were deemed authoritative, helpful, and/or otherwise sacred by various people and in various ways. Many of these "canon 1 books" from antiquity are still extant; they are the books that didn't get in to "*the* canon" (i.e., canon 2) and include compositions like *Jubilees*, *1 Enoch*, and *The Shepherd of Hermas*.[73]

Canon 2 is well and good but maintains its *authoritative function* only if it is also *used*, per the category of canon 1; otherwise it will simply become that which is officially "on the books" but not anywhere else. Linguistically speaking, it is only the *continued use* of the language that is canon 2 as an everyday resource that keeps it from becoming underused, unknown, and eventually otiose, especially in the face of the more powerful and functioning canon 1. Someone can have a "high view" of Scripture, even a carefully constructed doctrine about it (canon 2), but if the Bible isn't functioning authoritatively on a day-to-day basis (as per canon 1), then it is practically—that is, in terms of *actual practice*—dead.[74] And even if the pronouncement of death isn't accurate for the *entirety* of canon 2 (i.e., as a subset of canon 1, at least part of canon 2 might remain functionally authoritative), it is certainly true for a goodly portion of it. The Old Testament is precisely an example of this, with the previous chapters establishing its sickness and documenting its demise.

In brief, then, not all of canon 2 (the Bible) is canon 1 (functionally authoritative literature). What isn't *functionally* authoritative is *not* necessarily authoritative, even if it is technically or officially "canon" or "Scripture."

---

73. For these and other books, see OTP, NTA, and the Apostolic Fathers. For the OT Apocrypha, which is sacred in Catholic and Orthodox circles but not in Protestantism, see below. Note that *1 Enoch* is actually deemed canonical in Ethiopian Orthodox Christianity (cf. Jude 14–15, which cites it). For the larger issues of canonization, see McDonald, *Biblical Canon*; Sundberg, *Old Testament of the Early Church*; Campenhausen, *Formation of the Christian Bible*.

74. The death of canon 2 also means the loss of a way to evaluate (resist, recognize, redescribe) canon 1.

And if canon 2 (or large parts of it) is dead-in-practice, then any survival one might speak of will largely be a matter of antiquarian preservation akin to documenting dead or dying languages so that they can be kept "alive" (at some absolute minimum) in books that someone, God only knows who, might someday want to read. Then again, who wants to read a *grammar*, especially one of a *dead language*? Only a precious few. Old English is alive in this sort of way, as is Akkadian, Middle Egyptian, Ugaritic, and many others. That is fine and good: such languages are important and their mastery worthwhile for a host of reasons. But one can't imagine living communities—especially living communities *of faith*—predicated on these "preserved" languages, which are more like mummies, embalmed remains, than mommies, who can, via their skills in motherese, teach their children fluency in a living, used, and useful language, one by which they can and will live the rest of their lives.

Third and finally, poignant proof that even sacred writ can die lies near at hand: it may be found in the (non)status of the Old Testament Apocrypha in Protestantism. The Old Testament Apocrypha is a collection of books held by the majority of Christians for the majority of Christian history to be Sacred Scripture. The Protestant Reformation changed all that. Following Martin Luther (1483–1546), Protestant Christians quickly left the Apocrypha behind.[75] (Indeed, the very terminology "Apocrypha," which is at least slightly pejorative [it means "hidden (things)"], is largely a Protestant designation, though it traces back to Jerome [c. 345–420].) Within a short period of time, (Protestant) Bibles were printed without these books.[76] To this day, much Bible publishing outside strictly Catholic or Orthodox endeavors treats this corpus separately—either not translating it at all or translating it separately and subsequently, sometimes only after the rest of the Bible is complete.[77] Even in the translations that include the Apocrypha, it can be printed and issued independently or only included in "ecumenical editions," though even in the

75. For useful overviews, see "Apocrypha, the," in *ODCC*, esp. 84; Metzger, *Introduction to the Apocrypha*, esp. 175–204; briefly, Beal, *Rise and Fall of the Bible*, 128.

76. According to Greenslade, "The first edition of an English Bible deliberately issued without them was probably the Geneva Bible of A. Hard, Edinburgh, 1640, which retains the Prayer of Manasses only and gives reasons for omitting the rest" ("English Versions of the Bible," esp. 169), though still earlier editions omit the OTA (see already certain primitive manuscripts of the Syriac Peshitta; de Hamel, *Book*, 307). The Westminster Confession of 1648 explicitly stated that these books were "of no authority in the Church of God, nor to be otherwise approved, or made use of, than other human writings" (Greenslade, "English Versions of the Bible," 169). Luther did include the Apocrypha as an appendix in his 1534 translation, stating in his preface that they are "useful and good to be read." Even so, Luther also indicated that these books are "not to be esteemed as part of the Holy Scriptures." See Volz, "Continental Versions to c. 1600: German," esp. 100.

77. See Metzger, *Introduction to the Apocrypha*, 239–47.

latter the books are often not in their traditional locations but are instead lumped together between the Old and New Testaments.[78] Still further, the existence of "ecumenical editions" signals the existence of "nonecumenical" editions that exclude the Apocrypha altogether.

Once again, these present-day practices trace back to decisions made in the Reformation. Shortly thereafter, Protestant Christians simply stopped making much of the Apocrypha, whether that was in sermons based on it, commentaries written about it, or allusions to or citations of it of whatever sort.[79] The dearth of "Apocrypha practice" within Protestantism is entirely to be expected, since Protestant Bibles were being produced (in the vernacular) that no longer contained the Apocrypha. It is only relatively recently that Protestants have come back to the Apocrypha, realizing the significance of these writings, though it must be admitted that this significance is often limited to historical-critical concerns.[80]

To be sure, doubts about the apocryphal writings are as old as Jerome, who preferred the Hebrew truth (*Hebraica veritas*) of the Hebrew Old Testament books over those books known only in the Greek Septuagint (LXX).[81] Luther was thus not altogether de novo in his judgments about the Apocrypha. Nevertheless, detractors like Jerome were few and far between, with Augustine's defense of the apocryphal books carrying the day for more than a millennium, such that Luther, while not without precedent, was nevertheless a major innovator on this score. Further proof of his innovation on the matter of the Apocrypha is found in the objections to his position raised by his contemporaries at the time.

The upshot of all this is that Protestants have a Bible that differs from that of their Catholic and Orthodox brothers and sisters—a smaller, reduced Bible. While the merits of these different Bibles could be (and often are) debated, it is irrefutable that all Christians once had a fuller biblical "language" than the one that presently lives within the pages of most Protestant copies of the Bible. The continued use of the Apocrypha in the Anglican Book of Common Prayer (BCP) only proves the point: that use stems from the fact that the

78. Contrast, e.g., a Catholic translation like the NAB. The principal Greek witnesses do incorporate the apocryphal books throughout the OT canon—e.g., Wisdom and Sirach with Proverbs, Job, and Ecclesiastes; Tobit, Judith, and so forth with 1 Chronicles–Esther; and so on.

79. Cf. chap. 2 for the fact that sermons on texts from the Apocrypha in the Best Sermons series were only from Catholic priests.

80. But see the helpful collection of essays in Meurer, *Apocrypha in Ecumenical Perspective*.

81. Note, however, that Sirach, Tobit, Psalm 151, and the Letter of Jeremiah are now attested among the Dead Sea Scrolls, demonstrating that Hebrew versions of these books once existed. See Collins, "Apocrypha and Pseudepigrapha." The Greek versus Hebrew criterion is, therefore, not definitive.

roots of Anglicanism lie in Roman Catholicism; it thus is a holdover, a trace of or memory from the earlier, fuller language.[82] The main point, regardless, is that, for Protestantism, the writings of the Apocrypha, once deemed sacred Scripture, have died.[83] Language death can happen, then, even to the Bible, or at least to parts of it. That is exactly what I am arguing is happening to another part of the Bible, at least in North American Christianity. The death of the Apocrypha proves that another scriptural death is completely within the realm of possibility, though the affected portion is even larger and more ancient than the Apocrypha. Today we must contemplate the death of the majority of the Christian Bible, the entirety of the Old Testament, which is sick, endangered, and facing imminent demise.

Lest some readers of this book remain unconvinced, perhaps because they are Protestants who care little for the Apocrypha (though that would be just further evidence in support of my point), let me offer one final example: the phenomenon of New Testament–only Bibles. New Testament–only editions have a venerable heritage, going as far back as Erasmus (1466/9–1536) and scholarly editions of the Greek New Testament.[84] But they have become

82. The BCP draws extensively and organically from the apocryphal books, not only in the lectionary, which includes readings from Ecclesiasticus/Sirach (2:[1–7,] 7–11; 10:[7–11,] 12–18; 15:11–20 [2×]; 27:30–28:7; 38:1–4, 6–10, 12–14; 38:27–32 [2×]; 44:1–10, 13–14), Wisdom (1:16–2:1; 2:[6–11,] 12–22; 2:1, 12–24 [2×]; 3:1–9 [2×]; 7:7–14; 12:13, 16–19), Judith (9:1, 11–14), Baruch (5:1–9), 2 Esdras (2:42–48), Song of the Three Young Men (29–34, 35–65), and the Prayer of Manasseh (1–2, 4, 6–7, 11–15), but also in the daily office, which includes readings from Baruch (3:24–37; 4:21–29; 4:36–5:9), Ecclesiasticus (1:1–10, 18–27; 2:1–11; 2:7–18; 3:3–9, 14–17; 3:17–31; 4:1–10; 4:20–5:7; 6:5–17; 7:4–14; 10:1–8, 12–18; 11:2–20; 15:9–20; 18:19–33; 19:4–17; 24:1–12; 28:14–26; 31:3–11; 31:12–18; 31:25–32:2; 34:1–8, 18–22; 35:1–17; 36:1–17; 38:24–34; 39:1–10; 42:15–25 [2×]; 43:1–2, 27–32; 43:1–7, [27–33]; 43:1–22; 43:23–33; 44:1–15; 44:19–45:5; 45:6–16; 46:1–10; 46:11–20; 48:1–11 [2×]; 50:1, 11–24; 51:1–12; 51:6b–12; 51:13–22), 1 Maccabees (1:1–28; 1:42–63; 2:1–28, 2:29–43, 49–50; 3:1–24; 3:25–41; 3:42–60; 4:1–25, 4:36–59), Wisdom (1:1–15; 1:16–2:1, 12–22; 1:16–2:11; 2:21–24; 3:1–9 [2×]; 4:7–15; 4:16–5:8; 5:1–5, 14–16; 5:9–23; 6:12–23; 7:1–14; 7:3–14; 7:22–8:1; 9:1, 7–18; 9:1–12; 10:1–5, [5–12,] 13–21; 13:1–9; 14:27–15:3; 16:15–17:1; 19:1–8, 18–22), 2 Esdras (2:42–47), and Judith (4:1–15; 5:1–21; 5:22–6:4; 6:10–21; 7:1–7, 19–32; 8:9–17; 9:1, 7–10; 10:1–23; 12:1–20; 13:1–20). Several of the lectionary readings are optional, however. One should note the heavy emphasis on the wisdom genre in the lections used (esp. from Ecclesiasticus and Wisdom of Solomon); other genres and the majority of the books in the OTA are underrepresented. Only a few books enjoy full, *continua*-style reading—Ecclesiasticus and Wisdom primarily but also, to a lesser degree, 1 Maccabees, Baruch, and Judith (though in the latter case, the reading is optional for Esther in proper 20). The Song of the Three Young Men (vv. 29–34, 35–65) and the Prayer of Manasseh (vv. 1–2, 4, 6–7, 11–15) are used as canticles in response to the other scriptural readings in the two rites for morning prayer.

83. For brief summaries of the importance of the Apocrypha, including the theology contained therein, see "Apocrypha, the," in *ODCC* 84–85; Metzger, *Introduction to the Apocrypha*, 205–38.

84. See, "Erasmus, Desiderius," in *ODCC* 556–57. I thank Tim Beal for discussions on NT-only Bibles. See his *Rise and Fall of the Bible* for discussion of some editions thereof. Note also

especially prominent in modern times, thanks to the countless printings of New Testament–only Bibles by major publishers like Zondervan and distribution by the Gideons. Here too we should recall standard procedures in Bible translation and production like those encountered with the Apocrypha: most Bible translations begin with the New Testament and often release New Testament–only versions first before publishing the rest/entirety of the Bible (see, e.g., CEB, *The Message, The Voice*).[85]

The preceding considerations combine to suggest that it is far from unthinkable that the Old Testament might eventually be completely excluded from future versions of the Bible. Indeed, the publication of New Testament–only Bibles is already proof of the point! Software platforms and e-versions that can select the New Testament only while deselecting the Old are just the latest instantiations. In light of the Apocrypha's fate at the hands of the Reformers, one can see these phenomena as nothing if not a not-so-short step toward the total exclusion of the Old Testament. Indeed, the death of the Apocrypha in Protestant Christianity and the popularity of New Testament–only Bibles, especially among evangelical Protestants, shows that there is nothing to stand in the way of the complete elimination of the Old Testament—nothing, that is, except *continued use of the Old Testament*, which means *competent speakers of its language*.[86] But here is the most disturbing proof that the Old Testament could die, since it is precisely its lack of use—the fact that it is increasingly devoid of fluent users—that has prompted this study in the first place. In the next two chapters, however, I offer some suggestions on how the Old Testament might be saved despite its grim, imperiled situation.

---

that the Bogomils, adherents of a medieval heresy, accepted only the NT and the Psalms. See "Bogomils," in *ODCC* 219–20.

85. Compilers of these NT-only Bibles often feel compelled to include the Psalms. Thus the Psalms may yet retain some staying power, liveliness, or authority that other parts of the OT have lost. See further chap. 9, but note the problems besetting the Psalms in hymnody and lectionary as delineated in chap. 2.

86. To be clear, in my opinion the history of Christian doctrine and its use of the OT is, on its own, *insufficient* to prevent the OT's demise. On the one hand, that rich history demonstrates the existence of competent speakers, but on the other hand, that history and use—if left simply *back then* and *back there*—will not necessarily or automatically produce new speakers. Christianity in Germany, too, depended on and had access to the history of Christian doctrine (esp. Protestantism!) but nevertheless witnessed the near-death of the OT in the twentieth century (see chap. 5). One could easily say that it was only competent speakers, esp. among the Confessing Church, who prevented that death.

8

Saving the Old Testament

Can we rescue a word, and discover a universe?
Can we study a language, and awake to the Truth?
Can we bury ourselves in a lexicon, and arise in the presence of God?[1]

Despite the bitter facts regarding language death and the serious problems facing revitalization efforts recounted in chapters 3 and 7, the preceding chapter nevertheless claimed that there may yet be hope for the language that is the Old Testament. Perhaps it is not yet dead or so close to extinction that it cannot be brought back. If so, there is still the possibility of saving the Old Testament from what appears to be its terminal condition in so many Christian circles, at least in North America. This hope, however slim, is nevertheless a bright point, especially after the gloomy results of the testing in chapter 2 and the even more dismal signs of morbidity covered in chapters 4–6. Even so, since the matter under discussion is the *full* language of Scripture, and because the problems analyzed in chapters 4–6 at best reflect (re)pidginization and at worst reflect (de)creolization of that language, we shouldn't be too quick to sugarcoat matters or put too positive a spin on things. The Old Testament is, for all intents and purposes, still in critical condition. Moreover, as we saw at the end of the previous chapter, the fact that our patient could "pass on"—could actually, truly die—is not only not unthinkable, it is a very real possibility. This is due to *disuse* (chap. 2) and *misuse* as well as *abandonment* if not *total exclusion* (chaps. 4–6).[2]

1. Hoskyns, *Cambridge Sermons*, 70.
2. Recall too the phenomenon of "New Testament Churches," mentioned in chap. 1.

Additionally, since the language of the Old Testament is ancient and difficult, we must become familiar, if not altogether comfortable (i.e., fluent), with its more complex or darker hues, not afraid to turn away from the syrupy-sweet so as to linger over a hopeless lament like Ps. 88. Should someone object at this point, saying "But that's exactly the problem with the Old Testament: too dark, too depressing, too wrathful, and the like," I would simply recall what the previous chapters have repeatedly demonstrated: such an objection reflects a seriously distorted and pidginized view of the Bible as a whole, not just of the Old Testament. The Old Testament, too, contains the brightest of colors, just as the New Testament has its fair share of downsides (see chap. 9).

The upshot, in any event, is simply this: we shouldn't be too positive about the Old Testament's chances of survival, and certainly not too quickly. And so, even though this chapter and the next are about saving the Old Testament, we must consider additional evidence of our patient's decline, even if it serves only to underscore how difficult the treatment regimen will be. Terminal conditions are, after all, serious and require the most aggressive intervention if there is to be any hope for recovery. But, after touching on these distressing indicators, I turn in earnest to the question of what can be done to prevent the Old Testament's imminent demise, beginning with strategies found within the Old Testament itself, specifically within the book of Deuteronomy. The last chapter (chap. 9) contains further, concrete and specific recommendations on what should and should not be done to save the Old Testament.

Evidence of Further Decline

In C. S. Lewis's novel *The Great Divorce: A Dream*, a group of people take a bus ride from hell to heaven, where they are met by angelic figures—friends or family from their earthly lives who are now residents of heaven. These heavenly citizens try to talk the infernal visitors into staying, in which case the hell they knew previously would turn out to be only a kind of purgatory. Unfortunately, for various reasons, most of the visitors choose *not* to stay, preferring, as the old adage goes, the devil they already know. One vignette is particularly intriguing: it is an encounter between two friends who shared great theological interests in their former lives. As it happens, the visitor from hell is a theologian of no small fame who enjoyed great popularity, book sales, speaking invitations, "and finally a bishopric."[3]

3. C. S. Lewis, *Great Divorce*, 36.

Adding to the irony that a famous theologian and bishop happens to be residing in hell is the fact that he is one of the visitors who prefers to *return* rather than stay in heaven. His reasons for this choice are several, but are exemplified in the final remarks this theologian (called "the Ghost" in this passage due to his insubstantial nature vis-à-vis the heavenly realities) offers to his heavenly friend (named Dick), who has invited him to experience true happiness in heaven:

> "Happiness, my dear Dick," said the Ghost placidly, "happiness, as you will come to see when you are older, lies in the path of duty. Which reminds me . . . Bless my soul, I'd nearly forgotten. Of course I can't come with you. I have to be back next Friday to read a paper. We have a little Theological Society down there. Oh yes! there is plenty of intellectual life. Not of a very high quality, perhaps. One notices a certain lack of grip—a certain confusion of mind. . . ."[4]

In Lewis's novel, hell is thus not only replete with a famous theologian or two (maybe more) but is also stocked with theological societies, though not, admittedly, of a very high quality!

Despite the obvious humor, this is a sobering story. While Lewis may be a bit too hard on theologians at this point—one hopes that Old Testament specialists, at least (!), are not in danger of eternal torment—there is nevertheless a point to consider here because what Lewis is getting at is the failure of theologians to prevent their own demise. If that is true, might it also hold true for the demise of the Old Testament? Is it possible that "the professionals" are ineffectual here as well? If so, that would be an especially troubling sign of the Old Testament's sickness. If even the "doctors" can't save it, what then?

There are a number of issues to wonder and worry about at this point. One is the professionalization or "academicization" of theology (and biblical studies) into "a field" of study, one among a vast multitude, many (if not most) of which seem to be of far more immediate relevance to human society and thus likely to garner federal funding, not to mention national media attention.[5] To be sure, it has been centuries since theology was the "Queen of the Sciences": anyone imagining that the present situation will somehow reverse itself, with theology restored to its former glory and supreme status, is

---

4. Ibid., 43–44.

5. See the otherwise flawed and misguided critique of biblical studies in Avalos, *End of Biblical Studies*, though there is a note of truth in what he says on this particular point. More useful accounts, intended ultimately to help biblical and theological studies and not hurt them (as per Avalos), may be found in Martin, *Pedagogy of the Bible*; and Legaspi, *Death of Scripture*. Note also Moore and Sherwood, *Invention of the Biblical Scholar*; and the not entirely unrelated studies by Clines, "From Salamanca to Cracow" and "From Copenhagen to Oslo."

guilty of a pipe dream or is hoping for the eschaton. It has also been centuries since theology "turned" academic, attempting to justify itself by using the methods and tools of other humanistic sciences.[6]

Given the linguistic analogy, it should once again be stressed that all languages change (see chaps. 1 and 3 and below; also chap. 9), and so one should beware any and all notion of an altogether pristine past—not to mention our ability to (re)capture such. Normal linguistic change is not at issue here, however; instead, along with a number of other writers,[7] I wish to reflect on the nature and (non)efficacy of professional biblical scholarship such that so much of that scholarship doesn't seem to be proving very helpful in stopping the rapid decline of the Old Testament, as chronicled in earlier chapters.

Every year publishers churn out massive amounts of technical scholarly literature on the Bible. Even in a generous construal of this situation—something along the lines of trickle-down economics such that even the most technical studies eventually find their way into accessible commentaries, then into pastors' libraries, and then into sermons and adult education classes, and thus sooner or later (though only God knows how long this process must take) into everyday Christian life and practice—chapters 2 and 4–6 suggest that such a construal is simply not true. The trickle has stopped trickling. And what could one reasonably expect when it was only a trickle to begin with? It doesn't take much, especially in a warming climate, to dry up a trickle altogether.

Yet it is not just biblical studies proper that offers evidence of the Old Testament's further decline. To return to the initial tests conducted in chapter 2, one could observe that, if the trickle-down studies did somehow make it into a pastor's library, it could easily encounter a dam there prohibiting it from going any further. Indeed, if the Best Sermons series of the twentieth century are any indication, that is exactly what has happened. Stepping out of the pulpit, but remaining within the walls of the church, one could observe the hundreds of thousands if not millions of Bible studies taking place every week, if not every day, across the globe. But to what end? One is tempted to quote Ecclesiastes:

> What do people gain from all the hard work that they work so hard at under the sun? (Eccles. 1:3 CEB)

> But when I surveyed all that my hands had done, and what I had worked so hard to achieve, I realized that it was pointless—a chasing after wind. Nothing is to be gained under the sun. (Eccles. 2:11 CEB)

6. See esp. Charry, "Academic Theology"; Charry, *Renewing of Your Minds*; Charry, *God and the Art of Happiness*. Further, see Legaspi, *Death of Scripture*.
7. See note 5 above.

One is also tempted to wonder if the "hard work" ("toil," in many translations) mentioned in these verses might be a cipher for "Bible studies" or "Sunday school" and to conclude that there is no net gain to be derived therefrom. Maria, a character in Elie Wiesel's play *The Trial of God*, says that sometimes she wonders, when she hears the priest describe "our Lord's suffering," if "the Lord isn't suffering because He must listen to sermons!"[8] If she is right, the even greater number of toilsome Bible studies must be definitive proof of divine passibility.

The question facing all of these lower-level lay studies, no less than the high-level expertise of professional biblical scholarship, is whether any of it matters very much in terms of the overall bettering of humanity and the world (including the nonhuman elements thereof). Isn't the proof of the pudding in the eating? Is the lack of such eating just more proof that the moral critique of Christianity, or at least the moral critique of so many sermons and Bible studies within Christianity, is spot on?[9]

Before rushing to final judgment on these matters, the linguistic analogy should be considered once again. When deployed with reference to lay Scripture study, it raises the question of whether so many Bible studies are about language learning at all, especially about learning a full, robust version of the language. Quite apart from the fact that so many Bible studies seem like little more than opportunities to consume too many sugared pastries and drink too much weak coffee in Styrofoam cups made still worse (if that is even possible) by powdered cream packets, the linguistic analogy leads us to worry that many such gatherings are, at best, about learning a pidgin (or creole)—the "Happy Bible" pidgin (creole), for instance, or the "American Bible" pidgin (creole)[10]—*not* the full language. Acquisition of the pidginized or creolized version may not be the overt, intended, or even conscious curricular goal of

8. Wiesel, *Trial of God*, 46.

9. Again, see Charry, "Academic Theology," 90–104; Charry, *Renewing of Your Minds*; cf. also Eagleton, *Reason, Faith, and Revolution*, 47–108.

10. See chap. 6. For American civil religion, see Laderman, *American Civil Religion*; cf. the plethora of recent publications, such as Lee, *American Patriot's Bible, KJV*; Lee, *Young American Patriot's Bible*; D. Barton, *Founders Bible (NASB)*; Foster and Lillback, *1599 Geneva Bible: Patriot's Edition*. See Beal, *Rise and Fall of the Bible*, passim, for the problems that pertain to boutique Bible production and for the market-driven nature of Bible publishing. As he explains: "Rupert Murdoch didn't acquire Zondervan because he wanted to spread the Word any more than he acquired My-Space because he wanted to expand his friends list. As owner of HarperCollins, he also publishes occult classics like *The Satanic Bible* and *The Necronomicon*. Getting into Bible publishing is simply good business" (34–35). Cf. J. Smith, "Scriptures and Histories," 33, on "commercial Bible printers seeking a comparative advantage for their product which was, after all, identical to that of their competitors. The solution, as with soap powder, was found in varying the packaging and in the diversity of extra-biblical materials each edition included."

these meetings, just the unhappy result of interrupted learning or arrested development, especially if the Bible study in question is comprised of adults whose capacities for language learning are significantly limited.[11] Whatever the case, in whichever scenario, it is not surprising that there is little "net gain" (à la Ecclesiastes) and no real difference in outcome (hence the moral critique of Christianity). The end result of pidgin(ized) or creole(ized) Bible learning is *entirely what one would expect*: people who look and think exactly like everyone else, including those who have never read the Bible and would not claim to be Christian. But no worries: depending on the pidgin or creole, these well-meaning folks are often (for the most part) nice, "happy" consumers on their way to billionaire status and large donations to their favorite political party, or so the mythos goes, even though that is *not* how the Bible itself goes. Maybe so many Bible studies are hamstrung from the start. That's one option when they are seen through the linguistic analogy.

Here is another option: many people *may not want* to learn the language. Learning languages is hard work, after all, and it is made harder the more complex a language is. But, lest my critique seem unduly severe, let me soften it a bit by adding that the linguistic situation as described above indicates that many Christians have had little if any exposure to the full language at all. This means that many don't know what they are missing of the full language and so are innocent of blame, though perhaps only to the extent that one is innocent of systemic sin—a dubious compliment to be sure! Enough, then, with softening the critique. Then things get worse: If the linguistic analogy holds any water, and if (re)pidginization and (de)creolization are operative as I have suggested, then the very real possibility follows that the majority of what most Christians have heard, and for the majority of their lives, is at best a pidgin or a creole (whether a passionate version or not matters little), and so they have little to no idea that there is anything more to learn. The reduction of the original, fuller language of Scripture is, once again, a sign of its (imminent) death and so, to return to Frederick Buechner's line used as one of the *testimonia* to the present book, "If the language that clothes Christianity is not dead, it is at least, for many, dying; and what is really surprising, I suppose, is that it has lasted as long as it has."[12] Put differently, it's no small miracle that so many people go to church at all, given the smallness of the vision (that is, of the *language* in the linguistic analogy) that they've been given. If people ever are exposed to something bigger, grander, more

11. See McWhorter, *Language Interrupted*, for the fact that incomplete language acquisition can cause as many problems in language use and/or lead to as many differences in later stages of a language (vis-à-vis its original) as do pidginization and creolization.

12. Buechner, *Magnificent Defeat*, 110.

articulate—here and there, now and then—it may inspire momentarily, but its sheer oddity means that it is usually (and quickly) slotted into the much smaller grammatical structures that are already built in: into the memory and into the bones. Whatever the case, it's not accurate to say that all of this is malevolent. It is just pathetic. Or, perhaps better, *a*pathetic.

As for the apparent inefficacy of so much professional biblical scholarship—the inability of the never-ending flow of papers, publications, books, commentaries, and such to reverse the death of the Old Testament (the present book perhaps just one more instance of the same)—maybe "professionalization" itself is partly to blame. Disciplinary developments and increased specialization are also at work. Some fault should probably be laid at the door of at least some branches of historical criticism,[13] perhaps the comparative approach above all, insofar as these have often moved further and further *away* from the scriptural texts proper to the world behind the texts themselves, to extracanonical comparanda, and so have tended to emphasize diachronic and developmental growth, filleting the biblical materials into ever smaller and more disparate layers, often with little concern for the whole, whether that be unit, canonical book, Bible, or linguistic system.[14]

Without some basic language ability already in place, the cumulative effect of such work is often to distance a (potential) language user from the language that is Scripture. It effectively challenges and critiques—and, to be sure, these are crucial, important, and altogether appropriate tasks. And yet, without some prior knowledge (that is, a language user with some facility), challenge and critique are by themselves ineffective and inefficient to engender, inculcate, and teach the language proper.[15] Without prior knowledge, there's nothing there to challenge and critique; the subtraction from zero is thus less than zero.

13. See, e.g., Legaspi, *Death of Scripture*; Martin, *Pedagogy of the Bible*. It is fascinating to observe that Adolf von Harnack painted Marcion as the first historical critic (*History of Dogma*, 1:277–78).

14. See the incisive remarks of Levenson, "Eighth Principle of Judaism and the Literary Simultaneity of Scripture," in Levenson, *Hebrew Bible, the Old Testament, and Historical Criticism*, 62–81. Cf. Childs, *Isaiah*, xii:

> After having recently completed a lengthy project on biblical theology, . . . I am fully cognizant that its effect has been minimal on the field of biblical exegesis. Usually books on biblical theology have been relegated to a special subdiscipline, and thought to relate only to larger hermeneutical and theological concerns without any close relation to exegesis. Those engaged in biblical theology are often dismissed as "theologians," and not biblical interpreters. For my part, I have always considered biblical theology to be only an ancillary discipline that better serves in equipping the exegete for the real task of interpreting the biblical text itself.

15. For the crucial feedback loop of catechesis-and/with-criticism (and vice versa), see Strawn, "Teaching in a New Key."

In the end, then, such work may actually *undercut* if not completely *obliterate* a (potential) language user's capacity (or felt need) to learn the language at all (or in the first place). The technical nature of professional language (jargon) is also not conducive to initial language learning.[16]

Even so (and at the very same time), biblical scholarship, even of the most esoteric variety, is in its own way functioning at a very high level in terms of language preservation. On the ground (perhaps we should think here of low dialects), the Old Testament may be dying, yet it is receiving as much attention as ever (if not more) in the guild and in publishing. This flood of publications, especially in countless editions of the Bible, may be "a distress crop" and thus a sign of imminent death.[17] But the ever-increasing specialization of professional biblical studies (here the analogue is that of high dialects or technical professional jargons) coupled with the correlate distancing from ever-decreasing knowledge of the Bible on the ground, in everyday "speech" (the low dialect of real, practiced language), means that, in the end, *two distinct languages*—not just two dialects of the same language—will be spoken . . . or not spoken, as the case may be. Even the high dialect, that is, even though preserved, will cease to be a productive, living, spoken language by regular people in their regular lives. It will, for all intents and purposes, die as a practiced vernacular.[18] The low dialect, in the meantime, may drift so far through processes like (re)pidginiziation, (de)creolization, and so forth that it too will end up as a completely different language from the original—an original that, however exactly it transpired, has expired.

All that is to say that even the best of biblical scholarship, even when executed at the highest of levels and for the best of reasons, is insufficient for language preservation *as long as it is devoid of practiced language-use*. Lacking that, even the best of biblical scholarship, for the best of reasons, looks like nothing so much as documentation of a dying (or already dead) language, or even more specifically, like documentation of ever-more fine minutiae within such a language, such as the treatment of a specific preposition or analysis of a certain noun class. But even the best documentation does not suffice to save a dying language in the absence of living speakers.[19]

Here again the critique may be too harsh. I myself am a professional biblical scholar, after all, one trained in historical-critical approaches, especially of

16. On jargons, see Hock, *Principles of Historical Linguistics*, 456–62, 522–23.

17. The image is Beal's, in *Rise and Fall of the Bible*, 80–83.

18. Perhaps not completely; it could continue to survive as a technical jargon (see note 16 above and further below). Even so, see chap. 7 on dead vs. existing languages and the (non) possibilities of language revival.

19. See, inter alia, Harrison, *Last Speakers*.

the comparative variety. I continue to practice these brands of interpretation (along with others) and think they have their appropriate place and proper function.[20] I do not believe that any of these approaches (or others that might be mentioned) is inherently or somehow unavoidably antithetical to other, more theological and/or confessional approaches to the Old Testament as Christian Scripture.[21] I myself tend to think that as much depends on the practitioner's own self as on the methodological practice employed. The exegete's fundamental dispositions toward the text, ultimate commitments, and so on and so forth are far more determinative than the method of study chosen, though the import of method should not be underestimated. Still further, I do not wish to give the impression that every publication needs to be somehow "watered down," or have some sort of "immediate relevance" or impact. Theology, no less than medicine, various branches of the sciences, or indeed any area of academic inquiry, has its more esoteric aspects, some of which are relevant to other more pragmatic subjects somewhere down the line and some of which are not. That is fine and well and as it should be. Not every article in the *New England Journal of Medicine* should end with five concrete recommendations for pediatricians or primary-care doctors; it is enough that each article contributes to our understanding of medicine writ large. The same could certainly hold true for biblical studies, specifically, and theological studies more generally.[22] Finally, the impact of professional biblical scholarship is not felt solely in print publications of whatever sort, but also in *teaching*, even in *very basic introductory* teaching. The latter often looks quite a lot like language instruction; indeed, it often *is* language instruction, whether literally of the biblical languages proper, or analogically of the biblical "language." But even that kind of instruction isn't automatically effective. Teaching, even teaching of Scripture, will only be instruction in the Old Testament as (like) a language *if* it is actually executed as such.[23]

20. See, e.g., Strawn, "Comparative Approaches"; Strawn, "History of Israelite Religion."

21. Here I part company with, e.g., Legaspi, *Death of Scripture*, who overstates, I think, the malfeasance of certain branches of biblical study.

22. Linguistically speaking, jargons are not uncommon phenomena, and there is nothing wrong or bad about them. They are quite effective insider speech. In my linguistic analogy, a jargon is a problem only when it becomes incomprehensible to any and all others, including those who presumably would like to speak it generally or who think they already do. "Mechanic-ese," highly technical jargon about car repair, is perfectly well and good and highly effective among those fluent in the jargon, but it is problematic for those who don't speak the jargon and want to learn how to fix their own car.

23. Cf. chap. 1 on *how* and not just *if* the OT is present. See further chap. 9 below and also Strawn, "Teaching in a New Key." For a helpful example of how the entirety of the OT might be taught and be useful in instruction, see Brueggemann, *Creative Word*.

My observations about professional biblical studies on the one hand and lay Scripture studies on the other could be expanded or further nuanced, whether to make them sharper or softer.[24] Regardless, these observations suffice to evidence the Old Testament's continued decline. Neither the steady production of technical scholarship on the Old Testament nor the plethora of "Bible studies" has proved to be effective therapies with regard to our patient's malady. The Old Testament is still dying.

That dying was on special display above (see chaps. 2 and 4–6); thus evidence of further decline is not particularly surprising, even as certain aspects of it seem especially troubling. One hopes that this further evidence is *not*, à la Lewis's *Great Divorce*, proof that many students of the Bible, professional or otherwise, have already purchased their tickets for the bus trip *back* to hell. Even so, it is a worrisome possibility that this evidence of further decline could be the ultimate and final sign of morbidity, the death of the language of Scripture and most particularly of the Old Testament. Even the "doctors," those purportedly so fluent and dexterous in the language, along with the most devoted of adherents, those purportedly on board with the project, willing and able—all these simply can't stop it from happening. Jesus's pestering words in Matt. 23 start hitting close to home, but so do Job's words to his unhelpful friends (Job 13:4; 16:2), not to mention God's words to the same (Job 42:7–8).

Enough soaking in the problem. What, if anything, can be done to prevent the untimely death of the Old Testament?

Deuteronomy as a Model of/for Second-Language Acquisition (SLA)

The problems besetting the language that is the Old Testament are both several and significant. And yet, in the specific cases laid out here, it has repeatedly been seen that the full language of the Old Testament redresses these very real, very large problems. It is appropriate, then, to turn to the language of the Old Testament itself for help in the quest to save it. Furthermore, it is high time to do so: most of the arguments thus far have been *about* the Bible; what can be said *with* it or *from* it and *on the basis* of it?

The linguistic side of language survival was considered in chapter 7. Among other things, that chapter discussed how children learn languages, the problem

---

24. I have not mentioned, e.g., serious attempts to expose people to wide swaths of Scripture, which are certainly analogous to language immersion programs. The Disciple Bible Study or Covenant Bible Study programs come immediately to mind. What one often finds in the execution of these studies, however, is how hard it is for laypeople to recognize this material—esp. the OT—as their own, and as their own language. That is because it *isn't* their own language—not yet, at any rate—though the programs are designed to help remedy that situation.

of second-language acquisition, and some strategies for teaching languages, whether a first (L1) or a second (L2), so that they are effectively acquired. In what follows, I wish to consider Deuteronomy as a model of and for second-language acquisition (SLA).

Deuteronomy is an excellent book to consider for several reasons, the first of which is its ubiquity. This is captured memorably by J. G. McConville, when he writes that wherever one goes in the Old Testament, "Deuteronomy is always somehow there." It is, he continues, the "theological colossus that guards the entrance to Old Testament theology."[25] Deuteronomy's import extends into the New Testament as well, where it takes its place alongside Psalms and Isaiah as one of the three most important Old Testament books for the New.[26] If Deuteronomy is useful, then, as a model of language acquisition and thus language survival, its example may well carry significant weight and be broadly applicable, even beyond the confines of Deuteronomy proper.

Moreover, Deuteronomy is the book of teaching par excellence in the Old Testament. It repeatedly calls itself "Torah" (*tôrâ*) or *sēper (ha-)tôrâ* (book of the Torah) or is referred to as the same elsewhere in the Old Testament (see Deut. 1:5; 4:8, 44; 17:18–19; 27:3, 8, 26; 28:58, 61; 29:21, 29; 30:10; 31:9, 11–12, 24, 26; 32:46; Josh. 1:7–8; 8:31–32, 34; 22:5; 23:6; 24:26; 2 Kings 22:8, 11; 23:24–25; cf. Deut. 28:58; 29:20, 27; 31:24; 1 Kings 2:3; 2 Kings 10:31; 14:6; 17:13, 34, 37).[27] Etymologically, the word "Torah" derives from the verb √*yrh*, "to throw," and so carries with it connotations of that which is thrown (by a teacher) or, perhaps better, that which is caught (by a student), and therefore "Teaching" (NJPS) or "Instruction" (CEB) are valid translations; so also is "Law" (NRSV, NIV).[28]

Appealing to etymology is hardly definitive, sometimes even fallacious, but in this case its utility is confirmed by the *content* of Deuteronomy, which is everywhere about teaching.[29] Moses will not accompany the Israelites into Canaan. What they will have, instead, is his teaching—enshrined and encapsulated in Deuteronomy itself—in the book and in the poem (see below), which is to be placed with the ark of the covenant (Deut. 31:26) to go with the people of God from thence forward. Even this very brief summary of Deuter-

---

25. McConville, *Deuteronomy*, 10.

26. See, e.g., Lincicum, *Paul and the Early Jewish Encounter with Deuteronomy*.

27. For more on "Torah" in Deuteronomy, see Olson, *Deuteronomy and the Death of Moses*; and Vogt, *Deuteronomic Theology and the Significance of Torah*.

28. See, e.g., Seow, "Torah." As pointed out by Kaminsky and Lohr (*Torah: A Beginner's Guide*), in later periods and in its most expansive meaning, *Torah* "can refer to any part, or all, of the vast trove of Jewish law and lore from antiquity to today" (17, similarly 3).

29. See Olson, *Deuteronomy and the Death of Moses*; also Miller, "That the Children May Know"; and Firth, "Passing on the Faith in Deuteronomy."

onomy evokes the numerous ways it may pertain to the linguistic analogy. A few of these deserve more extended discussion, beginning with the occasion of the book.

The Occasion of Deuteronomy

At the end of the book of Numbers, all that is required for the story of Israel to proceed directly to the book of Joshua is an account of Moses's death. But that death, and that Moses will not accompany Israel into Canaan, means that the new generation (the second from Egypt, according to Numbers) must receive adequate instruction in the Lord's Torah. Despite the rhetoric of Deut. 5:3, not everyone now in the plains of Moab, across the Jordan from Jericho, would have been alive or of age at Sinai. When assessed through the linguistic analogy, then, the occasion of Deuteronomy sounds like nothing less than a fluent speaker, Moses (cf. Exod. 33:11; Deut. 34:10), whose time is now at an end and who, as a result, is desperate to ensure that he is not the last speaker of this language. He goes to great lengths, therefore, to make sure that the Torah, linguistically endangered as it is at this critical juncture, doesn't die with him.

Moses's skills in language instruction are manifest and his strategies for language instruction several. So, for example, not only does Moses himself teach this Torah, but he also consistently urges teaching of the same for all subsequent generations, thus commanding the parents to teach their children by using the same strategies he uses with them (see Deut. 6:7, 20–25).[30] Indeed, the next generation (the third from Egypt), the children, are a topic of central concern in Deuteronomy; it is clear, moreover, by how these children are talked about, that they are not limited solely to those who are biologically young, but include any and every "next generation" (see Deut. 29:14–15).[31] It's almost as if Moses knows that it only takes a generation for a language to die (see chap. 3), and it mustn't die, or else all is lost.

Deuteronomy places special emphasis on Moses's immediate successor, Joshua (1:38; 3:21, 28; 31:3, 7, 14, 23; 32:44; 34:9), but the book is primarily concerned with the entire language community, with *all* Israel (1:1; 5:1; 13:11; 21:21; 27:9; 29:2; 31:1, 7, 11; 32:45), not just with one person. So, although

---

30. One of these strategies is inscribing the audience into the earlier story. Note, e.g., the repetition of "we" language in the parent's response to the child's question about "you" in Deut. 6:20–25. This same sort of inscription happens throughout Deuteronomy in Moses's own discourse insofar as the new, second generation is consistently addressed as if it were the first one out of Egypt and present at Sinai (see, e.g., 1:6, 32; 4:15; 9:7; and passim). See further Strawn, "Slaves and Rebels."

31. See Miller, "That the Children May Know."

Joshua is important (see further below), the emphasis of the language learning is resolutely aimed at the whole community of Israel, as a group and as specific individuals.

The Strategies of Deuteronomy's Instruction, Especially Repetition

The strategies by which Deuteronomy accomplishes its language instruction are multiple. In terms of engaging Israel as a complex whole that is comprised of specific individuals, the book is famous for its grammatical alternation between second-person plural and second-person singular forms of address.[32] If nothing else, this phenomenon (which has never been fully explained satisfactorily) functions to keep the addressees engaged on two crucial levels: (1) that of *the corporate whole* and (2) that of *the specific individual*. Just when a hearer might be tempted to think that the instruction is generically communal, intended for the group but not specifically for "me," a second-person *singular* form of address disabuses the hearer of such a thought. And, lest the community think that the instructions are solely of the personal, individualist kind, the second-person *plural* form of address reminds Israel that these words are for "*all* of you."

While the devices Deuteronomy employs in its instruction are numerous, the most important by far is repetition.[33] Deuteronomy is highly repetitive on both macro- and microlevels. When the various instances of Deuteronomic repetition are analyzed, the result is that the book's rhetoric seems designed to drill the main points in, over and over and over again, until they are mastered and the desired result achieved. The main points involve the *key verbs* ("keep, observe, do") along with the *primary objects* of those verbs ("the commandments, the statutes, the ordinances"—that is, Deuteronomic Torah fully uttered), all within the primary time frame of the book ("right now, today"). The end result of this repetitive rhetoric, then, is someone who knows Deuteronomy's central vocabulary through and through and is clear as clear can be about what Deuteronomy is about. What Deuteronomy is about is keeping, observing, and enacting God's Torah, commandments, statutes, and ordinances in a whole host of ways, both now and, imminently, in the land of Canaan.

---

32. See Lundbom, *Deuteronomy*, 9–10; and the famous essay by Tillesse, "Sections 'tu' et sections 'vous' dans le Deutéronome."

33. For what follows, see Strawn, "Keep/Observe/Do!" For more on Deuteronomy's rhetoric, see Lenchak, "*Choose Life!*," 63–66; and Hur, "Rhetoric of the Deuteronomic Code." See also Lundbom, *Deuteronomy*; Lundbom, *Jeremiah*, esp. xix–xliii; Lundbom's collected essays, *Biblical Rhetoric and Rhetorical Criticism*, esp. chaps. 1, 11–13.

In brief, Deuteronomy's rhetoric helps to create fluency by its incessant, insistent repetition.[34] In this way, Deuteronomy's repetitive didacticism makes Moses a kind of mother vis-à-vis Israel, here construed as his child, if only because "in the instruction of the young . . . iteration prove[s] an effective device for stamping the mind with the things that must be remembered."[35] And yet, although Moses may adopt some practices of motherese, especially repetition, he is not content with pidgin-like baby talk. Deuteronomy is far too complex for that, despite its incessant repetition. Moses may speak motherese of a sort to his children, but he is ever the master of the language, the altogether-fluent mother, who presses his children into deeper and deeper linguistic expertise.

Practicing Deuteronomy

Repetition is a kind of practice, especially when the Torah leaves Moses's mouth and becomes a matter of Israelite concern, recitation, and enactment. Indeed, part of what Moses commands is precisely that these words be talked about regularly, indeed at all times (Deut. 6:7b: "when you are sitting around your house and when you are out and about, when you are lying down and when you are getting up" [CEB]) such that all of one's life and activities are dominated by these words. They are also to be taught to children (e.g., 4:9–10; 6:20–25; 11:19; 31:12–13; 32:46; cf. 31:19), even incisively (6:7a), and internalized "on the heart" or "in the mind" (so often CEB; see 6:6; 8:5; 11:18; cf. 4:39). Deuteronomic Torah is to mark the Israelite's external body as well, both hand and head (6:8), and it also marks the life of the corporate body: it is on every house and on the gates of every city (6:9). Given that the city gate was often the place of justice, it is fair to say that Deuteronomic Torah was intended to mark the body politic, as well. As if all this wasn't enough, the words of Deuteronomy are to be inscribed on monumental stones atop mountains in the very center of the land (27:1–26; cf. 11:26–32), and Moses commands that the Torah be read, in its entirety, regularly and periodically to all the people (31:9–13).

From internal organ to external limb, from individual self to extended family, from nearby to far away, from house to village, from center to periphery and back again, in passing moments and at high holy days—*all of space and time is to be marked by Deuteronomy and its "words."* This marking is because

34. For repetition in SLA, see Tomlin, "Repetition in Second Language Acquisition."

35. Muilenburg, "Study in Hebrew Rhetoric," esp. 100. For more on repetition and language acquisition, including with children, see Johnstone, "Introduction"; Tomlin, "Repetition in Second Language Acquisition"; and Lightbown and Spada, *How Languages Are Learned*, 10–15, 127, 138–39, 183–84.

that is what Deuteronomy is ultimately about: "these words" that Moses speaks and teaches to Israel are what Israel must speak and teach in turn.[36] In this way, Deuteronomy creates and represents a kind of language immersion program, one in which language learners are completely surrounded, even inundated, with the language they are trying to acquire. Such an environment also provides them with ample opportunities to practice—a crucial strategy in successful language acquisition.[37]

Deuteronomy's "Pastor"

The transition to Joshua demonstrates that Moses's instruction is effective: he will not prove to be the last speaker, a point to which I will return momentarily. The Old Testament also records how leadership continues beyond Joshua, through the judges, and into the monarchs. To be sure, some of these speak the language that is Deuteronomy better than others. In any event, long before any king formally steps on the stage, Deut. 17:14–20 presents the Pentateuch's only law concerning Israelite kingship. In it, the powers of the executive branch are carefully circumscribed, and with a degree of specificity that suggests, despite Deuteronomy's canonical placement *before* Kings, that the law is subsequent to the rise of monarchy and fully aware of Solomonic excess.[38]

Whatever the case, on virtually any account of kingship, what Deut. 17 advocates is not a monarch at all, certainly not by ancient Near Eastern standards, but at best a "designated reader": someone who sits around all day reading Torah. The Israelite king that is prescribed here is forbidden to acquire many horses, wives, or riches; he is also not allowed to exalt himself over his subjects, who are twice (vv. 15, 20) referred to by means of a kinship term (אֲחִים/*'aḥîm*; CEB: "fellow Israelites"). Instead, the king must be a *Torah scribe*, writing his own copy of the document in the presence of the Levitical priests (v. 18). And he must be a *Torah reader*, a completely obsessed and obsessive one at that, reading in it all the days of his life (v. 19). The king's encounter with Deuteronomy, at least in its written form, is thus even more regular and extensive than Israel as a whole: it is a *daily* preoccupation and *lifelong* pastime (v. 19a: "he must read in it every day of his life" CEB). The king's incessant and legislated attention to Torah not only makes him the ideal

36. The Hebrew name of Deuteronomy is, in fact, *dəbārîm*, "words" (see 1:1), which nicely summarizes the book on several levels. See Miller, *Deuteronomy*, 1–2.

37. See chap. 7 and note the problematic results of inadequate language practice detailed in chap. 2, esp. as captured in the U.S. Religious Knowledge Survey.

38. For more on this point and for what follows, see Strawn, "Designated Readers."

(or representative) Israelite; it also secures him a lasting dynasty (v. 20)—a dynasty, if he is any role model, that is made up not of despotic rulers but of designated readers.

In this way, Deuteronomy's scribe-king functions as something akin to Israel's "pastor"—one tasked with the community's instruction in the language of faith—and the model of the designated reader becomes a pregnant one for contemporary ministers (who are potentially the last speakers within their congregations), whether they are formally ordained or not. Just as the scribe-king of Deut. 17 serves as a model Israelite and designated reader for the community, so also the Deuteronomic law of the king suggests that more recent leaders must read and learn the language of God's word (Torah!) as representatives of and models for their people in order that this God-preoccupied designated reading on behalf of others never ends (cf. Deut. 17:20). These belated "scribe-pastors" are, as it were, "in-betweens," standing between the language (text) and the people (congregation) so as to facilitate their interaction and engagement, in order to, as Walter Brueggemann explains, "*re-text* this community: to turn the imagination and the practice of the community back to its most elemental assurances and claims."[39]

Re-texting a community will only happen by the creation of what Brueggemann calls "text-men" and "text-women." To be such a person means "to study [the text], to trust it, to engage it, to be led by it, to submit our modernist assumptions to it, and to have confidence that *this text*—despite all its vagaries and violence, its unbearable harshness and confounding cadences—is the one that merits our primal attention as a word of life."[40] That is what Deut. 17 wants to accomplish, in no less a person than the highest officer of the land, and so legislates as much, according to the chronology of Joshua and Judges, hundreds of years *before* the first Israelite king is anointed by Samuel. Not long after Deut. 17, but long before 1–2 Samuel, Joshua is required to maintain very similar habits of attention (Josh. 1:8),[41] which shows that the injunctions found in Deuteronomy apply to whomever leads God's people, regardless of their formal title, whether ecclesiastical or political. One needn't be a "pastor" to be instructed by the scribe-king of Deut. 17 or to be inspired by the model of the designated reader; neither must the "community"

39. Brueggemann, "Preacher as Scribe," 13, emphasis original.
40. Ibid., emphasis original. This is the first of two important re-texting tasks according to him; the second is to listen to the congregation, which is often textless—or, in the linguistic analogy—ignorant of the language.
41. Joshua 1:8 is the center of a chiasm with a verse on each side (vv. 7 and 9) enjoining Joshua to be strong and courageous. This envelope structure serves to highlight v. 8 and its injunctions to attend to "this book of Torah" (*sēper ha-tôrâ ha-zeh*), which is, again, Deuteronomy (see above and Josh. 1:7: "the law that Moses commanded you" CEB).

or "congregation" be a formal ecclesiastical body. After all, Deuteronomy's instruction is as interested in the next generation of children as with any other group (see above). The accent, that is, should be placed on the *scribe* part of "scribe-king" or "scribe-pastor." Perhaps equally fitting would be "scribe-parent" or "scribe-disciple."[42] In the latter case, Jesus's words in Matt. 13 are particularly striking. After presenting a series of parables about the kingdom of heaven, not all of which are completely transparent, Jesus turns to the disciples and asks them if they have understood everything. "Yes," they reply, to which he says: "Therefore every scribe who has been trained for the kingdom of heaven is like the master of a household who brings out of his treasure what is new and what is old" (Matt. 13:52 NRSV). It is not only the use of "scribe" (γραμματεύς/*grammateus*) that is noteworthy here but also that this scribe is "trained for the kingdom of heaven" and knows precisely what to bring out of "his treasure," apparently at exactly the right time. Even more remarkable is that, in Greek, the scribe's "treasure" is θησαυρός/*thēsauros*, which eventually comes into English (via Latin) as a loanword: "thesaurus." In the linguistic analogy, scribes trained for the kingdom, who are obsessed with the Torah of the Lord, have just the right word, new or old—as surely as a thesaurus is bound to have just the right term.

The Effectiveness of Deuteronomy

Did Deuteronomy work? Was Moses successful? The Old Testament suggests the answer to these questions is affirmative, at least to some degree. Again, per McConville, Deuteronomy is somehow present wherever one goes in the Old Testament. If nothing else, that remark demonstrates that Deuteronomic Torah really did "take"—at least in the final form of the Old Testament, which has Deuteronomy's fingerprints (or perhaps better, voiceprint, replete with dialectical isoglosses) all over it, most notably in the books of Joshua, Judges, Samuel, Kings, and Jeremiah.

Other ways the efficacy of the book is felt is in the immediate succession of Joshua (already noted above)—not only in how Joshua is repeatedly instructed and encouraged in the book of Deuteronomy itself but also in how the book that bears his own name immediately repeats the same instruction and encouragement, underscoring via repetition (once again!) that Joshua must be constantly or even exclusively formed in and by this language (Josh.

---

42. Note the nineteenth-century portraits of the family gathering around Scripture discussed in Beal, *Rise and Fall of the Bible*, 139–40. For the importance of parents in the religiosity of contemporary Christian teenagers, see Dean, *Almost Christian*, 109–30 (chap. 6, "Parents Matter Most: The Art of Translation"); and Smith with Denton, *Soul Searching*, 56–57.

1:6–9). This repetition to Joshua, no less than to Israel as a whole, shows that, whatever Joshua's age and status, he too belongs to Moses's "next generation," is equivalent to Moses's "child," and is thus a second-generation speaker.

Deuteronomy proves to be highly effective at several key points in the book of Joshua (see, e.g., Josh. 8:30–35), but perhaps nowhere more famously than in Joshua's last speech to the people of Israel before his death (Josh. 23–24). Here one finds nothing less than a miniversion of what one finds in the book of Deuteronomy.[43] In the end, Joshua's final words sound like nothing so much as his "father's" words: he too, like Moses, summons Israel to recommit to its covenant and its enactment (that is, to long-term language learning) before he dies and is no longer present to teach them the language in person. So then, not only in its large movement and its rhetorical devices, but also in the use of specific phrases and terms,[44] the book of Joshua, not just its lead character, shows that Deuteronomy can be learned and learned well.

Further proof of the same is found in the figure of Josiah, probably the best of Judah's kings (at least by Deuteronomic standards), who, upon hearing the words of "the book of the Torah" (once again, Deuteronomy or some part thereof), immediately grasps the significance of what has been read (2 Kings 22:11) and institutes a reform that, for all intents and purposes, looks like an attempt to put Deuteronomy's laws of cult centralization (Deut. 12) into practice centuries after Moses is said to have passed them along.[45]

Josiah takes the throne at the tender age of eight, and the book of the Torah is recovered in his eighteenth regnal year, making him only twenty-six at the time of this reform. Perhaps his youth may say something about Josiah's ability to pick up Deuteronomy quickly and expertly as an L2. Whatever the case, at the end of his life Josiah is valorized in a remarkable, indeed altogether singular, commendation: "There's never been a king like Josiah, whether before or after him, who turned to the LORD *with all his heart, all his being, and all his strength*, in agreement with everything in the Instruction from Moses" (2 Kings 23:25 CEB, emphasis added). Josiah thus was the very incarnation of the Shema of Deut. 6:4–9, where Israel is enjoined to "Love the LORD your God with all your heart, all your being, and all your strength" (6:5 CEB). This is high praise, indeed, made still more impressive by the fact that he is the only king—the

43. See, e.g., Strawn, "Commentary on Joshua 24:1–15."

44. See the classic study by Weinfeld, *Deuteronomy and the Deuteronomic School*, esp. 320–65.

45. See above on the phraseology. Lundbom ("Lawbook of the Josianic Reform"; repr. in Lundbom, *Biblical Rhetoric and Rhetorical Criticism*, 121–30; see also Lundbom, *Deuteronomy*, 13–18) argues that the book found in Josiah's time is actually the Song of Moses in Deut. 32. See further below and Strawn, "Reading Josiah Reading Deuteronomy."

only person, in fact—in the entire Bible of which this claim is made. Second Kings 23:25 suggests that not only did Josiah *acquire* Deuteronomy later, as an L2, but he also learned to speak it *natively*, without even a hint of an accent.

In sum then, yes, Deuteronomy's language program was highly effective: according to the flow of the canonical narrative, its language was successfully transmitted to the immediately following second generation (Joshua), and it was also successfully acquired by someone who lived many generations removed (Josiah), who thus had to learn it as an L2. Of course, not every Israelite learned the language or learned it so well; the Deuteronomistic History of Joshua–Kings goes to great lengths to point this out. There are numerous and even countless failures along the way. But the fact that those failures are presented in terms familiar to, even derived from, Deuteronomy—even in the most specific of ways, via the fine points of the phrasing used[46]—shows how profoundly the "language" of Deuteronomy left its impress on later Israel. It wasn't just a language that was passed on for posterity; it was interwoven into Israel's cultural memory, its understanding of its identity, and was a key factor in the formation of both. That sounds like nothing so much as a real language spoken by a real linguistic community that lives by the cultural forms located within and perpetuated by, in no small way, its common tongue.[47] And while other moments in that community's life might be mentioned, Joshua and Josiah are two important figures that bookend the beginning and end of the Deuteronomistic History and demonstrate that for individuals, too, Deuteronomy's Torah is both teachable and learnable.

Performing Deuteronomy

Joshua's and Josiah's instantiations of Deuteronomy show that its language "took": it was embodied and enacted, not simply memorized for the purposes of some singular moment or ultimately trite religious recitation. Joshua's and Josiah's instantiations are thus life performances of Deuteronomy and of its "language." Moreover, since each of these individuals is separated in time, not only from each other but also from Moses's original discourse in Deuteronomy, each one is of necessity a *different* performance. This is simply to underscore that time and circumstances matter, or in terms of the linguistic analogy, that real languages change (see chaps. 1 and 3 and further below; also chap. 9).

46. Again, see Weinfeld, *Deuteronomy and the Deuteronomic School.*
47. See the discussion of language and identity in chap. 7, which interacts with an important passage from Kutscher, *History of the Hebrew Language*, 298–99. Note also, and more recently, Schniedewind, *Social History of Hebrew.*

Deuteronomy itself knows this: the statutes and ordinances that Moses continually promises throughout chapters 1–11 are finally delivered in chapters 12–26. They are specifically and explicitly said to be for Israel's life *in the land* (12:1), which has not yet occurred in the narrative of the book. Moses himself speaks across the Jordan, in the plains of Moab, thus *not* in the land (1:1). What Moses says in Deuteronomy, therefore, must be enacted in different ways, in different places, and in different and later times.

The discipline of linguistics pays much attention to diachronic change. Language *use* means language *change* such that any language that is not changing—which is just another way of defining a language that is not being used—is dying.[48] This means that any and all enactments of Deuteronomy in different times and circumstances, which is *every* enactment subsequent to the literary audience of the book itself, are not only performances, they are also, and in no small way, *updates*: ways that the language survives in new times and later circumstances. The statutes and ordinances for life in the land in Deut. 12–26 represent just such an update for the Israel that will cross over the Jordan devoid of Moses, but the entirety of the book of Deuteronomy can be seen as such an update in how it receives, repeats, and revises earlier biblical legislation in various ways.[49]

Here again, repetition proves to be an important device, not only in terms of effective instruction in and acquisition of the language but also in proper maintenance of the language. Repetition ensures that the language that is (of necessity) updated nevertheless remains in recognizable continuity with its previous form(s). Repetition keeps the updating from becoming an entirely new language, whether via (re)pidginization, (de)creolization, or some other phenomenon.[50] It thus is not hard to discern that Joshua and Josiah instantiate Deuteronomic Torah and not something else. Joshua's "Deuteronomy" and Josiah's "Deuteronomy" may not be exactly identical one with the other, let alone with Moses's initial iteration, but they are both instances of Deuteronomy's language and evidence of its survival. Even if Joshua's and Josiah's versions are later "dialects"—which they no doubt are and of necessity must be due to diachronic change and language use—they are nevertheless later dialects *of the same language*. The way Deuteronomy's language survives intact is based not only on regular and repeated *performance* but equally also on performance that is marked by *regular(ized) repetition*. Performance ensures that the language is actually used (practiced) so that it continues to

48. See Aitchison, *Language Change*, 1–7.
49. See Strawn, "Deuteronomy"; and more extensively Levinson, *Deuteronomy*. Cf. also Stackert, *Rewriting the Torah*.
50. For the latter, see, e.g., McWhorter, *Language Interrupted*.

have a vibrant life in the linguistic community; repetition ensures that the language spoken is the *same language* and not some other—despite necessary and essential, even inevitable, updating. Sameness, of course, is a hallmark of repetition, even and despite the existence of difference, which also plays a significant role in repetition.[51] Difference, in the present case, is the linguistic change brought about by new times and circumstances and repeated language use, but the sameness is equally important: it is *repeated* use of the (same) language.

In his insightful study of repetition in literature and film, the literary critic Bruce Kawin argues that repetition can have a timeless quality, taking us somehow (at least for the duration of the repetition) out of time via its emphasis on the same/similar. Such repetition places us in the eternal now of the present moment.[52] This timeless aspect of repetition also helps to appropriately restrict the range of invariable diachronic change, making sure the latter doesn't drift so far as to end up as an entirely different language.

In sum, each part of "performing Deuteronomy" is crucial: both that Deuteronomy *is performed* and that the performance done is *of Deuteronomy*. In this way, performing Deuteronomy means that Deuteronomy is everywhere and always updated and yet always remains itself.

Singing Deuteronomy

The book of Deuteronomy ends with Moses's death, but Moses's teaching in the book ends with two poems.[53] Deuteronomy 33 contains Moses's blessing of the tribes, which is preceded by the poem in chapter 32. Although the poem in Deut. 32 is often referred to as the Song of Moses, its introduction in Deut. 31 makes clear that the poem is a piece of divine instruction in a way that Moses's blessing in chapter 33 is not. Deuteronomy 33 contains Moses's final words of blessing to Israel, but in chapter 32 we have God's final words of instruction to Israel in the book of Deuteronomy and in the Torah as a whole, as it now stands. Deuteronomy 32 is thus the ultimate climax, not only of Deuteronomy but of the entire Pentateuch as well. This climax comes in the form of a song.

In Deut. 31, in the introduction to this climactic song, God breaks the bad news to Moses: despite the extensive—and repetitive!—language instruction

---

51. See Strawn, "Keep/Observe/Do"; for a worked example on sameness/difference, see also Strawn, "X-Factor: Revisioning Biblical Holiness."

52. Kawin, *Telling It Again and Again.*

53. What follows is indebted to Strawn, "Deuteronomy," 74–75; see also Strawn, "Slaves and Rebels."

that Moses has been engaging in for thirty some chapters, as soon as he dies, Israel will stray (31:16; cf. 31:27–29). For these two reasons—Moses's departure and Israel's apostasy—Israel needs a witness (31:19). In light of the deadly results of Israel's straying (see 31:17–21), this witness is the only hope that Deuteronomic Torah has, the only hope that God through that Torah has, and the only hope that Israel by means of that same Torah has.

The witness is a song that will confront Israel (31:19, 21). Moses is instructed to write this song down and recite it to the people (31:19, 22, 30). Elsewhere in chapter 31 we learn that what Moses writes is the book of Torah (31:9, 24), meaning Deuteronomy itself (see above), and this book serves as a witness (31:26), just as the song is said to do (31:19, 21). The overlapping language suggests that the song that is written down and taught (31:22) and then sung (32:1–43) *is the same thing* as the Torah that has been taught for thirty chapters and is now written down in a book. If so, then what we have in chapter 32 is a poetic version of (the book of) Torah. Deuteronomic Torah, as powerful and effective as it is—both in its juggernaut status and its impressive rhetorical strategies—is incomplete without an ending that is poetic, even lyrical. Deuteronomic Torah, as powerful and effective as it is, must include poetry, must end with a musical version—probably because poetry, music, and song are so memorable (see below and chap. 9). Indeed, God promises that even after Moses's death and Israel's inevitable apostasy, the song will not be lost from the mouth of the children (31:21). Therefore the children will *remember*. And in Deuteronomy, remembering means *obeying* (see, e.g., 5:15; 8:2; 9:7; 11:2; 15:15; 16:12; 24:18, 22).

Ending Deuteronomy and the entire Torah with a song may sound beautiful and apropos, but it is also rather odd. The song of Deut. 32 is not very representative of what has come before—if what has come before is understood primarily or exclusively as the various statutes and ordinances found in chapters 12–26, let alone other legal corpora in the Pentateuch. On the other hand, the song of Deut. 32 is the perfect conclusion to the Torah: it is Torah itself, precisely because it captures the movement of the book of Deuteronomy and the Pentateuch, the ways of God with Israel.

The song begins with the perfect Rock that is God, whose well-cared-for children become spoiled and gluttonous (32:6–15a). The children in question are "children," the metaphorical children of Israel of all times and places, including everyone who belatedly reads or hears the poem. The immediacy of the song for the listening or reading audience is underscored by the fact that they are suddenly inscribed directly into the song at this very point (32:15b):

Jacob ate until he was stuffed;
Jeshurun got fat, then rebellious.
It was you who got fat, thick, stubborn! (32:15 CEB, emphasis added)

This satiety—"your" satiety, which becomes also *our* satiety whenever we read Deut. 32—leads to rebellion and idolatry (32:16–18; cf. 31:20; 6:10–15; 8:7–20), which in turn leads to God's punishment (32:19–26). But at the crucial point, God relents from destroying Israel. The turning point comes, in part, because the punitive tool of choice—the "no people" the Lord has chosen to use against Israel—has grown proud and has misunderstood its place and purpose (32:27; cf. 8:17). The success of these unnamed enemies is only because God has supported them (see 32:30).

The pride and misunderstanding of those used by God against God's own people changes everything: they are a nation that knows nothing, and certainly not the ways of the Lord (32:28–31). This leads to a new development in God's strategy of destruction. But just then something else happens that changes everything. As was the case in v. 15b, the Israelites once again find themselves—to borrow words from Pablo Neruda—"in the stanza," but this time, in v. 31, they are "cleansed of all evil."[54] At the very moment when it seems that all is lost, when God has handed Israel over to a deadly foe and is now engaged in personal dispute with that enemy nation—a dispute that may end up having little or nothing to do with the fate of God's people—suddenly, just then, Israel *reinserts* itself: "Their rock is not like *our* Rock," they say, as do all who read or hear this song after them (32:31 NRSV, italics added).

Two things must be said about this (re)insertion. First, in v. 15b, Israel found itself *inserted* passively, whether they wanted to be or not; and that insertion was for *judgment*: you grew fat! In v. 31, Israel *reinserts* itself, actively; and that (re)insertion is for *hope* if not also *doxology*: *our* Rock is incomparable! The shift from v. 15b to v. 31 is not solely a matter of *agency*, passive versus active, nor only one of *content*, judgment versus praise. It is also one of *language learning*: the Israel that speaks v. 31 has learned from v. 15b. Israel has learned a grammatical "rule," as it were, that they can find themselves "in the stanza" not only for judgment but also for hope. This linguistic "rule," if it may be called that, is thus successfully acquired and subsequently redeployed effectively, even salutarily.

This leads to the second thing that must be said about this (re)insertion: Israel's unexpected clinging to God at the point of no hope, when all seems lost, in the darkest night, leads directly to God clinging to them. Precisely at

54. Neruda, "Love," in Neruda, *Poetry of Pablo Neruda*, 5.

the moment of Israel's ultimate nadir, God promises to avenge God's people (32:35–36, 41–42; cf. Jer. 30:15–16). Although the poem itself does not make this explicit, it is tempting to suggest that Israel's language learning, from *v. 15b's insertion for judgment* to *v. 31's reinsertion for hope*, is precisely what preserves Israel's relationship with God—and God's relationship to Israel. Everything is up in the air in v. 30 until Israel demonstrates its mastery of the grammatical "rule": the self/community can and must be (re)inserted into the stanza. The deployment of this linguistic "rule" then changes everything. Now God is not manifest in judgment against Israel, but against Israel's enemies. What can Israel possibly do thereafter but respond in unrestrained praise (32:43)? And, as they do so, Israel's transformation is complete. They have been transformed from "degenerate children" (32:5), gluttonous idolaters (32:15), and those who suffer God's wrath (32:25): changed into those who cling to God in doxological hope (32:31) until finally, as victims, they are cared for and rescued by their Lord, and as a result, they praise God for divine justice and absolution in the end.

The poetic movement of Deut. 32 *is* Deuteronomic Torah. It is altogether consonant with the movement of the book of Deuteronomy as a whole, which takes Israel from past blessing (the ancestors, the covenant at Horeb/Sinai), into disobedience and judgment (Kadesh, the golden calf, exile), and out the other side again (the Moab covenant of chaps. 29–31) because of the inexplicable love of God for Israel, and the inexplicable mutuality of the covenant that binds God to Israel despite the worst disobedience and that binds Israel to God despite the worst punishment. Still further, the movement of Deuteronomic Torah is altogether consonant with the movement of the entire Pentateuch, which moves from creational blessing, to threats to that blessing, to deliverance, covenant, calf, wilderness, and Moab, until it arrives, at last, at Deuteronomy, where it receives an altogether crucial and thoroughly resonant and repetitive recapitulation. In this way, the song of Deut. 32 *is* Torah, and the Torah *is* (a) song.[55]

At the conclusion of Moses's song, we learn that it is actually a duet sung with Joshua (32:44). The duet is further proof of Moses's pedagogical abilities in the book and a foreshadowing of Joshua's penchant for language acquisi-

---

55. I cannot resist one aside about Torah/law at this point because Deut. 32, *the* song and climax of Torah, shows how so much Christian antinomianism is so thoroughly pidginized. Far better is Calvin, who wrote, "Whoever wants to do away with the law entirely for the faithful, understands it falsely" (*Institutes* 2.7.13); and the catechism of the BCP, 848: "Q. Since we do not fully obey them [the Ten Commandments], are they useful at all? A. Since we do not fully obey them, we see more clearly our sin and our need of redemption." See Miller, *Way of the Lord*, 265n47, for the notion that the ancient Greek laws were sung to the accompaniment of the kithara (lyre, harp; cf. Plato, *Laws* 4.722).

tion: he has a knack for Deuteronomy's language (see above). The duet also makes two additional items clear: first, Moses's death is truly imminent since he now needs explicit accompaniment; but also, second, the language of Deuteronomic Torah will most certainly live on with new speakers (singers!), like Joshua, ready to move forward, and with effective strategies of transmission in place, like the song of Torah itself, if and when all else fails (31:19, 21).

And the song worked! Joshua and Josiah have already been mentioned, but the song's efficacy was long lasting.[56] In 2 Macc. 7, a mother and her seven sons are martyred for their faith. After the death of the first son, the mother and the remaining brothers "encouraged each other to die honorably, saying, 'The Lord God truly watches over us and will come to our aid, just as Moses' song personally bore witness against them, clearly saying, "God will have compassion on his servants"'" (2 Macc. 7:5b–6 CEB). The citation comes from Deut. 32:36, but what is significant here is not only how the song lived on—it was not lost from the mouth of Israel's children even much, much later (see Deut. 31:21)—but also how the-Torah-that-is-a-song and the-song-that-is-the-Torah made a difference in this mother's and these children's living and dying. This Torah-song wasn't "just" words, a cultural-linguistic script living only in the left brain, devoid of actual practice.[57] No, this Torah-song was an *embodied language* that was *performed, enacted, and enfleshed*—even at the most treacherous of moments, even at the very moment of death.[58]

The story from 2 Macc. 7 is retold in 4 Macc. 18, only this time the mother gives credit to her husband, the boys' father, who is said to have been exemplary in teaching the language of faith to his children. Among the things the mother says her husband taught his sons—indeed, in the final climactic position in her list—is Deut. 32: "And he didn't forget to teach you the song that Moses taught, which says, *I kill and I bring things to life: this is your life and the length of your days*" (4 Macc. 18:18–19 CEB, italics original). This version

---

56. Given what is said in Deut. 31:16 concerning Israel's inevitable apostasy and in vv. 19, 21 about the function of the Torah-song after such apostasy, it may not be going too far to say that Deuteronomy's efficacy (see above) is a function of the Torah-song *primarily if not preeminently*. Note again Lundbom's opinion that the lawbook of Josiah's time was Deut. 32 ("Lawbook of the Josianic Reform"; and Lundbom, *Deuteronomy*, 13–18). Beyond the texts that are cited below from 2 Macc. 7, 4 Macc. 18, and Rev. 15, note also the Deuteronomic themes in Dan. 9 and the explicit mention of "the Law of Moses, the servant of God" and the curses and judgments written therein in Dan. 9:11 (also v. 13). The intercessory and rhetorical turns Daniel makes in his prayer (9:15–19) are not unlike Moses's own in Deuteronomy (e.g., Deut. 9:18–29) and in the turn from judgment to mercy in Deut. 32. Other pertinent texts that may also demonstrate the efficacy of Deuteronomy in later contexts and generations include Ezra 3:2; 6:18; Neh 1:7–9; 8:1, 14; 9:14; 10:29; and Mal. 4:4.

57. Cf. the criticisms of Lindbeck, some more effective than others, mentioned in chap. 1.

58. Note the importance of Scripture in, e.g., Erasmus's "Preparing for Death."

of the story demonstrates that knowledge of the Torah-song of Deut. 32 is dependent upon diligent *parental instruction* (see above and Deut. 6:20–25). As in the case of 2 Macc. 7, so also here, the Torah-song is explicitly mentioned, but the specific passage that is cited differs: here it is Deut. 32:39 but in combination with a phrase from Deut. 30:20. Learning the Torah-song at a parent's knee, that is, will inevitably involve branching out so as to include texts beyond just Deut. 32, encompassing more and more of God's Torah, God's instruction, God's teaching, God's ways.[59] That sounds like nothing so much as a developing capacity for full language fluency. One should also not miss that in 4 Maccabees, no less than 2 Maccabees, the Torah-song is recalled at a critical juncture and with crucial information that is needed at precisely such a deathly moment as this one: in this case, full fluency brings with it hope in God's resurrection power.

Then, finally, we can turn to Rev. 15, to the close of Christian Scripture and to the end of time (according to that book), where we find those who are victorious over the beast standing by a sea of glass, praising God with harps in hand:[60]

They sing the song of Moses, God's servant, and the song of the Lamb, saying,

> "Great and awe-inspiring are your works,
>   Lord God Almighty.
> Just and true are your ways,
>   king of the nations.
> Who won't fear you, Lord, and glorify your name?
>   You alone are holy.
> All nations will come and fall down in worship before you,
>   for your acts of justice have been revealed." (Rev. 15:3–4 CEB)

Specific citations from Deut. 32 are not as clear here as they are in 2 Maccabees or 4 Maccabees. The allusions in Rev. 15:3–4 run far and wide and are not limited solely to Deut. 32 as in 2 Macc. 7, or to the larger book of Deuteronomy as in 4 Macc. 18; this passage in Rev. 15 is truly a pastiche of Old Testament texts.[61] But that doesn't detract from the point; if anything,

---

59. See the following works that stress intertextual fields of allusion and citation in the ways the NT draws on the OT: R. Hays, *Echoes of Scripture*; R. Hays, *Conversion of the Imagination*; R. Hays, *Reading Backwards*; and J. Wagner, *Heralds of the Good News*.

60. See Charles (*Revelation*, 2:27) for the opinion that these saints are deceased martyrs. If so, they are still speaking the language, even beyond death.

61. Mounce, *Revelation*, 287: "Practically every phrase of the hymn comes from the rich vocabulary of the OT." Charles, *Revelation*, 2:36: "The Martyrs' Song is formed almost

it is further evidence of what was on display in the parental instruction of 4 Maccabees: the cultivation (and demonstration) of full fluency in the entire language of Scripture. Moses's song has clearly "stuck," and that Torah-song wasn't ultimately about the specifics of Deut. 32 per se but about the larger movement of Torah, about the perfect God (Deut. 32:4), the praiseworthy Lord, who sets things right for God's people and for the world. That movement is found in another "song of Moses," the Song of the Sea in Exod. 15,[62] but also elsewhere in Scripture—*all over* Scripture in fact (see above)—and so now, in the fullness of time according to Rev. 15, that movement incorporates yet another poem (!): the song of the Lamb. Two songs may be mentioned by name here, but there is ultimately just one melody. The language has changed, as all languages do; it has been updated, insofar as it now incorporates the Lamb, but it is still the same language, ultimately just one lyric, only one song: "the song of Moses and the song of the Lamb."

Based on the material from Deuteronomy that may serve as a model for SLA, the next chapter offers five specific recommendations for acquiring—and thus saving—the language that is the Old Testament.

---

wholly of O.T. expressions." See also Beasley-Murray, *Revelation*, 235–36; and Beale, *Revelation*, 793–99.

62. Many scholars favor Exod. 15 over Deut. 32 as the primary referent for "the song of Moses" in Rev. 15 (e.g., Mounce, *Revelation*, 286–87; Charles, *Revelation*, 2:34–36), but even these must admit to allusions to Deut. 32; cf. Witherington, *Revelation*, 206: "The song is a patchwork quilt of OT phrases, and its content owes more to Deuteronomy 32 than to Exodus 15."

9

Ways Forward and Not

The preceding foray into Deuteronomy proved to be remarkably generative. Deuteronomy manifests a concern for (second-)language acquisition and thus language survival. Moreover, the occasion of the book, its pedagogical strategies (above all, repetition), the evidence for the book's practice and performance, its "pastor," its efficacy, and its conclusion in song all demonstrate the utility of the linguistic analogy I have employed throughout the present book, even as they commended several specific strategies for moving forward. In this final chapter, I build on these gleanings from Deuteronomy to offer several concrete recommendations on how to save the language that is the Old Testament. Although I lift up four for special consideration, the various and specific insights from Deuteronomy retain their utility and should also be kept in mind. To these four positive recommendations, I then add a fifth, which is more cautiously formulated, since it includes an approach that is best avoided if we care to preserve the language that is the Old Testament.

The Most Basic (and Obvious) Recommendation: Regular Use

Whatever problems it may have in terms of test design or execution, the U.S. Religious Knowledge Survey (see chap. 2) offered definitive proof that education, especially at formative periods, along with time spent in discussing and practicing religion, correlated positively with greater knowledge about religion. The fact that nonreligious adherents like atheists/agnostics scored best does not disconfirm this finding, because such individuals (only a small percentage of the polled, who for that reason were oversampled) may well have had formative education in religion somewhere in their past (equivalent to *language learning*). In addition, given the heavily religious climate of the United States, they may have had to work their opinions out via vigorous dialogue and debate (which, in its own way, is a kind of [anti-] *language practice*).

Yet it remains clear that the Old Testament's health is imperiled for the very same reason that Anthony Towne wryly offered for God's untimely death in the 1960s: massive diminishing influence.[1] Beyond the U.S. Religious Knowledge Survey, I investigated three ways the language of Scripture is (or might be) practiced in Christian worship: in sermon, Scripture (reading), and song. In each case the Old Testament was shown to be in decline, suffering from ever-decreasing influence. While the language of the Old Testament *could* be practiced in these worship contexts, the three tests revealed that in point of fact it was *not*. As I argued in chapter 2, when these three tests are read in light of the U.S. Religious Knowledge Survey, it is easy to see how the dea(r)th of the Old Testament in these regular liturgical practices contributes directly to the overall dea(r)th of the Old Testament proper. Put most directly, the Old Testament is no longer "spoken here" in these crucial moments of Christian gathering and Christian formation; the opportunities to practice the language and to be educated in it and about it are thus missed, and missed *regularly*—week after week after week.

That's the bad news. The good news is that reversing this situation, redressing these practices, would immediately contribute to the health of the patient. This point was underscored in various ways above (see chaps. 4–8). Putting the pieces together, then, reveals the most basic (and most obvious) recommendation on how the Old Testament can be saved from its steady march toward language extinction. Indeed, in some ways, this first, most basic (and most obvious) recommendation is the only one necessary to prevent the Old Testament's demise. It is simply this: *the Old Testament must be used—extensively and regularly, certainly far more extensively and regularly than has been the case of late—in formative moments of Christian practice and education.*

This recommendation leads immediately and directly to some correlates: first, this recommendation means *more sermons and lessons preached and taught from the Old Testament*. Even if these sermons or lessons are not taken

1. Towne, "'Obituary' for God."

214

from the Old Testament exclusively (see further below), it must at least be the case that one hears the Old Testament from the pulpit (or lectern) *far* more frequently and more regularly than has been the case in the "Best Sermons" series for the past century or more. And let it be quickly added: one must hear the Old Testament from the pulpit (or lectern) in the best, most helpful, robust, and meaningful way. To return to the language of chapter 1, it is not just *if* the Old Testament is present (a question of *quantity*) but *how* it is present (a question of *quality*). In my judgment the best, most helpful, robust, and meaningful way the Old Testament is present and used is when, to echo Ellen F. Davis, it is understood to be an urgent speaking presence that exercises salutary pressure on our lives.[2]

Regular, extensive use of the Old Testament extends far beyond the pulpit or lectern, however. This recommendation also entails, second, the creation of *new and better hymns and songs* so that the church can sing its faith based on the full counsel of God, not just the final 22.1 percent (or less!) of it.[3] And then, third, there is the need for *new lectionaries* that do not suppress the Old Testament or its parts and for *brave liturgists and worship planners* who aren't afraid to round out abbreviated readings, avoiding well-meaning but unwise and ultimately injurious censorship.[4] To come full circle, better lectionaries would also mean *better lectionary preachers and teachers* who will (to say the very least) incorporate the Old Testament lesson into their sermons and teaching.

It is clear that this first recommendation places much responsibility on those tasked with preaching, teaching, and worship leadership. That is exactly as it should be because, in my judgment, most of the blame lies with the same. If Christian liturgical practices, especially sermon, lectionary, and song, showcase a dying of the Old Testament, who else to blame but those primarily responsible for the education of the congregation and charged with the public proclamation of Holy Scripture?

Let me add quickly that I don't believe that all "guilty parties" are necessarily malicious neo-Marcionites looking to make good on von Harnack's

2. See Davis, *Wondrous Depth*, xiv: The OT is "an urgent and speaking presence"; 2: the OT is "an immediate presence that exercises shaping force in Christian lives—indeed that serves as a source of salutary pressure on our lives." Note also Strawn, "Four Thoughts on Preaching and Teaching the Bible."

3. See chap. 5 for censorship of OT hymnody in Nazi Germany; and chap. 2 for Christian songs that do not capture the full witness of the Psalms and their covenantal dynamic. See further below for a contemporary Christian song that nicely models the largeness of God in a nonreductionist way.

4. Yet reading by itself will not be enough: "It shows no respect for the Old Testament passage when it is left unexpounded" (Rutledge, *And God Spoke to Abraham*, 12).

suggestion to throw the Old Testament out in our day and age.[5] But I also don't believe that all such persons are entirely innocent; neither are all those in the flock they shepherd always innocent, even if many are simply naive on the issues. But there can be no mistake: Marcion's heresy *is* malignant, even if one comes by it innocently (or ignorantly) enough. It must be cut out before the cancer spreads. It is clear, then, that any pastor (or other ecclesiastical leader) who is going to make a difference in these matters and on these points needs to be fluent in the language. Even a pastor who is the "last speaker of Old Testament" in the congregation must nevertheless keep speaking the language and do what is possible to educate the next generation so that, ultimately, this leader proves *not* to be the last speaker of that language. What one can do, in no small part (and in truth, it is far more than that), is to speak the language to the congregation, help them practice it, and make sure it is being taught to "children," whatever their age. Hence the leader must employ it constantly and consistently with all language users but *especially* with those new to the tongue. The leader *must* do this as the resident language expert and indeed, according to Deuteronomy's law of the king (Deut. 17:14–20), as *primarily* that kind of figure, not some other (see chap. 8).

The sad fact of the matter, however, is that most pastors seem less and less fluent in the language. This is no doubt due to a host of reasons that cannot be fully engaged or analyzed here. Here it suffices to make the point that, if religious leaders speak only a pidgin and pass only a pidgin along to their flock, it is not hard to extrapolate from such a scenario to the predicament we face presently. On the one hand, many Christians don't seem to have the foggiest idea of what's in their Bibles in the first place and are therefore completely incapacitated when it comes to responding to substantive critiques from the New Atheism (or elsewhere). On the other hand, many other Christians, like the happiologists of whatever stripe, are the entirely predictable result of the pidginization-to-creolization process: persons who speak an entirely new language, a creole that has emerged from a pidginized predecessor (see chap. 6). It is crucial, then—or rather, *absolutely imperative*—that the preacher know the full language of Scripture and communicate it effectively to the next generation of speakers. This language acquisition and the communication that leads to future acquisition are predicated fundamentally, ultimately, and perhaps solely on just this: *regular practice*—for both the language teacher and for the language students.

5. But note the continued debate on the status of the OT in recent German discussion, esp. the controversial support of von Harnack by Slenczka (e.g., "Texte zum Alten Testament"). See the reply by Hartenstein, "Zur Bedeutung des Alten Testaments." I thank Klaus Peter-Adam for bringing these items to my attention.

The Need for Adequate Linguistic Training

But, once again, the language of Scripture is a capacious, complex, and ancient one, especially since, as noted in chapter 1, the linguistic analogy applies equally well to both Testaments, New as well as Old, and yet more broadly still to how the entirety of the Christian Bible fits with and contributes to the language of faith. This fact, combined with the preceding remarks, leads to a second specific recommendation for those in the "pastoral" office.[6] *If pastors are to be fluent in the language in order to keep it alive, then they must have adequate linguistic training.* Formal education helps, of course (the U.S. Religious Knowledge Survey strikes again), but even a yearlong introduction to the Old Testament matched by a yearlong introduction to the New Testament in a master of divinity curriculum simply isn't enough. If the Old Testament is to survive, and if pastors are key loci for language dissemination, then seminaries will need to rethink their curricula, and pastors along with their ecclesiastical judicatories will need to reconsider what a seminary degree means.[7] Simply put, a diploma or certification, of whatever sort, is not proof of fluency.

To be sure, there is more to theological education than the Old Testament (alas!). There is a lot to cover, even in the traditional three-year master of divinity program, and an extra elective or two on the Old Testament will also not guarantee fluency. Quite to the contrary, in fact, because *fluency is a lifelong project*, precisely because speaking a language is a lifelong practice.[8] So, while education can help set pastors on the right path, it is up to them to keep walking it—and not just through continuing-education units (though those don't hurt), but by constant immersion and practice.[9] Happily, one of the best ways to learn and practice a language is by teaching it to others, so pastors needn't worry if they haven't yet mastered every nook and cranny—or, analogically, every irregular verb form—found in the Old Testament. With continued study and continued teaching, the pastor will become ever more adept. The same is true for all those who care to learn and practice the lan-

6. Once again, I employ scare quotes here because what I say is applicable beyond pastors, whether formally ordained or not. It can apply just as well to any tasked with the teaching of others, whatever their age.

7. See Webster, *Holy Scripture*, esp. 107–35; and Martin, *Pedagogy of the Bible*.

8. Some Algonquian languages are so difficult that even children raised from birth in the language are not considered competent until well into puberty. Such a situation concerns basic language *competency*, not yet the language mastery necessary for the highest of language arts (e.g., poetry). See further below.

9. *Apprenticeship* and *experience* are other terms to describe the issue at hand. See Dewey, *Experience and Education*; Lave and Wenger, *Situated Learning*; Gee, *Situated Language and Learning*; Gee, *Social Mind*. I thank Christy Lang Hearlson for discussions on this point and for directing me to this literature. See also Charry, *God and the Art of Happiness*, 252.

guage and who do not shy away from the high task of teaching—despite the sobering words of Matt. 18:6–7 and James 3:1.

Intentionality in Language Practice and Language Learning

This leads directly to a third suggestion: the language teacher (and language community) *must be intentional about communicating the language.* This includes being intentional about *how* the language is communicated, to be sure. The goal is full fluency, after all, and so one might again think of total saturation along the lines of language immersion programs. But still more basic is the point *that* the language is being communicated, appropriately and regularly, to learners. How can it be communicated appropriately and regularly? The three instruments assessed in chapter 2—homilies, hymnody, and the public reading of Scripture (preferably large swaths of it, not snippets)— are an excellent place to start, if only because they are already in place and constitute part and parcel of the expected rhythm of most Christian experience.[10] Immediate (and more extensive) attention to the Old Testament in sermon, song, and Scripture reading can build off these preexisting practices and would help stop the bleeding, but there are many more arenas to consider: religious education curricula for children and for adults spring immediately to mind, making sure that they are adequately and extensively engaged with the language that is the Old Testament.

Even in the best-case scenario involving a fully fluent pastor intent on teaching the full language to eager learners, *the teacher will need to vary the instruction for the sake of the pupils.* Not all of them will be equally far along in mastering the language. Some will be learning the alphabet ("Where's Zephaniah again? Is there a book of Hezekiah?"). Others will be capable of only a few short sentences, akin to reading a basic primer. A few will be quite adept indeed, with still others unfortunately manifesting poor linguistic habits due to inadequate prior education (whether on the part of a former teacher or the pupils themselves matters little). It is likely, then, that a pastor may find at least three different sets of students:

- some will need *initial formation* in the language;
- some will need *re-formation* to correct previous malformation;
- some will need *further information* to deepen skills and knowledge already in place.

10. See, inter alia, E. Anderson, *Worship and Christian Identity.*

It goes without saying that all three types will need *continued practice* in the language, because practicing is precisely how one learns and uses a language.

This is a challenging "classroom," to say the least. But pastors and other Christian leaders should take heart: language teachers face this sort of thing every day! It is far from impossible to bring students at different levels along together so that they all become more expert and adept in the study of a language. In addition to the strategies derived from best practices in language teaching,[11] a clue on how to do this effectively comes from Augustine.[12]

Augustine of Hippo (354–430) was a hugely popular preacher, preaching most days of the week to packed churches, with standing room only. The crowds were highly diverse, including catechumens training in the faith, pagans who wandered in off the street to hear him, and everything in between. His gifts as a rhetor and preacher are well known, and both are on display in how he often filleted his sermons to address the different constituents present in his congregation. At times he would stop and address the babes in Christ; at other times he would address those who were spiritually mature; at still other times he would address the "pagans."

What is Augustine doing in this setting? For one thing, he is not dumbing everything down to the least common denominator, for whatever reason. No doubt being sensitive to "seekers" or those new to the faith means well, but when it comes to the language of Scripture (and faith), we are dealing with a complex language that cannot be transmitted or appropriated simplistically—at least not *fully* and certainly not *always*. If things are forever and thoroughly "dumbed down," then we no longer have the full language on our lips but at best a pidgin, or worse. Another thing Augustine is doing—or rather, *not* doing—is giving up on the language, choosing to favor some other, whether a derivative creole or something else altogether. Instead, he is *teaching* the language, and in a savvy way that recognizes that the people listening to him are at different stages.

Augustine's practice of addressing his multiple constituents directly, even in the midst of the same sermon, is a helpful model for a pastor or teacher who must address a "congregation" or "class" comprised of users at many different levels of language learning.[13] For some of these users, "children" as it were, the pastor must speak motherese, a kind of pidgin designed for initial

---

11. See chap. 7 and the literature cited there, esp. Lightbown and Spada, *How Languages Are Learned*; and Klein, *Second Language Acquisition*.

12. For what follows I am indebted to Long, *Preaching from Memory to Hope*, 39–40; and his comments in "Preaching Moment 022." Long takes inspiration from Harmless, *Augustine and the Catechumenate*.

13. Long points out that this practice of "filleted address" (my phrasing) not only recognizes the complex plurality of the congregation, but also rhetorically disarms people from saying, "I didn't get anything out of that; it wasn't addressed to me."

language learners. That's perfectly fine, so long as pastors remember that they are operating in the role of parents, fluent adult speakers of the language who are tasked with bringing their kids to similar fluency. Mothers speak motherese, but they do so only for a limited period of time (infancy through early stages of childhood) and for a specific purpose (to teach a child how to talk). Speaking motherese, however, is not the same thing as being a mother, and being a mother will eventually involve *not* speaking motherese to a child. A young child's language can be cute and endearing, so much so that we hate to see our real children outgrow some of their early speech habits or (mis)pronunciations. But eventually, children must put childish things behind them (see the *testimonia* from 1 Cor. 13:11; Eph. 4:13a–14). Baby talk won't do in the now young adult's first job interview. Neither will Bible pidgins do in the real world. If nothing else, the signs of morbidity (cf. chaps. 4–6) suffice to make that abundantly clear. So pastors need to be intentional about bringing their "children" to "adult" levels of fluency. That won't happen if ministers speak only a pidginized motherese all the time, even though they will have to use a baby-talk pidgin some of the time to their most basic learners. Advanced learners, however, will need in-depth language training and, as advanced learners, are fully capable of the same. It goes without saying, but should be reiterated, that none of the learners, whether early or advanced, need instruction in a creole, since creoles are, by definition, different languages. The only exception would be the necessary re-formation needed by those who have been overly influenced or malformed by a creole.

On Creating Bilinguals

Given the linguistic analogy I am using here, the image of the minister as language teacher means that the language learners are acquiring (at least) a second language. The language of faith, of Scripture, of the Old Testament, is not their mother tongue, even for those who learn it at tender ages. This means that even the most fluent speaker of the language that is the Old Testament will be (at least) bilingual, and this raises the issue of code-switching (see chap. 7). This, then, is my fourth recommendation: *Not only must a second language be taught and acquired; one must then learn to switch between the languages—knowing how to do it, when to do it, and why one should do it.* If it is difficult to teach a language effectively, let alone to learn a language competently, it seems safe to say that teaching and learning (appropriate) code-switching is an even taller order.

Two brief clarifications are in order so as to prevent misunderstanding of the preceding discussion, especially since it is so heavily analogical. Once again a reminder: I do not intend to suggest that the only language expert in a community of faith is the ordained clergy or official ecclesiastical leader. Some of the "saints"—the ones who have been around the church barn a few times, who know their Bibles reasonably well, and so on and so forth—know the language much better than those "in charge," and this is especially true for those leaders who are not yet fully formed in the language themselves. The true saints—as in the Apostles' Creed's *sanctorum communionem*—certainly speak the language with a fluency that surpasses us lesser lights. In any event, church leaders need all the help they can get. They should learn from other skilled linguists in their flocks and should put those dexterous speakers to good use in training others. Those speakers will in turn learn still more in the process.

Second, I want to avoid the impression that what I am advocating is simply, purely, or merely a matter of *cognitive content*. The linguistic facility I am after cares little for people knowing, say, whether King Jehoiachin or King Jehoiakim came first. Fluency in the Old Testament is not worth having just to win some strange game of Bible trivia. Languages are not simply *mental* operations; they are *embodied, practiced* things. The tongue is involved, as is the voice and all that makes up the speech apparatus (vocal cords, palate, teeth, lungs, diaphragm). And this does not yet mention gestures, facial expressions, body posture—the entire range of nonverbal communicative elements that are operative in almost every instance of face-to-face human communication, not just in American Sign Language (ASL). Language learning, therefore, is not simply a matter of mastering a system of content, but learning a way of life, especially since languages are dense and complex cultural repositories (see chap. 3). Keeping this always and everywhere in mind helps avoid some of the critiques rightly leveled at George Lindbeck's notion of theology as a cultural-linguistic system, even as it draws from sources that Lindbeck himself also drew upon to make this very point (see chap. 1). The point in question can be nicely illustrated by James 1:27: "True devotion, the kind that is pure and faultless before God the Father, is this: to care for orphans and widows in their difficulties and to keep the world from contaminating us" (CEB). That is a statement about religious devotion (θρησκεία/*thrēskeia*) that is *practiced and embodied* in both negative, ascetic actions (remaining uncontaminated) and in positive, proactive ones (care for orphans and widows). It is also a definition of practiced, embodied religion that depends directly and extensively on the language of Scripture, which, for James, was the Old Testament.[14]

14. Note, e.g., that the collocation "orphans and widows" appears together only here in the NT, but it is commonly found in the OT. See, e.g., Exod. 22:22; Deut. 10:18; 14:29; 16:11, 14; 24:19–21; 26:12–13; 27:19; Ps. 68:5; Isa. 1:17. For more on James and the OT, see, among others, Carson, "James."

While learning how, when, and why to code-switch will be a process that is likely as lengthy as acquiring a language, one distinction seems crucial to make for those acquiring the (new) language of Scripture. It is simply this: that their new L2 is not identical or coterminous with their original L1, whatever that L1 might be. Stressing this difference will help prevent language interference from L1 that would otherwise complicate L2 acquisition; at the very least it will also help L2 learners realize such interference is possible and that not all aspects of L1 are beneficial. This is absolutely essential because *"language is the main instrument of [hu]man[ity]'s refusal to accept the world as it is."*[15] Without an L2 in place, L1 cannot be resisted or refused, especially at those points when it is in dire need of correction, particularly by the "strange new world within the Bible."[16] The formula L1 ≠ L2 is not only useful for *resisting* or critiquing L1; it is equally important for *recognizing* what is right and good about L1—or to put it in more explicitly theological language: not only to resist "the world" (so Steiner and the Epistle of James) but also to recognize where the Spirit might be at work in the world. In this way, L2 acquisition enables one to participate and further such work. Still further, L2 provides one with the ability to *redescribe* the world of L1,[17] which might well include alternative or even simultaneous resistance and recognition, but regardless, assessment by means of the primary lens provided by L2. It is rarely the case, after all, that multilingual speakers are equally proficient in the various languages they speak. One is almost always dominant over the others. In this light, because L1 ≠ L2, one must not only learn to code-switch between the languages but also acquire sufficient fluency so that L2 becomes the dominant tongue.

On "Bothness"

I come at last to my fifth recommendation, which begins with discussing a strategy that I do *not* believe will help prevent the death of the Old Testament; if anything, I think it will just accelerate the disease. I refer here to the many attempts to justify the Old Testament or warrant it somehow, primarily or exclusively, by reference to the New Testament. Although there are various

15. Steiner, *After Babel*, 228, emphasis original; cf. chap. 7 above.

16. The reference is to Barth, "Strange New World within the Bible." Cf. Rutledge, foreword to *Stewards of the Mysteries of God*, xi: "Without total and continual immersion in 'the strange new world of the Bible,' the preacher will only be able to tell stories from his or her personal human perspective, relating them almost incidentally to the readings for the day—thereby failing to transmit the world-overturning, *kosmos*-re-creating nature of the Voice of God."

17. See, e.g., Brueggemann, "That the World May Be Redescribed"; further Brueggemann, *Pathway of Interpretation*.

iterations of how this has been or might be done, one of the primary options could be titled "The Use of the Old Testament in the New." The argument runs something like this: "Jesus and Paul used the Old Testament, so, therefore, as a result (etc.), it must be really important."[18] The first part is true enough. Jesus and Paul *did* use the Old Testament, and such dependence demonstrates that they loved the Old Testament and treated it as Scripture, as did all the New Testament authors.[19] It is well known that the word *Scripture* (γραφή/*graphē*) in the New Testament means, without exception, the Old Testament, not the New Testament, which of course wasn't yet formed (2 Pet. 3:16 notwithstanding). Jesus, Paul, and the other New Testament writers thus show themselves to be language adepts, fluent speakers of "Old Testament." But is it enough to say that because Paul quoted from the Old Testament, then we should too? Perhaps it is, or at least *should* be, but the data presented in chapters 2 and 4–6 show that in much Christian practice and habit, it clearly *hasn't* been enough, even when the "quoter" in question is Jesus, not Paul. Strategies to save the Old Testament that are primarily or solely about the New Testament will thus not do; they seem, instead, to have exacerbated the problem.[20]

I suspect this is the case because many (though not, perhaps, all) iterations of this "New Testament" kind of approach seem predicated on some fundamental difference or distinction between the Testaments that is ultimately counterproductive for full fluency in the whole Bible. To be precise: too often the difference identified is an Old Testament *deficiency*, something the New Testament sets right, definitively improves upon, *supersedes*. Too much contrast leads, in the worst-case scenario, to (neo-)Marcionism and its inevitable problems; but even less strident forms of this approach can suggest a kind of Testamental bilingualism: one might sometimes, perhaps, but probably only

18. Cf. LaSor, Hubbard, and Bush, *Old Testament Survey*, 585–90. More recently, see Beale's tellingly titled *New Testament Biblical Theology*; and Brueggemann, "Review." See also Beale, *New Testament Use of the Old Testament*; Beale and Carson, *Commentary on the New Testament Use of the Old Testament*.

19. See Rutledge, *And God Spoke to Abraham*, 2: the OT is "the operating system for the New Testament. . . . The Second Testament simply will not work without its engine; it is 'powered on' by it." Also cf. Johnson, *Writings of the New Testament*, 2; and Seitz (*Word without End*, 69n17), who, speaking of the NT writers, wonders, "Is there a Gentile among them?"

20. One of the great biblical theologians of the recent past, Childs, recognized this point in the transition from his early work—*Biblical Theology in Crisis*, esp. 114–15, which posited an approach to doing biblical theology that focused on the use of the OT in the NT—to his later work, which proceeds quite differently, including extensive attention to what he called the "discrete" witnesses of the OT and the NT, esp. in his *Biblical Theology of the Old and New Testaments*. I thank Stephen B. Chapman for discussions on this matter. See also, and more briefly, Childs, "Nature of the Christian Bible." Despite this point, I believe Childs himself (or at least his followers) is sometimes guilty of favoring overmuch a kind of NT-centrism. See Strawn, "And These Three Are One."

rarely (!) speak "Old Testament," but one should speak "New Testament" as often as possible, and never the twain shall meet because the two are treated as discrete and distinct languages. Or at least it is very hard for "the twain" to meet for the selfsame reason, too hard for many people, at any rate, largely because they have lost fluency in the Old Testament. And so it is that we have New Testament–only Bibles, New Testament Biblical Theologies, New Testament Christians, and New Testament churches for the twenty-first century.

Christians cannot, of course, forget about the New Testament when they take up the Old. In point of fact, most Christians are probably equally deficient in the language that is the New Testament: previous chapters have shown that this is one of the unfortunate results of the death of the Old Testament.[21] Even so, it is equally true that the "two-Testamented" canon of Christian Scripture creates unique linguistic difficulties[22]—one that can suggest, and has created in certain moments of Christian history, a kind of Testamental bilingualism. This is a delicate and potentially dangerous issue (recall Marcion!), and so pastors must communicate clearly and in more than one way (both explicitly and implicitly) that they are speaking and teaching *one language, not two*. At most, then, we may admit to *diglossia* in the canon of Christian Scripture—two dialects, that is, *but two dialects of the same language* (see further below); we are *certainly not* dealing with two different languages (bilingualism proper) if for no other reason than the fact expressed above: that the New Testament authors all spoke "Old Testament" fluently.[23]

Once again, this is a very important issue, and it deserves more time and space than can be afforded here. Even so, I must register my concern with certain books that purportedly desire to address the Old Testament, even and especially in preaching, but often fall short in doing so precisely by suggesting a kind of Testamental bilingualism such that the Old Testament *somehow needs or requires* a New Testament text alongside it, or by suggesting that Christ must always somehow be preached from the Old Testament if the sermon is to be deemed sufficiently "Christian."[24] In contrast to these sorts

---

21. Cf. the *testimonia* to the present book, esp. that of Vischer: "Tell me what you would strike from the Old Testament and I'll tell you what defect there is in your Christian knowledge."

22. For discussion of the "two-Testamented" nature of Christian Scripture, see Childs, "Nature of the Christian Bible"; and esp. Seitz, *Character of Christian Scripture*.

23. In addition to the items already cited, see Jenson, *Canon and Creed*, esp. 19–26.

24. See, e.g., Achtemeier, *Old Testament and the Proclamation of the Gospel*; Achtemeier, *Preaching from the Old Testament*; McCurley, *Proclaiming the Promise*; Greidanus, *Preaching Christ from the Old Testament*; Greidanus, *Preaching Christ from Genesis*; Greidanus, *Preaching Christ from Ecclesiastes*; Greidanus, *Preaching Christ from Daniel*; and the discussion of Eric Seibert's work in chap. 5. Contrast Strawn, "And These Three Are One"; more extensively, Goldingay, *Do We Need the New Testament?*

of practices, well-meaning or otherwise, I think preachers can find a far better model in Walter Brueggemann. As I noted in chapter 2 (see also apps. 5–6), 10.4% of his published sermon corpus is composed of New Testament–only sermons, but even more surprisingly, a much smaller percentage (5.9%) is devoted solely to the Old Testament. The vast majority (83.5%) of Brueggemann's sermons are taken from *both* Old and New Testament texts. This is no doubt largely because Brueggemann is a lectionary preacher.[25] Despite the fair criticisms that can be leveled at the lectionary (see chap. 2), Brueggemann's sermonic practice showcases that the lectionary can be a helpful tool in uniting the Testaments in the liturgical practices of, and thus the mind(s) of, a listening congregation.[26] Of course, given Brueggemann's penchant for connecting different passages intertextually—and his excellent mastery of Scripture—one suspects that he didn't need the lectionary to help him on this point; his remarkable dexterity and fluency in the language of Scripture more than suffice.[27] Regardless, this kind of intertexual linkage, whether facilitated by the lectionary or constructed by the fluent preacher, is a key way pastors can help their congregants learn the *entire* language of Scripture, Old and New Testaments *together*.[28] This togetherness, the integral unity of the Bible, is on display throughout the New Testament,[29] is absolutely crucial in the history of Christian theology (witness the counterexample provided by Marcion), and is employed in various ways by the best Old Testament preachers and interpreters.[30]

For these reasons and others, I argue that the Old Testament cannot be saved by any strategy that focuses exclusively or even overmuch on the New Testament, especially on the way the New Testament treats the Old.[31] As I noted in chapter 1 and have repeatedly observed in subsequent chapters, the fates of the two Testaments are intertwined, and the death of one means the death of the other, just as saving one means saving the other. Both Testaments

---

25. See C. Campbell's foreword to *Threat of Life*, ix.

26. See also West, *Scripture and Memory*; and O. Allen, *Preaching and Reading the Lectionary*.

27. Appendix 6 demonstrates this dexterity insofar as Brueggemann's corpus, which is significantly smaller than the Best Sermons series (134 sermons vs. 879 sermons, respectively, or 6.5 times smaller; see tables 3–4 in chap. 2 and apps. 1–3), outperforms those three series combined in every biblical book he preaches from.

28. An amazing repository of such linkage may be found in the margins and app. 3 of Aland et al., *Novum Testamentum Graece*.

29. See the previous note and the works cited in note 59 in chap. 8 above.

30. See Miles, "Proclaiming the Gospel of God," esp. chap. 3; and Davis, *Wondrous Depths*.

31. In point of fact, there is no one such "way," but numerous ways—as many ways as two lines of poetry relate to each other in Hebrew parallelism. For this evocative analogue for relating the Testaments, see Miles, "Proclaiming the Gospel of God"; and more briefly, LeMon and Strawn, "Parallelism," esp. 513–14.

are involved in the present plight, even if the Old Testament is far more imperiled at the moment; and so *both* must be involved in rectifying it.

Let us view matters from a slightly different perspective. The problems that face the Old Testament, especially in so many "folk" understandings, also face the New. The fact that so many people think that the problems of, say, law, violence and war, the wrath and judgment of God, or even the issue of cursing one's enemies (see chap. 3) live only in the Old Testament is proof not only of pidginization of their Old Testament knowledge but also of their New Testament language facility, since all these problems are also found in the New Testament, although in somewhat different form(s).[32] If "New Testament Christians" don't know this, it is simply because they don't know their New Testaments very well. Marcion knew better, which is why his New Testament canon was so thoroughly streamlined (i.e., *pidginized*), greatly reduced from the form we now have; and so did Christopher Hitchens, who wrote that the New Testament was worse than the Old.[33] As I've repeatedly stressed throughout this book, only a *full* knowledge of the *full* language of Scripture, *both* Old *and* New Testaments, can appropriately handle these problems, not to mention others, or begin to redress the signs of morbidity that the Bible, *both* Old *and* New Testaments, is clearly manifesting. The problems and the solutions face these two Testaments *together*. This is largely what I mean by "bothness." *Both* Testaments are in this predicament together, *both* have their fair share of problems (esp. for modern sensibilities), and *both* have their fair share of solutions to the same. It is certainly *not* the case that the problems live only in the Old Testament and the solutions live only in the New. Proceeding (or teaching) as if that were the case inevitably leads to a supersession that Marcion would be more than happy to welcome into his pulpit on Sunday morning (or house church on Wednesday night).

This point duly made, it remains true that (1) most Christians (think they) know their New Testaments better than their Old and (2) (presumably) would never countenance the death of the New, even if they are less concerned about the health of the Old, and so one way to ensure that the Old Testament

32. See, briefly, Strawn, "Teaching the Old Testament"; more extensively, de Villiers and van Henden, *Coping with Violence in the New Testament*; and (despite the title) H. Thomas, J. Evans, and Copan, *Holy War in the Bible*. Similarly, Rutledge (*And God Spoke to Abraham*, 5n7), noting the contrast between the wrath of God in the OT and the love of God in the NT, rightly observes: "This contrast, all too frequently drawn, requires not only the ignoring of large parts of the Old Testament but also a willful disregard of the many passages of judgment in the words of Jesus." The reverse problem, that the "good stuff" comes only from the NT, is similarly ignorant or illiterate. On its own, Isa. 54:9–10 suffices as definitive proof to the contrary.

33. See chap. 5 above for Marcion and chap. 4 for Hitchens. The specific chapter in Hitchens, *God Is Not Great*, 109–22, is titled "The 'New' Testament Exceeds the Evil of the 'Old' One."

survives is by consistent linkage to the New. I repeat that such linkage must *not* be supersessionistic, implying that every Old Testament text must be "balanced" or "fixed" by a New Testament text, or that every Old Testament sermon must be "walked by the cross" for it to count as Christian. Instead, the Testaments can be united in, for example, their consistent witness to God's brutal judgment on those guilty of injustice (see, e.g., Exod. 22:21–24; Matt. 25:31–46) or in their stunning affirmation that it is okay for God's people to beg for vengeance—which is to say that both Testaments show the saints praying for divine payback (see, e.g., Ps. 137; Rev. 6:9–11). In the case of the former example, what difference is there, really, between God's killing sword or God's unending fire of eternal punishment (Exod. 22:24; Matt. 25:41, 46)? *Both* Exod. 22 and Matt. 25 show how serious God is about justice being done to "the least of these brothers and sisters of mine" (Matt. 25:40, 45 CEB). In the case of the latter example, what the psalmist prays for in Ps. 137 is no worse than what the martyrs under God's altar in heaven (!) cry out for in Rev. 6. Both ask God to set the record straight and act on their behalf, even if for the time being they must "wait a little longer" (Rev. 6:11 NIV). Both examples illustrate the point made nicely by Fleming Rutledge: "We must read the New Testament in light of the Old," not just vice versa.[34] As further examples one might think of texts like 1 Tim. 2:11–15 and 1 John 3:12 and the need to read them vis-à-vis the fine details of Gen. 3 and 4, respectively; or of a text like Rom. 13:1–7, which must be discussed in concert with, say, Exod. 1–3 or the political theologies found in the book of Daniel.[35]

"Bothness" signifies, then, the inextricably intertwined relationship of the Testaments and that both must proceed together, equally yoked, as it were.[36] In John Donne's apt phrasing, "the two Testaments grow one Bible."[37] The old clichéd and tired ways of relating the Testaments will have to go since they have proven ineffective for preserving the language that is the Old Testament. Thus promise-fulfillment schemas, while not entirely inaccurate, are also only so helpful and are far from foolproof. If one continues to speak of "promise-fulfillment," one must be clear that such a schema works only with some texts, certainly not all, and that not all of the fulfillment is found in the New Testament; some is already realized in the Old Testament. More

---

34. Rutledge, *And God Spoke to Abraham*, 4.

35. On the latter, see Newsom with Breed, *Daniel*; and Portier-Young, *Apocalypse against Empire*.

36. The relationship of the Testaments is a massive topic. For a beginning, see Barr, *Old and New in Interpretation*; Hasel, *Old Testament Theology*, 172–93; Reventlow, *Problems of Biblical Theology*, 10–144; Seitz, *Character of Christian Scripture*.

37. From Donne's sermon "The Fear of the Lord," cited by Rutledge, *And God Spoke to Abraham*, 10. The sermon itself is in Davis, *Imagination Shaped*, 96–113, here citing 113.

in concert with my point about "bothness," however, would be to stress that what ultimately matters in promise-fulfillment scenarios is not simply or only the fulfillment but rather the faithfulness of God, which permeates and undergirds both the promise and its realization.[38]

Other old saws will also have to go. So, per Rutledge: "It is true that we can't understand the New Testament without the Old, but that is an inadequate account of its importance."[39] Or then there is the plethora of language about "development" in and between the Testaments that somehow comes to a covenantal "climax" in the New Testament and in the New Testament alone.[40] Such sequencing is, first and foremost, an imposition on the biblical text, which, considered as a whole, is not a narrative at all and certainly far from evincing any simplistic, unilinear, plot-driven "story." At its worst, such narrative impositions result (invariably, it seems) in the Old Testament being only so much "building action," "background information," or—perhaps worse—"ancient history," mere preface to where the real action is (the New Testament). The Old Testament might well be present in such constructions, even if only to some minor degree, but *how* it is present is exactly the problem (cf. chap. 1 above).[41] These sorts of approaches consistently privilege the New Testament *at the expense of the Old*, and as such they simply will not contribute to the long-term health and survival of the language that is the Old Testament. Quite to the contrary, in the process they will (inadvertently) end up contributing directly to the demise of the New Testament as well, since if the Old Testament dies, the New is not far behind. Though space precludes a full discussion, I think the same judgment holds true for those approaches to the Bible that are overly Christocentric, which is to say, Christomonic. Orthodox Christianity, after all, is robustly trinitarian.[42] Or, to cite that thoroughly Christocentric theologian Dietrich Bonhoeffer once more: "In my opinion it

38. For this point, see (from the perspective of the lectionary) Ramshaw, "First Testament in Christian Lectionaries"; and Stookey, "Marcion, Typology, and Lectionary Preaching"; as well as (from the perspective of systematic theology) Downing, *Has Christianity a Revelation?*

39. Rutledge, *And God Spoke to Abraham*, 2. See also the insightful remarks of Smend, "Unconquered Land," 259.

40. See, e.g., N. Wright, *Scripture and the Authority of God*, 42–45. Note that Blackman found Marcion guilty of "committing the error of trying to possess the climax without the antecedents, which alone gave it a setting and made it intelligible" (*Marcion and His Influence*, 120).

41. As Rutledge declares, the "widespread misunderstanding" of the relationship of the Testaments, which so easily becomes incipiently anti-Judaic, "is so deeply lodged in the minds of many church members that only a very concerned, intentional remedial program . . . extending over a period of years can displace it. The primary way to do this is to preach the gospel from the Old Testament in an ongoing, comprehensive fashion" (foreword to Miller, *Stewards of the Mysteries of God*, esp. xii–xiii).

42. See further Strawn, "And These Three Are One."

is not Christian to want to take our thoughts and feelings too quickly and too directly from the New Testament."[43]

And yet, even with these important cautions registered, it remains true that many Christians know (or think they know) their New Testaments better than their Old Testaments. This can be a useful starting point from which to build a robust full-canon fluency, if that strategy is intentionally adopted. If it is, those tasked with the language instruction of a community of faith will want to repeatedly hold the two Testaments together, consistently cross-reference them one with the other, constantly show how the New relies on the Old, and so on and so forth, as a way to expand a greatly reduced biblical vocabulary to a far more fulsome and ultimately fluent one. There is, after all, always hope for a pidgin, even a New Testament one, as long as language teachers know the full language and are intent on getting their students there.

By "bothness" I intend at least one further meaning: the full language of Scripture will not tolerate reductionism of whatever sort, especially along the lines found in (re)pidginization and (de)creolization. As I mentioned in chapter 5, if "Dick and Jane ran" is an utterly simplistic sentence, so also is "God is love" or "God is good," especially when adding "all the time."[44] Such pithy reductions may at times be necessary to communicate certain truths, particularly at certain stages in basic language instruction, but they are not sufficient and certainly not for long. If they were, we would have a small collection of three-word sentences rather than the thick, complicated, often horrifically opaque two-Testamented (!) canon of Holy Scripture.[45]

The best interpreters (language users) of Scripture are able to capture such dense "bothness"—the full range of, say, God's presentation in Scripture in both wrath and mercy (not privileging one over the other).[46] But this kind of

---

43. Bonhoeffer, *Letters and Papers from Prison*, 157. Cf. further Downing, *Has Christianity a Revelation?*

44. I am not unaware of texts like 1 John 1:5. My point is that 1 John 1:5 must be set in conversation with other texts, such as Isa. 45:7.

45. Cf. Beal's evocative description of the Bible as a "library of questions" (*Rise and Fall of the Bible*, 146–79). An interesting case study in reading the whole Bible, which he calls "messier" and "infinitely more complex" than what people often think about it—and the benefits of doing so—may be found in Plotz, *Good Book*, though even attempts to reckon with the whole aren't foolproof, which is also on display in Plotz's work (see further below).

46. See Beal (*Rise and Fall of the Bible*, 148–49) on "impoverishment by univocality" (a phrase from Derrida). One might contrast the multilevel approach that marked early Jewish and Christian exegesis. See, e.g., Gunneweg, *Understanding the Old Testament*, 7; Dawson, *Christian Figural Reading*. For "bothness" in action, see, e.g., Heschel, *Prophets*, 358–92, on God's wrath; cf. the discussion in Strawn and Strawn, "Prophecy and Psychology," esp. 619–21. For additional examples of attempts (and metaphors) to hold the entirety of the OT together, see Brueggemann, *Theology of the Old Testament*; and Knohl, *Divine Symphony*. Once again contrast Marcion, who, when faced with the "unmanageable abundance" and diversity of the

"bothness" can be captured effectively even for young children or within the compass of a very short song. As an example of the former, David Helm's *Big Picture Story Bible* speaks of the "hard and happy history" of Israel.[47] That is exactly right, and the child may go on to learn later that "hard and happy" in that construction is actually a hendiadys. As an example of the latter, consider the following lyrics from the contemporary Christian song "You Are," by Andrew Thomas (featuring Kawan Moore):

> God is not a Muslim, nor is he a Christian
> He's bigger than an atheist, bigger than a religion.
> He is world-changing, earth-shaking, hard not to hear of him,
> but God is not a white man, nor is he American,
> God is not a Baptist, a Methodist, a Catholic,
> he's bigger than denominations, that's not even half of it.
> Love, he is bigger than
> Hate, he is bigger than . . .[48]

These lines, while brief, are a poetic presentation of a capacious, nonreductionist understanding of God's "bothness." If the lyrics make some readers uncomfortable, that may be precisely because they actively resist several kinds of pidginized reductionisms that mar and mark so much of contemporary North American Christianity, especially when it comes to the full language of the Old Testament and Christian Scripture.

The Challenge of Future Change

The recommendations offered above for saving the Old Testament can basically be boiled down to the first suggestion, which is why it headed the list and why I indicated that it was so basic and fundamental, if not also so self-evident and obvious. The key insight for saving the language that is the Old Testament, and maybe the only hope for its continued existence, is regular and repeated use of the Old Testament. This should involve not only *practice in the language* but also cultivation of *language practices*, which includes the fact that the language must be *performed* and *enacted*. It is clear that the survival of the Old Testament depends on the presence of fluent speakers,

revealed material in the OT, was stupefied by this abundance and "especially the *complexion oppositorum* [combination of opposites]" (von Harnack, *Marcion: The Gospel*, 6).

47. Helm, *Big Picture Story Bible*. See Strawn, "Triumph of Life," esp. 315–20.

48. Andrew Thomas (featuring Kawan Moore), "You Are" (2011). Thanks to Andrew Thomas for his permission to cite this song; this part of the lyric is rapped by Kawan Moore.

who are expert in the full language in all its complexity, irregularity, and nuance. It is equally clear that the survival of the Old Testament depends on such speakers' incessant teaching of this language to the next generation, whatever their biological age. Each of these points was on display in a remarkable way in Deuteronomy (chap. 8) along with another crucial factor that must not be neglected: real languages change through the course of time and repeated use (see also chaps. 1 and 3). It is necessary to return to the subject of language change at the end of my recommendations since it, too, is a rather important matter that deserves careful consideration. Three points must be stressed.

First and foremost, one must always remember that real, living, vibrant languages *do* in fact change. Living languages are languages that are spoken and practiced, which means they are spoken and practiced diachronically, and the passage of time involves linguistic change by necessity and as a matter of course. Old English is not the same as Middle English, which is not the same as modern English, let alone the various idiomatic vernaculars, peppered with slang, loanwords, dialectical differences and the like, running from New Jersey to Southern California.[49] The language that is the Old Testament (or Christian Scripture) is no different on this point.[50] That is why, already in chapter 1, I warned against any simplistic notion of a "pure" Old Testament language that could be easily (re)acquired and/or (re)appropriated. The oddity of enacting the language of the Bible as if it hasn't changed in two thousand years, give or take a millennium, is what lends books like *The Year of Living Biblically* their humor and what fuels the disdain of the New Atheists and other critics of all things biblical. But again, real languages *do* change. This is why, in the Christian canon, we have not only the Old Testament but also the New and why Christian theology has not only Holy Scripture but also creeds and councils and so forth—up to and including present-day performances of Scripture.[51] Such things are signs of linguistic life, signs that the language is being practiced and so is not only living but also developing and changing.

49. See, inter alia, McWhorter, *Our Magnificent Bastard Tongue*; and Crystal, *Cambridge Encyclopedia of the English Language*.

50. Beal, *Rise and Fall of the Bible*, 145: "The only constant in the history of the Bible is change. The history of the Bible is one of perpetual revolution. In that light, we might begin to think about the Bible not so much as a fixed thing but as a dynamic, vital tradition, . . . less like a rock than a river, continually flowing and changing, widening and narrowing, as it moves downstream"—or, as the linguistic analogy would have it, as a language being constantly practiced and changing in the process.

51. See Jenson, *Canon and Creed*, and note the musical and dramatic analogues of old and new found in McClure, *Mashup Religion*; and Martoia, *Bible as Improv*, respectively. See also Brueggemann, *Creative Word*.

Languages that do not change are, by definition, dead.[52] So linguistic change is automatic, something that is entirely natural and to be expected, and can be celebrated as a vibrant sign of linguistic health and life.[53]

Second, a very quick qualifier should be entered, however, and that is that not all linguistic change is good—not if one wants to keep speaking the *same* language. Here we enter into murky waters: Quite apart from more obvious instances of linguistic change caused by language contact (pidginization) and/or subsequent developments thereafter (creolization), how far can two dialects drift before they are no longer dialects of the same original tongue? There is often no clear or obvious dividing line between stages in a language's diachronic and dialectical development, but I suggested earlier that one way to think about this issue is along the lines of speciation. When two animals can no longer interbreed and produce offspring, they are no longer considered the same species. Analogically, then, we might say that when two speakers can no longer understand each other, they no longer speak two dialects of the same language but two different languages since they now require a translator or some other sort of mediation. Old English, for example, is, for all intents and purposes (in this functional definition), a very different language than the one spoken today. Middle English is closer but still in need of translation. Shakespeare's Elizabethan English is probably still understandable to most contemporary English speakers, but it takes some getting used to, and in more than a few cases clarifying annotations are necessary.

This means, then, that while the language that is the Old Testament (and Christian Scripture) in the course of its practice and use will and must change, caution and care must be exercised about such change lest the language suffer overmuch in the process and get lost, in one way or another, via one linguistic process or another (or several!), with the end result being the effective death of the original. In modern times, the existence of an organization like the Academy of the Hebrew Language in Israel offers this kind of service, tasked as it is with making decisions about the Modern Hebrew language that are binding on all governmental agencies.[54] As seen in the section on Deuteronomy as a model of SLA (chap. 8), the nature and function of Deuteronomic repetition is another example of how a language can change but nevertheless remain in continuity with what has gone before. Moses "amends the constitution," as it were—and indeed, must do so, for the changed circumstances

---

52. See Aitchison, *Language Change*.

53. Note Hagège (*Death and Life of Languages*, 319), who argues that even creolization is a response to—specifically a struggle against—language death.

54. See their website at http://hebrew-academy.huji.ac.il/English/Pages/Home.aspx.

of life in the land (see Deut. 12:1)—but this amendment is in recognizable continuity with what has come before, despite an unavoidable (and healthy) degree of variance.[55] Or, as noted in the case of Joshua or Josiah, their versions of Deuteronomy aren't exactly the same as Moses's or as each other's, but one can see, nevertheless, that what they are updating and transmitting is, despite diachronic development, still recognizable as "dialects" of Deuteronomy. Change can, will, and must happen, then, to a language that is living and in order for a language to survive, but great care must be taken to make sure the language somehow remains itself: too much is at stake if things prove otherwise (see chaps. 4–8).[56] To put the matter in an idiom familiar from the New Testament, Jesus's comment about not putting new wine into old wineskins is well known (Matt. 9:17; Mark 2:22; Luke 5:37–38), but he never said anything against putting old wine into new wineskins! Luke's version of this "parable" culminates with an intriguing but less well-known remark by Jesus that is equally instructive: "No one who drinks a well-aged wine wants new wine, but says, 'The well-aged wine is better'" (5:39 CEB).[57]

Music, Memory, Poetry . . . and Children (Again)

Putting well-aged wine into new wineskins isn't a bad description of linguistic repetition, which always traffics in repeating what is prior, earlier, or old with something different or new—a new change or addition, for example, or at the very least, a new circumstance or time frame that differs from the initial iteration. This repetition-with-updating, this old wine in new wineskins, is on display in many places in Scripture but was on display in many ways in Deuteronomy as a model of SLA (chap. 8)—a point that has proved to be very generative for the

55. Note the axiom of St. Stephen I: *nihil novandum, nisi quod traditum est,* "no innovation, except from tradition" (cited in Grant and Tracy, *Short History of the Interpretation of the Bible,* 82). Once again, with reference to the OT and this issue, see Brueggemann, *Creative Word,* and the literature cited there, esp. J. Sanders, *Torah and Canon.*

56. See Jenson (*Canon and Creed,* esp. 3–5, 33, 40–41) on the problem of the "telephone game," in which transmission over time often results in a disintegration of the original message. Jenson argues that canon, creed, and episcopacy (church governance) are ways the more deleterious aspects of diachronic change are resisted. Indeed, he evocatively suggests that "perhaps in his youth Marcion had been impressed by an abrupt round of the telephone game," though he apparently lacked the prophylactics offered by canon, creed, and episcopacy. Cf. Grant and Tracy, *Short History of the Interpretation of the Bible,* 82: "The possibility of fresh and creative insights remains open. Unless, however, the continuity is maintained it is difficult to understand how the word 'Christian' can be employed in describing the insights."

57. On the passage, see Green, *Gospel of Luke,* 249–50. It is telling that Marcion excised v. 39 from his version of this pericope in Luke (see ibid., 250).

linguistic analogy I have developed here.[58] As a way of concluding my discussion of recommended treatment to save the language that is the Old Testament, I'd like to return to the way Deuteronomy ends in song (see chap. 8 above). I believe this may be one of the most significant strategies of all, if only because—as Deuteronomy itself knows (and from God no less!)—music is so eminently memorable and because so much hangs on the "children" remembering.

We may begin with Deut. 31:21: "Then, when all kinds of bad things and misfortunes happen to them, this poem will witness against them, giving its testimony, because it won't be lost from the mouths of their descendants" (CEB). The CEB's translation of the Hebrew word שִׁיר/šîr as "poem" (cf. NRSV "song") is both reasonable and evocative. Much of the Bible's best poetry, at least in terms of musical memory, is now forgotten in the way contemporary hymnody and the Revised Common Lectionary select and interpret, if not also excise and censor, so much of the Psalms in (or rather out of) Christian worship. This is a grave situation, given the power of music and lyric—the poetry that accompanies music and the poetry that is itself musical—to dominate our imagination and brains.[59] Lyrics (and melodies) last in no small part due to their memorability, the power of their images and tunes, and the way they have a tendency to worm their way into our brains so that we can recite song lyrics we haven't thought of for years if only the first few bars of the tune are heard, or conversely, how we can hum a tune if the right lyric is invoked.

That is precisely the kind of memory that God seeks in Deut. 31–32. The poem/song of Torah must be learned because once it is learned well, it will never be forgotten (Deut. 31:21). It will be like the tongue that returns to a sore, only in this specific case the return does not elicit pain but redemption. Even the most dread and deadly circumstances of punishment and exile—indeed, especially those moments!—can remind Israel of the song/poem of Torah, at which point that lyric kicks in and does its work, eventuating in a restored, redeemed, and praiseful people of God (see chap. 8).

Mariano Magrassi puts the matter perfectly for people of the Book today:

A proverb says, "The tongue ever turns to the aching tooth." This is what happens in the case of popular songs, is it not? Could not the psalms, which Christians

---

58. This is clearly quite different from "rebranding" or "remarketing" the Bible. As Beal (*Rise and Fall of the Bible*) reminds us, consumerism of Scripture is not the same as (and far from) literacy.

59. See chap. 2 and, e.g., Boyd, *Why Lyrics Last*; and Sacks, *Musicophilia*, esp. 32–53 (on "brainworms"). Boyd states that narrative is "the default task orientation of the human mind" but that "*all* kinds of pattern appeal to our appetite for ordered information" (3, emphasis original). Lyrics that are lasting "blend the appeal of pattern with other strategies for attention" (5). In this way, lasting lyrics (even the very same lyric) are able to call us "again and again to discover new patterns and new pleasures from endless new perspectives" (6).

sing over and over in the assembly, rise from the lips of farmers, artisans and laborers during their work? Would this not be normal, at least for consecrated religious [people]? The texts return spontaneously to the lips of those who carry them in their heart and strive each day to fix them ever deeper. As they come to mind during the day, they are expressed in ejaculations, sometimes purely mental, sometimes formed by the lips in the language of the Bible. Often some unexpected illumination sheds new light on those words, and their meaning is seen more clearly than ever before. It is not the monotonous repetition of trite texts but the joyful discovery of a Word ever fresh and new. What solidity and vigor it brings to our whole spiritual life![60]

Way back when, in Deut. 32, it was precisely this sort of enacted memory that permitted Israel to move from its *insertion for judgment* ("It was *you* who got fat, thick, stubborn!" v. 15 CEB) to its *reinsertion for hope* ("Their rock is not like *our* Rock," v. 31 NRSV). Something new, "some unexpected illumination," shed "new light on those words" in that transition from v. 15 to v. 31, and the same holds true, even more true, for the mother and children of 2 and 4 Maccabees. In each case, it was not "monotonous repetition of trite texts but the joyful discovery of a Word ever fresh and new."

It is, then, a grave situation if—or rather *that*—so much of our biblical "lyric" is now lost from Scripture reading, sermon, and song. Equally grave is the *engraving* on our imaginations and brains (what Deuteronomy calls our "hearts") of so many lyrics that are not biblical at all,[61] as well as those that are only partially so: "pidgin-songs," as it were, or "creole-tunes."[62] But if the climactic finale of Torah found in Deut. 31–32 is any clue, *the Old Testament needs to be sung if it is to survive.* Only lyrics that work their way deep into our memories, those that are thoroughly internalized and "written on our hearts"—keeping us up at night because we can't get them out of our heads (cf. Deut. 6:4–9; Pss. 1:2; 42:8; 63:6; 92:2; 119:55, 148)—only this kind of language will be remembered, will come to mind when we need it most, when the chips are down.[63] And it

---

60. Magrassi, *Praying the Bible*, 112.

61. Cf. Strawn, "Sanctified and Commercially Successful Curses"; and again, the distinction between canon 1 and canon 2 made in chap. 7 above. According to Blackman (*Marcion and His Influence*, 64–65), Marcion may have made up psalms of his own to support his theology.

62. Cf. Rutledge, *And God Spoke to Abraham*, 11: "In the mainline church environment of today, it is much easier to find information about Celtic spirituality, labyrinth-walking, Jungian dream interpretation, the latest findings of the Jesus seminar, and other such eclectic topics than it is to find in-depth teaching about the Old Testament."

63. See the intriguing essay by Sauter ("Jonah 2: A Prayer out of the Deep") in which he posits that Jonah's otherwise ill-timed and mismatched psalm from the belly of the fish may be a piece of memorized liturgy: it is all Jonah can remember to pray in his moment of distress. The irony is that even this ill-timed prayer is effective! Bergen (*Twisted Cross*, 143) reports that

will be this kind of language that springs to our lips, that we can speak accurately, maybe automatically, even if we hear only a few bars of the instrumental accompaniment.

We need, then, new and excellent songs of Torah, songs *of* the Old Testament, songs *about* the Old Testament, songs *of* Scripture and *about* Scripture that will introduce and encapsulate, teach and remind singers of the full language of faith. And we need them as soon as possible, *especially for use with children*—real, chronologically young children—whose brains are plastic enough to learn a language thoroughly and deeply and who are ready, able, and willing to do so.[64] So much depends upon the children![65]

If the specific recommendations for saving the Old Testament boiled down to "the great commandment" of *regular and repeated use*, the current point adds a "second which is like it": *make such use memorable*. On these two commandments hang (the survival of) all the Law and the Prophets . . . as well as the Psalms, and the Gospels and Epistles to boot. And lyric, poetry, and song are the most memorable of artistic-literary types. Memorable use need not be restricted to song, of course; the point is simply that this sort of effective use is not only recommended but required lest we lose people, especially young people, when their language facility is at its peak.[66] Poor language instruction and training, practice, and use—especially at formative moments or periods (ages)—can have profoundly negative and destructive consequences.[67]

---

the only area where the German Christian "assault on Jewish influence" made "less significant inroads" was in the area of church music.

64. In addition to the literature cited in chap. 7 on language learning and children, one might take as an instructive anecdote how many of the translators of the King James Version of the Bible (1611) were what might be called "child prodigies," introduced to the biblical languages at very young ages. See G. Campbell, *Bible: The Story of the King James Version 1611–2011*, 276–301. For a delightful example of the power of religious lyric for children, see Stephen Dunn's poem "At the Smithville Methodist Church."

65. See above, also chaps. 3 and 7 and these additional biblical texts: Josh. 8:30–35; Neh. 13:24; and Matt. 21:15–16 (quoting Ps. 8:1–2).

66. See Dean, *Almost Christian*; Kinnaman with Hawkins, *You Lost Me*; and C. Smith with Denton, *Soul Searching*, 268: "A major challenge for religious educators of youth, therefore, seems to us to be fostering articulation, helping teens to *practice talking about* their faith, providing practice at using vocabularies, grammars, stories, and key messages of faith. Especially to the extent that the language of faith in American culture is becoming a foreign language, educators, like real foreign-language teachers, have that much more to work at helping their students learn to practice speaking that other language of faith. Our observation is that religious education in the United States is currently failing with youth when it comes to the articulation of faith" (emphasis original).

67. In addition to the literature cited in the previous note, one might note how various children's Bibles often paraphrase, rewrite, and/or sanitize the Bible in various ways, for various reasons, and with varying effects. See Frerichs, "Children's Bibles," 108–9; and further, Bottigheimer, *Bible for Children*. As a poor example of how a children's Bible handles

Let me stress once more that the survival of this language, its use and retention, is not a matter of simple *information* but one of *formation*. Learning and singing life-transforming lyrics is not just an example of practicing the language; it is an instance of formative language practice. Shannon Craigo-Snell presents an apt formulation:

> We teach our children to sing "Jesus Loves Me" not as an affirmation of something they [already] know, *but as a way for them to know it*. We bow our heads, bend our knees, lift our arms and raise our voices, not merely to express an understanding previously gained, but *in order to comprehend more fully the reality and meaning of the Word of God*.[68]

Singing the Old Testament is thus a way for us to *know* it—not just to learn it but to learn from it—and a way for us to "comprehend more fully the reality and meaning of the Word of God." In biblical language, such comprehension—such knowledge—is never solely cognitive but practiced and real, a point already underscored by the biblical language of *word*, which connotes both "message" and "address."

Of course no one song, given its brevity, could possibly do justice to the whole language of Scripture.[69] Then again, in some ways, that is what Deut. 32 seems to be wanting to do vis-à-vis the Torah by means of its repetition and recitation, when all these words "find" the Israelites (see Deut. 4:30; cf. 31:17, 21). But even if so, the genre of lyric poetry knows that it cannot say everything. What it says is *enough*, however, and what is said it says *well enough*. Lyric says it *well* because the language that it uses is beautiful, artful, and memorable. The best poetry is high art: dense and rich in imagery and nuance, as far from pidginization as one could possibly imagine. Lyric says *enough* because by its very terseness and economy, the poem/song requires

---

the relationship of the Testaments, see Milton, *Family Story Bible*, which divides its table of contents of paraphrased Bible stories between the "Hebrew Scriptures" and the "Christian Scriptures."

68. Craigo-Snell, "Command Performance," 482, emphasis added.

69. But see Magrassi (*Praying the Bible*, 50) on the clarity of the abbreviated divine word, which in his case concerns the christological reading of Scripture. Despite this clarity, it is important that Magrassi recognizes that even "Jesus" is an abbreviation, not coterminous with the full extent of the whole of Scripture. One might contrast the work of Seibert (*Disturbing Divine Behavior*), which, in its privileging of the "actual God" revealed by Jesus rather than the "textual God" (169–81), cannot avoid "rejecting major sections of the Old Testament, a bit like Marcion," according to Lamb (*God Behaving Badly*, 102), and maybe more than a bit. A further problem: Seibert's "actual God" *is* the "textual God," but *just part* of that God—the part Seibert most likes. The issue is made still clearer once Seibert admits to struggling with the problem of inconsistency in the Bible's presentation of God's character (*Disturbing Divine Behavior*, 173). But, once again, *bothness* is required to achieve the full picture.

continued speaking/singing and reflection.[70] One must always come back to such an artful and evocative composition, each time finding more to sing about, think upon, and offer praise for. If these kinds of songs are learned early and deeply by children of whatever age (including novices in the language), then these lyrics will be at the ready, forming people who can speak, sing, and enact the language at exactly the right times. They will be scribes trained for the kingdom of heaven, with their scriptural thesauruses at the ready (Matt. 13:52). No language with practitioners like that would ever die out. The creation, transmission, and repetition of life-giving, life-forming, and life-transforming biblical lyrics are thus absolutely imperative.

Of course only the most gifted in the arts of the word will be able to write the poetry we must have to live our lives and die our deaths. Thankfully, it is not a matter of creating such poetry from scratch, because the language of Scripture already contains this high art if only we have tongues to learn it, ways to re-perform it, and the will to do *both*.

Conclusion

Many of the great texts of Christian faith are precisely these types of great "poems"—terse compositions that open up, yielding more the more we reflect on them, the more we recite them, the more we "sing" them. One thinks of the Ten Commandments or the Lord's Prayer or the creeds. Nicholas Lash's motto about the Apostles' Creed is apropos at this point: "short words, endless learning."[71] By this he means that the words of the Apostles' Creed are few in number (only seventy-seven in the standard Latin text) such that they can be easily memorized by any four- or five- or six-year-old, but it will take a lifetime to learn what they mean and how to live them out with any measure of faithfulness.

If "short words, endless learning" is true of the creed, "long words, even longer learning" would be a better motto when it comes to the language that is the Old Testament and Scripture as a whole. Even thorough acquaintance with something like Deuteronomy, which is always somehow there in the Old Testament, will not suffice as a replacement for the whole. As dominant as Deuteronomy is, it is ultimately just *one bit*—a piece of the grammar, a verbal paradigm or nominal declension, as it were—of the full language that is Scripture. And Deut. 32, as summative and important as it is, won't

---

70. See Strawn, "Lyric Poetry"; Dobbs-Allsopp, *On Biblical Poetry*; and Brueggemann, *From Whom No Secrets Are Hid*.

71. Lash, *Believing Three Ways in One God*, chap. 2.

suffice either. As 2 Maccabees, 4 Maccabees, and Revelation demonstrate, the Song of Moses keeps expanding outward to encompass other texts, even as it is embodied and practiced amid different, even deadly circumstances. Such reuse with expansion is a sign that those who sing Moses's song are *fluent* in the full language of Scripture, not just a chapter or two—nor even a book therein—even as it shows that they are real language *users*: they are not merely students of a dead language, but practitioners of a living one, even unto death.

Long words, even longer learning. But this comes as no surprise: everyone knows that acquiring a language, even one's own native tongue, takes a long time and hard work, and it involves making countless mistakes along the way. When we are talking about a second language (L2), and that L2 is an ancient one, something like the Old Testament or Scripture as a whole, it is abundantly clear that acquisition is not going to happen overnight. It's going to take more than reading the Bible once or twice, even if you blog about it at the same time,[72] and it's going to take more than memorizing a few verses here or there. It's going to take *a lot* more, though (re)reading and memorization are essential parts of language acquisition. Formal and formative instruction, too, will be required—*learning*, that is, and *long* learning at that, which means time to soak and steep in the language and to practice it with others who are also doing their best to acquire it so as to speak it fluently.

When it comes to the language that is the Old Testament, for many people it will simply be too late. They may not have the capacity, the time, or the desire to master a new (but very old) L2. Similarly, in many Christian communities—"New Testament Churches," for example, full of "New Testament Christians"—the Old Testament may well be dead already, too far gone to recover, almost impossible to bring back to life. And these dire situations do not yet include mention of the need to correct so much (re)pidginization or (de)creolization of the Old Testament, if such can be corrected (see chap. 7).

All of that sounds like *very* long and *very* hard work. Indeed, when we are talking about the fullness and richness of Scripture and the faith it engenders, we might well wonder if anyone but God could hope for full fluency. But the length and difficulty of the task doesn't mean we are released from it. To reapply words from Rabbi Tarphon found in the Mishnah, "It's not your job to finish the work, but neither are you free to walk away from it" (*m. 'Abot* 2.16). Or to borrow from another rabbi, the great Hillel, one shouldn't say,

---

72. The reference is to Plotz, whose *Good Book* began as "Blogging the Bible" for Slate.com. The above judgment holds equally true for John Hartung's work discussed in chap. 4 ("Love Thy Neighbor"), despite his claim to have read the Bible for years and his disavowal of needing any instruction (!) in reading.

"'When I have time, I shall study,' for you may never have time" (*m. 'Abot* 2.4).[73] In other words, hard work like the acquisition of the language of Scripture shouldn't be put off until later; one may not have such time later, let alone the proper brain plasticity.

In the specific case of the language that is the Old Testament, the task is made yet more difficult because of the specific content of this language.[74] I have tried not to gloss over the very real difficulties presented by (and in) the Old Testament. These are real and must somehow be accounted for, not by ignoring them or simply pointing to the easy parts, thinking they somehow cancel out the others or at least balance them out somewhat. I hope that some of what I've said in previous chapters gestures toward ways that the hard parts of *the whole Bible* (since they live in both Testaments) might be understood, especially when seen within the language analogy. Space has prevented me from saying more, though I reiterate that the most difficult parts of the language of the Old Testament prove its complexity and antiquity if only because the most difficult and most ancient languages are the hardest to learn and have the most irregularities.[75] I add that only the most dexterous language users, such as *our best poets*, are able to traffic in all the nooks and crannies of a language, gleaning and using what is there, at the right time and for the right purposes, in just the right, artful, and poetic ways—ways that cannot be reduced to formal logic or flat prose.[76] Such poetry recalls the "tried-and-true worker" of 2 Tim. 2:15, "who doesn't need to be ashamed" (due to ignorance in the language or lack of linguistic skill?) but "who interprets the message of truth correctly" (CEB; KJV: "rightly dividing the word of truth") and sounds a lot like those scribes trained for the kingdom in Matt. 13.[77] And that is the kind of linguistic skill needed to handle the ins

73. The translations of *'Abot* are from Neusner, *Mishnah*, 678 and 676, respectively.

74. Morgan with Barton, *Biblical Interpretation*, 3: "Language is the necessary vehicle here, but the heart of the problem lies in understanding the *subject-matter* being discussed. In biblical interpretation also, learning the languages is a first step, but the major difficulties arise over the subject-matter."

75. Even modern and more familiar languages have more than their fair share of complexities like mood and modality. See, e.g., Palmer, *Mood and Modality*. It is again telling that so much common reflection on the Bible is not marked by such nuance.

76. This is not entirely unrelated to the issue of "picking and choosing" discussed in chap. 4, which was the bane of the New Atheists (though they proved to be subject to their own critique!). The difference here is that the poet's selection is intentional and predicated on linguistic dexterity and skill, as well as knowledge of the whole, *not* the result of ignorance or arbitrariness. It is a matter of linguistic *phronēsis*, poetic practical wisdom.

77. See Brueggemann with Sharp, *Living Countertestimony*, 115: "Kingdom scribes, scholars who serve the secret of God, work at the artistic pivot point of old and new, of tradition and interpretation, of crucifixion and resurrection. At their best, scribes preclude the dumbing down to which the Church is deeply tempted in its effort to domesticate. They

and outs, the ups and downs, the zeniths and nadirs of the language that is the Old Testament, specifically, and the entirety of Christian Scripture more generally. Whenever such work is done, it is evidence of the best language use *in practice*.

In this book, however, I have been concerned, not with the specific difficulties offered at various points in the Old Testament, so much as with the difficulties of acquiring it as a (second) language and all that hangs on such acquisition (or its lack). I end by underlining once more how hard this work is and will be. By all accounts language learning is strenuous. First, we have to learn the alphabet and phonics so as to proceed to reading short sentences, then long ones, then paragraphs, and eventually whole books. Unfortunately, language learning doesn't stop at accurate pronunciation or reading comprehension. Learning how to carry on a conversation will be every bit as difficult: how to use a word correctly and, subsequently, how to generate new sentences, thoughts, discourse, even how to compose poetry by using the language we have acquired. It will be very difficult work. Frustrating work. But rewarding work that will come, slowly, with time.

And, one day, we might even dream in the language of Scripture.

Listen, my people, to my teaching;
  tilt your ears toward the words of my mouth.
I will open my mouth with a proverb.
  I'll declare riddles from days long gone—
    ones that we've heard and learned about,
    ones that our ancestors told us.
We won't hide them from their descendants;
  we'll tell the next generation
  all about the praise due the Lord *and his strength—*
    the wondrous works God has done.
He established a law for Jacob
  and set up Instruction for Israel,
    ordering our ancestors
    to teach them to their children.
This is so that the next generation
  and children not yet born will know these things,
    and so they can rise up and tell their children

---

insist that what is familiar and comfortable must be recognized as strange. He [Jesus] left them with the parables; and he left them with the heavy lifting to do." See also Brueggemann, "Preacher as Scribe."

to put their hope in God—
  never forgetting God's deeds,
  but keeping God's commandments—
and so that they won't become like their ancestors:
a rebellious, stubborn generation,
  a generation whose heart wasn't set firm
  and whose spirit wasn't faithful to God.
                    (Ps. 78:1–8 CEB, italics added)

Appendix 1

Newton Series

Year	Total sermons	OT-only sermons	NT-only sermons	Combination sermons[a]	No-text sermons	Ratio of NT to OT	% OT to all	% NT to all	% of combined	% of no-text	OT texts for combined	Texts for OT-only sermons[b]
1924	20	3	14	3	0	4.67	15%	70%	15%	0%	Exod. 5:1 (with 1 NT text); 33:23 (with 1 NT text); Ps. 36:9 (with 1 NT text)	(1) Gen. 3:24; (2) Ps. 36:5–6; (3) Ps. 36:9
1925	21	6	15	0	0	2.5	29%	71%	0%	0%	n/a	(1) Exod. 39:14; (2) Num. 13:33; (3) Hosea 11:8–9; (4) Amos 8:11–12;[c] (5) Ps. 5:3; (6) Ps. 81:5
1926	25	6	17	1	1	2.83	24%	68%	4%	4%	Gen. 13:12 (with 1 NT text)	(1) Gen. 3:23–24; (2) 1 Kings 22:14; (3) Isa. 2:4; (4) Jon. 1:3; (5) Ps. 84:1; (6) Pss. 9:9, 46:1; 68:5; 90:1
1927	25	3	21	1	0	7	12%	84%	4%	0%	Job 14:14 (with 1 NT text)[d]	(1) Josh. 24:15;[c] (2) Ps. 121:1; (3) Ps. 142:5
Totals	91	18	67	5	1	3.72	19.7%	73%	5.4%	1%		

[a] The OT text is given as a "reading," not as "Scripture" or the theme verse for the sermon.

[b] OT texts are listed in the order of the Hebrew Bible.

[c] This sermon is by a rabbi.

[d] This sermon is by the noted homiletician G. A. Buttrick.

Appendix 2

Butler Series

Year	Total	OT-only sermons	NT-only sermons	Combination sermons[a]	No-text sermons	Ratio of NT to OT	% OT to all	% NT to all	% of combined	% of no-text	OT texts for combined[b]	Texts for OT-only sermons[b]
1944	52	14	33	0	5	2.36	27%	63%	0%	9%		(1) Isa. 26:9; (2) Isa. 40:31; (3) Jer. 2:31;[c] (4) Ezek. 48:35; (5) Joel 3:14; (6) Ps. 11:3; (7) Ps. 22:21; (8) Ps. 42:3;[c] (9) Ps. 89:16;[c] (10) Ps. 103:3–4; (11) Ps. 121:1; (12) Ps. 125:2; (13–14) Dan. 7:14
1946[d]	52	12	21	2	16	1.75	23%	40.4%	3.8%	30.7%	(1) Exod. 2:11 (with 1 NT text); (2) Josh. 24:15 (with 1 NT text)	(1) Gen. 13:8;[e] (2) Exod. 3:5; (3) 1 Kings 17:3; (4) Isa. 5:4;[c] (5) Hab. 1:16;[c] (6) Ps. 8:4–5; (7) Ps. 25:1; (8) Ps. 46:1; (9) Ps. 119:18; (10) Ps. 126:5; (11) Ps. 139:10; (12) 2 Chron. 30:8
1947–48	52	13	20	2	17	1.54	25%	38.4%	3.8%	32.6%	(1) Gen. 9:11–16 (with 1 NT text); (2) Lam. 3:39 (with 3 NT texts)[f]	(1) Gen. 11:7; (2) Gen. 45:8 with 50:20; (3) Gen. 45:26–28; (4) Deut. 30:14;[c] (5) Isa. 28:24, 26; (6) Isa. 44:17; (7) Isa. 52:10; (8) Jer. 44:4; (9) Ps. 23:5; (10) Ps. 40:3; (11) Ps. 77:7–9, 14; (12) Ps. 137:1–4 with Ezek. 1:1; (13) Job 16:4
1949–50	52	13[g]	27	1	12	2.07	25%	52%	1.9%	23%	1 Sam. 27:10 (with 1 NT text)	(1) 1 Kings 19:9; (2) Isa. 32:2; (3) Jer. 22:16 and Deut. 16:20;[c] (4) Ps. 8:4a; (5) Ps. 37:1a;[h] (6) Ps. 95:6; (7) Ps. 99:1; (8) Ps. 127:1; (9) Ps. 139;[i] (10) Ps. 139:1–2, 4–5, 7–8; (11) Ps. 119:54; (12) Ps. 119:97; (13) Sir. 15:14; 31:10[j]
1951–52	52	12	20	0	20	1.66	23%	38.4%	0%	38.4%		(1) Exod. 25:8;[c] (2) Isa. 31:1; (3) Isa. 40:8; (4) Isa. 55:2; (5) Isa. 50:2; (6) Ps. 11:3; (7) Ps. 24:1–2; (8) Ps. 33:12; (9) Ps. 121:8; (10) Prov. 9:1; (11) Dan. 12:12–13; (12) Neh. 2:18

1955	52	6	29	0	17	4.83	11.5%	55.7%	0%	32.6%		(1) Isa. 1:18; (2) 1 Sam. 12:7; (3) 1 Kings 22:8 and Jer. 1:9–10; (4) Job 8:7; (5) Job 23:3 and Ps. 139:7;[k] (6) Song 4:16
1959–60	42	12	18	0	12	1.5	28.5%	42.8%	0%	28.5%		(1) Gen. 9:21; (2) Gen. 32:26; (3) Exod. 32:19–20; (4) Lev. 16:2–3; (5) 1 Sam. 7:12; (6) 2 Sam. 18:31–33; (7) Isa. 6:1; (8) Isa. 25:9; (9) Hosea 11:1; (10) Ps. 30:5; (11) Ps. 51:11; (12) Ps. 73:17
1962	42	4	11	0	27	2.75	9.5%	26.1%	0%	64.2%		(1) Isa. 35:7; (2) Isa. 49:22–23; (3) Amos 5:18; (4) book of Jonah
1964	35	5	10	0	20	2	14%	28.5%	0%	57.1%		(1) 2 Kings 20:2, 7; (2) Mal. 2:10; (3) Ps. 8:3–4; (4) Ps. 90:12; (5) 2 Chron. 12:9–10
1966–68	52	8	17	1	26	2.12	15.3%	32.6%	1.9%	50%	(1) Prov. 4:7–9 (with 1 NT text)	(1) Exod. 16:2, 8; (2) Exod. 16:19–20, (3) Jer. 18:1–6; (4) Ezek. 47:12; (5) Hab. 3:18; (6) Ps. 13:1; (7) Ps. 23:4; (8) Ps. 42:3
Totals	483	99	206	6	172	2.08	20.5%	42.6%	1.2%	35.6%		

[a] The OT text is given as a "reading," not as "Scripture" or the theme verse for the sermon.

[b] OT texts are listed in the order of the Hebrew Bible.

[c] This sermon is by a rabbi.

[d] In the copy available to me, sermon 6 was ripped out, so the final tallies are not precise.

[e] This sermon is by the noted Jewish scholar and rabbi Louis Finkelstein.

[f] The second sermon is by the noted theologian Martin Niemöller.

[g] This includes one sermon based on the OT Apocrypha.

[h] This sermon is by Norman Vincent Peale. The text is Ps. 37:1a, though the Scripture is said to be Ps. 37:1–11. See further chap. 6.

[i] This sermon is by the famous systematic theologian Paul Tillich.

[j] This sermon is by a Roman Catholic priest.

[k] This sermon is by the NT scholar John Knox.

Appendix 3

Cox Series

Year	Total sermons	OT-only sermons	NT-only sermons	Combination sermons[a]	No-text sermons	Ratio of NT to OT	% OT to all	% NT to all	% of combined	% of no-text	OT texts for combined[b]	Texts for OT-only sermons[b]
1988	52	16	26	7	3	1.65	30.7%	50%	13.4%	5.7%	(1) Gen. 1:27–31 (with 3 NT texts); (2) 1 Kings 16:19–33; 17:10–16 (with 1 NT); (3) Isa. 53:3–5 (with 2 NT); (4) Zech. 8:1–8 (with 1 NT);[c] (5) Ps. 8 and Gen. 1:26–28 (with 1 NT); (6) Ps. 84 and Jer. 14:7–10, 19–22 (with 2 NT); (7) Ps. 139:7–12 (with 1 NT)	(1) Gen. 2:18; (2) Gen. 3:1–6; (3) Gen. 11:31–12:3; (4) Gen. 15; (5) Deut. 6:4–5; (6) Deut. 34:1–12; (7) Josh. 1:1–11; (8) 1 Sam. 28–31; (9) Isa. 55:6; (10) Jer. 9:23–24; (11) Hosea 11:1–4; (12) Ps. 25; (13) Ps. 77:3, 6; (14) Ps. 88; (15) Ps. 100; (16) Eccles. 3:1
1989	52	11	29	8	4	2.63	21.1%	55.7%	15.3%	7.6%	(1) Gen. 22:1–9 (with 1 NT text);[c] (2) Num. 13:17–14:2 (with 2 NT); (3) Josh. 3:4 (with 1 NT); (4) Josh. 4:1–9 (with 1 NT); (5) 1 Sam. 31:1–6 and 2 Sam. 1:2–4, 11–12, 17–27 (with 1 NT); (6) Jon. 3:1–5, 10 (with 2 NT); (7) Ps. 86:11–17 (with 2 NT); (8) Ps. 139 (with 1 NT)	(1) Gen. 1:1–2:3; (2) Exod. 20:14; (3) 2 Sam. 21:14–22; (4) Isa. 9:2; (5) Ezek. 36:22–32;[d] (6) Amos 5:18–24; (7) Mal. 1:1–2, 6; 2:10; 3:13–17;[e] (8) Ps. 23; (9) Ps. 33:20; (10) Ps. 90:12; (11) Neh. 3 (selected verses)
1990	40	7	22	7	4	3.14	17.5%	55%	17.5%	10%	(1) Gen. 1:26–27 (with 1 NT text); (2) Gen. 2:21–24 (with 2 NT); (3) Deut. 8:1–10 (with 1 NT); (4) 1 Kings 17:17–24 (with 1 NT); (5) 2 Kings 5:18–19 (with 1 NT); (6) Isa. 40:1–8 (with 2 NT); (7) Neh. 8:2–4, 5–6, 8–10 (with 2 NT)	(1) Gen. 12:1–9; (2) Gen. 45:1–15; (3) Exod. 3:1–12; (4) Exod. 33:14; (5) Num. 22:6, 28, 32; (6) 1 Kings 18:20–29, 36–39; (7) 1 Chron. 29:10–25

1991	40	10	18	9	3	1.8	25%	45%	22.5%	7.5%	(1) Josh. 2:1–24 and 6:20–26 (with 2 NT texts); (2) Isa. 60:1–6 and Ps. 71 (with 2 NT); (3) Isa. 61:1–11 (with 1 NT); (4) Jer. 8:8–13 (with 1 NT);[c] (5) Jer. 15:10–21 (with 1 NT); (6) Ezek. 34:11–24 (with 1 NT); (7) Ps. 24:1–5 (with 2 NT);[f] (8) Ps. 51 (with 2 NT); (9) Job 3:1–4 and 20:4–6 (with 1 NT)	(1) Gen. 3:6–12, 16; (2) Gen. 32:22–31; (3) Isa. 40:29–31 and Ps. 138; (4) Isa. 42:1–4; (5) Isa. 43:1–5; (6) Isa. 46:1–4; (7) Ps. 119:105;[g] (8) Ps. 121; (9) Song 2:8–17; (10) Lam. 1:1–22
1992	40	14	14	6	6	1	35%	35%	15%	15%	(1) Exod. 20:1–2, 17 (with 1 NT text); (2) Exod. 1:8–2:10 (with 1 NT);[h] (3) Lev. 19:1–2, 15–18 (with 1 NT); (4) Deut. 25:1–6 (with 1 NT); (5) Hosea 11:1–11 (with 1 NT);[c] (6) Eccles. 3:1–15 (with 1 NT)	(1) Gen. 22:1–18; (2) Exod. 3:6; (3) Exod. 4:10; (4) Exod. 20:7; (5) Num. 13:1–31 [sic], 25–28a, 30–32, 33b; 14:1–4; (6) Judg. 17–18; (7) Isa. 11:6–9; (8) Isa. 40:1–11;[i] (9) Ps. 1:3; (10) Ps. 23:6; (11) Ps. 71; (12) Ps. 98; (13) Ezra 3:10–13; (14) Wis. 7:27b

[a] The OT text is given as a "reading," not as "Scripture" or the theme verse for the sermon.

[b] OT texts are listed in the order of the Hebrew Bible.

[c] This sermon is by the OT scholar and homiletician Elizabeth Achtemeier, well known for her method of correlating OT and NT texts (see chap. 9).

[d] This sermon is by the noted preacher William H. Willimon.

[e] This sermon is by the OT scholar Page H. Kelley.

[f] This sermon is by the OT scholar W. Sibley Towner.

[g] This sermon is by the well-known NT scholar Bruce M. Metzger.

[h] This sermon is by the homiletician Anna Carter Florence.

[i] This sermon is by the OT scholar H. G. M. Williamson.

Year	Total sermons	OT-only sermons	NT-only sermons	Combination sermons[j]	No-text sermons	Ratio of NT to OT	% OT to all	% NT to all	% of combined	% of no-text	OT texts for combined[k]	Texts for OT-only sermons[k]
1993	40	7	26	4	3	3.71	17.5%	65%	10%	7.5%	(1) 1 Kings 17:8–16 (with 1 NT text); (2) Joel 3:1–2, 9–17 (with 1 NT); (3) Jon. 3:10–4:11 (with 1 NT); (4) Eccles. 2:20–3:15 (with 1 NT)	(1) Gen. 4:1–16; (2) Gen. 9:8–17;[l] (3) Exod. 3:7–12; (4) Zech. 4:1–14; (5) Ps. 8;[m] (6) Ps. 8:4; (7) Job 1:20–21
1994	41	4	24	7	6	6	9.7%	58.5%	17%	14.6%	(1) Gen. 1:1–5 (with 2 NT texts); (2) Exod. 20:1–6 (with 1 NT); (3) Exod. 33:12–13, 17–23 (with 1 NT); (4) 2 Sam. 18:24–33 and Ps. 102:1–12 (with 2 NT);[n] (5) Amos 3:1–8 (with 2 NT); (6) Ps. 145 (with 1 NT); (7) Dan. 3:13–18 (with 2 NT)	(1) Num. 13:25–33; (2) Jer. 1:4–10; (3) Jer. 32:1–15; (4) Jer. 48:11
Totals	305	69	159	48	29	2.3	22.6%	52.1%	15.7%	9.5%		

[j]The OT text is given as a "reading," not as "Scripture" or the theme verse for the sermon.

[k]OT texts are listed in the order of the Hebrew Bible.

[l]This sermon is by former US Vice President Al Gore.

[m]This sermon is by a professor of homiletics.

[n]This sermon is by a theology professor.

Appendix 4

Size of Testaments

Bible version	Books	Chapters	Verses	Words
NRSV (OT/OTA/NT)	85	1,398	37,791	913,140
NIV (OT/NT)	66	1,189	31,086	726,628
NRSV (OT)	39	929		
NRSV (OT/OTA)	58	1,138		
NRSV (OTA)	19	209		
NIV (OT)	39	929		
NJPS (OT)	39	929	23,203	548,210
HB (WTT)	39	929	23,213	309,976
NRSV (NT)	27	260		
NIV (NT)	27	260		
GNT	27	260	7,941	138,020
Ratio of OT chapters to NT chapters	3.57			
Ratio of OT + OTA chapters to NT chapters	4.37			
% of OT chapters to whole	78.1%			
% of OT + OTA chapters to whole	81.4%			

Appendix 5

Sermon Data
from Walter Brueggemann

The corpus is by Brueggemann: *Collected Sermons of Walter Brueggemann*, 2 vols.; *Inscribing the Text*, ed. A. C. Florence; and *The Threat of Life*, ed. C. L. Campbell.

Volume	Total sermons	OT-only sermons	NT-only sermons	Combination sermons	No-text sermons	Ratio of NT to OT	% OT to all	% NT to all	% of combined	% of no-text	OT texts for combined[a]	Texts for OT-only sermons[a]
Collected Sermons, vol. 1	67	4	7	56	0	1.75	5.9%	10.4%	83.5%	0%	(1) Gen. 17:1–10, 15–19 and Ps. 105:1–11 (with 2 NT texts); (2) Gen. 41:11–32, 46–49 and 47:13–26 (with 1 NT); (3) Gen. 45:2–15 and Ps. 37:1–11 (with 1 NT); (4) Exod. 1:15–22 and 15:20–21 (with 1 NT); (5) Exod. 3:7–10 (with 2 NT); (6) Exod. 14:4–18 (with 2 NT); (7) Exod. 17:1–7 and Ps. 95 (with 1 NT); (8) Exod. 20:10–7 (with 2 NT); (9) Exod. 34:29–35 and Ps. 99 (with 2 NT); (10) Lev. 25:8–24 and Isa. 61:1–4 (with 1 NT); (11) Num. 6:22–27 (with 5 NT); (12) Deut. 5:1–6 (with 2 NT); (13) Deut. 30:10–14 (with 2 NT); (14) 1 Kings 17:17–24 (with 2 NT); (15) 1 Kings 19:19–21 (with 1 NT); (16) 2 Kings 2:9–15 (with 1 NT); and 2 Kings 4:42–46 (with 1 NT); (16) 2 Kings 5:1–14 and Ps. 30 (with 1 NT); (17) 2 Kings 5:1–14 and Ps. 30 (with 1 NT); (18) Isa. 1:21–27 (with 2 NT); (19) Isa. 11:1–10 and Ps. 72:1–7, 18–19 (with 1 NT); (20) Isa. 25:1–9 and Ps. 23 (with 2 NT); (21) Isa. 35:1–10 and Ps. 124 (with 2 NT); (22) Isa. 43:1–5 (with 1 NT); (23) Isa. 43:15–21 (with 1 NT); (24) Isa. 43:16–21 (with 1 NT); (25) Isa. 49:7–13 (with 1 NT); (26) Isa. 51:1–3 and NT);	(1) Exod. 19:4–6; (2) Jer. 5:20–29; (3) Mic. 4:1–5; (4) Ps. 69:2, 14

43:15–21; 55:12–13 (with 1 NT); (27) Isa. 51:1–6 (with 1 NT); (28) Isa. 55:1–13 (with 1 NT); (29) Isa. 58:1–9 (with 1 NT); (30) Isa. 60:1–7 (with 1 NT); (31) Isa. 65:17–25 (with 2 NT); (32) Jer. 9:23–24 (with 1 NT); (33) Jer. 9:23–24 and Ps. 87 (with 1 NT); (34) Jer. 31:31–34 and Ps. 51:10–17 (with 2 NT); (35) Jer. 45 and Ps. 131 (with 1 NT); (36) Ezek. 11:17–20 (with 2 NT); (37) Hosea 13:12–14 (with 1 NT); (38) Mic. 4:1–5 and Ps. 98:1–5 (with 2 NT); (39) Hab. 1:1–3; 2:1–4 and Ps. 119:137–44 (with 2 NT); (40) Zeph. 3:14–20 and Isa. 12:2–6 (with 2 NT); (41) Mal. 4:5–6 (with 3 NT); (42) Ps. 1 (with 3 NT); (43) Ps. 23 (with 1 NT); (44) Ps. 23 and 1 Sam. 16:1–13 (with 2 NT); (45) Ps. 30:4–11 (with 1 NT); (46) Ps. 32 (with 1 NT); (47) Ps. 50:1–23 (with 2 NT); (48) Ps. 68:1–10, 32–35 (with 2 NT); (49) Ps. 73 (with 1 NT); (50) Ps. 97 (with 2 NT); (51) Ps. 107:1, 33–43 (with 2 NT); (52) Job 26:1–3 and 27:1–6 (with 1 NT); (53) Prov. 15:17 (with 2 NT); (54) Lam. 1:1–6 and 3:19–26 (with 2 NT); (55) Dan. 1:3–21 (with 1 NT); (56) 1 Chron. 29:10–13 and Ps. 148 (with 2 NT)

ᵃOT texts are listed in the order of the Hebrew Bible.

Volume	Total	OT-only sermons	NT-only sermons	Combination sermons	No-text sermons	Ratio of NT to OT	% OT to all	% NT to all	% of combined	% of no-text	OT texts for combined[b]	Texts for OT-only sermons[b]
Collected Sermons, vol. 2	54	2	5	47	0	2.5	3.7%	9.2%	87%	0%	(1) Gen. 9:8–17 and Ps. 25:1–10 (with 2 NT texts); (2) Gen. 17:1–7, 15–16 and Ps. 22:23–31 (with 2 NT); (3) Gen. 25:19–34 and Ps. 119:105–22 (with 2 NT); (4) Gen. 37:1–6, 12–28 and Ps. 85:8–13 (with 1 NT); (5) Deut. 26:1–11 (with 1 NT); (6) Deut. 26:1–11 and Ps. 91:1–2, 9–16 (with 2 NT); (7) Deut. 30:15–20 and Ps. 119:1–8 (with 2 NT); (8) 1 Sam. 16:1–13 and Ps. 23 (with 1 NT); (9) 1 Kings 19:15–16, 19–21 and Ps. 77:1–2, 11–20 (with 2 NT); (10) 2 Kings 4:42–44 and Ps. 145:10–19 (with 2 NT); (11) 2 Kings 6:8–23 (with 1 NT); (12) 2 Kings 22:3–13 and Jer. 36:4–8, 14–26 (with 1 NT); (13) Isa. 11:1–9 (with 1 NT); (14) Isa. 42:10–13 (with 1 NT); (15) Isa. 49:8–16a and Ps. 131 (with 2 NT); (16) Isa. 55:1–8 and Ps. 63:1–9 (with 2 NT); (17) Isa. 55:1–11 and Ps. 92:1–4, 12–15 (with 2 NT); (18) Isa. 58:1–9a and Ps. 112:1–10 (with 2 NT); (19) Isa. 63:7–9 (with 2 NT); (20) Isa. 65:17–25 (with Ps. 98 and 2 NT); (21) Jer. 22:1–6 and Ps. 46 (with 2 NT); (22) Jer. 31:31–34 and Ps. 119:9–16 (with 1 NT);	(1) Ps. 104:24–35; (2) Isa. 11:1–9

The Threat of Life	6	2	0	4	0	0	33.3%	0	66%	0%

(23) Jer. 32:1–15 (with 2 NT); (24) Ezek. 18:1–4, 25–32 (with 2 NT); (25) Ezek. 34:1–6, 11–16, 20–24 (with 1 NT); (26) Hosea 1:2–10 and Ps. 85 (with 2 NT); (27) Hab. 1:1–4; 2:1–4 and Ps. 119:137–44 (with 1 NT); (28) Ps. 4 (with 3 NT); (29) Ps. 23 (with 3 NT); (30) Ps. 23 (with 3 NT);c (31) Ps. 25:1–10 (with 1 NT); (32) Ps. 29 (with 2 NT); (33) Ps. 30 (with 2 NT); (34) Ps. 31:9–16 (with 2 NT); (35) Ps. 40:1–11 (with 2 NT); (36) Ps. 66:1–12 and Jer. 29:1–4, 7 (with 2 NT); (37) Ps. 97 (with 3 NT); (38) Ps. 98 (with 3 NT); (39) Ps. 103 (with 2 NT); (40) Ps. 104:24–35 and Ezek. 37:1–14 (with 1 NT); (41) Ps. 113 (with 1 NT); (42) Ps. 116:1–3, 10–17 (with 3 NT); (43) Ps. 121 (with 2 NT); (44) Ps. 146 (with 2 NT); (45) Ps. 148 (with 3 NT); (46) Ps. 150 (with 2 NT); (47) Job 19:23–27 and Ps. 17:1–9 with 2 NT)

(1) Exod. 3:1–12 and Ps. 103:1–13 (with 2 NT texts);(2) Exod. 11:4–8 and 12:29–32 (with 2 NT); (3) Exod. 33:18–34:10 (with 1 NT); (4) Dan. 3:14–20 (with 1 NT)

(1) Ps. 69:13–14a, 16–18, 33; (2) Ps. 69:19–29

b OT texts are listed in the order of the Hebrew Bible.

c The three NT texts here differ from the three used with the previous sermon on Ps. 23.

Volume	Total	OT-only sermons	NT-only sermons	Combination sermons	No-text sermons	Ratio of NT to OT	% OT to all	% NT to all	% of combined	% of no-text	OT texts for combined[d]	Texts for OT-only sermons
Inscribing the Text	7	0	2	5	0	2	0%	28%	71%	0%	(1) 1 Kings 17:8–16 (with 1 NT text); (2) 2 Kings 8:1–6 (with 1 NT); (3) Isa. 6:9–10 and 55:1–3 (with 1 NT); (4) Isa. 43:16–21 (with 1 NT); (5) Jer. 20:7–13 (with 1 NT)	n/a
Totals	134	8	14	112	0	1.75	5.9%	10.4%	83.5%	0%		

[d]OT texts are listed in the order of the Hebrew Bible.

Appendix 6

Old Testament Texts
Used by Walter Brueggemann

No differentiation is made in Brueggemann's corpus regarding whether the text is from an OT-only sermon or a combined one. Totals in boldface indicate outperformance vis-à-vis the Best Sermons series (see apps. 1–3 above and chaps. 2 and 9) as determined by percentage. Out of the 39 biblical books, Brueggemann's corpus outperforms the Best Sermons series 22 times, with the Best Sermons series outperforming Brueggemann's corpus only 12 times (in each of those instances Brueggemann's corpus lacks a sermon on that book of the OT). Both corpora lack sermons on five books: Ruth, Esther, Obadiah, Nahum, and Haggai.

Book	Texts	Brueggemann totals (out of 134; with % of whole)	Newton/ Butler/Cox totals (out of 879; with % of whole)
Genesis	9:8–17; 17:1–7, 15–16; 17:1–10, 15–19; 25:19–34; 37:1–6, 12–28; 41:11–32, 46–49; 45:2–15; 47:13–26;	8 (5.9%)	29 (3.2%)
Exodus	1:15–22; 3:1–12; 3:7–10; 11:4–8; 12:29–32; 14:4–18; 15:20–21; 17:1–7; 19:4–6; 20:10–7; 33:18–34:10; 34:29–35	12 (8.9%)	20 (2.7%)
Leviticus	25:8–24	**1 (0.74%)**	2 (0.22%)
Numbers	6:22–27	**1 (0.74%)**	6 (0.68%)
Deuteronomy	5:1–6; 26:1–11 (2×); 30:10–14; 30:15–20	**5 (3.7%)**	6 (0.68%)
Joshua		0 (0%)	7 (0.79%)

261

Book	Texts	Brueggemann totals (out of 134; with % of whole)	Newton/Butler/Cox totals (out of 879; with % of whole)
Judges		0 (0%)	1 (0.11%)
Ruth		0 (0%)	0 (0%)
1 Samuel	16:1–13 (2×)	2 (1.49%)	5 (0.56%)
2 Samuel		0 (0%)	4 (0.45%)
1 Kings	17:8–16; 17:17–24; 19:15–16, 19–21; 19:19–21	4 (2.9%)	9 (1.02%)
2 Kings	2:9–15; 4:42–44; 4:42–46; 5:1–14; 6:8–23; 8:1–6; 22:3–13	7 (5.2%)	2 (0.22%)
1 Chronicles	29:10–13	1 (0.74%)	1 (0.11%)
2 Chronicles		0 (0%)	2 (0.22%)
Ezra		0 (0%)	1 (0.11%)
Nehemiah		0 (0%)	3 (0.34%)
Esther		0 (0%)	0 (0%)
Job	19:23–27; 26:1–3; 27:1–6	3 (2.2%)	7 (0.79%)
Psalms	1 (whole psalm); 4 (whole psalm); 17:1–9; 22:23–31; 23 (whole psalm, 6×); 25:1–10 (2×); 29 (whole psalm); 30 (whole psalm, 2×); 30:4–11; 31:9–16; 32 (whole psalm); 37:1–11; 40:1–11; 46 (whole psalm); 50:1–23; 51:10–17; 63:1–9; 66:1–12; 68:1–10, 32–35; 69:2, 14; 69:13–14a, 16–18, 33; 69:19–29; 72:1–7, 18–19; 73 (whole psalm); 77:1–2, 11–20; 85 (whole psalm); 85:8–13; 87 (whole psalm); 91:1–2, 9–16; 92:1–4, 12–15; 95 (whole psalm); 97 (whole psalm, 2×); 98 (whole psalm, 2×); 98:1–5; 99 (whole psalm); 103 (whole psalm);103:1–13; 104:24–35; 105:1–11; 107:1, 33–43; 112:1–10; 113 (whole psalm); 116:1–3, 10–17; 119:1–8; 119:9–16; 119:105–122; 119:137–144 (2×); 121 (whole psalm); 124 (whole psalm); 131 (whole psalm, 2×);145:10–19; 146 (whole psalm); 148 (whole psalm, 2×); 150 (whole psalm)	66 (49%)	76 (8.6%)
Proverbs	15:17	1 (0.74%)	2 (0.22%)
Ecclesiastes		0 (0%)	3 (0.34%)
Song of Songs		0 (0%)	2 (0.22%)

Book	Texts	Brueggemann totals (out of 134; with % of whole)	Newton/ Butler/Cox totals (out of 879; with % of whole)
Isaiah	1:21–27; 6:9–10; 11:1–9; 11:1–10; 12:2–6; 25:1–9; 35:1–10; 42:10–13; 43:1–5; 43:15–21 (2×); 43:16–21 (2×); 49:7–13, 49:8–16a; 51:1–6; 51:1–3; 55:1–3, 55:1–8; 55:1–11; 55:1–13; 55:12–13; 58:1–9a; 58:1–9; 60:1–7; 61:1–4; 63:7–9; 65:17–25 (2×)	29 (21.6%)	28 (3.18%)
Jeremiah	5:20–29; 9:23–24 (2×); 20:7–13; 22:1–6; 29:1–4, 7; 31:31–34 (2×); 32:1–15; 36:4–8, 14–26; 45 (whole chap.)	11 (8.2%)	12 (1.36%)
Lamentations	1:1–6; 3:19–26	2 (1.4%)	2 (0.22%)
Ezekiel	11:17–20; 18:1–4, 25–32; 34:1–6, 11–16, 20–24; 37:1–14	4 (2.98%)	5 (0.56%)
Daniel	1:3–21; 3:14–20	2 (1.4%)	3 (0.34%)
Hosea	1:2–10; 13:12–14	2 (1.4%)	4 (0.45%)
Joel		0 (0%)	2 (0.22%)
Amos		0 (0%)	4 (0.45%)
Obadiah		0 (0%)	0 (0%)
Jonah		0 (0%)	4 (0.45%)
Micah	4:1–5 (2×)	2 (1.4%)	0 (0%)
Nahum		0 (0%)	0 (0%)
Habakkuk	1:1–4 and 2:1–4; 1:1–3 and 2:1–4	3 (2.2%)	2 (0.22%)
Zephaniah	3:14–20	1 (0.74%)	0 (0%)
Haggai		0 (0%)	0 (0%)
Zechariah		0 (0%)	2 (0.22%)
Malachi	4:5–6	1 (0.74%)	4 (0.45%)

Bibliography

Abley, Mark. *Spoken Here: Travels among Threatened Languages*. New York: Mariner, 2005.

Academy of the Hebrew Language, The. Website: http://hebrew-academy.huji.ac.il/English/Pages/Home.aspx.

Achtemeier, Elizabeth. *The Old Testament and the Proclamation of the Gospel*. Philadelphia: Westminster, 1973.

———. *Preaching from the Old Testament*. Louisville: Westminster John Knox, 1989.

Ackroyd, Peter R., ed. *The Cambridge History of the Bible*. 3 vols. Cambridge: Cambridge University Press, 1963–70.

Aitchison, Jean. *Language Change: Progress or Decay?* 3rd ed. Cambridge: Cambridge University Press, 2001.

———. *Linguistics*. 6th ed. Chicago: McGraw-Hill, 2003.

Aland, Barbara, et al., eds. *Novum Testamentum Graece*. 28th ed. Stuttgart: Deutsche Bibelgesellschaft, 2012.

Allen, Horace T., Jr. "Introduction: Preaching in a Christian Context." In *Handbook for the Revised Common Lectionary*, edited by Peter C. Bower, 1–24. Louisville: Westminster John Knox, 1996.

Allen, O. Wesley, Jr. *Preaching and Reading the Lectionary: A Three-Dimensional Approach to the Liturgical Year*. St. Louis: Chalice, 2007.

Anderson, Bernard W. *The Old Testament and Christian Faith: A Theological Discussion*. New York: Herder & Herder, 1969.

———. *Understanding the Old Testament*. 4th ed. Englewood Cliffs, NJ: Prentice Hall, 1986.

Anderson, E. Byron. *Worship and Christian Identity: Practicing Ourselves*. Collegeville, MN: Liturgical Press, 2003.

Arnold, Bill T., and David B. Weisberg. "Babel und Bibel und Bias." *BR* 18.1 (2002): 32–40.

———. "A Centennial Review of Friedrich Delitzsch's 'Babel und Bibel' Lectures." *JBL* 121 (2002): 441–57.

———. "Delitzsch in Context." In *God's Word for Our World*, edited by Deborah L. Ellens, J. Harold Ellens, Rolf Knierim, and Isaac Kalimi, 2:37–45. 2 vols. JSOTSup 388–89. London: T&T Clark, 2004.

Auslander, Shalom. *Foreskin's Lament: A Memoir*. New York: Riverhead, 2007.

Avalos, Hector. *The End of Biblical Studies*. Amherst, NY: Prometheus, 2007.

Bailey, Lloyd R. "The Lectionary in Critical Perspective." *Int* 31 (1977): 139–53.

Balás, D. L. "Marcion Revisited: A 'Post-Harnack' Perspective." In *Texts and Testaments: Critical Essays on the Bible and Early Church Fathers*, edited by W. E. March, 96–108. San Antonio: Trinity University Press, 1980.

Barr, James. *Holy Scripture: Canon, Authority, Criticism*. Philadelphia: Westminster, 1983.

———. *Old and New in Interpretation: A Study of the Two Testaments*. New York: Harper & Row, 1966.

Barrett, C. K. *The Gospel according to St. John: An Introduction with Commentary and Notes on the Greek Text*. 2nd ed. Philadelphia: Westminster, 1978.

Barth, Karl. *Dogmatics in Outline*. Translated by G. T. Thomson. San Francisco: Harper & Row, 1959.

———. "The Strange New World within the Bible." In *The Word of God and the Word of Man*, translated by Douglas Horton, 28–50. Gloucester, UK: Peter Smith, 1978.

Bartlett, David L. "Lectionaries." In *The New Interpreter's Bible One-Volume Commentary*, edited by Beverly Roberts Gaventa and David Petersen, 992–94. Nashville: Abingdon, 2010.

Bartlett, David L., and Barbara Brown Taylor, eds. *Feasting on the Word: Preaching the Revised Common Lectionary*. 12 vols. Louisville: Westminster John Knox, 2008–10.

Barton, David, ed. *The Founder's Bible (NASB)*. Newbury Park, CA: Shiloh Road, 2013.

Barton, John. "Marcion Revisited." In *The Canon Debate*, edited by Lee Martin McDonald and James A. Sanders, 341–54. Peabody, MA: Hendrickson, 2002.

Bauer, Hans, and Pontus Leander. *Historische Grammatik der hebräischen Sprache des Alten Testamentes*. 1922. Reprint, Hildesheim: Georg Olms, 1965.

Bayard, Pierre. *How to Talk about Books You Haven't Read*. Translated by Jeffrey Mehlman. New York: Bloomsbury, 2007.

Beal, Timothy. *The Rise and Fall of the Bible: The Unexpected History of an Accidental Book*. Boston: Houghton Mifflin Harcourt, 2011.

Beale, G. K. *The Book of Revelation*. NIGTC. Grand Rapids: Eerdmans, 1999.

———. *Handbook on the New Testament Use of the Old Testament: Exegesis and Interpretation*. Grand Rapids: Baker Academic, 2012.

———. *A New Testament Biblical Theology: The Unfolding of the Old Testament in the New*. Grand Rapids: Baker Academic, 2011.

Beale, G. K., and D. A. Carson, eds. *Commentary on the New Testament Use of the Old Testament*. Grand Rapids: Baker Academic, 2007.

Beasley-Murray, George R. *The Book of Revelation*. NCB. Grand Rapids: Eerdmans, 1974.

———. *John*. WBC. Waco: Word, 1987.

Ben-Shahar, Tal. *Being Happy: You Don't Have to Be Perfect to Lead a Richer, Happier Life*. New York: McGraw Hill, 2010.

Bentley, G. E. "Illustrated Bibles." In Metzger and Coogan, *Oxford Companion to the Bible*, 298–300.

Bergen, Doris L. *Twisted Cross: The German Christian Movement in the Third Reich*. Chapel Hill: University of North Carolina Press, 1996.

Berger, Peter L., and Thomas Luckman. *The Social Construction of Reality: A Treatise in the Sociology of Knowledge*. New York: Anchor, 1966.

Bergler, Thomas E. *From Here to Maturity: Overcoming the Juvenilization of American Christianity*. Grand Rapids: Eerdmans, 2014.

———. *The Juvenilization of American Christianity*. Grand Rapids: Eerdmans, 2012.

Bergmann, Michael, Michael J. Murray, and Michael C. Rea, eds. *Divine Evil? The Moral Character of the God of Abraham*. Oxford: Oxford University Press, 2011.

Bernard of Clairvaux. *On the Song of Songs*. Translated by Kilian Walsh and Irene M. Edmunds. 4 vols. Kalamazoo, MI: Cistercian, 1971–80.

Beyer, Franz-Heinrich, and Michael Waltermathe. "The Good, the Bad and the Undecided: Cultural Echoes of the Decalogue—An Educational Perspective." In *The Decalogue in Jewish and Christian Tradition*, edited by Yair Hoffman and Henning Graf Reventlow, 148–63. LHBOTS 509. New York: T&T Clark, 2011.

Billman, Kathleen D., and Daniel L. Migliore. *Rachel's Cry: Prayer of Lament and Rebirth of Hope*. Cleveland: United Church Press, 1999.

Blackman, E. C. *Marcion and His Influence*. London: SPCK, 1948.

Blake, Frank R. *A Resurvey of Hebrew Tense with an Appendix: Hebrew Influence on Biblical Aramaic*. Rome: Pontifical Biblical Institute, 1951.

Blount, Brian K. *Cultural Interpretation: Reorienting New Testament Criticism*. Minneapolis: Fortress, 1995.

Bly, Robert. *The Eight Stages of Translation*. Boston: Rowan Tree, 1986.

Boda, Mark J., and J. Gordon McConville, eds. *Dictionary of the Old Testament: Prophets*. Downers Grove, IL: IVP Academic, 2012.

Bonhoeffer, Dietrich. *Letters and Papers from Prison*. Edited by Eberhard Bethge. Enlarged ed. New York: Collier, 1972.

Booth, Wayne C. *The Company We Keep: An Ethics of Fiction*. Berkeley: University of California Press, 1988.

Booth, Wayne C., Gregory G. Colomb, and Joseph M. Williams. *The Craft of Research*. 3rd ed. Chicago: University of Chicago Press, 2008.

Borg, Marcus J. *Speaking Christian: Why Christian Words Have Lost Their Meaning and Power—and How They Can Be Restored*. New York: HarperOne, 2011.

Bottigheimer, Ruth. *The Bible for Children: From the Age of Gutenberg to the Present*. New Haven: Yale University Press, 1996.

Bower, Peter C., ed. *Handbook for the Revised Common Lectionary*. Louisville: Westminster John Knox, 1996.

Bowler, Kate. *Blessed: A History of the American Prosperity Gospel*. Oxford: Oxford University Press, 2013.

Boyce, Richard Nelson. *The Cry to God in the Old Testament*. SBLDS 103. Atlanta: Scholars Press, 1988.

Boyd, Brian. *Why Lyrics Last: Evolution, Cognition, and Shakespeare's Sonnets*. Cambridge, MA: Harvard University Press, 2012.

Boyer, Pascal. *Religion Explained: The Evolutionary Origins of Religious Thought*. New York: Basic Books, 2001.

Braulik, Georg. "The Sequence of the Laws in Deuteronomy 12–26 and in the Decalogue." In *A Song of Power and the Power of Song: Essays on the Book of Deuteronomy*, edited by Duane L. Christensen, 313–35. SBTS 3. Winona Lake, IN: Eisenbrauns, 1993.

Bright, John. *The Authority of the Old Testament*. Grand Rapids: Baker, 1975.

Brown, Raymond E. *The Birth of the Messiah: A Commentary on the Infancy Narratives in the Gospels of Matthew and Luke*. ABRL. New York: Doubleday, 1993.

———. *The Gospel according to John: Introduction, Translation, and Notes*. 2 vols. AB. Garden City, NY: Doubleday, 1966–70.

Brown, Warren S., and Brad D. Strawn. *The Physical Nature of Christian Life: Neuroscience, Psychology, and the Church*. New York: Cambridge University Press, 2012.

Brown, William P. "Happiness and Its Discontents in the Psalms." In *The Bible and the Pursuit of Happiness: What the Old and New Testaments Teach Us about the Good Life*, edited by Brent A. Strawn, 95–115. Oxford: Oxford University Press, 2012.

Brueggemann, Walter. *The Book That Breathes New Life: Scriptural Authority and Biblical Theology*. Minneapolis: Fortress, 2005.

———. *The Collected Sermons of Walter Brueggemann*. 2 vols. Louisville: Westminster John Knox, 2001–15.

———. "The Costly Loss of Lament." *JSOT* 36 (1986): 57–71.

———. "The Costly Loss of Praise." In *The Psalms and the Life of Faith*, edited by Patrick D. Miller, 98–111. Minneapolis: Fortress, 1995.

———. *The Creative Word: Canon as a Model for Biblical Education*. 2nd ed. Minneapolis: Fortress, 2015.

———. *Divine Presence amid Violence: Contextualizing the Book of Joshua*. Eugene, OR: Cascade, 2009.

———. "'Exodus' in the Plural (Amos 9:7)." In *Texts That Linger, Words That Explode*, edited by Patrick D. Miller, 89–103, 125–29. Minneapolis: Fortress, 2000.

———. *From Whom No Secrets Are Hid: Introducing the Psalms*. Edited by Brent A. Strawn. Louisville: Westminster John Knox, 2014.

———. *Inscribing the Text: Sermons and Prayers of Walter Brueggemann*. Edited by Anna Carter Florence. Minneapolis: Fortress, 2004.

———. *The Land: Place as Gift, Promise, and Challenge in Biblical Faith*. 2nd ed. OBT. Minneapolis: Fortress, 2002.

———. *A Pathway of Interpretation: The Old Testament for Pastors and Students*. Eugene, OR: Cascade, 2008.

———. "The Preacher as Scribe." In *Inscribing the Text: Sermons and Prayers of Walter Brueggemann*, edited by Anna Carter Florence, 5–19. Minneapolis: Fortress, 2004.

———. "Preaching a Sub-Version." *ThTo* 55 (1998): 195–212.

———. *The Prophetic Imagination*. 2nd ed. Minneapolis: Fortress, 2001.

———. Review of *A New Testament Biblical Theology*, by G. K. Beale. *Int* 67 (2013): 74–76.

———. "Sometimes Wave, Sometimes Particle." *CBR* 8 (2010): 376–85.

———. "That the World May Be Redescribed." *Int* 56 (2002): 359–67.

———. *Theology of the Old Testament: Testimony, Dispute, Advocacy*. Minneapolis: Fortress, 1997.

———. *The Threat of Life: Sermons on Pain, Power, and Weakness*. Edited by Charles L. Campbell. Minneapolis: Fortress, 1996.

Brueggemann, Walter, with Carolyn J. Sharp. *Living Countertestimony: Conversations with Walter Brueggemann*. Louisville: Westminster John Knox, 2012.

Buechner, Frederick. *The Magnificent Defeat*. San Francisco: HarperSanFrancisco, 1985.

Bullock, Barbara E., and Almeida Jacqueline Toribio, eds. *The Cambridge Handbook of Linguistic Code-Switching*. Cambridge: Cambridge University Press, 2009.

Butler, G. Paul, ed. *Best Sermons: 1944 Selection*. Chicago: Ziff Davis, 1944.

———, ed. *Best Sermons: 1946 Edition.* New York: Harper & Bros., 1946.

———, ed. *Best Sermons: 1947–1948 Edition.* New York: Harper & Bros., 1947.

———, ed. *Best Sermons: 1949–1950 Edition.* New York: Harper & Bros., 1949.

———, ed. *Best Sermons: 1951–1952 Edition.* New York: Macmillan, 1952.

———, ed. *Best Sermons: 1955 Edition.* New York: McGraw-Hill, 1955.

———, ed. *Best Sermons.* Vol. 7, *1959–1960 Protestant Edition.* New York: Crowell, 1959.

———, ed. *Best Sermons.* Vol. 8, *1962 Protestant Edition.* Princeton: D. Van Nostrand, 1962.

———, ed. *Best Sermons.* Vol. 9, *1964 Protestant Edition.* Princeton: D. Van Nostrand, 1964.

———, ed. *Best Sermons.* Vol. 10, *1966–1968 Protestant Edition.* New York: Trident, 1968.

Caine, Kenneth W. *The Positive Bible: From Genesis to Revelation; Scripture That Inspires, Nurtures and Heals.* 1998. Reprint, New York: HarperCollins, 1999.

Callen, Barry L. *Beneath the Surface: Reclaiming the Old Testament for Today's Christian.* Lexington: Emeth, 2012.

Calvin, John. *Institutes of the Christian Religion.* Edited by John T. McNeill and translated by Ford Lewis Battles. 2 vols. LCC 20. Philadelphia: Westminster, 1960.

Campbell, Charles L. Foreword to *The Threat of Life: Sermons on Pain, Power, and Weakness*, by Walter Brueggemann, vii–xi. Minneapolis: Fortress, 1996.

Campbell, Gordon. *Bible: The Story of the King James Version 1611–2011.* Oxford: Oxford University Press, 2010.

Campenhausen, Hans von. *The Formation of the Christian Bible.* Translated by J. A. Baker. Philadelphia: Fortress, 1972. Original German ed., 1968.

Cariello, Sergio. *The Action Bible: New Testament.* Colorado Springs: David C. Cook, 2011.

Carlson, Melody, and Alexi Natchev. *The Prayer of Jabez for Little Ones.* Nashville: Nelson, 2001.

Carr, David M. *Writing on the Tablet of the Heart: Origins of Scripture and Literature.* Oxford: Oxford University Press, 2005.

Carroll, Robert P. *Wolf in the Sheepfold: The Bible as Problematic for Theology.* 2nd ed. London: SCM, 1997.

Carson, D. A. "James." In *Commentary on the New Testament Use of the Old Testament*, edited by G. K. Beale and D. A. Carson, 997–1013. Grand Rapids: Baker Academic, 2007.

Catholic Church: Liturgy and Ritual. *Ordo lectionum Missae.* Vatican City: Typis Polyglottis Vaticanis, 1969.

Center for the Study of Religion and American Culture. "The Bible in American Life." March 6, 2014. http://www.raac.iupui.edu/files/2713/9413/8354/Bible_in_American_Life_Report_March_6_2014.pdf.

Chapman, Stephen B. *The Law and the Prophets: A Study in Old Testament Canon Formation.* FAT 27. Tübingen: Mohr Siebeck, 2000.

———. "Martial Memory, Peaceable Vision: Divine War in the Old Testament." In *Holy War in the Bible: Christian Morality and an Old Testament Problem*, edited by Heath Thomas, Jeremy Evans, and Paul Copan, 47–67. Downers Grove, IL: IVP Academic, 2013.

Charles, R. H. *A Critical and Exegetical Commentary on the Revelation of St. John.* 2 vols. ICC. New York: Charles Scribner's Sons, 1920.

Charlesworth, James H. *Jesus within Judaism: New Light from Exciting Archaeological Discoveries.* ABRL. New York: Doubleday, 1988.

Charry, Ellen T. "Academic Theology in Pastoral Perspective." *ThTo* 50 (1993): 90–104.

———. *By the Renewing of Your Minds: The Pastoral Function of Christian Doctrine.* New York: Oxford University Press, 1997.

———. *God and the Art of Happiness.* Grand Rapids: Eerdmans, 2010.

Chaves, Mark. *American Religion: Contemporary Trends.* Princeton: Princeton University Press, 2011.

Childs, Brevard S. *Biblical Theology in Crisis.* Philadelphia: Westminster, 1970.

———. *Biblical Theology of the Old and New Testaments: Theological Reflection on the Christian Bible.* Minneapolis: Fortress, 1992.

———. *Isaiah: A Commentary.* OTL. Louisville: Westminster John Knox, 2000.

———. "The Nature of the Christian Bible: One Book, Two Testaments." In *The Rule of Faith: Scripture, Canon, and Creed in a Critical Age*, edited by Ephraim Radner and George Sumner, 115–25. Harrisburg, PA: Morehouse, 1998.

———. *The New Testament as Canon: An Introduction.* 1984. Reprint, Valley Forge, PA: Trinity, 1994.

Chomsky, Noam. *On Language: Chomsky's Classic Works "Language and Responsibility" and "Reflections on Language."* New York: New Press, 2007.

———. *Syntactic Structures.* The Hague: Mouton, 1957.

Chomsky, William. *Hebrew: The Eternal Language.* Philadelphia: Jewish Publication Society, 1957.

Clabeaux, John J. *A Lost Edition of the Letters of Paul: A Reassessment of the Text of the Pauline Corpus Attested by Marcion.* CBQMS 21. Washington, DC: Catholic Biblical Association, 1989.

———. "Marcion." *ABD* 4:514–16.

———. "Marcionite Prologues to Paul." *ABD* 4:520–21.

Clines, David J. A. "From Copenhagen to Oslo: What Has (and Has Not) Happened at Congresses of the IOSOT." In *On the Way to the Postmodern: Old Testament Essays, 1967–1998*, 1:194–221. 2 vols. JSOTSup 292–293. Sheffield: Sheffield Academic, 1998.

———. "From Salamanca to Cracow: What Has (and Has Not) Happened at SBL International Meetings." In *On the Way to the Postmodern: Old Testament Essays, 1967–1998*, 1:158–93. 2 vols. JSOTSup 292–93. Sheffield: Sheffield Academic, 1998.

Cohen, Benyamin. *My Jesus Year: A Rabbi's Son Wanders the Bible Belt in Search of His Own Faith.* New York: HarperCollins, 2008.

Cohen, Shaye J. D. *The Beginnings of Jewishness: Boundaries, Varieties, Uncertainties.* Berkeley: University of California Press, 1999.

Collins, John. J. "Apocrypha and Pseudepigrapha." In *Encyclopedia of the Dead Sea Scrolls*, edited by Lawrence H. Schiffman and James C. VanderKam, 1:35–39. New York: Oxford University Press, 2000.

Copan, Paul. *Did God Really Command Genocide? Coming to Terms with the Justice of God.* Grand Rapids: Baker Books, 2014.

———. *Is God a Moral Monster? Making Sense of the Old Testament God.* Grand Rapids: Baker Books, 2011.

Corner, Mark. Review of *The Nature of Doctrine: Religion and Theology in a*

Postliberal Age, by George A. Lindbeck. *MoTh* 3 (1986): 110–13.

Cotterell, Peter, and Max Turner. *Linguistics and Biblical Interpretation*. Downers Grove, IL: InterVarsity, 1989.

Cowles, C. S., Eugene H. Merrill, Daniel L. Gard, and Tremper Longman III. *Show Them No Mercy: 4 Views on God and Canaanite Genocide*. Grand Rapids: Zondervan, 2003.

Cox, James W., ed. *Best Sermons*. Vols. 1–3. San Francisco: Harper & Row, 1988–90.

———, ed. *Best Sermons*. Vols. 4–7. San Francisco: HarperSanFrancisco, 1991–94.

Craigie, Peter C. *The Problem of War in the Old Testament*. 1978. Reprint, Eugene, OR: Wipf & Stock, 2002.

Craigo-Snell, Shannon. "Command Performance: Rethinking Performance Interpretation in the Context of Divine Discourse." *MoTh* 16 (2000): 475–94.

Creach, Jerome F. D. *Violence in Scripture*. Interpretation. Louisville: Westminster John Knox, 2013.

Crystal, David. *The Cambridge Encyclopedia of the English Language*. 2nd ed. Cambridge: Cambridge University Press, 2003.

———. "The Death of Language." *Prospect* (November 1999): 56–58.

———. *Language Death*. Cambridge: Cambridge University Press, 2000.

———. *A Little Book of Language*. New Haven: Yale University Press, 2010.

Davis, Ellen F. *Getting Involved with God: Rediscovering the Old Testament*. Cambridge: Cowley, 2001.

———. *Imagination Shaped: Old Testament Preaching in the Anglican Tradition*. Valley Forge, PA: Trinity, 1995.

———. "Losing a Friend: The Loss of the Old Testament to the Church." In *Jews, Christians, and the Theology of the Hebrew Scriptures*, edited by Alice Ogden Bellis and Joel S. Kaminsky, 83–94. SymS 8. Atlanta: Society of Biblical Literature, 2000.

———. *Wondrous Depth: Preaching the Old Testament*. Louisville: Westminster John Knox, 2005.

Dawkins, Richard. *The God Delusion*. Boston: Houghton Mifflin, 2006.

———. *River out of Eden: A Darwinian View of Life*. London: Weidenfeld & Nicholson, 1995.

Dawson, John David. *Christian Figural Reading and the Fashioning of Identity*. Berkeley: University of California Press, 2002.

Day, John, ed. *The Recovery of the Ancient Hebrew Language: The Lexicographical Writings of D. Winton Thomas*. Sheffield: Sheffield Phoenix, 2013.

Dean, Kenda Creasy. *Almost Christian: What the Faith of Our Teenagers Is Telling the American Church*. Oxford: Oxford University Press, 2010.

De Hamel, Christopher. *The Book: A History of the Bible*. London: Phaidon, 2001.

Delaney, Carol. *Abraham on Trial: The Social Legacy of Biblical Myth*. Princeton: Princeton University Press, 1998.

Delitzsch, Friedrich. *Babel and Bible: Two Lectures on the Significance of Assyriological Research for Religion*. Translated by Thomas J. McCormack and W. H. Carruth. Chicago: Open Court, 1903.

———. *Die grosse Täuschung*. Stuttgart: Deutsche Verlags-Anstalt, 1921.

Dennett, Daniel C. *Breaking the Spell: Religion as a Natural Phenomenon*. New York: Penguin, 2006.

Detmers, Achim. "Die Interpretation der Israel-Lehre Marcions im ersten Drittel des 20. Jahrhunderts." In *Marcion und seine kirchengeschichtliche Wirkung / Marcion and His Impact on Church History*, edited by Gerhard May and Katharina

Greschat, 275–92. TU 150. Berlin: de Gruyter, 2002.

Deutscher, Guy. *Through the Language Glass: Why the World Looks Different in Other Languages*. New York: Metropolitan, 2010.

de Villiers, Pieter G. R., and Jan Willem van Henden, eds. *Coping with Violence in the New Testament*. STR 16. Leiden: Brill, 2012.

Dewey, John. *Experience and Education: The 60th Anniversary Edition*. West Lafayette, IN: Kappa Delta Pi, 1998.

Dobbs-Allsopp, F. W. *On Biblical Poetry*. Oxford: Oxford University Press, 2015.

Dollar, Creflo. *The Holy Spirit, Your Financial Advisor: God's Plan for Debt-Free Money Management*. New York: FaithWords, 2013.

Dorian, Nancy C., ed. *Investigating Obsolescence: Studies in Language Contraction and Death*. Studies in the Social and Cultural Foundations of Language 7. Cambridge: Cambridge University Press, 1989.

———. "The Problem of the Semi-Speaker in Language Death." *International Journal of the Sociology of Language* 12 (1977): 23–32.

Douthat, Ross. "God and the Details." *New York Times*, October 6, 2010. http://douthat.blogs.nytimes.com/2010/10/06/god-and-the-details/.

Downing, F. Gerald. *Has Christianity a Revelation?* Philadelphia: Westminster, 1964.

Dunn, Stephen. "At the Smithville Methodist Church." In *New and Selected Poems, 1974–1994*, 183–84. New York: Norton, 1995.

Eagleton, Terry. *Reason, Faith, and Revolution: Reflections on the God Debate*. New Haven: Yale University Press, 2009.

Earl, Douglas S. "The Christian Significance of Deuteronomy 7." *JTI* 3 (2009): 41–62.

———. *The Joshua Delusion? Rethinking Genocide in the Bible*. Eugene, OR: Cascade, 2010.

———. *Reading Joshua as Christian Scripture*. JTISup 2. Winona Lake, IN: Eisenbrauns, 2010.

Eco, Umberto. *Experiences in Translation*. Toronto: University of Toronto Press, 2001.

Eller, Vernard. *The Language of Canaan and the Grammar of Feminism*. Grand Rapids: Eerdmans, 1982.

Elliot, Alison J. *Child Language*. CTL. Cambridge: Cambridge University Press, 1981.

Elson, John Truscott. "Changing Theologies for a Changing World." *Time*, December 26, 1969.

———, ed. "The God Is Dead Movement." *Time*, October 22, 1965.

———. "Is God Coming Back to Life?" *Time*, December 26, 1969.

———. "Theology: Toward a Hidden God." *Time*, April 8, 1966.

Enns, Peter. *Inspiration and Incarnation: Evangelicals and the Problem of the Old Testament*. Grand Rapids: Baker Academic, 2005.

Episcopal Church, The. *The Book of Common Prayer*. New York, Seabury, 1979.

Erasmus, Desiderius. "Preparing for Death: *De praeparatione ad mortem*." In *Collected Works of Erasmus*, translated and annotated by John N. Grant and edited by John W. O'Malley, 390–450. Toronto: University of Toronto Press, 1998.

Ericksen, Robert P. *Theologians under Hitler: Gerhard Kittel, Paul Althaus, and Emanuel Hirsch*. New Haven: Yale University Press, 1985.

Evans, Ernest, ed. and trans. *Tertullian: Adversus Marcionem*. 2 vols. Oxford: Clarendon, 1972.

Evans, Rachel Held. *A Year of Biblical Womanhood: How a Liberated Woman*

Found Herself Sitting on Her Roof, Covering Her Head, and Calling Her Husband "Master." Nashville: Nelson, 2012.

Farrar, Frederic W. *History of Interpretation.* Grand Rapids: Baker, 1961.

Fassberg, Stephen E., and Avi Hurvitz, eds. *Biblical Hebrew in Its Northwest Semitic Setting: Typological and Historical Perspectives.* Jerusalem: Magnes; Winona Lake, IN: Eisenbrauns, 2006.

Fawcett, Bruce, and Jody Linkletter. "Bible Reading and Adolescents' Attitudes toward Sexual Practices and Substance Abuse." In *From Biblical Criticism to Biblical Faith: Essays in Honor of Lee Martin McDonald,* edited by William H. Brackney and Craig A. Evans, 406–21. Macon, GA: Mercer University Press, 2007.

Firth, David G. "Passing on the Faith in Deuteronomy." In *Interpreting Deuteronomy: Issues and Approaches,* edited by David G. Firth and Philip S. Johnston, 157–76. Downers Grove, IL: IVP Academic, 2012.

Fishbane, Michael. *Biblical Interpretation in Ancient Israel.* Oxford: Clarendon, 1988.

———. *The Exegetical Imagination: On Jewish Thought and Theology.* Cambridge, MA: Harvard University Press, 1998.

Fitzmyer, Joseph A. *The Gospel according to Luke: Introduction, Translation, and Notes.* 2 vols. AB. New York: Doubleday, 1981–85.

Ford, David F. *Theology: A Very Short Introduction.* 2nd ed. Oxford: Oxford University Press, 2013.

Foster, Marshall, and Peter A. Lillback, eds. *1599 Geneva Bible: Patriot's Edition.* 2nd ed. White Hall, WV: Tolle Lege Press, 2010.

Fox, Michael V. *Proverbs 10–31: A New Translation with Introduction and Commentary.* AB. New Haven: Yale University Press, 2009.

Frankfort, Harry G. *On Bullshit.* Princeton: Princeton University Press, 2005.

Fredricksen, Paula. *Augustine and the Jews: A Christian Defense of Jews and Judaism.* New York: Doubleday, 2008.

Frei, Hans W. *The Eclipse of Biblical Narrative: A Study in Eighteenth and Nineteenth Century Hermeneutics.* New Haven: Yale University Press, 1974.

Frerichs, Ernest S. "Children's Bibles." In Metzger and Coogan, *Oxford Companion to the Bible,* 108–9.

Fretheim, Terence E. "God, Creation, and the Pursuit of Happiness." In *The Bible and the Pursuit of Happiness: What the Old and New Testaments Teach Us about the Good Life,* edited by Brent A. Strawn, 33–55. Oxford: Oxford University Press, 2012.

Frye, Northrop. *The Great Code: The Bible and Literature.* New York: Harcourt Brace Jovanovich, 1982.

Frymer-Kensky, Tikva. *Studies in the Bible and Feminist Criticism.* Philadelphia: Jewish Publication Society, 2006.

Garber, Zev. "Amalek and Amalekut: A Homiletical Lesson." In *Jewish Bible Theology: Perspectives and Case Studies,* edited by Isaac Kalimi, 147–59. Winona Lake, IN: Eisenbrauns, 2012.

Gardner-Chloros, Penelope. *Code-Switching.* Cambridge: Cambridge University Press, 2009.

———. "Sociolinguistic Factors in Code-Switching." In *The Cambridge Handbook of Linguistic Code-Switching,* edited by Barbara E. Bullock and Almeida Jacqueline Toribio, 97–113. Cambridge: Cambridge University Press, 2009.

Garman, Michael. *Psycholinguistics.* CTL. Cambridge: Cambridge University Press, 1990.

Garrison, Becky. *The New Atheist Crusaders and Their Unholy Grail: The Misguided*

Quest to Destroy Your Faith. Nashville: Nelson, 2007.

Gee, James Paul. *Situated Language and Learning: A Critique of Traditional Schooling*. New York: Routledge, 2004.

———. *The Social Mind: Language, Ideology, and Social Practice*. New York: Bergin & Garvey, 1992.

Geertz, Clifford. *The Interpretation of Cultures*. New York: Basic Books, 1973.

Gillingham, Susan E. *One Bible, Many Voices: Different Approaches to Biblical Studies*. Grand Rapids: Eerdmans, 1999.

Glinert, Lewis. *The Grammar of Modern Hebrew*. Cambridge: Cambridge University Press, 1989.

Goldhagen, Daniel Jonah. *Hitler's Willing Executioners: Ordinary Germans and the Holocaust*. New York: Knopf, 1996.

Goldingay, John. *Do We Need the New Testament? Letting the Old Testament Speak for Itself*. Downers Grove, IL: IVP Academic, 2015.

———. *Key Questions about Christian Faith: Old Testament Answers*. Grand Rapids: Baker Academic, 2010.

Goodman, Nelson. *Ways of Worldmaking*. Indianapolis: Hackett, 1978.

Gortner, E. M., S. S. Rude, and J. W. Pennebaker. "Benefits of Expressive Writing in Lowering Rumination and Depressive Symptoms." *Behavior Therapy* 37 (2006): 292–303.

Grant, Robert M. "Marcion, Gospel of." *ABD* 4:516–20.

Grant, Robert M., and David Tracy. *A Short History of the Interpretation of the Bible*. 2nd ed. Philadelphia: Fortress, 1984.

Green, Joel B. *The Gospel of Luke*. NICNT. Grand Rapids: Eerdmans, 1997.

Greenslade, S. L. "English Versions of the Bible, A.D. 1525–1611." In *The Cambridge History of the Bible*, vol. 3, *The West from the Reformation to the Present Day*, edited by S. L. Greenslade, 141–74. Cambridge: Cambridge University Press, 1963.

Greidanus, Sidney. *Preaching Christ from Daniel: Foundations for Expository Sermons*. Grand Rapids: Eerdmans, 2012.

———. *Preaching Christ from Ecclesiastes: Foundations for Expository Sermons*. Grand Rapids: Eerdmans, 2010.

———. *Preaching Christ from Genesis: Foundations for Expository Sermons*. Grand Rapids: Eerdmans, 2007.

———. *Preaching Christ from the Old Testament: A Contemporary Hermeneutical Method*. Grand Rapids: Eerdmans, 1999.

Grenoble, Lenore A., and Lindsay J. Whaley. *Saving Languages: An Introduction to Language Revitalization*. Cambridge: Cambridge University Press, 2006.

Gunneweg, A. H. J. *Understanding the Old Testament*. Translated by John Bowden. OTL. Philadelphia: Westminster, 1978.

Hadaway, C. Kirk, Penny Marler, and Mark Chaves. "Overreporting Church Attendance in America: Evidence That Demands the Same Verdict." *ASR* 63 (1998): 122–30.

———. "What the Polls Don't Show: A Closer Look at U.S. Church Attendance." *ASR* 58 (1993): 741–52.

Hagège, Claude. *On the Death and Life of Languages*. Translated by Jody Gladding. New Haven: Yale University Press, 2009.

Hale, Ken, et al. "Endangered Languages." *Language* 68 (1992): 1–42.

Hall, Stuart George. "Marcion." In *The SCM Dictionary of Biblical Interpretation*, edited by R. J. Coggins and J. L. Houlden, 422–24. London: SCM, 1990.

Hancock, Ian F. "On the Origins of the Term Pidgin." In *Readings in Creole Studies*, edited by I. F. Hancock et al., 81–88. Ghent: E. Story-Scientia, 1979.

Harmless, William. *Augustine and the Cat-echumenate*. Collegeville, MN: Liturgical Press, 1995.

Harnack, Adolf von. *History of Dogma*. Translated by Neil Buchanan et al. 7 vols. Boston: Little, Brown, 1898–1901.

———. *Marcion: Das Evangelium vom fremden Gott; Eine Monographie zur Geschichte der Grundlegung der katholischen Kirche*. Leipzig: Hinrichs, 1921. 2nd ed., 1924.

———. *Marcion: The Gospel of the Alien God*. Translated by John E. Steely and Lyle D. Bierma. Eugene, OR: Wipf & Stock, 2007. Original German eds., 1921, 1924.

———. *Militia Christi: The Christian Religion and the Military in the First Three Centuries*. Translated by David McInnes Gracie. Philadelphia: Fortress, 1981. Original German ed., 1905.

———. *Outlines of the History of Dogma*. Translated by Edwin Knox Mitchell. Boston: Beacon, 1957. Original German ed., 1893.

Harris, Sam. *The End of Faith: Religion, Terror, and the Future of Reason*. New York: Norton, 2004.

———. *Letter to a Christian Nation*. 2006. Reprint, New York: Vintage, 2008.

Harrison, K. David. *The Last Speakers: The Quest to Save the World's Most Endangered Languages*. Washington, DC: National Geographic, 2010.

———. *When Languages Die: The Extinction of the World's Languages and the Erosion of Human Knowledge*. Oxford: Oxford University Press, 2007.

Hart, David Bentley. *Atheist Delusions: The Christian Revolution and Its Fashionable Enemies*. New Haven: Yale University Press, 2009.

Hartenstein, Friedhelm. "Zur Bedeutung des Alten Testaments für die evangelische Kirche: Eine Auseinandersetzung mit den Thesen von Notger Slenczka." *TLZ* 140 (2015): 738–51.

Hartley, John E. *Leviticus*. WBC. Nashville: Nelson, 1992.

Hartung, John. "Love Thy Neighbor: The Evolution of In-Group Morality." *Skeptic* 3, no. 4 (1995): 86–99. Forum discussion thereon. *Skeptic* 4, no. 1 (1996): 24–31. http://strugglesforexistence.com/?p =article_p&id=13.

Hasel, Gerhard F. *Old Testament Theology: Basic Issues in the Current Debate*. 4th ed. Grand Rapids: Eerdmans, 1991.

Hauerwas, Stanley. *Unleashing the Scripture: Freeing the Bible from Captivity to America*. Nashville: Abingdon, 1993.

———. *Working with Words: On Learning to Speak Christian*. Eugene, OR: Cascade, 2011.

Haught, John F. *God and the New Atheism: A Critical Response to Dawkins, Harris, and Hitchens*. Louisville: Westminster John Knox, 2008.

Hays, Christopher B. *Death in the Iron Age II and in First Isaiah*. FAT 79. Tübingen: Mohr Siebeck, 2011.

Hays, Richard B. *The Conversion of the Imagination: Paul as Interpreter of Israel's Scripture*. Grand Rapids: Eerdmans, 2005.

———. *Echoes of Scripture in the Letters of Paul*. New Haven: Yale University Press, 1989.

———. *Reading Backwards: Figural Christology and the Fourfold Gospel Witness*. Waco: Baylor University Press, 2014.

Helm, David. *The Big Picture Story Bible*. Wheaton: Crossway, 2004.

Hens-Piazza, Gina. *The New Historicism*. GBS. Minneapolis: Fortress, 2002.

Heschel, Abraham J. *The Prophets*. 1962. Reprint, New York: Perennial Classics, 2001.

Hitchens, Christopher. *God Is Not Great: How Religion Poisons Everything.* New York: Twelve, 2007.

Hock, Hans Henrich. *Principles of Historical Linguistics.* 2nd ed. Berlin: Mouton de Gruyter, 1991.

Holladay, William L. "How the Twenty-Third Psalm Became an American Secular Icon." In *The Psalms through Three Thousand Years: Prayerbook of a Cloud of Witnesses,* 359–71. Minneapolis: Fortress, 1993.

———. *The Psalms through Three Thousand Years: Prayerbook of a Cloud of Witnesses.* Minneapolis: Fortress, 1993.

Holland, Scott. *How Do Stories Save Us? An Essay on the Question with the Theological Hermeneutics of David Tracy in View.* Louvain Theological and Pastoral Monographs 35. Louvain: Peeters; Grand Rapids: Eerdmans, 2006.

Holm, John. *An Introduction to Pidgins and Creoles.* CTL. Cambridge: Cambridge University Press, 2000.

Holmer, Paul L. *The Grammar of Faith.* San Francisco: Harper & Row, 1978.

Holmes, Peter, trans. "The Five Books against Marcion." By Tertullian. In *The Ante-Nicene Fathers,* vol. 3, *Latin Christianity: Its Founder, Tertullian,* edited by Alexander Roberts and James Donaldson, 269–475. New York: Christian Literature, 1885–96. Reprint, Grand Rapids: Eerdmans, 1950–51.

Hoskyns, Edwyn Clements. *Cambridge Sermons.* London: SPCK, 1938.

Houtman, Cornelis. *Exodus.* 4 vols. HCOT. Kampen: Kok, 1993–2002.

Hunter, Rodney J. "Ministry—or Magic?" *PSB* 1 (1977): 61–67.

Hur, Shin Wook. "The Rhetoric of the Deuteronomic Code: Its Structures and Devices." PhD diss., Emory University, 2013.

Jacobs, A. J. *The Year of Living Biblically: One Man's Humble Quest to Follow the Bible as Literally as Possible.* New York: Simon & Schuster, 2007.

Jacobson, Claire. "Translator's Preface." In *Structural Anthropology,* by Claude Lévi-Strauss, translated by Claire Jacobsen and Brooke Grundfest Schoepf. New York: Basic Books, 1963.

Jameson, Fredric. *The Prison-House of Language: A Critical Account of Structuralism and Russian Formalism.* Princeton: Princeton University Press, 1972.

Janzen, J. Gerald. "'And Not We Ourselves': Psalm 100:3 and the Eschatological Reign of God." In *When Prayer Takes Place: Forays into a Biblical World,* edited by Brent A. Strawn and Patrick D. Miller, 99–133. Eugene, OR: Cascade, 2012.

———. "Revisiting 'Forever' in Psalm 23:6." In *When Prayer Takes Place: Forays into a Biblical World,* edited by Brent A. Strawn and Patrick D. Miller, 188–208. Eugene, OR: Cascade, 2012.

Jasper, David. "The Death and Rebirth of Religious Language." *Religion and Literature* 28 (1996): 5–19.

Jenkins, Philip. *Laying Down the Sword: Why We Can't Ignore the Bible's Violent Verses.* San Francisco: HarperOne, 2011.

Jenson, Robert W. *Canon and Creed.* Interpretation. Louisville: Westminster John Knox, 2010.

———. *Systematic Theology.* 2 vols. New York: Oxford University Press, 1997–99.

Johnson, Luke Timothy. "Imagining the World Scripture Imagines." *MoTh* 14 (1998): 165–80.

———. *The Writings of the New Testament: An Interpretation.* 3rd ed. Minneapolis: Fortress, 2010.

Johnstone, Barbara. "An Introduction." *Text* 7 (1987): 205–14.

Jones, Laurie Beth. *Jesus, Career Counselor: How to Find (and Keep) Your Perfect Work.* New York: Howard, 2010.

———. *Jesus, CEO: Using Ancient Wisdom for Visionary Leadership*. New York: Hyperion, 1995.

———. *Jesus, Entrepreneur: Using Ancient Wisdom to Launch and Live Your Dreams*. New York: Crown Business, 2002.

———. *Jesus, Inc.: The Visionary Path*. New York: Crown Business, 2001.

———. *Jesus, Life Coach: Learn from the Best*. Nashville: Nelson, 2006.

Joüon, Paul, and T. Muraoka. *A Grammar of Biblical Hebrew*. 2 vols. SB 14.1–2. Rome: Pontifical Biblical Institute, 1993.

Juel, Donald. "A Disquieting Silence: The Matter of the Ending." In *The Ending of Mark and the Ends of God: Essays in Memory of Donald Harrisville Juel*, edited by Beverly Roberts Gaventa and Patrick D. Miller, 1–14. Louisville: Westminster John Knox, 2005.

———. *Messianic Exegesis: Christological Interpretation of the Old Testament in Early Christianity*. Philadelphia: Fortress, 1987.

Kaltner, John, and Steven L. McKenzie. *The Back Door Introduction to the Bible*. Winona, MN: Anselm Academic, 2012.

Kaminsky, Joel S. "New Testament and Rabbinic Views of Election." In *Jewish Bible Theology: Perspectives and Case Studies*, edited by Isaac Kalimi, 119–46. Winona Lake, IN: Eisenbrauns, 2012.

———. *Yet I Loved Jacob: Reclaiming the Biblical Concept of Election*. Nashville: Abingdon, 2007.

Kaminsky, Joel S., and Joel N. Lohr. *The Torah: A Beginner's Guide*. Oxford: Oneworld, 2011.

Kang, Sa-Moon. *Divine War in the Old Testament and in the Ancient Near East*. BZAW 177. Berlin: de Gruyter, 1989.

Katsh, Abraham I. *The Biblical Heritage of American Democracy*. New York: Ktav, 1977.

Kaufman, Gordon D. Review of *The Nature of Doctrine: Religion and Theology in a Postliberal Age*, by George A. Lindbeck. *ThTo* 42 (1985): 240–41.

Kaufman, Stephen A. "The Structure of the Deuteronomic Law." *Maarav* 1 (1978–79): 105–58.

Kawin, Bruce F. *Telling It Again and Again: Repetition in Literature and Film*. Boulder: University Press of Colorado, 1989.

Keel, Othmar, and Christoph Uehlinger. *Gods, Goddesses, and Images of God in Ancient Israel*. Translated by Thomas H. Trapp. Minneapolis: Fortress, 1998.

Kellman, Steven G., ed. *Switching Languages: Translingual Writers Reflect on Their Craft*. Lincoln: University of Nebraska Press, 2003.

Kelsey, David H. *Proving Doctrine: The Uses of Scripture in Modern Theology*. 1975. Reprint, Valley Forge, PA: Trinity, 1999.

Kennedy, X. J., and Dana Gioia. *An Introduction to Poetry*. 11th ed. New York: Pearson Longman, 2005.

Kenyon, E. W. *The Two Kinds of Faith: Faith's Secret Revealed*. 1942. Reprint, Lynnwood, WA: Kenyon's Gospel Publishing Society, 1998.

Kierkegaard, Søren. *Fear and Trembling, and The Sickness unto Death*. Translated with introductions and notes by Walter Lowrie. Garden City, NY: Doubleday, 1954.

Kim, Eo Kon. "'Outcry': Its Context in Biblical Theology." *Int* 42 (1988): 229–39.

King, Philip J., and Lawrence E. Stager. *Life in Biblical Israel*. LAI. Louisville: Westminster John Knox, 2001.

Kingsmill, Edmée. "The Psalms: A Monastic Perspective." In *The Oxford Handbook of the Psalms*, edited by William P. Brown, 596–607. Oxford: Oxford University Press, 2014.

————. *The Song of Songs and the Eros of God: A Study in Biblical Intertextuality*. OTM. Oxford: Oxford University Press, 2009.

Kinnaman, David, with Aly Hawkins. *You Lost Me: Why Young Christians Are Leaving Church . . . and Rethinking Faith*. Grand Rapids: Baker Books, 2011.

Kinzig, Wolfram. "Ein Ketzer und sein Konstrukteur: Harnacks Marcion." In *Marcion und seine kirchengeschichtliche Wirkung / Marcion and His Impact on Church History*, edited by Gerhard May and Katharina Greschat, 253–74. TU 150. Berlin: de Gruyter, 2002.

Klassen, William. "Marcion." In *The Dictionary of Biblical Interpretation*, edited by John H. Hayes, 2:123. 2 vols. Nashville: Abingdon, 1999.

Klein, Wolfgang. *Second Language Acquisition*. CTL. Cambridge: Cambridge University Press, 1986.

Knohl, Israel. *The Divine Symphony: The Bible's Many Voices*. Philadelphia: Jewish Publication Society, 2003.

Kort, Wesley A. *"Take, Read": Scripture, Textuality, and Cultural Practice*. University Park: Pennsylvania State University Press, 1996.

Kraeling, Emil G. *The Old Testament since the Reformation*. New York: Schocken, 1969.

Kristof, Nicholas D. "Test Your Savvy on Religion." *New York Times*, October 9, 2010. http://www.nytimes.com/2010/10/10/opinion/10kristof.html.

Kroskrity, Paul V., ed. *Telling Stories in the Face of Danger: Language Renewal in Native American Communities*. Norman: University of Oklahoma Press, 2012.

Kugel, James L. *The Idea of Biblical Poetry: Parallelism and Its History*. New Haven: Yale University Press, 1981.

Kutscher, Eduard Yechezkel. *A History of the Hebrew Language*. Edited by Raphael Kutscher. Jerusalem: Magnes; Leiden: Brill, 1982.

————. *The Language and Linguistic Background of the Isaiah Scroll (1 Q Isaᵃ)*. STDJ 6. Leiden: Brill, 1974.

Laderman, Gary. *American Civil Religion*. Minneapolis: Fortress, 2013.

Lakoff, George, and Mark Johnson. *Metaphors We Live By*. Chicago: University of Chicago Press, 2003.

————. *Philosophy in the Flesh: The Embodied Mind and Its Challenge to Western Thought*. New York: Basic Books, 1999.

Lamb, David T. *God Behaving Badly: Is the God of the Old Testament Angry, Sexist and Racist?* Downers Grove, IL: InterVarsity, 2001.

Langacker, Ronald W. *Cognitive Grammar: A Basic Introduction*. Oxford: Oxford University Press, 2008.

Lash, Nicholas. *Believing Three Ways in One God: A Reading of the Apostles' Creed*. Notre Dame, IN: University of Notre Dame Press, 1993.

LaSor, William Sanford, David Allan Hubbard, and Frederic William Bush. *Old Testament Survey: The Message, Form, and Background of the Old Testament*. 2nd ed. Grand Rapids: Eerdmans, 1996.

Lave, Jean, and Etienne Wenger. *Situated Learning: Legitimate Peripheral Participation*. Cambridge: Cambridge University Press, 1991.

Lebreton, Jules. "Bulletin d'histoire des origines chrétiennes." *Recherches de science religieuse* 15 (1925): 320–90.

Lebreton, Jules, and Jacques Zeiller. *The History of the Primitive Church*. Translated by Ernest C. Messenger. 4 vols. London: Burns, Oates & Washbourne, 1942–48.

Lee, Richard, ed. *The American Patriot's Bible, KJV: The Word of God and the Shaping of America*. Nashville: Nelson, 2012.

————, ed. *The Young American Patriot's Bible: The Word of God and the Heroes That Shaped America*. Nashville: Nelson, 2011.

Legaspi, Michael C. *The Death of Scripture and the Rise of Biblical Studies*. Oxford: Oxford University Press, 2010.

LeMon, Joel M., and Brent A. Strawn. "Parallelism." In *Dictionary of the Old Testament: Wisdom, Poetry and Writings*, edited by Tremper Longman III and Peter Enns, 502–15. Downers Grove, IL: IVP Academic, 2008.

Lenchak, Timothy A. *"Choose Life!" A Rhetorical-Critical Investigation of Deuteronomy 28,69–30,20*. AnBib 129. Rome: Pontifical Biblical Institute, 1993.

Levenson, Jon D. *The Death and Resurrection of the Beloved Son: The Transformation of Child Sacrifice in Judaism and Christianity*. New Haven: Yale University Press, 1993.

————. *The Hebrew Bible, the Old Testament, and Historical Criticism: Jews and Christians in Biblical Studies*. Louisville: Westminster/John Knox, 1993.

————. *Resurrection and the Restoration of Israel: The Ultimate Victory of the God of Life*. New Haven: Yale University Press, 2008.

Levine, Baruch A. *Leviticus*. JPS Torah Commentary. Philadelphia: Jewish Publication Society, 1989/5749.

Levinson, Bernard M. *Deuteronomy and the Hermeneutics of Legal Innovation*. Oxford: Oxford University Press, 1997.

Lévi-Strauss, Claude. *Structural Anthropology*. Translated by Claire Jacobson and Brooke Grundfest Schoepf. New York: Basic Books, 1963.

Lewis, C. S. *The Great Divorce: A Dream*. 1946. Reprint, San Francisco: HarperSanFrancisco, 2001.

————. *The Lion, the Witch, and the Wardrobe*. 1950. Reprint, New York: HarperCollins, 1997.

Lewis, Sarah. *Positive Psychology at Work: How Positive Leadership and Appreciative Inquiry Create Inspiring Organizations*. Oxford: Wiley-Blackwell, 2011.

Lightbown, Patsy M., and Nina Spada. *How Languages Are Learned*. 3rd ed. Oxford: Oxford University Press, 2006.

Lincicum, David. *Paul and the Early Jewish Encounter with Deuteronomy*. WUNT 2.284. Tübingen: Mohr Siebeck, 2010.

Lind, Millard C. *Yahweh Is a Warrior: The Theology of Warfare in Ancient Israel*. Scottdale, PA: Herald Press, 1980.

Lindbeck, George A. *The Nature of Doctrine: Religion and Theology in a Postliberal Age*. 1984. Reprint, Louisville: Westminster John Knox, 2009.

————. "Postcritical Canonical Interpretation: Three Modes of Retrieval." In *Theological Exegesis: Essays in Honor of Brevard S. Childs*, edited by Christopher Seitz and Kathryn Greene-McCreight, 26–51. Grand Rapids: Eerdmans, 1999.

Löhr, Winrich. "Did Marcion Distinguish between a Just God and a Good God?" In *Marcion und seine kirchengeschichtliche Wirkung / Marcion and His Impact on Church History*, edited by Gerhard May and Katharina Greschat, 131–46. TU 150. Berlin: de Gruyter, 2002.

Long, Thomas G. *Preaching from Memory to Hope*. Louisville: Westminster John Knox, 2009.

————. "Preaching Moment 022." http://www.workingpreacher.org/preachingmoments.aspx?video_id=30.

Lundbom, Jack R. *Biblical Rhetoric and Rhetorical Criticism*. HBM 45. Sheffield: Sheffield Phoenix, 2013.

————. *Deuteronomy: A Commentary*. Grand Rapids: Eerdmans, 2013.

———. *Jeremiah: A Study in Ancient Hebrew Rhetoric*. 2nd ed. Winona Lake, IN: Eisenbrauns, 1997.

———. "The Lawbook of the Josianic Reform." *CBQ* 38 (1976): 293–302.

Lust, Barbara C. *Child Language: Acquisition and Growth*. CTL. Cambridge: Cambridge University Press, 2006.

Luther, Martin. "To the Councilmen of All Cities in Germany That They Establish and Maintain Christian Schools." In *Martin Luther's Basic Theological Writings*, edited by Timothy F. Lull and William R. Russell, 456–74. 3rd ed. Minneapolis: Fortress, 2012.

Madigan, Kevin J., and Jon D. Levenson. *Resurrection: The Power of God for Christians and Jews*. New Haven: Yale University Press, 2008.

Magrassi, Mariano. *Praying the Bible: An Introduction to Lectio Divina*. Collegeville, MN: Liturgical Press, 1998.

Mankowski, Paul V. *Akkadian Loanwords in Biblical Hebrew*. HSS 47. Winona Lake, IN: Eisenbrauns, 2000.

Marini, Stephen A. "Family Bible." In Metzger and Coogan, *Oxford Companion to the Bible*, 224–25.

Marsden, Richard, and E. Ann Matter, eds. *The New Cambridge History of the Bible*. Vol. 2, *From 600 to 1450*. Cambridge: Cambridge University Press, 2012.

Marshall, Bruce D. "Introduction: *The Nature of Doctrine* after 25 Years." In *The Nature of Doctrine: Religion and Theology in a Postliberal Age*, by George A. Lindbeck, vii–xxvii. Louisville: Westminster John Knox, 2009.

———. "Israel: Do Christians Worship the God of Israel?" In *Knowing the Triune God: The Work of the Spirit in the Practices of the Church*, edited by James J. Buckley and David S. Yeago, 231–64. Grand Rapids: Eerdmans, 2001.

Martin, Dale B. *Pedagogy of the Bible: An Analysis and Proposal*. Louisville: Westminster John Knox, 2008.

Martoia, Ron. *The Bible as Improv: Seeing and Living the Script in New Ways*. Grand Rapids: Zondervan, 2010.

Matras, Yaron. *Language Contact*. CTL. Cambridge: Cambridge University Press, 2009.

Matthews, P. H. *Oxford Concise Dictionary of Linguistics*. 3rd ed. Oxford: Oxford University Press, 2014.

May, Gerhard. "Marcion in Contemporary Views: Results and Open Questions." *The Second Century* 6 (1987–88): 129–51.

———. "Marcion ohne Harnack." In *Marcion und seine kirchengeschichtliche Wirkung / Marcion and His Impact on Church History*, edited by Gerhard May and Katharina Greschat, 1–7. TU 150. Berlin: de Gruyter, 2002.

May, Gerhard, and Katharina Greschat, eds. *Marcion und seine kirchengeschichtliche Wirkung / Marcion and His Impact on Church History*. TU 150. Berlin: de Gruyter, 2002.

McArthur, Thomas Burns, ed. *The Oxford Companion to the English Language*. Oxford: Oxford University Press, 1992.

McCann, J. Clinton. *A Theological Introduction to the Book of Psalms: The Psalms as Torah*. Nashville: Abingdon, 1993.

McClure, John S. *Mashup Religion: Pop Music and Theological Invention*. Waco: Baylor University Press, 2011.

McConnell, D. R. *A Different Gospel*. Peabody, MA: Hendrickson, 1988.

McConville, J. G. *Deuteronomy*. Apollos Old Testament Commentary 5. Leicester, UK: Apollos; Downers Grove, IL: InterVarsity, 2002.

McCrum, Robert. *Globish: How the English Language Became the World's Language*. New York: Norton, 2010.

McCurley, Foster R., Jr. *Proclaiming the Promise: Christian Preaching from the Old Testament.* Philadelphia: Fortress, 1974.

McDonald, Lee Martin. *The Biblical Canon: Its Origin, Transmission, and Authority.* 3rd ed. Peabody, MA: Hendrickson, 2007.

McKane, William. *Proverbs: A New Approach.* OTL. Philadelphia: Westminster, 1970.

McKibben, Bill. *The End of Nature.* New York: Random House, 2006.

McWhorter, John. *Defining Creole.* Oxford: Oxford University Press, 2005.

———. *Doing Our Own Thing: The Degradation of Language and Music and Why We Should, Like, Care.* New York: Gotham, 2003.

———. *The Language Hoax: Why the World Looks the Same in Any Language.* Oxford: Oxford University Press, 2014.

———. *Language Interrupted: Signs of Non-native Acquisition in Standard Language Grammars.* Oxford: Oxford University Press, 2007.

———. "Linguistics from the Left: The Truth about Black English That the Academy Doesn't Want You to Know." In *The Politically Correct University: Problems, Scope, and Reforms,* edited by Robert Maranto, Richard E. Redding, and Frederick M. Hess, 175–91. Washington, DC: AEI Press, 2009.

———. *The Missing Spanish Creoles: Recovering the Birth of Plantation Contact Languages.* Berkeley: University of California Press, 2000.

———. *Myths, Lies, and Half-Truths of Language Usage.* Chantilly, VA: Great Courses, 2012.

———. *Our Magnificent Bastard Tongue: The Untold History of English.* New York: Gotham, 2008.

———. *The Power of Babel: A Natural History of Language.* New York: Perennial, 2003.

———. *Spreading the Word: Language and Dialect in America.* Portsmouth, NH: Heinemann, 2000.

———. *The Story of Human Language.* 3 parts. Chantilly, VA: Teaching Company, 2004.

———. *Towards a New Model of Creole Genesis.* Studies in Ethnolinguistics 3. New York: Peter Lang, 1997.

———. *What Language Is: And What It Isn't and What It Could Be.* New York: Gotham, 2011.

———. *The Word on the Street: Fact and Fable about American English.* New York: Plenum, 1998.

Meisel, Jürgen M. *First and Second Language Acquisition: Parallels and Differences.* CTL. Cambridge: Cambridge University Press, 2011.

Metzger, Bruce M. "Curious Bibles." In Metzger and Coogan, *Oxford Companion to the Bible,* 143–44.

———. *An Introduction to the Apocrypha.* New York: Oxford University Press, 1957.

Metzger, Bruce M., and Michael D. Coogan, eds. *The Oxford Companion to the Bible.* Oxford: Oxford University Press, 1993.

Meurer, Siegfied, ed. *The Apocrypha in Ecumenical Perspective: The Place of the Late Writings of the Old Testament among the Biblical Writings and Their Significance in the Eastern and Western Church Traditions.* Translated by Paul Ellingworth. UBS Monograph Series 6. New York: United Bible Societies, 1991.

Michalson, Gordon E., Jr. "The Response to Lindbeck." *MoTh* 4 (1988): 107–20.

Miles, Carol Antablin. "Proclaiming the Gospel of God: The Promise of a Literary-Theological Hermeneutical

Approach to Christian Preaching of the Old Testament." PhD diss., Princeton Theological Seminary, 2000.

Miller, Patrick D. *Deuteronomy*. Interpretation. Louisville: John Knox, 1990.

———. *The Divine Warrior in Ancient Israel*. Cambridge, MA: Harvard University Press, 1973. Reprint, Atlanta: Society of Biblical Literature, 2006.

———. "God's Other Stories: On the Margins of Deuteronomic Theology." In *Realia Dei: Essays in Archaeology and Biblical Interpretation in Honor of Edward F. Campbell, Jr. at His Retirement*, edited by Prescott Williams Jr. and Theodore Hiebert, 185–94. Atlanta: Scholars Press, 1999.

———. "God the Warrior: A Problem in Biblical Interpretation and Apologetics." *Int* 19 (1965): 39–46.

———. *Stewards of the Mysteries of God: Preaching the Old Testament—and the New*. Eugene, OR: Cascade, 2013.

———. "That the Children May Know: Children in Deuteronomy." In *The Child in the Bible*, edited by Marcia J. Bunge, Terence E. Fretheim, and Beverly Roberts Gaventa, 45–62. Grand Rapids: Eerdmans, 2008.

———. *The Way of the Lord: Essays in Old Testament Theology*. FAT 39. Tübingen: Mohr Siebeck, 2004.

Miller-Naudé, Cynthia, and Ziony Zevit, eds. *Diachrony in Biblical Hebrew*. LSAWS 8. Winona Lake, IN: Eisenbrauns, 2012.

Milton, Ralph. *The Family Story Bible*. Louisville: Westminster John Knox, 1996.

Moberly, R. W. L. *The Bible, Theology, and Faith: A Study of Abraham and Jesus*. CSCD. Cambridge: Cambridge University Press, 2000.

———. *The Old Testament of the Old Testament: Patriarchal Narratives and Mosaic Yahwism*. OBT. Minneapolis: Fortress, 1992.

———. *Old Testament Theology: Reading the Hebrew Bible as Christian Scripture*. Grand Rapids: Baker Academic, 2013.

———. *The Theology of the Book of Genesis*. OTT. Cambridge: Cambridge University Press, 2009.

———. "Toward an Interpretation of the Shema." In *Theological Exegesis: Essays in Honor of Brevard S. Childs*, edited by Christopher Seitz and Kathryn Greene-McCreight, 124–44. Grand Rapids: Eerdmans, 1999.

Moll, Sebastian. *The Arch-Heretic Marcion*. WUNT 250. Tübingen: Mohr Siebeck, 2010.

Moore, Stephen D., and Yvonne Sherwood. *The Invention of the Biblical Scholar: A Critical Manifesto*. Minneapolis: Fortress, 2011.

Morgan, David. *Visual Piety: A History and Theory of Popular Religious Images*. Berkeley: University of California Press, 1998.

Morgan, Robert, with John Barton. *Biblical Interpretation*. Oxford: Oxford University Press, 1988.

Moule, C. F. D. *The Meaning of Hope: A Biblical Exposition with Concordance*. Philadelphia: Fortress, 1953.

Mounce, Robert H. *The Book of Revelation*. NICNT. Grand Rapids: Eerdmans, 1977.

Muilenburg, James. "A Study in Hebrew Rhetoric: Repetition and Style." In *Congress Volume: Copenhagen, 1953*, edited by George W. Anderson, 97–111. VTSup 1. Leiden: Brill, 1953.

Neruda, Pablo. *The Poetry of Pablo Neruda*. Edited by Ilan Stavans. New York: Farrar, Straus & Giroux, 2003.

Nettle, Daniel, and Suzanne Romaine. *Vanishing Voices: The Extinction of the*

World's Languages. Oxford: Oxford University Press, 2000.

Neusner, Jacob. *The Mishnah: A New Translation*. New Haven: Yale University Press, 1988.

Newsom, Carol A. *The Book of Job: A Contest of Moral Imaginations*. Oxford: Oxford University Press, 2003.

Newsom, Carol A., with Brennan W. Breed. *Daniel: A Commentary*. OTL. Louisville: Westminster John Knox, 2014.

Newton, Joseph Fort, ed. *Best Sermons 1924*. New York: Harcourt, Brace, 1924.

———, ed. *Best Sermons 1925*. New York: Harcourt, Brace, 1925.

———, ed. *Best Sermons 1926*. New York: Harcourt, Brace, 1926.

———, ed. *Best Sermons*. Vol. 4. New York: Harcourt, Brace, 1927.

Ngũgĩ wa Thiong'o. *Decolonising the Mind: The Politics of Language in African Literature*. Nairobi: East African Educational Publishers, 1986.

Nietzsche, Friedrich. *The Gay Science*. Translated by Walter Kaufmann. New York: Random House, 1974.

Norris, Kathleen. *Amazing Grace: A Vocabulary of Faith*. New York: Riverhead, 1998.

North, Robert. "Could Hebrew Have Been a Cultic Esperanto?" *ZAH* 12 (1999): 202–17.

Notre Dame, University of. National Study of Youth and Religion. Research Project, directed by Christian Smith and Lisa Pearce. 2001–. http://youthandreligion.nd.edu.

Olson, Dennis T. *Deuteronomy and the Death of Moses: A Theological Reading*. OBT. Minneapolis: Fortress, 1994.

Osteen, Joel. *Daily Readings from Your Best Life Now: 90 Devotions for Living at Your Full Potential*. New York: FaithWords, 2005.

———. *Every Day a Friday: How to Be Happier 7 Days a Week*. New York: FaithWords, 2011.

———. *I Declare: 31 Promises to Speak over Your Life*. New York: FaithWords, 2012.

———. *Scriptures and Meditations for Your Best Life Now*. New York: FaithWords, 2006.

———. *Your Best Life Begins Each Morning: Devotions to Start Every New Day of the Year*. New York: FaithWords, 2008.

———. *Your Best Life Now: 7 Steps to Living at Your Full Potential*. New York: FaithWords, 2004.

———. *Your Best Life Now for Moms*. New York: FaithWords, 2008.

———. *Your Best Life Now Journal: A Guide to Reaching Your Full Potential*. New York: FaithWords, 2005.

———. *Your Best Life Now Study Guide: 7 Steps to Living at Your Full Potential*. New York: FaithWords, 2005.

Palmer, F. R. *Mood and Modality*. 2nd ed. CTL. Cambridge: Cambridge University Press, 2001.

Patton, Kimberly Christine. *Religion of the Gods: Ritual, Paradox, and Reflexivity*. Oxford: Oxford University Press, 2009.

Peale, Norman Vincent. *The Power of Positive Thinking*. New York: Prentice-Hall, 1952.

Pennebaker, James W. "The Effects of Traumatic Disclosure on Physical and Mental Health: The Values of Writing and Talking about Upsetting Events." *International Journal of Emergency Mental Health* 1 (1999): 9–18.

———. *Opening Up: The Healing Power of Confiding in Others*. New York: William Morrow, 1990. Reprint, New York: Guilford, 1997.

———. "The Social, Linguistic, and Health Consequences of Emotional Disclosure." In *Social Psychological Foundations of*

Health and Illness, edited by J. Suls and K. A. Wallston, 288–313. Malden, MA: Blackwell, 2003.

———. "Telling Stories: The Health Benefits of Narrative." *Literature and Medicine* 19 (2000): 3–18.

———. "Writing about Emotional Experiences as a Therapeutic Process." *Psychological Science* 8 (1997): 162–66.

Pennebaker, J. W., and C. K. Chung. "Expressive Writing, Emotional Upheavals, and Health." In *Foundations of Health Psychology*, edited by H. Friedman and R. Silver, 263–84. New York: Oxford University Press, 2007.

Pennebaker, J. W., C. F. Hughes, and R. C. O'Heeron. "The Psychophysiology of Confession: Linking Inhibitory and Psychosomatic Processes." *Journal of Personality and Social Psychology* 52 (1987): 781–93.

Pennebaker, J. W., and R. C. O'Heeron. "Confiding in Others and Illness Rate among Spouses of Suicide and Accidental-Death Victims." *Journal of Abnormal Psychology* 93 (1984): 473–76.

Pennebaker, J. W., and J. R. Susman. "Disclosure of Traumas and Psychosomatic Processes." *Social Science and Medicine* 26 (1988): 327–32.

Peterson, Christopher. *A Primer in Positive Psychology*. Oxford: Oxford University Press, 2006.

Pew Forum on Religion and Public Life. *U.S. Religious Knowledge Survey*. September 2010. Washington, DC: Pew Research Center, 2010. http://www.pewforum.org/files/2010/09/religious-knowledge-full-report.pdf.

Pinker, Steven. *Language, Cognition, and Human Nature: Selected Articles*. Oxford: Oxford University Press, 2013.

———. *The Language Instinct: How the Mind Creates Language*. New York: Perennial, 1994.

———. *The Stuff of Thought: Language as a Window into Human Nature*. New York: Viking, 2007.

Plate, S. Brent. "Why Pollsters Still Don't Get Religion." *Religion Dispatches*. September 29, 2010. http://religiondispatches.org/why_pollsters_still_dont_get_religion/.

Plotz, David. *Good Book: The Bizarre, Hilarious, Disturbing, Marvelous, and Inspiring Things I Learned When I Read Every Single Word of the Bible*. New York: HarperCollins, 2009.

Porter, Stanley E., and Matthew Brook O'Donnell, eds. *The Linguist as Pedagogue: Trends in the Teaching and Linguistic Analysis of the Greek New Testament*. NTM 11. Sheffield: Sheffield Phoenix, 2009.

Portier-Young, Anathea E. *Apocalypse against Empire: Theologies of Resistance in Early Judaism*. Grand Rapids: Eerdmans, 2011.

Powell, Mark Allan. *What Do They Hear? Bridging the Gap between Pulpit and Pew*. Nashville: Abingdon, 2007.

Prothero, Stephen. *Religious Literacy: What Every American Needs to Know—and Doesn't*. New York: HarperOne, 2008.

Pyper, Hugh S. *The Unchained Bible: Cultural Appropriations of Biblical Texts*. LHBOTS 567. London: T&T Clark, 2012.

———. *An Unsuitable Book: The Bible as Scandalous Text*. Bible in the Modern World 7. Sheffield: Sheffield Phoenix, 2005.

Rad, Gerhard von. *God at Work in Israel*. Translated by John H. Marks. 1974. Reprint, Nashville: Abingdon, 1980.

———. *Holy War in Ancient Israel*. Translated by Marva J. Dawn. Reprint, Eugene, OR: Wipf & Stock, 2000. Original German ed., 1951.

Radner, Ephraim. *Leviticus*. Brazos Theological Commentary on the Bible. Grand Rapids: Brazos, 2008.

Ramshaw, Gail. "The First Testament in Christian Lectionaries." *Worship* 64 (1990): 484–510.

Raynal, Charles E. Review of *The Nature of Doctrine: Religion and Theology in a Postliberal Age*, by George A. Lindbeck. *Int* 41 (1987): 81–85.

Rendsburg, Gary A. "A Comprehensive Guide to Israelian Hebrew: Grammar and Lexicon." *Orient* 38 (2003): 5–35.

———. *Diglossia in Ancient Hebrew*. AOS 72. New Haven: American Oriental Society, 1990.

Reventlow, Henning Graf. *Problems of Biblical Theology in the Twentieth Century*. Philadelphia: Fortress, 1986.

———. *Problems of Old Testament Theology in the Twentieth Century*. Philadelphia: Fortress, 1985.

Richards, Jack C., and Theodore S. Rodgers. *Approaches and Methods in Language Teaching: A Description and Analysis*. Cambridge: Cambridge University Press, 1986.

Ricoeur, Paul. *The Rule of Metaphor: Multidisciplinary Studies of the Creation of Meaning in Language*. Translated by Robert Czerny et al. 1975. Reprint, Toronto: University of Toronto Press, 1977.

Roberts, Alexander, and James Donaldson, eds. *The Ante-Nicene Fathers*. Vol. 3, *Latin Christianity: Its Founder, Tertullian*. Edinburgh: T&T Clark, 1993.

Robinson, Armin, ed. *The Ten Commandments: Ten Short Novels of Hitler's War against the Moral Code*. New York: Simon & Schuster, 1944.

Rorty, Richard. *The Linguistic Turn: Recent Essays in Philosophical Method*. Chicago: University of Chicago Press, 1967.

Rumscheidt, Martin, ed. *Adolf von Harnack: Liberal Theology at Its Height*. Making of Modern Theology. Minneapolis: Augsburg Fortress, 1989.

———. "Harnack, Karl Gustav Adolf von." In *Dictionary of Major Biblical Interpreters*, edited by Donald K. McKim, 504–7. Downers Grove, IL: IVP Academic, 2007.

Rutledge, Fleming. *And God Spoke to Abraham: Preaching from the Old Testament*. Grand Rapids: Eerdmans, 2011.

———. Foreword to *Stewards of the Mysteries of God: Preaching the Old Testament—and the New*, by Patrick D. Miller, xi–xiv. Eugene, OR: Cascade, 2013.

Sacks, Oliver. *Musicophilia: Tales of Music and the Brain*. Rev. and expanded ed. New York: Vintage, 2008.

Sáenz-Badillos, Angel. *A History of the Hebrew Language*. Translated by John Elwolde. Cambridge: Cambridge University Press, 1993.

Sahlins, Marshall. *How "Natives" Think: About Captain Cook, for Example*. Chicago: University of Chicago Press, 1995.

Sanders, E. P. *Jesus and Judaism*. Philadelphia: Fortress, 1985.

———. *Paul and Palestinian Judaism: A Comparison of Patterns of Religion*. Philadelphia: Fortress, 1977.

Sanders, James A. "Canon: Hebrew Bible." *ABD* 1:837–52.

———. *Torah and Canon*. Philadelphia: Fortress, 1972.

Sanders, Seth L. *The Invention of Hebrew*. Urbana: University of Illinois Press, 2009.

Saperstein, Marc. *Jewish Preaching, 1200–1800: An Anthology*. New Haven: Yale University Press, 1989.

Sauter, Gerhard. "Jonah 2: A Prayer out of the Deep." In *A God So Near: Essays on Old Testament Theology in Honor of Patrick D. Miller*, edited by Brent A.

Strawn and Nancy R. Bowen, 145–52. Winona Lake, IN: Eisenbrauns, 2003.

Sawyer, John F. A. *Sacred Languages and Sacred Texts*. London: Routledge, 1999.

Schniedewind, William M. "Aramaic, the Death of Written Hebrew, and Language Shift in the Persian Period." In *Margins of Writing, Origins of Cultures*, edited by Seth L. Sanders, 137–47. Chicago: Oriental Institute of the University of Chicago, 2006.

———. *A Social History of Hebrew: Its Origins through the Rabbinic Period.* AYBRL. New Haven: Yale University Press, 2013.

Schökel, Luis Alonso. *The Inspired Word: Scripture in the Light of Language and Literature*. Translated by Francis Martin. New York: Herder & Herder, 1965.

Schweizer, Bernard. *Hating God: The Untold Story of Misotheism*. Oxford: Oxford University Press, 2011.

Seibert, Eric A. *Disturbing Divine Behavior: Troubling Old Testament Images of God*. Minneapolis: Fortress, 2009.

———. *The Violence of Scripture: Overcoming the Old Testament's Troubling Legacy*. Minneapolis: Fortress, 2012.

Seitz, Christopher R. *The Character of Christian Scripture: The Significance of a Two-Testament Bible*. STI. Grand Rapids: Baker Academic, 2011.

———. *Figured Out: Typology and Providence in Christian Scripture*. Louisville: Westminster John Knox, 2001.

———. *Word without End: The Old Testament as Abiding Theological Witness*. Grand Rapids: Eerdmans, 1998.

Seitz, Christopher R., and Kent Harold Richards, eds. *The Bible as Christian Scripture: The Work of Brevard S. Childs*. Atlanta: Society of Biblical Literature, 2013.

Seow, C. L. *Ecclesiastes: A New Translation with Introduction and Commentary*. AB. New York: Doubleday, 1997.

———. "Torah." In *Dictionary of Deities and Demons in the Bible*, edited by Karel van der Toorn, Bob Becking, and Pieter W. van der Horst, 874–76. 2nd ed. Grand Rapids: Eerdmans, 1999.

Sharp, Carolyn J. *Old Testament Prophets for Today*. Louisville: Westminster John Knox, 2009.

———. *Wrestling the Word: The Hebrew Scriptures and the Christian Believer*. Louisville: Westminster John Knox, 2010.

Sheppard, Gerald T. "Canon." In *The Encyclopedia of Religion*, edited by Mircea Eliade et al., 3:62–69. 16 vols. New York: Macmillian, 1987.

Simmons, Dale H. *E. W. Kenyon and the Postbellum Pursuit of Peace, Power, and Plenty*. London: Scarecrow, 1997.

Slenczka, Notger. "Texte zum Alten Testament" (2015–16). https://www.theologie.hu-berlin.de/de/st/AT.

Sluga, Hans. "Wittgenstein, Ludwig." In *The Cambridge Dictionary of Philosophy*, edited by Robert Audi, 976–80. 2nd ed. Cambridge: Cambridge University Press, 1999.

Smend, Rudolf. *"The Unconquered Land" and Other Old Testament Essays: Selected Studies by Rudolf Smend*. Translated by Margaret Kohl and edited by Edward Ball and Margaret Barker. Burlington: Ashgate, 2013.

———. *Yahweh War and Tribal Confederation: Reflections upon Israel's Earliest History*. 1963. Reprint, Nashville: Abingdon, 1970.

Smit, Dirk J. "'Pidgin or Pentecost'? On Translation and Transformation." *Scriptura* 58 (1996): 305–28.

Smith, Christian. *The Bible Made Impossible: Why Biblicism Is Not a Truly Evangelical Reading of Scripture*. Grand Rapids: Brazos, 2011.

Smith, Christian, with Melinda Lundquist Denton. *Soul Searching: The Religious and Spiritual Lives of American Teenagers*. Oxford: Oxford University Press, 2005.

Smith, Jonathan Z. "Scriptures and Histories." In *On Teaching Religion: Essays by Jonathan Z. Smith*, edited by Christopher I. Lehrich, 28–36. Oxford: Oxford University Press, 2013.

Smith, Mark S. "The Heart and Innards in Israelite Emotional Expressions: Notes from Anthropology and Psychology." *JBL* 117 (1998): 427–36.

Smith, Wilfred Cantwell. *Believing: An Historical Perspective*. Boston: Oneworld, 1998.

———. *Faith and Belief*. Princeton: Princeton University Press, 1987.

Social Science Research Council. "Surveying Religious Knowledge." *The Immanent Frame: Secularism, Religion, and the Public Sphere*. 2010. http://blogs.ssrc.org /tif/2010/10/05/religious-knowledge/.

Sommer, Benjamin D. *The Bodies of God and the World of Ancient Israel*. Cambridge: Cambridge University Press, 2009.

———. "The Scroll of Isaiah as Jewish Scripture; or, Why Jews Don't Read Books." In *Society of Biblical Literature 1996 Seminar Papers*, 225–42. Atlanta: Scholars Press, 1996.

Sparks, Kenton L. *Sacred Word, Broken Word: Biblical Authority and the Dark Side of Scripture*. Grand Rapids: Eerdmans, 2012.

Spellman, Chad. *Toward a Canon-Conscious Reading of the Bible: Exploring the History and Hermeneutics of the Canon*. NTM 34. Sheffield: Sheffield Phoenix, 2014.

Sperber, Alexander. *A Historical Grammar of Biblical Hebrew*. Leiden: Brill, 1966.

Stackert, Jeffrey. *Rewriting the Torah: Literary Revision in Deuteronomy and the Holiness Legislation*. FAT 52. Tübingen: Mohr Siebeck, 2007.

Stager, Lawrence E. "The Archaeology of the Family in Ancient Israel." *BASOR* 260 (1985): 1–35.

Stark, Thom. *The Human Faces of God: What Scripture Reveals When It Gets God Wrong (and Why Inerrancy Tries to Hide It)*. Eugene, OR: Wipf & Stock, 2011.

Stavans, Ilan. *Resurrecting Hebrew*. New York: Schocken, 2008.

Steiner, George. *After Babel: Aspects of Language and Translation*. 3rd ed. Oxford: Oxford University Press, 1998.

Steinmetz, David C. "The Superiority of Pre-critical Exegesis." In *The Theological Interpretation of Scripture: Classic and Contemporary Readings*, edited by Stephen E. Fowl, 26–38. Malden: Blackwell, 1997.

Stewart, Anne W. *Poetic Ethics in Proverbs: Wisdom Literature and the Shaping of the Moral Self*. New York: Cambridge University Press, 2016.

Stone, Lawson G. "Ethical and Apologetic Tendencies in the Redaction of the Book of Joshua." *CBQ* 53 (1991): 25–36.

Stookey, Laurence Hull. "Marcion, Typology, and Lectionary Preaching." *Worship* 66 (1992): 251–62.

Strawn, Brent A. "And These Three Are One: A Trinitarian Critique of Christological Approaches to the Old Testament." *PRSt* 31 (2004): 191–210.

———. "Authority: Textual, Traditional, or Functional? A Response to C. D. Elledge." In *Jewish and Christian Scriptures: The Function of "Canonical" and "Non-canonical" Religious Texts*, edited by James H. Charlesworth and Lee Martin McDonald, 104–12. JCTCRS 7. London: T&T Clark, 2010.

———, ed. *The Bible and the Pursuit of Happiness: What the Old and New Testaments Teach Us about the Good Life*. Oxford: Oxford University Press, 2012.

———. "Canaan and Canaanites." In *The Oxford Encyclopedia of the Bible and Theology*, edited by Samuel E. Balentine, 1:104–11. 2 vols. Oxford: Oxford University Press, 2015.

———. "Commentary on Joshua 24:1–15" (October 12, 2014). https://www.workingpreacher.org/preaching.aspx?commentary_id=2227.

———. "Comparative Approaches: History, Theory, and the Image of God." In *Method Matters: Essays on the Interpretation of the Hebrew Bible in Honor of David L. Petersen*, edited by Joel M. LeMon and Kent Harold Richards, 117–42. RBS 56. Atlanta: Society of Biblical Literature, 2009.

———. "Designated Readers: Deuteronomy's Portrait of the Ideal King—or Is It Preacher?" *Journal for Preachers* 32 (2008): 35–40.

———. "Deuteronomy." In *Theological Bible Commentary*, edited by Gail R. O'Day and David L. Petersen, 63–76. Louisville: Westminster John Knox, 2009.

———. "Exodus." In *The New Interpreter's Bible One-Volume Commentary*, edited by Beverly Roberts Gaventa, David L. Petersen, et al., 33–56. Nashville: Abingdon, 2010.

———. "Four Thoughts on Preaching and Teaching the Bible—Mostly the Old Testament." In *The Bible Tells Me So: Reading the Bible as Scripture*, edited by Richard P. Thompson and Thomas Jay Oord, 33–42. Nampa, ID: SacraSage, 2011.

———. "The History of Israelite Religion." In *The Cambridge Companion to the Hebrew Bible / Old Testament*, edited by Stephen B. Chapman and Marvin A. Sweeney, 86–107. Cambridge: Cambridge University Press, 2016.

———. "Introduction: The Bible and . . . Happiness?" In *The Bible and the Pursuit of Happiness: What the Old and New Testaments Teach Us about the Good Life*, edited by Brent A. Strawn, 3–27. Oxford: Oxford University Press, 2012.

———. "'Israel, My Child': The Ethics of a Biblical Metaphor." In *The Child in the Bible*, edited by Marcia J. Bunge, Terence E. Fretheim, and Beverly Roberts Gaventa, 103–40. Grand Rapids: Eerdmans, 2008.

———. "Jonah and Genre." Oxford Biblical Studies Online. Oxford: Oxford University Press, 2013. http://global.oup.com/obso/focus/focus_on_jonah/.

———. "Keep/Observe/Do—Carefully—Today! The Rhetoric of Repetition in Deuteronomy." In *A God So Near: Essays on Old Testament Theology in Honor of Patrick D. Miller*, edited by Brent A. Strawn and Nancy R. Bowen, 215–40. Winona Lake, IN: Eisenbrauns, 2003.

———. "Leviticus 19:1–2, 9–18." In *The Lectionary Commentary: Theological Exegesis for Sunday's Texts*, vol. 1, *The Old Testament and Acts (the First Readings)*, edited by Roger E. Van Harn, 115–20. Grand Rapids: Eerdmans, 2001.

———. "Lyric Poetry." In *Dictionary of the Old Testament: Wisdom, Poetry and Writings*, edited by Tremper Longman III and Peter Enns, 437–46. Downers Grove, IL: IVP Academic, 2008.

———. "On Walter Brueggemann: (A Personal) Testimony, (Three) Dispute(s), (and on) Advocacy." In *Imagination, Ideology, and Inspiration: Walter Brueggemann and Biblical Studies*, edited by Jonathan Kaplan and Robert Williamson Jr., 9–47. Hebrew Bible Monographs. Sheffield: Sheffield Academic, 2015.

———. "Poetic Attachment: Psychology, Psycholinguistics, and the Psalms." In *The Oxford Handbook of the Psalms*, edited by William P. Brown, 404–23. Oxford: Oxford University Press, 2014.

———. "The Psalms and the Practice of Disclosure." In *From Whom No Secrets Are Hid: Introducing the Psalms*, by Walter Brueggemann, edited by Brent A. Strawn, xiii–xxiv. Louisville: Westminster John Knox, 2014.

———. "The Psalms: Types, Functions, and Poetics for Proclamation." In *Psalms for Preaching and Worship*, edited by Roger E. Van Harn and Brent A. Strawn, 34–36. Grand Rapids: Eerdmans, 2009.

———. "Reading Josiah Reading Deuteronomy." In *Reading for Faith and Learning*, edited by Douglas L. Gragg and John B. Weaver. Abilene, TX: Abilene Christian University Press, forthcoming.

———. "Sanctified and Commercially Successful Curses: On Gangsta Rap and the Canonization of the Imprecatory Psalms." *ThTo* 69 (2013): 403–17.

———. "Slaves and Rebels: Inscription, Identity, and Time in the Rhetoric of Deuteronomy." In *Sepher Torat Mosheh: Studies in the Composition and Interpretation of Deuteronomy*, edited by Daniel I. Block and Richard M. Schultz. Peabody, MA: Hendrickson, forthcoming.

———. "Teaching in a New Key: The Pedagogical Formation of Theological Faculty." In *How Youth Ministry Can Change Theological Education—If We Let It: Reflections from the Lilly Endowment's High School Theology Program Seminar*, edited by Kenda Creasy Dean and Christy Lang Hearlson, 247–64. Grand Rapids: Eerdmans, 2016.

———. "Teaching the Old Testament: When God Seems Unjust." *Circuit Rider* 36, no. 4 (August–October 2012): 7–9.

———. "Trauma, Psalmic Disclosure, and Authentic Happiness." In *Bible through the Lens of Trauma*, edited by Elizabeth Boase and Christopher G. Frechette. Semeia Studies 86. Atlanta: SBL Press, forthcoming.

———. "The Triumph of Life: Towards a Biblical Theology of Happiness." In *The Bible and the Pursuit of Happiness: What the Old and New Testaments Teach Us about the Good Life*, edited by Brent A. Strawn, 287–322. Oxford: Oxford University Press, 2012.

———. "What Is Cush Doing in Amos 9:7? The Poetics of Exodus in the Plural." *VT* 63 (2013): 99–123.

———. "The X-Factor: Revisioning Biblical Holiness." *ATJ* 54 (1999): 73–92.

———. "Yhwh's Poesie: The *Gnadenformel*, the Book of Exodus, and Beyond." In *Close Reading: Biblical Poetry*, edited by J. Blake Couey and Elaine James. Cambridge: Cambridge University Press, forthcoming.

Strawn, Brent A., and Brad D. Strawn. "Prophecy and Psychology." In *Dictionary of the Old Testament: Prophets*, edited by Mark J. Boda and J. Gordon McConville, 610–23. Downers Grove, IL: IVP Academic, 2012.

Sundberg, Albert C., Jr. *The Old Testament of the Early Church*. HTS 20. Cambridge, MA: Harvard University Press; London: Oxford University Press, 1964.

Tanner, Kathryn. *Theories of Culture: A New Agenda for Theology*. Guides to Theological Inquiry. Minneapolis: Fortress, 1997.

Taylor, Mark C., ed. *Critical Terms for Religious Studies*. Chicago: University of Chicago Press, 1998.

Thomas, Heath, Jeremy Evans, and Paul Copan, eds. *Holy War in the Bible: Christian Morality and an Old Testament Problem*. Downers Grove, IL: IVP Academic, 2013.

Tillesse, Georges Minettede. "Sections 'tu' et sections 'vous' dans le Deutéronome." *VT* 12 (1962): 29–87.

Tomlin, Russell S. "Repetition in Second Language Acquisition." In *Repetition in*

Discourse: Interdisciplinary Perspectives, edited by Barbara Johnstone, 1:172–94. 2 vols. Norwood, NJ: Ablex, 1994.

Towne, Anthony. "An 'Obituary' for God." *New York Times*, March 6, 1966, E5 (Religion).

Towner, W. Sibley. "'Without Our Aid He Did Us Make': Singing the Meaning of the Psalms." In *A God So Near: Essays on Old Testament Theology in Honor of Patrick D. Miller*, edited by Brent A. Strawn and Nancy R. Bowen, 17–34. Winona Lake, IN: Eisenbrauns, 2003.

Toy, Crawford H. *A Critical and Exegetical Commentary on the Book of Proverbs*. ICC. New York: Charles Scribner's Sons, 1902.

Tracy, David. *The Analogical Imagination: Christian Theology and the Culture of Pluralism*. New York: Crossroad, 1981.

———. "Lindbeck's New Program for Theology: A Reflection." *The Thomist* 49 (1985): 460–72.

Treier, Daniel J. *Introducing Theological Interpretation of Scripture: Recovering a Christian Practice*. Grand Rapids: Baker Academic, 2008.

Trible, Phyllis. *Texts of Terror: Literary-Feminist Readings of Old Testament Narratives*. OBT. Philadelphia: Fortress, 1984.

Trigg, Joseph W. *Origen*. Early Church Fathers 60. London: Routledge, 1998.

United Nations Educational, Scientific and Cultural Organization. *Aspects of Literacy Assessment: Topics and Issues from the UNESCO Expert Meeting*. 10–12 June 2003, Paris. ED-2005/WS/23. http://unesdoc.unesco.org/images/0014/001401/140125eo.pdf.

VandeCreek, L., M. D. Janus, J. W. Pennebaker, and B. Binau. "Praying about Difficult Experiences as Self-Disclosure to God." *International Journal for the Psychology of Religion* 12 (2002): 29–39.

Van Harn, Roger E., ed. *The Lectionary Commentary: Theological Exegesis for Sunday's Texts*. 3 vols. Grand Rapids: Eerdmans, 2001.

Van Harn, Roger E., and Brent A. Strawn, eds. *Psalms for Preaching and Worship: A Lectionary Commentary*. Grand Rapids: Eerdmans, 2009.

Vanhoozer, Kevin J. *The Drama of Doctrine: A Canonical Linguistic Approach to Christian Theology*. Louisville: Westminster John Knox, 2005.

Vischer, Wilhelm. "Das alte Testament als Gottes Wort." *Zwischen den Zeiten* 5 (1927): 377–95.

———. *The Witness of the Old Testament to Christ*. Translated by A. B. Crabtree. London: Lutterworth, 1949.

Vita, Juan-Pablo. *Canaanite Scribes in the Amarna Letters*. AOAT 406. Münster: Ugarit-Verlag, 2015.

Vogt, Peter T. *Deuteronomic Theology and the Significance of Torah: A Reappraisal*. Winona Lake, IN: Eisenbrauns, 2006.

Volz, Hans. "Continental Versions to c. 1600: German." In *The Cambridge History of the Bible*, vol. 3, *The West from the Reformation to the Present Day*, edited by S. L. Greenslade, 94–109. Cambridge: Cambridge University Press, 1963.

Vygotsky, Lev S. *Thought and Language*. Cambridge, MA: MIT Press, 1962.

Wagner, J. Ross. *Heralds of the Good News: Isaiah and Paul in Concert in the Letter to the Romans*. NovTSup 101. Boston: Brill, 2003.

Wagner, J. Ross, C. Kavin Rowe, and A. Katherine Grieb, eds. *The Word Leaps the Gap: Essays on Scripture and Theology in Honor of Richard B. Hays*. Grand Rapids: Eerdmans, 2008.

Wagner, Max. *Die lexikalischen und grammatikalischen Aramaismen im alttestamentlichen Hebräisch*. BZAW 96. Berlin: Töpelmann, 1966.

Waldman, Nahum M. *The Recent Study of Hebrew: A Survey of the Literature with Selected Bibliography*. Cincinnati: Hebrew Union College Press; Winona Lake, IN: Eisenbrauns, 1989.

Walton, John H. "The Decalogue Structure of the Deuteronomic Law." In *Interpreting Deuteronomy: Issues and Approaches*, edited by David G. Firth and Philip S. Johnston, 93–117. Downers Grove, IL: IVP Academic, 2012.

Webster, John. *Holy Scripture: A Dogmatic Sketch*. Cambridge: Cambridge University Press, 2003.

Weinfeld, Moshe. *Deuteronomy and the Deuteronomic School*. Oxford: Oxford University Press, 1972.

Wenham, Gordon J. *The Book of Leviticus*. NICOT. Grand Rapids: Eerdmans, 1979.

———. *Psalms as Torah: Reading Biblical Song Ethically*. Grand Rapids: Baker Academic, 2012.

Wesley, John. "An Address to the Clergy." In *The Works of the Rev. John Wesley, MA*, edited by Thomas Jackson, 10:480–500. 3rd ed. 14 vols. 1872. Reprint, Grand Rapids: Baker, 1979.

West, Fritz. *Scripture and Memory: The Ecumenical Hermeneutic of the Three-Year Lectionaries*. Collegeville, MN: Liturgical Press, 1997.

Westermann, Claus, ed. *Essays on Old Testament Hermeneutics*. 1960. Reprint, Richmond, VA: John Knox, 1963.

———. *Praise and Lament in the Psalms*. Translated by Keith R. Crim and Richard N. Soulen. 1965. Reprint, Atlanta: John Knox, 1981.

Wheeler, David L. "The Death of Languages." *Chronicle of Higher Education*. April 20, 1994.

Wheeler, Rebecca S. *Code-Switching: Teaching Standard English in Urban Classrooms*. Theory & Research into Practice. Urbana, IL: National Council of Teachers of English, 2006.

White, James F. "Our Apostasy in Worship." *Christian Century* 94 (September 28, 1977): 842–45.

White, Lydia. *Second Language Acquisition and Universal Grammar*. CTL. Cambridge: Cambridge University Press, 2003.

———. *Universal Grammar and Second Language Acquisition*. LALD 1. Amsterdam: John Benjamins, 1989.

Wiesel, Elie. *The Trial of God*. New York: Schocken, 1995.

Wilkinson, Bruce. *The Prayer of Jabez: Bible Study*. Portland: Multnomah, 2001.

———. *The Prayer of Jabez: Breaking through to the Blessed Life*. Portland: Multnomah, 2000.

———. *The Prayer of Jabez: Devotional*. Portland: Multnomah, 2001.

———. *The Prayer of Jabez for Kids*. Portland: Multnomah, 2001.

———. *The Prayer of Jabez for Teens*. Portland: Multnomah, 2001.

———. *The Prayer of Jabez Journal*. Portland: Multnomah, 2001.

Wilkinson, Darlene Marie. *The Prayer of Jabez for Women*. Portland: Multnomah, 2010.

Williams, D. S. "Reconsidering Marcion's Gospel." *JBL* 109 (1989): 477–96.

Wilson, Eric G. *Against Happiness: In Praise of Melancholy*. New York: Farrar, Straus & Giroux, 2008.

———. *The Mercy of Eternity: A Memoir of Depression and Grace*. Evanston, IL: Northwestern University Press, 2010.

Wilson, Marvin R. *Exploring Our Hebraic Heritage: A Christian Theology of Roots and Renewal*. Grand Rapids: Eerdmans, 2014.

Winedt, Marlon. "'Honor Your Father and Mother' or 'Honor Your Mother and

Father'? A Case Study in Creole Bible Translation." *BT* 58 (2007): 57–64.

Witherington, Ben, III. *Revelation*. NCBC. Cambridge: Cambridge University Press, 2003.

Witten, Marsha G. *All Is Forgiven: The Secular Message in American Protestantism*. Princeton: Princeton University Press, 1993.

Wolff, Hans Walter. *Anthropology of the Old Testament*. Translated by Margaret Kohl. Reprint, Mifflintown, PA: Sigler, 1996. Original German ed., 1974.

Woolard, Kathryn A. "Language Convergence and Language Death as Social Processes." In *Investigating Obsolescence: Studies in Language Contraction and Death*, edited by Nancy C. Dorian, 355–67. Studies in the Social and Cultural Foundations of Language 7. Cambridge: Cambridge University Press, 1989.

Wright, Christopher J. H. *The God I Don't Understand: Reflections on Tough Questions of Faith*. Grand Rapids: Zondervan, 2008.

Wright, G. Ernest. *The Challenge of Israel's Faith*. Chicago: University of Chicago Press, 1944.

Wright, N. T. *Scripture and the Authority of God: How to Read the Bible Today*. New York: HarperOne, 2013.

Wyatt, Nicolas. *The Mythic Mind: Essays on Cosmology and Religion in Ugaritic and Old Testament Literature*. London: Equinox, 2005.

———. "The Vocabulary and Neurology of Orientation: The Ugaritic and Hebrew Evidence." In *Ugarit, Religion and Culture: Proceedings of the International Colloquium on Ugarit, Religion and Culture, Edinburgh, July 1994; Essays Presented in Honour of Professor John C. L. Gibson*, edited by N. Wyatt, W. G. E. Watson, and J. B. Lloyd, 351–80. UBL 12. Münster: Ugarit-Verlag, 1996.

Wycliffe Bible Translators. *Da Jesus Book: Hawaii Pidgin New Testament*. 2nd ed. Orlando: Wycliffe Bible Translators, 2011.

Young, Frances. *Biblical Exegesis and the Formation of Christian Culture*. Cambridge: Cambridge University Press, 1997.

Young, Frances, Lewis Ayres, and Andrew Louth, eds. *The Cambridge History of Early Christian Literature*. Cambridge: Cambridge University Press, 2004.

Young, Ian, Robert Rezetko, and Martin Ehrensvärd. *Linguistic Dating of Biblical Texts*. 2 vols. London: Equinox, 2008.

Zuckermann, Ghil'ad. *Language Contact and Lexical Enrichment in Israeli Hebrew*. Palgrave Studies in Language History and Language Change. New York: Palgrave Macmillan, 2003.

Scripture and Ancient Sources Index

The appendixes have not been indexed; please see there for additional references.

Modern Authors Index

The appendixes have not been indexed; please see there for additional names.

Subject Index